Long-Term Athlete Development

Istvan Balyi, MA

Advanced Training and Performance, Ltd

Richard Way, MBA

Canadian Sport for Life and Citius Performance Corp.

Colin Higgs, PhD

Professor Emeritus, Memorial University, Canada

Human Kinetics

Library of Congress Cataloging-in-Publication Data

Balyi, Istvan.
   Long-term athlete development / Istvan Balyi, Richard Way, Colin Higgs.
      p. ; cm.
   Includes bibliographical references and index.
   I. Way, Richard, 1957- II. Higgs, Colin, 1945- III. Title.
   [DNLM: 1. Athletic Performance--physiology. 2. Athletic Performance--psychology. 3. Athletes--education. QT 260]
   RC1235
   612'.044--dc23

                                      2013008554

ISBN: 978-0-7360-9218-0 (print)

The web addresses cited in this text were current as of March 2013, unless otherwise noted.

Acquisitions Editor: Myles Schrag; **Developmental Editor:** Amanda S. Ewing; **Assistant Editors:** Casey A. Gentis, Jacqueline Eaton Blakley, and Anne Rumery; **Copyeditor:** Patsy Fortney; **Indexer:** Katy Balcer; **Permissions Manager:** Dalene Reeder; **Graphic Designer:** Nancy Rasmus; **Graphic Artist:** Yvonne Griffith; **Cover Designer:** Julie Denzer; **Photograph (cover):** iStockphoto/U Star PIX; **Photographs (interior):** © Human Kinetics, unless otherwise noted; photos on pages 33 and 79 courtesy of Richard Way and Citius Performance Corp.; photo on page 285 (top) courtesy of Istvan Balyi; photo on page 285 (bottom) courtesy of Richard Way; photo on page 286 courtesy of Colin Higgs; **Photo Asset Manager:** Laura Fitch; **Photo Production Manager:** Jason Allen; **Art Manager:** Kelly Hendren; **Associate Art Manager:** Alan L. Wilborn; **Illustrations:** © Human Kinetics, unless otherwise noted; **Printer:** Total Printing Systems

Printed in the United States of America   10 9 8 7 6 5 4

The paper in this book is certified under a sustainable forestry program.

Human Kinetics
P.O. Box 5076
Champaign, IL 61825-5076
Website: www.HumanKinetics.com

In the United States, email info@hkusa.com or call 800-747-4457.
In Canada, email info@hkcanada.com.
In the United Kingdom/Europe, email hk@hkeurope.com.

For information about Human Kinetics' coverage in other areas of the world, please visit our website: **www.HumanKinetics.com**

E5121

Contents

Part III   Stages of Long-Term Athlete Development

Preface

This book describes a new approach to athlete-centered sport—the emerging concept of long-term athlete development (LTAD). This stage-by-stage approach gives every child, youth, and adult the greatest opportunity to engage in lifelong, health-enhancing physical activity, and if they have the talent and the drive, to reach their highest sport performance potential.

The book addresses a number of target groups. It is suitable as an undergraduate text for students in kinesiology, physical education, sport management, coaching, recreation, and education, while also meeting the needs of coaches, especially those working with children and youth. Because LTAD addresses the changes needed in sport systems to meet the developmental needs of participants, this book is also helpful for sport organizations and those with management roles within the sport system. Last, it is a valuable resource for parents and guardians who want to make sure that the sport in which their children engage meets each child's developmental needs, is ethical, and is organized with the best interest of the child as the key goal.

This book evolved from the work of a group of sport experts tasked with changing the sport system in Canada from one that produced "champions by chance" to one that would give athletes the best chance to reach their full potential. An analysis of existing sport programs around the world showed that most developed athletes by doing the same things in the same ways regardless of the athlete's age or—more important—stage of development. Based on an evaluation of the problems inherent in many sport systems, and a careful review of the existing knowledge about healthy child development, these experts developed a systematic approach to optimal sport and physical activity development. That process was called long-term athlete development, and it is now being implemented in many sports and in many countries around the world.

Too often, coaches deliver adult versions of sport (often adult male versions of sport) to children and youth of both sexes because they are unaware of the need for different types of training at different stages of human development. LTAD addresses this issue while also removing the artificial barrier between high-performance sport and engagement in lifelong, health-enhancing physical activity. LTAD recognizes that both high performance and lifelong engagement are built on the same foundation of physical literacy, and that an effective sport system builds a solid foundation before moving toward sport specificity.

This text, for the first time, brings together the large body of LTAD knowledge that has been developed over the past decade. The basic ideas of LTAD have been sharpened through the development of more than 100 sport-specific LTAD models in more than a dozen countries.

Part I of the text addresses the concepts that underpin long-term athlete development and explains how those concepts can be applied to all participants, including those with physical and intellectual disabilities. In part II the foundation concepts are expanded through the description of the key factors that guide and shape LTAD, including physical literacy; the differences between early and late specialization sports; variations in trainability across the life span (including windows of optimum trainability); and the importance of taking into consideration the

eBook
available at
HumanKinetics.com

stages of participants' intellectual, emotional, and moral development. Information is also presented on the time needed to develop excellence in sport and how periodization of training is related to the stage of athlete development. Because LTAD is about changing the whole sport system to improve the quality of the sport experience for participants, the amount, type, and rules of competition for different stages of athlete development are examined. Also addressed is how the many systems that affect athletes (e.g., sport organizations, schools, recreation systems) can work together to enhance the sport experience, rather than making conflicting demands. The key issue is that LTAD is a process of continuous improvement.

Part III looks at the seven stages of human development, from Active Start (the first six years of life), in which basic human movements are mastered, through the FUNdamentals stage (ages 6 to 9 for boys, 6 to 8 for girls), during which fundamental movement skills are developed, and through to the Learn to Train stage (approximately 9 to 12 for boys and 8 to 11 for girls), during which it is critical that children master a wide range of foundational sport skills. These three stages combined cover the period of development of physical literacy, after which people can pursue high-performance sport excellence. This occurs in the three stages of Train to Train (adolescent growth period), Train to Compete (postadolescent period), and Train to Win (early adulthood). This part of the text outlines optimum programs for participants at each stage of the LTAD model. The goal is to enable everyone to reach the final stage, Active for Life, which offers a variety of physical activities ranging from informal recreation to masters competitions.

This text is a road map to the development of high-performance athletes and the creation of healthy, active citizens. The LTAD model recognizes that athletes often change their focus. Some drop out of the high-performance stream, but they can rejoin that stream at any time if they maintain their sport engagement. You can use this book as an overview of athletic development from birth to adulthood and beyond, or, if your interest is more focused, to plan detailed programs for a particular group of athletes or participants at a specific stage of life. How you use it is up to you.

Acknowledgments

The authors acknowledge the contributions of the LTAD Expert Group and CS4L Leadership Team, the many colleagues who continually educate us, and Sport Canada for their willingness to support Canadian Sport for Life over an extended period of time.

Part I

Introduction to Long-Term Athlete Development

Today, children, teens, and adults of all ages face greater challenges than ever before. Obesity has become an epidemic and a major threat to the health of nations as obese people avoid sport and physical activity to escape stigma and embarrassment. Parents with visions of Olympic glory or professional riches for their children think that early specialization is the key to ultimate success and put their children in specialized programs far too soon. Meanwhile, the video game industry pours billions of dollars into entertainment that keeps children (and adults) more sedentary than ever before, while promoting virtual sports and virtual physical activity with new pseudo motion games. These problems are global and become more pressing every day.

Despite these problems, we have all seen and been awed by the transformation of a young boy or girl from awkward sport beginner to superb athlete. We instinctively know there have been coaching and training along the way, as well as support from caring adults and opportunities for meaningful competition. And we know, without a doubt, that there have been glorious moments of success, but also moments of crushing disappointment along the way. Some athletes' development has been haphazard, even random, creating "champions by chance," whereas others' has been planned, systematic, progressive, and developmentally appropriate.

This planned, systematic, and progressive development of individual athletes is called long-term athlete development (LTAD; also often called LTPD for long-term participant development or long-term player development). LTAD is the answer to one fundamental question: *What needs to be done at each stage of human development to give every child the best chance of engaging in lifelong, health-enhancing physical activity; and for those with the drive and talent, the best chance of athletic success?* Effective long-term athlete development focuses not on short-term gains and early success, but on what is best for the sport participant throughout life.

Many sport leaders are reinventing sport to better contribute to the well-being of society, the ethical development of athletes, and the development of higher-quality sporting experiences for everyone. To do this, they work diligently to link traditionally disconnected institutions (within sport and physical activity) as well as to link sport and physical activity to other sectors of civil society, such as education and health. This collaboration is needed so that the developing athlete is not harmed by the cumulative, and sometimes contradictory, demands of school, club, and representative teams, on which they might play a single sport. Because athletes develop within a number of systems, those systems need to work together to ensure optimum player development.

Part I of this text is organized into two chapters. Chapter 1 provides an overview of LTAD that briefly covers the history of athlete development models. Following a description of the shortcomings of current sport systems, and the consequences for individuals, sport, and society that result from these shortcomings, is a description of the evolution and development of the LTAD model.

Because LTAD represents a fundamental shift in the way sport is delivered, chapter 1 identifies the desired changes to sport and outlines the three major goals of the model: developing physical literacy, improving sport performance, and increasing levels of physical activity. The current fragmentation of the sport experience caused by the "us versus them" mentality of physical education, school sport, club teams, and national and regional representative and development programs is addressed along with the need to ensure that programs do what is best for the participant rather than what is best for the program.

LTAD is both a guide for developing athletes and physical activity participants and a powerful tool for change within sport systems. Its goals are to make sport more inclusive, more integrated, and of higher quality, while making the development of high-performance athletes more systematic.

Chapter 2 reinforces the critical idea that LTAD is a process for everyone by describing how the model can be applied to people with disabilities. Following a brief description of the way sport for those with disabilities is organized, and the types of people with disabilities who engage in sport, the chapter presents the LTAD process for athletes born with disabilities (congenital disabilities) and those who acquire disability through accident or illness.

In addition to the seven stages of the able-bodied LTAD model, the model for those with disabilities has two additional stages (awareness and first contact). Variations in the seven stages of LTAD as a result of disability are presented, along with some special considerations when dealing with specific types of disability.

Chapter 2 presents ways to support athletes with disabilities throughout their development and emphasizes the importance of properly classifying these athletes. Guidance is given concerning ways to audit facilities to ensure that they are accessible to all athletes, and changes to the sport system that would encourage participation in sport by athletes with disabilities are presented.

Chapter 2 concludes with the observation that there are far more similarities between LTAD for able-bodied athletes and LTAD for athletes with disabilities than there are differences. Adapting LTAD for athletes with disabilities is relatively easy if there is a willingness on the part of coaches and sport administrators.

Limitations of LTAD

Any attempt to fundamentally change an institution as old and as important as sport will face challenges, and for this reason it is important to address the limitations of the LTAD model. The strength of the LTAD model is that it is based on three solid foundations:

1. What is known about the stages of human growth and development
2. The academic and scientific information regarding enhancing physical capacity, particularly for children and youth
3. What effective youth sport coaches have found to work

Combining theory and practice into a single model is both the great strength of long-term athlete development and the focus of criticism aimed against it. The model is an attempt to be "roughly right" about the whole process rather than "exactly right" in every detail while risking missing the big picture.

LTAD also fills a void. In the past, information about how to systematically develop sporting excellence and increase active participation has been lacking. In fact, in many instances high performance and participation have been seen as an either-or choice for sport systems and particularly for national sport organizations (NSOs). NSOs were originally developed to govern participation in particular sports and to organize and sanction events and championships, and they were good at these tasks. In more recent years, NSOs have invested more time and energy in development, although this development is more frequently of the sport than of the athletes in the sport.

One criticism of LTAD is the lack of proof that it is better than the "old" way of developing athletes. In one sense this is true. First, there is no single "old" way of developing athletes, just an accumulation of practices and activities passed down within every sport. Second, no real-world experiment could ever be conducted in which young athletes are assigned to traditional or LTAD development pathways for the decade or two required for full athlete development. What we do understand are the many problems with the unsystematic athlete development systems currently in place. LTAD is designed to eliminate as many of those problems as possible. It is a model that relies on face validity. The question, based on what we know about children and youth and about sport, is: Does it make sense?

LTAD is based on the Japanese concept of *kaizen*, a word that can be translated as "improvement," or "change for the better." This philosophy has been imported to North America and applied to many types of business and social undertakings. At its heart is the idea that everyone in the system is responsible for the quality of the final product; as such, everyone is responsible for looking for ways to reduce errors and make things better. It is in this spirit of continuous improvement that leaders have developed, and continue to develop, LTAD.

As new information becomes available, and as the body of evidence from sports that have adopted LTAD increases, continual fine-tuning of the process will take place. There is no claim that LTAD as currently formulated is "exactly right," but a great interest exists in getting it right, and that will require a process of constant evolution and updating.

Long-Term Athlete Development Model

Bill filled the van with equipment, preparing for another big weekend of sports with the kids. Today was special, though, because Grandpa (his father) was coming to this morning's games. He hadn't been to a game in a long time, and with Grandpa getting older, there wouldn't be too many games left for him to see.

As Bill loaded the equipment, he reflected on the Youth Sport Association meeting he'd attended the previous evening. An approach called long-term athlete development (LTAD) had been introduced. Based on LTAD, a number of changes were suggested with regard to how the association ran its competitions. The leaders also talked about the need to focus on the needs and stages of development of the participants. Other things were said at the meeting, but, he had to admit, he had stopped listening because he just wasn't comfortable with all of the recommended changes.

Bill snapped back to reality. Where were the kids? They had to get going to pick Grandpa up and make it to the game on time. He found the kids where they usually were—in front of the screen, gaming. This drove Bill crazy because he felt he had little control over how much time the kids spent playing these games. He set limits at home, but the kids always seemed to find friends who had no limits. What really troubled Bill was that he could see that his kids were a bit heavy. Not really heavy, but heavier than he had been as a child.

Finally, they were out the door. They picked up Grandpa and they were soon in the stands. It was a good game—a bit of a blowout, but Bill's kids were on the winning team when the game ended so he didn't care. "So Dad, what did you think of the game?" he asked. Much to Bill's surprise, Grandpa launched into a rant about how the game wasn't like it had been when he was a kid. "There were girls playing! The equipment was different! Everything was different!" he railed. This hit Bill hard. Just the night before at the meeting, he had been arguing to keep the game the same because that was how it was traditionally played. But Grandpa was saying that many changes had happened even since his day.

Bill wondered if he was behind the times. Was he thinking about sport too conventionally? He was shocked that his father couldn't enjoy his kids' game just because of a few changes in format and style. Considering his own reaction to LTAD, was he thinking like Grandpa? Bill's mind came back to reality again as he looked around for his children. He noticed that when the game was over, only a few players remained on the field to play around; his kids were already in the van with their eyes locked on their handheld screens. Their definition of fun sure was different from his. Perhaps it was time for Bill to consider these LTAD changes.

This chapter provides a brief history of the evolution of the LTAD model and outlines the seven stages and 10 key factors of the model. It also describes how participation and performance work together to promote excellence and make people active for life. The shortcomings and consequences of the current sport system are also addressed, as is how LTAD can be used as a philosophy, guide, and tool for positive change.

Beginnings of LTAD

In 1983 Harsanyi reviewed the literature of athlete development models from the 1950s to the 1980s and concluded that most of them were characterized by four stages: child, juvenile, junior, and adult—or basic, intermediate, advanced, and elite. All of the models were based on chronological age and did not consider biological or developmental age. This pyramid model, shown in figure 1.1, systematically excludes people along the sport development pathway, focusing only on athletes who make the cut to the next level. As the arrow depicts in figure 1.1, the pyramid system eliminates participants at every level until only a few remain to represent their country. In this system of exclusion, those not progressing to the next level are not valued. This traditional pyramid model, created in the 1960s, is still used in many sports today. The systematic elimination of participants from the club and national levels results in only a few high performers remaining at the highest level. The sport system did not care where these excluded participants went. This pyramid model disconnected sport and recreation in North America: recreation valued participating outside the athlete development pathway, whereas many in sport did not.

In 1989 Sanderson introduced an athlete development model in his article "Growth and Development Considerations for the Design of Training Plans for Young Athletes." This model took into consideration the growth and maturation processes of young, developing athletes. Sanderson's work was important because it considered developmental age a crucial factor in athlete development, whereas other models were based only on chronological age. In 1995

Balyi and Way developed a four-stage model called long-term athlete development that, by 2005, had evolved into seven stages. This book is based on this model.

The original impetus of the Balyi and Way LTAD model was to improve the quality of sport programs so all participants, including top athletes, could reach their potential. In 2005 Balyi and colleagues built on the 1995 model to develop LTAD as a practical pathway incorporating empirical coaching observations and experiences; coaching science; and human growth, development, and maturation principles. Similarities also exist between LTAD and the emerging field of developing expertise in sport.

LTAD was created to improve the quality of sport and physical activity so participants could realize their potential, whatever it may be. To improve the current sport system's structure for people at all levels of involvement, a fundamental change is necessary. Central to this change is the clear identification of principles and guidelines that focus on the needs and goals of participants throughout the life cycle. This is the aim of LTAD: to address the many shortcomings and resulting consequences that impede the current system and to provide positive experiences for participants of all abilities.

The shortcomings of the current system of developing athletes to become excellent or to become active for life are the following:

Poor Training, Practice, and Competition Theories

- In team sports, young athletes overcompete and undertrain.
- Adult training and competition programs are superimposed on developing athletes.
- Training methods and competition programs designed for male athletes are superimposed on female athletes.
- Preparation is geared toward the short-term outcome (winning) and not toward the process of long-term development.
- Chronological rather than developmental age is used in training and competition planning.

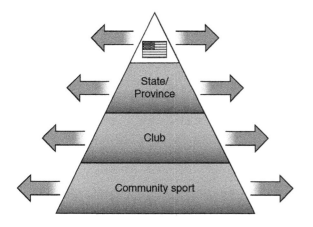

FIGURE 1.1 The traditional athlete development model.

- Coaches largely neglect the sensitive periods of accelerated adaptation to training.
- Fundamental movement skills and sport skills are either not taught properly or not taught at all.
- The developmental training needs of athletes with disabilities are not well understood.

Ill-Structured Programs

- The most knowledgeable coaches work at the elite level; volunteers coach at the developmental level, where quality, trained coaches are essential.
- Parents are not educated about LTAD.
- In most sports, the competition system interferes with athlete development.
- There are ineffective talent identification (TID) systems.
- There is no integration of school physical education programs, recreational community programs, and elite competitive programs.
- Sports have athletes specialize too early in an attempt to attract and retain participants.

Inactive and Unhealthy Lifestyles

- An unhealthy, sedentary lifestyle dominates everyday life.
- People lack knowledge about active and healthy lifestyles.
- People have poor nutritional habits.

Lack of Working Together

The following areas lack integration and communication:

- Education
- Health
- Sport
- Recreation

The consequences of these shortcomings are the following:

Serious Health Issues

- Lack of participation resulting in a sedentary way of life
- Significant pressure on government revenues to deliver rehabilitation programs

Limits to Athletic Development

- Poor movement abilities
- Lack of proper fitness
- Poor skill development
- Bad habits developed from a focus on winning
- Children not having fun as they play adult-based programs
- Undeveloped and unrefined skills as a result of undertraining
- Female athletes not reaching their potential because of inappropriate programs
- Athletes failing to reach their genetic potential and optimal performance level

Ineffective Collaboration and Inefficient Delivery of Programs

- Lack of coordinated policies
- Lack of communication and collaboration among education, health, sport, and recreation
- Failure to reach optimal performance levels in international competitions
- Athletes pulled in different directions by school, club, and provincial teams because of the structure of competition programs
- Lack of remedial programs, implemented by provincial and national team coaches, to counteract the shortcomings of athlete preparation
- No systematic development of the next generation of successful international athletes
- Fluctuating national performances as a result of a lack of TID and a developmental pathway

One major consequence of the current system is that when fundamental movement skills and sport skills are either not taught properly or not taught at all, children lose many options for participating in physical activities and sports. This is shown in figure 1.2.

LTAD Model Explained

The LTAD model is a seven-stage framework to guide the participation, training, competition, and recovery pathways in sport and physical activity, from infancy through all phases of adulthood. The seven stages are as follows:

1. Active Start
2. FUNdamentals
3. Learn to Train
4. Train to Train
5. Train to Compete
6. Train to Win
7. Active for Life

Each stage is discussed in more detail in part III. The LTAD seven-stage model is built on the following 10 factors:

1. Physical literacy
2. Specialization
3. Age
4. Trainability
5. Intellectual, emotional, and moral development
6. Excellence takes time
7. Periodization
8. Competition
9. System alignment and integration
10. Continuous improvement

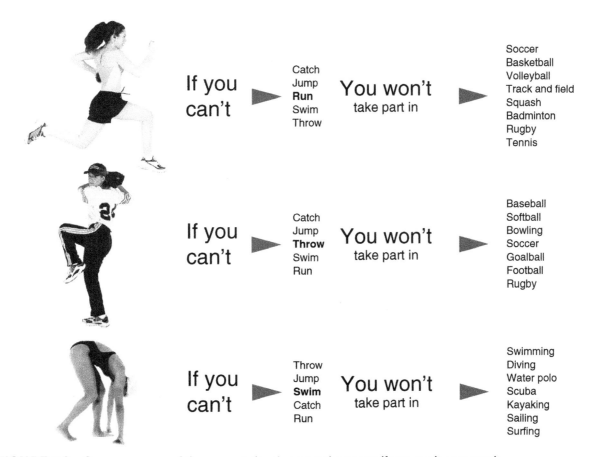

FIGURE 1.2 Consequences of the current developmental system: If you can't, you won't.

Reprinted, by permission, from C. Higgs, I. Balyi, and R. Way, 2008, *Developing physical literacy: A guide for parents of children ages 0 to 12* (Vancouver, BC: Canadian Sport Centres), 13.

Each of these factors is discussed in detail in part II. Any organization interested in incorporating LTAD into its programming should use these factors when educating parents, coaches, administrators, and participants about the benefits of the LTAD approach.

LTAD focuses on the needs of participants and their individual stages of development and provides a point of reference for coaches, administrators, sport scientists, parents, and others involved in supporting the delivery of sport at all levels. The model recognizes both participation and performance-oriented pathways in sport and physical activity, preceded by the fun-based development of physical literacy (i.e., being competent in both fundamental movement skills and fundamental sport skills) in the early years. The framework provides guidance to improve the quality of sport and physical activity by helping all children to become physically literate.

Within the performance-oriented pathway, athletes whose experiences are informed by the LTAD model experience developmentally appropriate training and competition programs at all ages, to increase their participation and optimize performance. For those choosing more participation-oriented involvement, LTAD provides the core skills and capabilities to support and promote lifelong engagement.

People develop physical literacy during the first three stages of LTAD, which, in turn, helps them move to the later stages (figure 1.3). Those with disabilities go through two additional stages: awareness and first contact. Awareness is about discovering the opportunities that are available, and first contact is about ensuring that the athlete's first experience in the sport is positive and meaningful.

LTAD recognizes that people go through stages of growth and development from birth to death. At each stage, a range of physical, psychological, social, and environmental factors affect their ability to participate, train, and compete in physical activity. LTAD presents an optimal pathway from pond or playground to podium, as well as a catalyst for lifelong physical activity. It offers athletes the opportunity

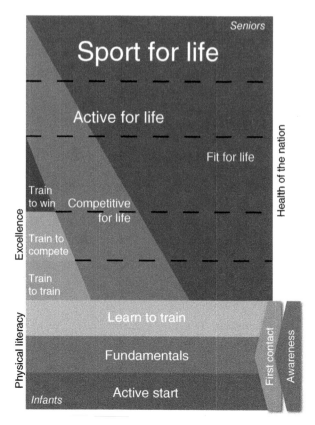

FIGURE 1.3 Basic sport for life LTAD rectangle.
Reprinted, by permission, from Canadian Sports for Life.

to reach their full athletic potential, whether that means competing for select club teams, earning college scholarships, competing in the Olympics or Paralympics, or becoming sport professionals. Participation-oriented people derive greater enjoyment in one or more sports, which helps them remain active for life. The model also provides the tools to help people progress within and between the participation- and performance-oriented pathways.

Administrators, coaches, and parents should remember that moving from one stage to another is based on ability and not chronological age; however, chronological age is used as a guide. Some stages also identify a developmental age, which broadly relates to the connection between growth and maturation.

Table 1.1 highlights the differences between where we are now and where we want to be, which is a sport system based on LTAD principles.

Sport for Life

Sport for life (S4L) is a movement to improve the quality of sport and physical activity. It links sport, education, recreation, and health and aligns community, provincial and state, and national programming. S4L's vision is quality programs for everyone based on developmentally appropriate sport and physical activity. Its mission is to improve the health and sporting experiences of everyone by advancing physical literacy, improving performance, and increasing lifelong participation in physical activity. When enacted, S4L links and integrates programs delivered in the areas of health, recreation, education, and sport and aligns programming in clubs, provincial and state organizations, and national sport and multisport organizations. S4L addresses the overarching system and structure of sport and physical activity, including the relationships among school sport, physical education, and organized sport at all levels, from policy to program delivery.

TABLE 1.1 Where We Are Now and Where We Want to Be

Where we are now . . .	Where we want to be . . .
Parents believe that focusing children on a single sport is advantageous.	Parents ensure that their children become physically literate (more athletic) through multisport activities.
Sport programs and competitions are based on chronological age.	Developmental age and the specific LTAD stage guides participation.
International standard annual age cutoffs for youth are in place.	Competition is reformatted to increase enjoyment and development and considers relative age (see chapter 5).
Traditional programming is based on guessing what programs are best for the participant.	Programs identify participants' biological markers to tailor programs specific to their needs.
Adult periodization is based on a single sport and intended for national-level athletes.	Periodization considers junior athletes who may be participating in more than one sport as well as attending school.
Adult training programs are superimposed on developing athletes.	Developmentally appropriate programs using the sensitive periods of accelerated adaptation are included in training program designs.
Male training programs are superimposed on female athletes.	Programs for females are designed specifically to consider their physiological stages of development.
Participants of all ages overvalue winning but lack a developmentally appropriate competition structure.	Participants of all ages participate in developmentally appropriate and meaningful competition.
Systems lead to exclusion at all stages, because only a small percentage of athletes qualify for the highest levels of performance.	Systems promote the inclusion of all athletes by ensuring that they have the skills necessary for remaining physically active, either competitively or recreationally, for life.
A singular approach allows administrations to serve their organizations only.	A global vision in an integrated system allows organizations to work toward a better future for all.

Designed to address a person's unique goals, needs, and stage of athletic development, LTAD provides the guidance required for participants in sport and physical activity to achieve three key outcomes: physical literacy, improved performance, and lifelong participation. Physical literacy is the foundation for improved performance and lifelong participation (figure 1.4). By developing physical literacy, people learn the fundamental movement and sport skills necessary to engage in sport and physical activity for the rest of their lives, whether for competition or fitness.

LTAD was developed with a strong emphasis on the development of fundamental skills and sport-specific skills to create viable pathways for young athletes wishing to progress within competitive sport. This approach came about as a result of a recognition of the dangers of identifying talent based on early physical maturity, as discovered in extensive research on "the relative age effect" (Mujika et al., 2009). It also provided specific recommendations for training interventions that take into account the developmental, rather than chronological, age of the participant.

From the outset, researchers indicated that lifelong physical activity and related health benefits could be a significant by-product of an effectively implemented LTAD system. From the early 1990s onward, the success of LTAD as a planning and policy tool has highlighted the need to more clearly articulate the nature of and relationship between performance- and participation-oriented pathways. This relationship has since been acknowledged in sport systems around the world, including in Canada (Balyi, Cardinal, Higgs, Norris, & Way, 2005), Ireland (Duffy et al., 2003), Bahrain (Balyi et al., 2012), England (Stafford, 2005), and South Africa (Vardhan, Balyi, & Duffy, 2012), as well as by international organizations (International Sport Coaching Framework, 2012). LTAD has also been a part of a wider recognition of the need for longer-term views of sport participation, best exemplified by the developmental model of sport participation (Cote, Baker, & Abernethy, 2003).

Sport for Life Philosophy

The LTAD model and philosophy acknowledge first that physical education, school sports, competitive sports, and recreational activities are mutually interdependent and contribute to the development of healthy, active kids. Traditionally, physical education in schools, recreational sports, and elite sports have all been developed separately. This approach is ineffective and expensive. It fails to ensure that all children, including those who may have the potential to become elite athletes, are given a solid foundation and knowledge base—physical, technical, tactical, and mental—on which to build their athletic abilities. LTAD is an inclusive model that encourages children to get involved in lifelong physical activity by connecting and integrating school physical education programs with elite sport club programs and recreational sport programs in the community. Through its holistic approach, LTAD considers physiological, psychological, and social development so each athlete develops as a complete person.

Also, although not typical in most parts of the world, sports in North America have traditionally operated independently from one another, as well as from schools and community (city) programs. Consequently, sport systems are riddled with an "us versus them"

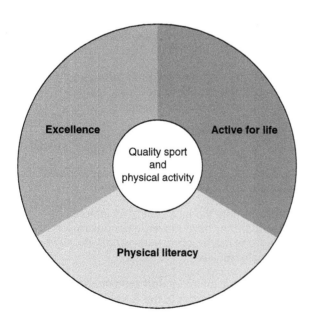

FIGURE 1.4 Three outcomes of LTAD.

"In youth hockey, in most cases, it's really important for kids to play other sports—whether it's indoor lacrosse or soccer or baseball. I think what that does is two things. One, each sport helps the other sport. And then I think taking time off in the off-season—that three- or four-month window—really rejuvenates kids so when they come back at the end of August, they're more excited. They think, 'All right, hockey's back, I'm ready to go.'" Wayne Gretzky (as cited in Duhatschek, 2008)

mentality. This individualistic and oppositional approach results in organizations and coaches competing for good players instead of helping these players develop fundamental movement and sport skills and preparing them for the sport that best suits them. The current approach in North America is often not in the best interest of athletes and contradicts the successful sport systems of other nations, where sport organizations and coaches work together to fully develop athletes for high-performance achievement and long-term participation.

Framework for Working Together

By establishing specific terms for the seven stages and their components, LTAD gives individuals and organizations a common vocabulary through which to connect. Working together involves connections

- within sport and physical activity organizations;
- between sport and physical activity organizations; and
- among the areas of sport, recreation, education, and health.

Components within sport and physical activity organizations must work in harmony to provide the most productive services possible. This is the first layer of a three-dimensional approach. Once individual organizations are aligned, their next step is to connect with other sport and physical activity organizations and provide combined services to make participants' experiences as complete as possible.

All organizations can use LTAD to determine their roles and responsibilities in the development of athletes throughout their careers. They can also help athletes who are at the end of their careers remain active for life and give back to their sports in volunteer roles.

As a framework for working together, LTAD provides a platform for discussion. For example, those concerned about inactive children express the following:

- Health practitioners are concerned about poor health due to weight gain that can cause a number of issues, including the early onset of diabetes.
- Educators are concerned about poor grades due to children's lack of attention span stemming from improper nutrition and insufficient physical activity.
- Recreation programmers are concerned about diminished participation due to children's lack of interest in exerting themselves.
- Sport coaches are concerned about inadequate physical and skill development due to reduced participation.
- Parents are concerned about their children's inactivity and seek support to change this behavior.

Staff in all sectors may have different concerns, but *they all are concerned*. LTAD allows the sectors to support each other in the interest of igniting activity in inactive children. For example, if all staff use physical literacy as an outcome, they can identify gradual steps to increase children's enjoyment of physical activity by learning new fundamental movement and sport skills. Parents can engage by understanding what their children need to become physically literate, thus ensuring that they are in the right programs to achieve the goal.

Guide for Participating in Sport and Physical Activity

The first three stages of LTAD—Active Start, FUNdamentals, and Learn to Train—are imperative for both the development of physical literacy and the enjoyment of sport and physical activity. Once children pass through the Learn to Train stage, they have acquired the fundamental movement and sport skills necessary to participate in whatever activities they choose. At this point, the knowledge and skills they have gained will lead to either excellence or continued participation in physical activity for life. Either way, they have the necessary means to remain active for life.

Once athletes have passed through the Learn to Train stage and become physically literate, the Train to Train, Train to Compete, and Train to Win stages become possibilities. As they enter these later stages, their levels of competition and performance increase. If they choose not to pursue the highest levels of competition, they may leave any of the excellence stages at any time and enter the Active for Life stage.

Tool for Change

Change can be a difficult process to begin, particularly when things have been static for a long time. This is the problem many sport organizations face today. They recognize that changes are necessary to properly develop athletes and create a more physically active and healthy nation, but they fear moving out of their comfort zone.

LTAD has been created to incite organizations to change to improve the quality of sport and physical activity. By following LTAD, sport systems will be better equipped to do the following:

- Move from exclusion to inclusion by finding a place for all to play rather than cutting kids from sport teams.

- Shift from independence to integration by helping organizations and sectors work together to ensure the holistic development of children and youth through access to a range of activities and facilities.

- Promote quality over quantity by considering the quality of participants' experiences instead of providing funds solely based on the number of participants.

- Plan for success (instead of watching it randomly happen) by properly developing talent.

- Place more emphasis on the quality of a program and less on the immediate results it produces.

- Consider what is best for athletes' or participants' longevity by allowing them to play other sports or on different teams that might fit them better, instead of trying to keep them in a certain sport or on a specific team just because they are achieving.

- Focus on long-term goals over short-term goals by considering participants' experiences and ensuring that they all have the chance to play and contribute, regardless of whether they are all-stars or bench players.

Summary

With obesity and inactivity rates increasing and technology enveloping today's youth, it's time to act. LTAD is the catalyst for improving the quality of sport by challenging the underlying beliefs and theories that have stagnated it. When children enjoy activity—whether a sport or general physical activities—they are more likely to engage. LTAD is a guide for action that begins with instructing parents about the sports their children could participate in and moves all the way to creating a national sport policy.

All of us face significant challenges in being and staying healthy—and so do our children. LTAD, with its goals of developing physical literacy, improving performance, and promoting lifelong physical activity, is a tool that

LTAD-Based Actions Checklist

The following checklist of actions can be used by any organization's board of directors to improve the quality of their sport or recreation programs through the implementation of LTAD.

Adopt a sport for life *philosophy*.

☐ Use LTAD in decision making.

☐ Determine roles and mandates based on LTAD stages.

☐ Build relationships based on LTAD language, values, and principles.

☐ Implement LTAD-centered governance structures.

☐ Implement LTAD-centered strategic planning.

☐ Use LTAD-based criteria to budget and fund.

Use sport for life and LTAD as a *framework* to review and align sport training, competition, and recovery programming for the following:

☐ School sports

☐ Community sport

☐ Pro club academies

☐ University or college athletics

☐ Sport schools

☐ Recreation centers

☐ Physical education (to strive to develop physical literacy)

Use LTAD as a *guide* to create quality standards.

☐ Modify coaching practices.

☐ Improve training programs.

☐ Improve planning and periodization.

☐ Time specialization correctly (sport, discipline, event, position).

☐ Upgrade stage-specific skills training.

☐ Ensure the use of LTAD stage–appropriate equipment and clothing.

☐ Design a new generation of facilities.

Use LTAD as a *guide* to review and update the following:

☐ Rules of the game

☐ Tournament or league formats

☐ Season schedules

☐ Officiating practices

Use sport for life and LTAD as a *tool for change* to communicate and improve sport for the following:

☐ Coaches

☐ Officials

☐ Volunteers

☐ Parents

☐ Administrators

A very effective tool for change is knowledge. To be able to trigger change for good, the first task is to learn more about your sport. You should do simple research to become a student of your sport. For example, does the program have a relative age effect? Find this by reviewing the birth month of the children who have registered. Ask parents why they registered their children and, more important, if they didn't sign up for the next season, why they didn't want to come back.

everyone can use to improve the quality of sport and physical activity. The LTAD model permits individuals and organizations to make sound decisions about the best possible training, competition, and recovery programs for all members. Implementing a stage-by-stage LTAD approach can facilitate change in the culture of club sport because clubs develop their own LTAD programs and work with various partners in the community (schools and local government), with the goal of getting more people active and excelling in sport. LTAD is a philosophy, a guide, a framework, and a tool for change. It can serve as a catalyst for getting organizations to work together to improve the experiences people have while participating in sport and physical activity.

Using the LTAD 10 key factors, administrators, coaches, and parents can develop physically literate children, world-class athletes, and healthy, active people for life.

Questions for Reflection

- What does the LTAD model recognize in addition to performance that makes it different from the traditional athlete development model?
- Most athlete development models have been based on chronological age. What is the primary type of age that guides LTAD?
- What is likely to happen to someone who doesn't have fundamental sport skills?
- How many stages are in the typical LTAD model?
- How many factors influence LTAD?
- Is LTAD a philosophy, guide, tool, or all of these?

References

Balyi, I., Cardinal, C., Higgs, C., Norris, S., & Way, R. (2005). *Canadian sport for life: Long-term athlete development* [Resource paper]. Vancouver, BC: Canadian Sport Centres.

Balyi, I., & Way, R. (1995). Long-term planning of athlete development: The training to train phase. *B.C. Coach*, 2-10.

Balyi, I., et al. (2012). *Bahrain sport for life*. Bahrian: Bahrain Sport Commission.

Cote, J., Baker, J., & Abernethy, B. (2003). From play to practice: A developmental framework for acquisition of expertise in team sports. In Starkes, J.L. & Ericsson, K.A. (Eds.), *Expert performance in sport: Advances in research on sport expertise* (pp. 89-113). Champaign, IL: Human Kinetics.

Duffy, P., Balyi, I., Aboud, S., Gregg, et al. (2003). *Building pathways in Irish sport: Towards a plan for the sporting health and well-being of the nation*. Limerick, Ireland: National Coaching and Training Centre.

Duhatschek, E. (2008, September 26). The Great One's message to parents: Let your kids have fun. *The Globe and Mail* (n.p.).

Harsanyi, L. (1983). A 10-18 eves atletak felkeszitesenek modellje. *Utanpotlasneveles, 10* (n.p.).

International sport coaching framework. (2012). Champaign, IL: Human Kinetics.

Mujika, I., Vaeyens, R., Matthys, S. J., Santisteban, J., Goiriena, J., & Philippaerts, R. (2009). The relative age effect in a professional football club setting. *Journal of Sports Sciences, 27* (11), 1153-1158.

Sanderson, L. (1989). Growth and development considerations for the design of training plans for young athletes. *SPORTS: Science Periodical on Research and Technology in Sport, 10* (2), 1-7.

Stafford, I. (2005). *Coaching for long-term athlete development: To improve participation and performance in sport*. West Yorkshire, UK: SportscoachUK & Coachwise Business Solutions.

Vardhan, D., Balyi, I., & Duffy, P. (2012). *South African sport for life*. Johannesburg, South Africa: South African Sport Commission.

To Learn More

Bar-Or, O. (1996). *The child and the adolescent athlete*. Oxford, UK: Blackwell Science.

Barnsley, R.H., Thompson, A.H., & Barnsley, P.E. (1985). Hockey success and birthdate: The relative age effect. *Canadian Association for Health, Physical Education, and Recreation, 51*, 23-28.

Dick, F.W. (1985). *Sports training principles*. London: Lepus Books.

Gladwell, M. (2008). *Outliers: The story of success*. New York: Little, Brown.

Higgs, C., Balyi, I. & Way, R. (2006). *No accidental champions: Long-term athlete development for athletes with a disability*. Vancouver, BC: Canadian Sport Centres.

Higgs, C., Balyi, I. & Way, R. (2008). *Developing physical literacy: A guide for parents of children ages 0 to 12: A supplement to Canadian sport for life*. Vancouver, BC: Canadian Sport Centres.

Higgs, C., & Way, R. (Eds.). (2005). *Sport Canada: Strategic leadership for sport* [Figure]. Modified from *Sport England*, 2004. Victoria, BC: Canadian Sport Centres.

Malina, R.M., Bouchard, C., & Bar-Or, O. (2004). *Growth, maturation, and physical activity* (2nd ed.). Champaign, IL: Human Kinetics.

Robinson, M.J. (2010). *Sport club management.* Champaign, IL: Human Kinetics.

Starkes, J.A., & Ericsson, K.A. (2003). *Expert performance in sport: Recent advances in research on sport expertise.* Champaign, IL: Human Kinetics.

United States Olympic Committee. (2000). *The path to excellence: A comprehensive view of development of U.S. Olympians who competed from 1984 to 1998.* Colorado Spring, CO: USOC.

Way, R., Balyi, I., & Grove, J. (2007). *Canadian sport for life: A sport parent's guide.* Ottawa, ON: Canadian Sport Centres.

Active for Life magazine: www.a4l.ca

Canadian Sport for Life: www.cs4l.ca

Canadian Sport for Life, physical literacy: www.physical-literacy.ca

International Sport for Life Society: www.is4ls.org

Also, search the Internet for the keywords *sport-specific LTAD models worldwide.*

Athletes With Disabilities

John didn't remember anything about the accident. He and some friends had been competing at a regional track and field meet, and the last thing he could remember was being in the passenger seat of the car on the way home. He remembered that it had started to rain, and that he was leaning over to try to get some better music on the radio. Next thing he knew was waking up in the hospital with no feeling in his legs and unable to move them. He was the lucky one. His two friends, the only other passengers in the car, had both been killed; and the doctors had told him that he would be spending the rest of his life in a wheelchair as a result of his spinal cord injury.

John was surprised that, other than his family, one of his first visitors was a young woman in a wheelchair whom he had never met before. She introduced herself as Colleen and explained that she was a counselor in the hospital's rehab center and would be working with him to help make sure he lived a full and productive life. The first thing they were going to work on was getting John active again to build up his strength. Then he would learn how to get into and out of his wheelchair and become mobile. Colleen promised he would be able to try wheelchair basketball, and if he was interested, wheelchair racing and cross-country skiing.

John, who was familiar with long-term athlete development from track and field, was thinking about what Colleen had said. With a laugh he realized that he was going back to the beginning: active start, then the *fun*damentals of using his wheelchair, and then he would have to learn to train again, but this time in wheelchair sport.

Athletes with disabilities have either had their disabilities since birth (congenital disabilities) or have become disabled later in life (acquired disabilities). Athletes with either congenital or acquired disabilities go through the same LTAD stages as their able-bodied peers, although there are two additional substages early in the process. This chapter addresses the kinds of support athletes with disabilities need to reach their full athletic potential.

Sport for People With Disabilities

A person with any kind of disability can take part in just about any sport for fun, excitement, and healthy recreation, but high-performance organized sport is widely organized for those with specific types of disability.

The Paralympic Games, the highest level of sport for people with disabilities, are organized by the International Paralympic Committee. These Games are held about two weeks after the Olympic Games and in the same city. This means that Paralympic Summer Games and Paralympic Winter Games are each held once every four years. National Paralympic Committees organize a range of sporting activities within their own countries for people with the following types of disability:

- **Wheelchair user.** Sport for wheelchair users is for those who use a wheelchair for locomotion. This can include people with spinal cord injury, amputees, people with cerebral palsy or who are post-polio, or those with other mobility disabilities that require the use of a wheelchair.

- **Amputee.** Amputees are those who lack limbs or limb segments.

- **Cerebral palsy.** *Cerebral palsy* (CP) is a term used to cover a range of movement difficulties that are nonprogressive and noncontagious, and that are most often caused by injury to the brain before, during, or after birth. One or more limbs may be involved, and the disability ranges from mild to severe.

• **Visually impaired.** Athletes with a visual impairment range from those with total blindness (no reaction to light) to those who are partially sighted.

• **Les autres.** The term for these athletes is derived from the French and means "the others." It covers athletes with a mobility impairment who do not fall into any other group (e.g., people with dwarfism or multiple sclerosis).

• **Intellectual impairment.** This category includes people who have demonstrated such significant impairment in their intellectual or cognitive ability that they have associated limitations to their adaptive behavior and their ability to take part in sport.

Because athletes have differing degrees of disability, they compete in classes of approximately equal degrees of disability. Different sports have different classification systems; in some sports athletes with different disabilities compete together, and in other sports only those with the same disability compete.

LTAD Stages for Athletes With Disabilities

Some disabilities, such as cerebral palsy, are present from birth, which makes them congenital. People with congenital disabilities pass through the same stages of LTAD as their able-bodied peers (figure 2.1), although the nature of the disability may change the age at which they pass from one stage to the next. For example, those with intellectual impairment may start their adolescent growth spurt earlier than others, but may take longer to complete it, resulting in their being in the train to train stage longer than their peers.

The situation is slightly more complex for people with acquired disabilities; for them, the age at which they acquired the disability is an important factor. A person who has acquired

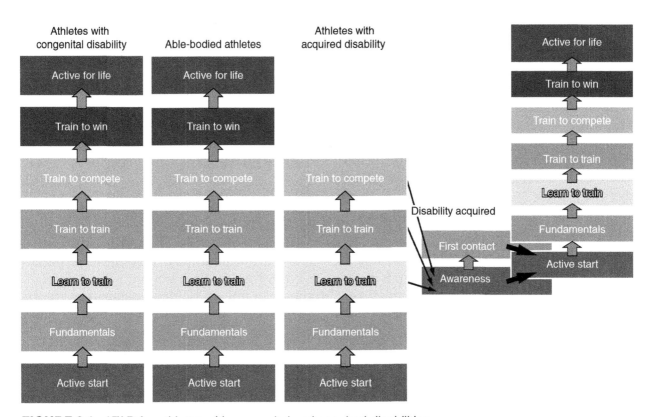

FIGURE 2.1 LTAD for athletes with congenital and acquired disabilities.

a disability very early in life will pass through most stages of LTAD along with able-bodied peers. Someone who acquired a disability later in life needs to repeat the early stages of LTAD using the body's newly changed capabilities. People in this category also need to pass through the two additional LTAD substages for those with disabilities.

Active Start

For those with congenital disabilities, the Active Start stage is the same as it is for able-bodied athletes. This stage is a time to learn basic human movements (modified as necessary to accommodate different abilities), to develop a positive attitude toward physical activity, to build the vast web of brain connections that control movements, and to develop habits of being physically active. This is also a time when parents and caregivers need to support young children, but not smother them. Too frequently, loving parents want to protect children with disabilities from further hurt. However, in protecting them from the normal bumps and bruises of childhood rough-and-tumble, they also prevent them from developing their physical skills and their confidence to move.

For the person with a traumatically acquired disability, the Active Start stage is about making the transition from medical treatment to reengaging in life and once again becoming physically active. It is about learning the basic human movements that are possible with whatever functional capacity remains following the trauma, and developing or redeveloping a positive attitude toward physical activity.

FUNdamentals

For the able-bodied child and the child with a congenital disability, the FUNdamentals stage is about learning all of the fundamental movement skills. It's about learning to run and jump and hop and catch and throw and kick and also about learning to use a prosthetic arm or leg, or to become mobile using a wheelchair or walker. It is about learning all of those skills that can be used in sport and physical activity later in life.

For those with acquired disabilities, it is about relearning to use their bodies, with their new strengths and weaknesses. This means learning such skills as transferring from a bed or chair to a wheelchair, and being comfortable wheeling around under various conditions. It means learning mobility skills in the absence of vision, or learning to walk and run using a prosthesis. For both the able bodied and those with congenital disabilities, this stage is not about learning sport skills; rather, it is about learning all the skills that may be used later in sport. It is also the time for those with acquired disabilities to build up their remaining functional musculature.

Learn to Train

In the Learn to Train stage, people learn and polish fundamental sport skills; this is true for athletes with acquired or congenital disabilities. As with able-bodied children, this is a time to engage in many different sport activities, not to start becoming a specialist. It is a time to find out the sports for which their talents make them best suited and to find the sports that best meet their physical, mental, emotional, and social needs. Athletes with acquired disabilities often want to jump straight into a single sport immediately after the transition from the FUNdamentals stage, but this is a mistake. The Learn to Train stage is a time to sample what is out there in order to make an informed choice about the two or three sports on which to focus.

Train to Train

The Train to Train stage is the time to "build the engine" in athletes with congenital disabilities, because, like their able-bodied peers, they are going through their adolescent growth spurt. It is also a time for them to become more specialized in their sport selection, narrowing their choice to one or two complementary sports (e.g., wheelchair racing in the summer and cross-country skiing in the winter).

For the athlete with an acquired disability, this is still the time to seriously develop the physical capacities of strength, stamina, suppleness (flexibility), and skill in the chosen sport(s). As with able-bodied athletes, there is a need to increase the volume of training with care to avoid overuse injuries. This can be particularly difficult for wheelchair users, who must use the smaller muscles of the shoulders and arms for both sport training and performance and the mobility demands of daily living. Given that almost all wheelchair propulsion in daily living and in sport is used to drive the wheelchair and athlete forward, there is a risk that muscular development in the shoulder and arms will be greater in the muscles that drive the wheelchair forward than in those that drive the wheelchair backward. This asymmetrical muscle development can make the athlete more susceptible to injury. This stage, as it is for able-bodied athletes, is the one that makes or breaks the developing athlete. Too little training at this stage and athletes will not reach their full potential; too much training and they will fail to fully develop because of overuse injuries.

Train to Compete

The athlete at the Train to Compete stage is starting to compete nationally and perhaps internationally. Because this stage occurs in postadolescence for athletes with either acquired or congenital disabilities, both have the same needs. This is a time when athletes with high-performance aspirations should have a clear focus on a single sport, and within that sport a single discipline or, in team sport, a single position. Everything in the Train to Compete stage for the able-bodied athlete is applicable to the athlete with a disability.

Train to Win

Athletes in the Train to Win stage are competing on the world stage and are in contention for medals (or at least for the finals) in their sport at continental and world championships, and at the Paralympic Summer and Winter Games. They are elite athletes like their able-bodied peers and need to train and compete in exactly the same manner.

Additional Stages

For athletes with disabilities, there are two additional LTAD stages: awareness and first contact (see figure 2.1).

Awareness

For a child with a congenital disability, the early years are often filled with medical interventions and therapy, and with parents working hard to ensure that the child receives the needed medical, educational, and social support. During this critical early childhood period, physical activity and sport involvement are often not high priorities for parents. A lack of awareness of the benefits that taking part in physical activity can bring may result in little effort being expended in getting children involved.

The situation is slightly different for people who acquire disabilities. Prior to being injured, few people are aware of, or knowledgeable about, sport for those with disabilities, and the newly disabled are therefore unaware of the wide range of sport and recreation opportunities available to them. They are also likely unaware of the enhanced quality of life from the improved strength and fitness that results from sport participation. For these reasons, sport organizations need to make sport opportunities for people with disabilities better known, particularly to doctors, physiotherapists, and rehabilitation specialists.

First Contact

It takes a great deal of courage for a person with a disability to arrive at a sport venue and say, "I want to learn this sport." Therefore, the moment of first contact between a person with a disability and the sport system is critical. That contact can have a huge impact on whether the person stays, learns the sport, and becomes fully involved—or withdraws. If during first contact the person is made to feel welcome, the probability of returning is high. If, on the other hand, the person feels unwelcome or rejected, the likelihood of continuing in the sport is slim.

People with disabilities (and their parents) generally have no expectation that the coach or sport leader will have all the answers as to exactly how they will fit in the sport. Often, all they want to hear is something along the lines of, "Come on in—and welcome. I'm not sure how, but together we can find ways to get you playing."

Special Considerations

Despite the overwhelming similarities between able-bodied athletes and athletes with disabilities, there are some special disability considerations that athletes and coaches need to be aware of. Consider the following:

- **Blind athletes.** For athletes with congenital blindness, learning a new skill is much more difficult than it is for athletes with vision. Without vision, the athlete has difficulty building a mental map of what the skill should look like. Often, visually impaired athletes have to have their limbs moved repeatedly through the action they are trying to learn; they may have to do this six or seven times to understand the skill as well as a sighted athlete would having seen it performed only once. Blind sport organizations and national organizations for the blind have a wealth of experience working with blind and visually impaired athletes, and coaches should call on these organizations for their knowledge and expertise.

- **Athletes with cerebral palsy.** In the past there was concern that resistance training might increase the spasticity of muscles in athletes with cerebral palsy. Spasticity is the uncontrolled (or difficult-to-control) involuntary spasms that result from muscles continually receiving messages to contract, and people feared that strengthening the muscles might make these spasms more pronounced. Recent research has shown that this is not the case (Verschuren et al., 2011).

- **Quadriplegics.** Damage to the spinal cord in the neck region results in nerves that control blood flow to the skin over most of the surface of the body being unable to connect with the subcutaneous arteries that control blood flow to the skin (Thijssen et al., 2011). When able-bodied people are cold, their arteries contract so that less blood can flow through them, preserving the body's heat in their core. When their core body temperature rises, their arteries relax so that more blood can flow to the skin, where it is cooled. Because quadriplegics' bodies are unable to open and close these subcutaneous blood vessels, they are much less able to control their body temperature. For this reason, care must be taken that they do not get too hot or too cold (Thijssen et al., 2011).

- **Athletes with high support needs.** In sport terminology, athletes with the greatest degree of disability are called athletes with high support needs. These athletes sometimes need assistance with issues of daily living. Athletes with severe intellectual disability, those with no vision, and some quadriplegics may not be able to travel alone to sporting events, and may need help getting around, particularly in strange environments. Too often coaches and team officials are expected to undertake this daily living support of athletes, which distracts from their ability to focus on the sport performance aspects of their jobs.

Supporting Athletes With Disabilities

Throughout the LTAD process, athletes with disabilities need specific support in a number of areas. These areas are addressed in this section.

Training and Competition Partners

In some sports for people with disabilities there is a need for training and competition partners. For example, a totally blind athlete (or one with very restricted vision) cannot run or cycle on her own and therefore needs a guide or pilot to train with her to ensure her safety. This presents two problems: finding someone prepared to train whenever the athlete needs to and finding a training partner who can keep up with the athlete as she progresses. This sometimes requires that the athlete leave a training partner behind to work with a faster or stronger partner.

Having training and competition partners is important throughout the LTAD process, but it becomes critical in the Train to Train, Train to Compete, and Train to Win stages. At these stages, training speeds, intensity, and volume are high, and an inability to train because of the lack of a training partner disrupts periodization.

Spotlight on Brian McKeever

Brian McKeever is a superb cross-country skier and was a member of the Canadian National Cross Country Ski Team at the 2010 Winter Olympics. As a reserve, he didn't get to race, and that was a huge disappointment.

He is also legally blind and has won multiple gold medals at the Paralympic Winter Games. His problem is that he needs to train and race with a guide, and there are few, in fact very few, skiers in Canada fit enough and fast enough to train with him or keep up with him in a race. Fortunately, his brother Robin is one such athlete. Together they have been in the Train to Win stage and have been winning internationally for many years.

Classification

Classification is a fundamental part of sport for people with disabilities. The purpose of classification is to ensure that each athlete competes against others with approximately the same degree of disability. Regardless of the nature of the disability, there is always a full spectrum of levels of disability from minimal to very severe. For competition, this continuum is divided into a discrete number of classes, and this always leaves some athletes very close to the dividing line between classes. Athletes very close to the margins of one class, who are classified at the least disabled end of the more severely disabled class, have a significant athletic advantage over those with more severe disabilities in their class. If they are judged to be only very slightly less disabled, they could be placed at the most-disabled end of the less-disabled class. Because classification is not an exact science, athletes need to be sure of their level of classification.

Early in their sporting careers, athletes are more likely to be classified by local, less qualified classifiers, and there is always a risk that an error of classification might be made. It is therefore important that athletes with disabilities get accurately and permanently classified as soon as possible. This often happens at their first national or international event.

Athletes also need to know, early in their playing careers, whether they are in a classification that will permit them to compete at the highest level. There are two issues that may prevent an athlete from being able to compete at the Paralympics: minimum disability and type of disability. Most sports have minimum disability criteria. In track events for amputees, for example, it would be hard to justify including a person who had lost the tip of his little finger! In other events (e.g., boccia), a significant number of people who have disabilities that make them ineligible to compete at world championships or Paralympic Games take part in the sport for recreational reasons. The reason for making sure that athletes understand early in their athletic careers whether they can compete at the highest level is not to discourage them from taking part; rather, it is to ensure that they are not disappointed later in their careers when their Paralympic dreams are dashed.

Equipment

Specialized equipment such as wheelchairs and prostheses is needed for some sports for athletes with disabilities. Some require the adaptation of regular sport equipment so athletes can make maximum use of their physical capabilities. Although this can be a problem for adult athletes, it is almost always a problem for children and youth with disabilities who can grow out of expensive artificial limbs or wheelchairs very rapidly. For this reason, and because sometimes no child-sized equipment is available, children and youth with disabilities can find themselves using adult equipment that may be too large or too heavy for them to use safely and effectively. To ensure long-term

What Is Boccia?

Similar to curling or lawn bowls, boccia is played indoors on a flat, smooth surface. The objective is to throw, kick, or use an assistive device to propel six leather balls as close as possible to a white target ball (called a jack). A match has four ends, and after each end, players receive 1 point for each ball closer to the jack than the opponent's closest ball. Played mostly by cerebral palsy athletes, boccia is played in single, pair, and team formats and is coeducational.

athlete development, parents and coaches should borrow or otherwise obtain correctly sized equipment, particularly at the Learn to Train and Train to Train stages.

To progress from the Train to Train to the Train to Compete stage, athletes need access to high-quality equipment that will not put them at a disadvantage compared to their competitors. To reach the highest levels of success in the Train to Win stage, athletes need to work with sport scientists and equipment manufacturers to develop equipment that will provide them with a competitive advantage.

Accessible Facilities

To progress, athletes with disabilities must be able to access facilities. This means all parts of the facility, not just the playing surface. Local organizations for people with disabilities can help coaches and parents audit facilities for accessibility. The following items should provide a starting point:

- *Entrance:* Is the entrance to the building free of steps that would prevent a wheelchair user from entering without assistance?
- *Changing facilities:* Is it possible to get into the changing rooms, shower facilities, and toilets, and is there a degree of privacy that a person with a disability might desire?
- *Playing surface:* Is there a barrier-free way to get from the changing facilities to the playing surface?

- *Signage:* Does the signage indicate barrier-free routes? Are signs in braille for the visually impaired?
- *Welcome:* Does the facility welcome people with disabilities, or simply tolerate them?

One often-overlooked aspect of accessibility is transportation. Athletes at the Active Start, FUNdamentals, and Learn to Train stages are often dependent on parents or others to transport them to and from practices. However, this dependency often extends through the Train to Train and later stages for athletes with disabilities. This extended dependency can be due to a lack of accessible public transport or the difficulty of using public transport when needing to carry both daily living and sport wheelchairs. For athletes with high support needs, travel alone may not be possible, and in many communities sport training facilities are not well served by public transport. Once the athlete is old enough to drive, some of the transportation issues may be resolved, but because people with disabilities are statistically less likely to be gainfully employed, a lack of funds to purchase and modify a vehicle may pose a problem.

Knowledgeable Coaches and Officials

In the past many of the people working with athletes with disabilities came from disability groups. Although they were very knowledgeable about disability and adapting physical activity, they were generally not the most knowledgeable about sport and coaching. More recently, with the mainstreaming of sport, athletes with disabilities work more frequently with coaches who are very knowledgeable about their sport—and less knowledgeable about disability (Gregan, Bloom, & Reid, 2007). Coaches, therefore, need to work with those most knowledgeable about disability, and with the athlete, to ensure that the athlete gets coaching expertise coupled with a deep knowledge of disability.

At the earlier stages of LTAD, athletes with disabilities need coaches with positive attitudes about disability as well as technical expertise so they develop sound technical skills from the beginning and do not develop bad habits that have to be unlearned later. As the athlete progresses toward the Train to Train, Train to Compete, and Train to Win stages, the focus shifts as quality coaching and correctly prescribed periodized training programs become critical. At the highest levels of sport performance, athletes with disabilities often train with able-bodied national team athletes under the same coaching staff.

Athletes with disabilities need officials familiar with the rules specific to the way the sport is conducted for people with disabilities, as well as with LTAD, so they can interpret and explain the rules at a level consistent with the athletes' stage of development.

Competition

Meaningful competition for athletes with disabilities can be difficult to achieve, especially at the Learn to Train and Train to Train stages. The difficulty comes from the system of classification used in disability sport, and the low number of athletes with a specific disability in any given community.

To ensure that sport for people with disabilities is as fair as possible, athletes compete against others with approximately the same degree of disability. In the vast majority of small and medium-sized communities, the number of people with the same degree of disability who are at the same stage of athlete development and in the same sport is often very low. Quite often, an athlete is the only one in his community at a particular stage of development with a specific disability.

To overcome the lack of similar-stage athletes against whom to compete, coaches and event organizers need to be creative in allowing those who would not normally compete against each other to do so. This may well mean holding nonstandard events; for example, people without disabilities could be recruited to play wheelchair basketball to ensure that there are enough players on each team, or younger or less developed athletes could start before the others in a wheelchair race, or start at the same time but farther down the track.

In able-bodied sport, we know that excellence takes time—about 8 to 12 years of deliberate practice to reach the top. This also holds true in the most highly competitive sports for those with disabilities, such as wheelchair racing, wheelchair basketball, and swimming. Some sports or events are less competitive (e.g., throwing events in track and field); in these events a person who had a fairly high level of athletic performance before a traumatic injury may be able to progress very quickly to competing at the international level. This very rapid advancement through the stages of Train to Train, Train to Compete, and Train to Win can be problematic because the athlete may not have systematically developed his physical capacity in the Train to Train stage, which may leave him more prone to injury.

Sport Science

Little research has been conducted on sport for people with disabilities, and currently most training programs for these athletes are based on what has been learned from working with able-bodied athletes. At the Train to Win stage, athletes with disabilities need state-of-the-art physiological, biomechanical, and psychological testing and training prescriptions. Coaches need to understand sport science, and sport scientists need to undertake original research on sport performance techniques, training methods, and equipment designed to give athletes with disabilities a competitive advantage at the international level.

At the Learn to Train, Train to Train, and Train to Compete stages, sport science can best contribute through optimization of performance techniques and creating a better understanding of how adaptive and sporting equipment can be modified or adjusted to best fit the needs of the athlete. In addition, the refinement of training loads based on periodic evaluations of athletes' physiological status and the development of sound sport psychology programs, both based on the developmental age of athletes, is important.

Sport scientists can make major contributions to LTAD at the FUNdamentals and Learn to Train stages by researching skill acquisition, effective learning environments, and the activities and teaching methods that best enhance the learning of fundamental movement skills by people with disabilities. Particular emphasis needs to be placed on finding out more about the early skill learning of children and adults with disabilities, about which little is currently known.

Summary

Sport for people with disabilities is more like able-bodied sport than it is different. Athletes with congenital disabilities need to pass through the same stages of development, and those with acquired disabilities need to relearn their skills and redevelop their physical capacity by passing through the same stages again. In addition, there are two more stages: awareness and first contact, which involve making sure that people with disabilities are aware of the many sporting and recreational opportunities available to them, and ensuring that the first contact between an athlete with a disability and the sport system is a positive one.

Questions for Reflection

- In a small to medium-sized community in which there are relatively few young people with disabilities, how could you ensure that these people have meaningful competition in sitting volleyball, swimming, and goalball?
- In your own community, what sports for people with disabilities are available? Where are they conducted?

- Visit a local community center and see whether it could be used by a person in a wheelchair. Where would a wheelchair user have the greatest difficulty? What if the person were blind?
- Research the sports that are contested at the Paralympic Summer Games and Paralympic Winter Games. Which would you most and least like to take part in if you had or developed a disability?

References

Gregan, K., Bloom, G.A., & Reid, G. (2007). Career evolution and knowledge of elite coaches of swimmers with a physical disability. *Research Quarterly for Exercise & Sport, 78* (4), 339-350.

Thijssen, D.J., Eijsvogels, T.H., Hesse, M., Ballak, D.B., Atkinson, G., & Hopman, M.E. (2011). The effects of thoracic and cervical spinal cord lesions on the circadian rhythm of core body temperature. *Chronobiology International: The Journal of Biological & Medical Rhythm Research, 28* (2), 146-154.

Verschuren, O., Ada, L., Maltais, D.B., Gorter, J., Scianni, A., & Ketelaar, M. (2011). Muscle strengthening in children and adolescents with spastic cerebral palsy: Considerations for future resistance training protocols. *Physical Therapy, 91* (7), 1130-1139.

To Learn More

Bhambhani, Y., & Higgs, C. (n.d.). *Training athletes with a physical disability. A supplement to Canadian Sport for Life.* Retrieved from www.canadiansportforlife.ca/resources/training-athletes-physical-disability

Canadian Cycling Association. (2010). *Long-term development para-cycling.* Ottawa, ON: Canadian Cycling Association.

Higgs, C., Balyi, I. & Way, R. (2006). *No accidental champions: Long-term athlete development for athletes with a disability.* Vancouver, BC: Canadian Sport Centres.

Royal Yacht Association. (n.d.). *Sailability.* Southampton, UK: RYA.

Smith, A., Whiting, J., & Higgs, C. (2009). *Cross country skiing: A sport for life.* Canmore, AB: Cross Country Canada.

Canadian Paralympic Committee: www.paralympic.ca

International Paralympic Committee: www.paralympic.org

National Center on Health, Physical Activity, and Disability: www.ncpad.org

U.S. Paralympic Committee: www.usparalympics.org

Part II

Key Factors in Long-Term Athlete Development

Part II outlines the 10 key factors that influenced the development of LTAD. Any coach or organization implementing an LTAD approach needs to take these factors into consideration.

1. **Physical literacy**. Physical literacy is the mastering of basic human movements, fundamental movement skills, and foundational sport skills. Such mastery permits children to read their environments and make appropriate decisions, allowing them to move confidently and with control in a wide range of physical activity situations. It supports long-term participation and performance to the best of one's ability. Physical literacy is the cornerstone of both participation and excellence in physical activity and sport. Ideally, physical literacy is developed prior to the adolescent growth spurt. It has been adopted as the foundation of the sport for life concept in Canada.

2. **Specialization**. Specialization in sport occurs when athletes limit their participation to a single sport, which they train for and compete in year-round. Sports can be divided into the categories of early or late specialization. In early specialization sports (mostly acrobatic and artistic sports such as gymnastics, diving, and figure skating), early training (by ages 5 to 7) is necessary for future excellence. Most sports are late specialization, and some are very late specialization; however, the time to specialize for each sport is unique. Late specialization sports such as soccer, hockey, basketball, and baseball can still be mastered for elite levels of competition as long as specialization begins between the ages of 12 and 15. It is essential, however, that these athletes have already acquired physical literacy prior to the adolescence growth spurt.

3. **Age**. Children develop at different rates. When considering training, competition, and recovery programs for athletes, regardless of the LTAD stage, parents, coaches, and administrators must consider the age of the athlete. This cannot be done simply by checking the date of birth. A number of age categories must be considered:

- Chronological age—the number of years and days that have elapsed since birth
- Relative age—the differences in age among children born in the same calendar year
- Developmental age—physical, mental, cognitive, and emotional maturity
- Skeletal age—the maturity of the skeleton based on bone development
- General training age—the number of years in training and the sampling of sports
- Sport-specific training age—the number of years since the athlete specialized

4. **Trainability**. To create optimal training and competition programs, coaches and administrators need to be aware of the sensitive periods in which training for different body systems, including for stamina, strength, speed, skill, and suppleness (flexibility) have optimal effects.

5. **Intellectual, emotional, and moral development**. Children develop intellectually, emotionally, and morally at different rates, and within each child one or more of these factors may be advanced or still developing. This variation in the rate of development affects the child's capacity to make decisions and deal with the strong emotions that are part of the sport experience. It is common for a child to be in different stages of intellectual and emotional development (e.g., advanced intellectually but behind emotionally), and coaches and administrators need to be aware of how this affects training and competition.

6. **Excellence takes time**. Some research has suggested that a minimum of 10 years of practice (sometimes stated as 10,000 hours) is needed for experts in any field to reach elite levels of performance (Ericsson et al., 1993; Ericsson et al., 2007). Other experts believe that talent is based on genetics and can be nurtured at an accelerated rate. Regardless of whether the young athlete is gifted (or talented), many years of training and practice are required to become the best in a sport. During those many hours of practice, a progression of interventions (i.e., developmentally appropriate training competition and recovery programs delivered by quality coaches) is required to ensure optimal development.

7. **Periodization**. Periodization is time management in sport, ensuring that the right kind of training is done at the right time. As a planning technique, it provides the framework for arranging the complex array of training processes into a logical schedule to bring about optimal improvements in performance. Periodization is the process of integrating and sequencing sport science, sports medicine, and sport-specific technical and tactical activities. It sequences the training components into weeks, days, and sessions and is situation specific depending on priorities and the time available to bring about the required training and competition improvements. Periodization organizes and manipulates the aspects of volume, intensity, and frequency of training through long-term (multiyear) and short-term (annual) training, competition, and recovery programs to achieve peak performances when required.

8. **Competition**. Competition drives the actions in sport. Coaches instruct based on competitions, and parents, administrators, and politicians define success based on the outcome of competitions. Thus, designing developmentally appropriate competition is key to LTAD. Following are several types of competition:

- Training (scrimmages)
- Simulations (exhibitions, friendlies)
- Performance-oriented (regular season)
- Decisive (playoffs, finals, games)

To create proper stage-specific competition formats, coaches and administrators must address a variety of issues. Designing individual sport competitions is dramatically different from designing competition in team sports.

9. **System alignment.** Being involved in sport and physical activity exposes participants to a variety of settings and situations that collectively can be defined as a system. System alignment from an individual's perspective provides a guide for parents and athletes to consider as they progress through the LTAD pathway. The alignment of systems from an organizational perspective is how the four key sectors (health, education, recreation, and sport) interact. LTAD is athlete centered; coach driven; and administration, sport science, and sponsor supported. LTAD can drive the core business of a sport organization whether it be a club, school, recreation organization, or health-based physical activity program. LTAD can also have a strong impact on the coaching education curriculum. Developmental readiness replaces ad hoc decision making about programming preparation. LTAD can serve as the common thread that brings together school-based, community-based, and sports club programs in athlete development.

10. **Continuous improvement**. The concept of continuous improvement, which permeates LTAD, is drawn from the respected Japanese industrial philosophy known as kaizen. The world of sport and athleticism is changing all the time, and if it is to keep pace, continuous change must be implemented. Change is difficult and challenging for many people. However, taking no actions to improve the quality of sport has resulted in declining participation and increased obesity, among other issues. Thus, LTAD strives to be a catalyst for continuous improvement.

Limitations of LTAD

The 10 factors covered in part II are the key factors, but clearly not the only factors that influence the long-term development of any athlete. Additional factors such as genetic predisposition, social support for involvement, and access to financial resources (to name just a few) can have an impact on both development and performance. Thus, it is likely that with increasing knowledge, details of these factors will change over time.

A more fundamental limitation of LTAD is that very little is known about the ways the various factors interact and, more specifically, how changes in one factor affect others. For example, although we have a better understanding of sensitive periods of training, we have essentially no knowledge about how using early sensitive periods might change the timing or strength of later sensitive periods and thus affect, for example, the 10 Ss.

In addition, there is still much to be learned about individual variations in response to training. We do not know, for example, whether people with different genetic makeups respond differently to different types of training at different points in their maturation. As this knowledge becomes available, it may well change our view of the optimization of training.

In addition, the possible interactions between and among the 10 factors are probably beyond our ability to comprehend, and adding factors increases this complexity exponentially. The 10 factors presented here represent those that were considered most important during the development of LTAD. Others might wish to include alternate or additional factors and show both why they should be included and how that additional information changes what should be done with athletes. That is their prerogative and demonstrates the key component of LTAD's philosophy of continuous improvement.

References

Ericsson, K.A., Krampe, R. Th., & Tesch-Roemer, C. (1993). The role of deliberate practice in the acquisition of expert performance. *Psychological Review*, 100, 363-406.

Ericsson, K.A., Roring, R.W., & Nandagopal, K. (2007). Giftedness and evidence for reproducibly superior performance: an account based on the expert performance framework. *High Ability Studies* Vol. 18, No. 1, June 2007, pp. 3–56.

Physical Literacy

Karen had played basketball all her life. Then, at the age of 20, she blew out her knee and was cut from the team. Always a competitor, though, she decided that if she could no longer play basketball, she'd win at something else—but what? She had never learned to swim, so swim racing and triathlon were out, and although cross-country skiing would have been gentle on her knees, she'd never skated or done sliding or skiing sports. Without the opportunity early in life to hit a ball, she wasn't very good at it, so softball, baseball, tennis, squash, and badminton were all out as well. She found this pretty depressing.

Sitting enjoying a book one day, Karen realized that early in life she had learned to read well, and because of that could read anything she chose. This started her thinking that if she had learned to do a range of physical and sport skills well when she was young, she would be able to easily take up many different sports now. She would be physically literate.

When we see an adult enjoying a novel or scanning a newspaper, we sometimes forget how much practice it took to reach that level of literacy. At an early age, the reader had to recognize individual letters of the alphabet, associate those letters and letter pairs with sounds, and then string those sounds together into meaningful words. In the same way, an adult or youth who can perform fluid, skillful movements in a dance routine or sport competition had to, as a child, learn basic human movements, fundamental movement skills, and foundation sport skills, and then learn to combine them into meaningful movement patterns. This is the essence of physical literacy— learning individual movements, combining them in varied ways, and then using them alone and in combination in a wide variety of physical activity and sport circumstances.

The development of physical literacy is a key component of long-term athlete development (LTAD). It is important whether an athlete wants to be active in recreation or an Olympic or Paralympic champion. Learning and practicing age-appropriate movement skills are the basic building blocks for the development of physical literacy and are critical for feeling confident in physical activity for fun and for health, or for competing or pursuing excellence later in life. Physical literacy is also a critical component of a child's development of self-awareness and self-confidence.

The chapter addresses the origins of the term *physical literacy* and considers some of its multiple definitions. It outlines the components of physical literacy, describes the consequences of not acquiring physical literacy early in life, and explains the role physical literacy plays in the development of both high-performance athletes and people who want to take part in sport as a form of lifelong, health-enhancing physical activity.

Physical Literacy Definitions

Although the term *physical literacy* has been used by a number of authors over the years, and there is some confusion over its earliest use, the term has now become most closely associated with Dr. Margaret Whitehead of Bedford University (United Kingdom) and her seminal paper "The Concept of Physical Literacy," published in 2001. Whitehead subsequently revised and expanded her definition of physical literacy in papers published in 2006, 2007, and 2009. "In short, physical literacy can be defined as the motivation, confidence, physical competence, understanding and knowledge to maintain physical activity at an individually appropriate level, throughout life" (Whitehead & Murdock, 2006). A longer definition of physical literacy is as follows (see figure 3.1 as well):

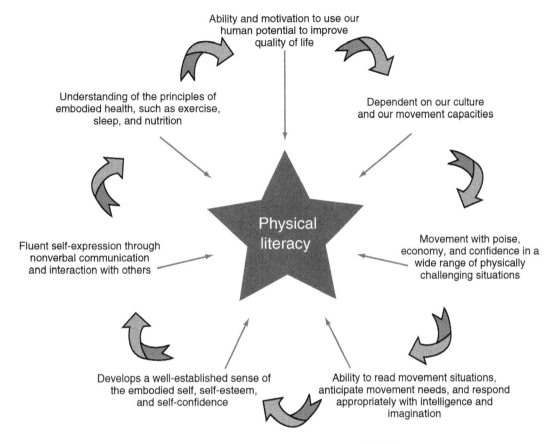

FIGURE 3.1 Components of physical literacy based on the work of Whitehead.

- "Physical literacy can be described as the ability and motivation to capitalise on our movement potential to make a significant contribution to the quality of life.

- As humans we all exhibit this potential, however its specific expression will be particular to the culture in which we live and the movement capacities with which we are endowed.

- An individual who is physically literate moves with poise, economy and confidence in a wide variety of physically challenging situations.

- The individual is perceptive in 'reading' all aspects of the physical environment, anticipating movement needs or possibilities and responding appropriately to these, with intelligence and imagination.

- A physically literate individual has a well established sense of self as embodied in the world. This together with an articulate interaction with the environment engenders positive self esteem and self confidence.

- Sensitivity to and awareness of our embodied capacities leads to fluent self expression through non-verbal communication and to perceptive and empathetic interaction with others.

- In addition the individual has the ability to identify and articulate the essential qualities that influence the effectiveness of his/her own movement performance, and has an understanding of the principles of embodied health, with respect to basic aspects such as exercise, sleep and nutrition" (Whitehead & Murdock, 2006).

Reprinted, by permission, from M. Whitehead and E. Murdoch, 2006, *Physical literacy and physical education: Conceptual mapping*. Available: www.physical-literacy.org.uk/conceptualmapping2006.php

Another definition of *physical literacy* is offered by Canadian Sport for Life (Balyi et al., 2005) and Physical and Health Education Canada (2011): "Individuals who are physically literate move with competence and confidence in a wide variety of physical activities that benefit the healthy development of the whole person." This means that physically literate people can do the following:

- Consistently develop the motivation and ability to understand, communicate, apply, and analyze various forms of movement.

- Demonstrate a variety of movements confidently, competently, creatively, and strategically across a wide range of health-related physical activities.

- Make healthy, active choices that are both beneficial to and respectful of their whole self, others, and their environment.

A third definition of *physical literacy*, as used in the LTAD model, describes the accumulated skills and attitudes that need to be developed prior to the onset of the adolescent growth spurt. It refers to the combination of basic human movements, fundamental movement skills, and fundamental sport skills necessary for engaging in health-enhancing physical activity, the pursuit of excellence in sport, or both. It is the combination of the successful completion of the Active Start, FUNdamentals, and Learn to Train stages (figure 3.2).

So what does an understanding of the definitions of physical literacy mean in practice? Whitehead's more academic definition has implications for practitioners using LTAD. Based on her definition, LTAD practitioners need to do the following:

- Help all children develop their physical capabilities and to do so in a supportive environment that fosters a positive attitude toward physical activity so that they will want to take part. We need to make physical activity fun and provide children with adequate opportunities to play!

- Be aware of the cultural importance of physical activities and how learning

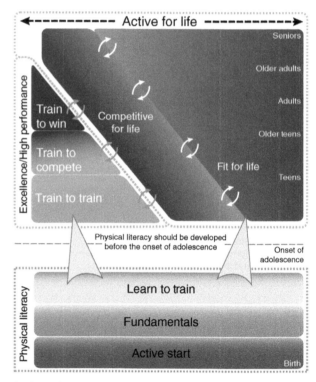

FIGURE 3.2 Physical literacy as the foundation for lifelong physical activity and sport excellence.

culturally appropriate activities can help children and youth fit into their communities. This is of critical importance with new immigrants. We also need to be aware of the physical capacities and limitations of all children—especially those with chronic health problems or disabilities—to ensure that the activities they engage in use their capabilities to the greatest degree possible, and that we do not marginalize those who are "differently abled."

- Ensure that children have the opportunity to engage in a wide variety of activities in various environments. This is one of the reasons to avoid specialization too early in a single sport.

- Provide opportunities for unstructured play so children learn to read and react in a wider range of movement situations than can be found in formal sports.

- Build self-esteem and self-confidence in children by setting tasks that are challenging to them—but within their ability to perform—because success at such tasks builds genuine self-esteem.

- Provide opportunities for children to express themselves through movement—mime, dance, and other creative movement activities.

- Teach children about the importance of exercise, nutrition, and sleep, and question them to evaluate their understanding about what they are doing and why.

An understanding of the definitions of physical literacy can also help practitioners fight childhood obesity and the rising inactivity among children that threatens the health of North America and that of much of the developed and developing world. The problem needs to be addressed now if we are to prevent a generation of children from growing up with such chronic health problems as coronary heart disease, type 2 diabetes, high cholesterol, stroke, high blood pressure, sleep and respiratory problems, and certain types of cancer (Centers for Disease Control and Prevention, 2011). Research shows that without the development of physical literacy, many children and youth withdraw from physical activity and sport and turn to more inactive and unhealthy choices during their leisure time (Kirk, 2005). We also know to be physically active later in life, people need to feel confident in activity settings; that confidence in adulthood most often comes from having learned fundamental movement and sport skills as a child. As stated by Le Masurier and Corbin (2006):

"To date, research has demonstrated that programs exhibiting the characteristics of quality physical education lead to increased physical activity levels (Dale, Corbin, & Dale, 2000; McKenzie et al., 2004; Pate et al., 2005; Sallis et al., 1997), improved self-concept (Goni & Zulaika, 2000), increased self-efficacy (Dishman et al., 2004), improved motor skills (Emmanouel, Zervas, & Vagenas, 1992), increased enjoyment (Dishman et al., 2005), increased motivation (Prusak et al.,

2004), reduced sedentary behaviors following graduation from high school (Dale & Corbin, 2000), and increased physical activity over the long term in women (Trudeau, Laurencelle, Trembley, Rajic, & Shephard, 1998)" (p. 44)

Therefore, for the population to be active and healthy, all children need a sound foundation of movement and sport skills to build on later in life. This is why developing physical literacy is so important.

Physical Literacy Development in Children

As discussed, physical literacy is the development of basic human movements, fundamental movement skills, and foundational sport skills that permit a child to move confidently and with control in a wide range of physical activity, rhythmic (dance), and sport situations. Physical literacy also includes the ability to "read" what is going on in an activity setting and react appropriately to those events.

For complete physical literacy, children should learn fundamental movement and sport skills in four basic sport environments:

- On the ground—the basis for most games, sports, dances, and physical activities
- In the water—the basis for all aquatic activities
- On snow and ice—the basis for all winter sliding activities
- In the air—the basis for gymnastics, diving, and other aerial activities

As we saw in the previous section (and will discuss in detail in the following sections), physical literacy is developed during the first three stages of the LTAD model, meaning the time from birth to the onset of the adolescent growth spurt (approximately age 11 for girls and age 12 for boys). Missing out on learning specific skills limits future sport and fitness opportunities (see figure 1.2 in chapter 1), but having fundamental skills—that is, having physical literacy—opens many activity doors (figure 3.3).

Failure to develop physical literacy puts children and youth at a great disadvantage when it comes to full engagement in a range of physical and sport activities. This is particularly true for children with disabilities. During the early stages of life, children are often dependent on parents and caregivers for opportunities to engage in physical activity, because these people control most aspects of their daily lives. The parents or guardians of children with disabilities are often focused on ensuring that they receive the necessary medical and rehabilitation services. Also, wanting to protect them from the bumps and bruises of childhood, they may be reluctant to permit them to take part in the general rough-and-tumble that characterizes young children's active play. Thus, for these children, play and physical activity opportunities are often far down the list of priorities, which may be one reason people with disabilities are more likely than their nondisabled peers to be inactive and overweight later in life.

Developing physical literacy in all children requires the combined efforts of parents or guardians, day care providers, school personnel, community recreation leaders, and everyone else involved in the sport, recreation, and education systems (figure 3.4). Also critical is that professionals involved in the development of children and youth have a common understanding of what is meant by physical literacy and how it can be developed in all children.

FIGURE 3.3 The benefits of having physical literacy in fundamental skills.

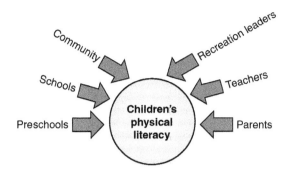

FIGURE 3.4 Developing children's physical literacy is everyone's responsibility.

During this period of physical literacy development, we must remember that children are not just miniature adults. Although children mature and learn at different rates, almost all children learn their fundamental movement skills in the same sequence and go through the same phases. For almost every skill, children need to pass through a series of developmental stages. Few can skip a particular developmental stage and still learn the skill, although some may pass through a developmental stage of a given skill within a very short period of time. The goal for caregivers should therefore be to help children move to the next version of the skill they are learning, rather than pushing them to perform the skill the way an adult would. Professionals working with young children need to be familiar with the developmental stages of learning the skills they want to introduce to the children in their care.

Physical Literacy During Active Start

During the Active Start stage (from infancy to age 6), the physical literacy objectives are to learn fundamental movements and link them together in play. Physical activity is essential for healthy development during the critical first six years of life. It is especially important during the first three years because brain growth at this time is extremely rapid and learning creates more brain cell connections at this time than in later years (Dobbing & Sands, 1973). Among its other benefits, physical activity during this time does the following:

- Lays the foundation for future success in skill development by helping children enjoy being active, learn to move efficiently, and improve coordination and balance.
- Creates neural connections across multiple pathways in the brain (Twist & Hutton, 2008), particularly when rhythmic activities are used.
- Enhances the development of brain function, coordination, social skills, gross motor skills, emotional control, leadership skills, and imagination.
- Helps children build confidence and develop positive self-esteem.
- Builds strong bones and muscles, improves flexibility, develops good posture, improves fitness, promotes a health body weight, reduces stress, and improves sleep.

At this age, physical activity should always be a fun part of children's day, not something they are required to do. Active play in a safe and challenging environment is the best way to keep children physically active.

Organized physical activity and active play are particularly important for the healthy development of children with disabilities if they are to acquire habits of lifelong activity. Because this is a period in which children with disabilities rapidly outgrow their mobility aids, communities need to find effective ways (e.g., equipment swaps or rentals) to ensure that all children have access to the equipment they need to be active. Children with sensory disabilities (visual impairment or hearing loss) often require more repetitions and different ways of getting information from the instructor to learn movement skills. To find out more, contact a local organization that provides support for people with the specific disability you are researching.

Physical Literacy During FUNdamentals

During the FUNdamentals stage (boys 6 to 9, girls 6 to 8), the objective is to learn all fundamental movement skills and build overall motor skills. This is a critical stage for the development

Active Start Physical Literacy Activities

- Encourage children to run—not just in a straight line, but with stops and starts and changes in direction. Tag and chasing games are excellent.

- Play catching games. Use a wide range of soft objects and balls of various sizes. Start with having the children catch a large ball with two hands, and progress toward smaller balls, eventually using only one hand. Remember that balls that don't bounce too much are great for learning, as are beanbags.

- Play games making body shapes (upside down and right-side up). Have the children pretend to slither like snakes and roll like rolling pins on the floor or down a small grassy slope.

- Play throwing games, starting with soft objects that the children can hold easily. Try to get them to throw at a target, sometimes as hard as possible. Have them use both their left and right hands when throwing.

- For quiet times, or when in small spaces, play balancing games. Have the children stand on one foot and then the other, try balancing on different body parts, and try walking along any painted lines on the ground.

- Play jumping games. Have the children jump and make shapes in the air, or jump to see how high or far they can go. Make imaginary rivers and get them to jump from one bank to the other. Have them try jumping from one foot or both, and make sure they bend at the knees when they land.

- Introduce the children to water activities and learn-to-swim programs. Get them on skates or skis and out on the ice or snow so they learn to slide.

- Have the children ride a tricycle or a bike—with or without training wheels—to develop dynamic balance.

of physical literacy. During this time, the foundations of many advanced skills are laid.

Skill development for children at this stage is best achieved using unstructured play in a safe and challenging environment. Quality instruction from knowledgeable teachers, leaders, or coaches in community recreation activities, schools, and minor sport programs is key. Skill development during this stage should be well structured, positive and fun, and should concentrate on developing the ABCs (agility, balance, coordination, and speed) as well as rhythm.

Hand and foot speed can be developed especially well during the FUNdamentals stage. Missing this window of opportunity to develop speed may result in compromised body speed later in life.

This also is a great stage in which to take part in a wide range of sports—land-based, water-based and ice- and snow-based activities depending on the time of the year. Strength, endurance, and flexibility need to be developed, but through games and fun activities rather than a training regimen. Learning to read the movements going on around them and learning to make sound decisions during games are critical skills that children should develop at this stage.

All children, including those with disabilities, should master fundamental movement skills before being introduced to sport-specific skills. Children at the FUNdamentals stage should not specialize in a single sport. Although they may have a sport that they take part in once or twice a week, they should take part in other sports or activities at least three times per week. Children at this stage have a strong sense of what is fair and should be introduced to the simple rules and ethics of sports. Basic tactics and decision making can be introduced. Using equipment that is the right size and that fits well makes learning activities much more enjoyable and safer. Equipment swaps and rentals are ways to keep the cost of participation down, which is particularly important for children with disabilities who need specialized sport equipment.

FUNdamentals Physical Literacy Activities

- Encourage children to engage in unstructured physical play with their friends every day, regardless of the weather.
- Continue to play catching, throwing, hitting, running, and other physically demanding games with both boys and girls.
- If possible, enroll children in programs that offer a wide range of activities (multisport programs). Have them try as many activities as possible.
- Attend parent–teacher or other school meetings and advocate for quality physical education programs in the school taught by a qualified physical educator. Ask that sufficient time be allocated (the recommendation is 150 minutes per week, 30 minutes per day).
- Don't be concerned with game scores. At this stage, many programs that involve competition don't keep score. This puts the focus of the program on learning and having fun, rather than on doing whatever it takes to win matches or games.
- Don't believe the myth that early specialization in sports such as soccer and hockey will lead to far greater performance later in life. Developing all-around athletes at this stage is far better (but remember that a few sports, such as gymnastics and figure skating, do require early specialization; see chapter 4 for more information on specialization).

Developing the ABCs

An important part of physical literacy is learning agility, balance, coordination, and speed (ABCs) skills, all of which are valuable in daily activities and almost all sports. The ABCs can be learned and refined in a number of activities. Some sports and activities are better at developing one or more of the ABCs than others are.

- Gymnastics is a great way for young children to learn and develop agility, balance, and coordination; athletics (track and field) develops speed and coordination.
- Skating and skiing provide opportunities for the development of balance, coordination, and speed; soccer helps with speed, agility, and coordination.
- Swimming and synchronized swimming develop balance, coordination, and a feel for the water; they also develop confidence and a respect for the importance of safety.
- Cycling, skateboarding, and horse riding build balance and the judgment of speed.

Parents and caregivers should try to ensure that their children have the opportunity to take part in all of these activities during the critical physical literacy years. In communities with limited recreational opportunities, and for parents with limited financial resources, this may be difficult to achieve. This makes school physical education programs especially important, because they provide the only opportunities for the development of physical literacy in every child.

Community recreation and sport programs also play a role. Community recreation organizations should create programs for prepubescent children that cover a range of physical literacy skills, rather than single-sport programs. Programs offered by minor sport organizations are obviously going to focus on their own sports, but they could do a much better job of teaching broad physical literacy skills particularly in warm-ups and small-game activities, rather than teaching only sport-specific skills in isolation. Fortunately, there is a national move in some countries for sports to work cooperatively on introducing children to clusters of sports.

Physical Literacy During Learn to Train

During the Learn to Train stage (boys 9 to 12 and girls 8 to 11; ends with the onset of puberty), the objective is to learn foundational sport skills. This is the most important stage for the development of sport-specific skills, because it is a period of accelerated learning of coordination and fine motor control. It is also a time when children enjoy practicing skills they learn and seeing their own improvement.

The Learn to Train stage is still too early for specialization in late specialization sports. Although many children at this stage have developed a preference for one sport or another, they need to engage in a broad range of activities to ensure full athletic develop-ment, playing at least two sports. Although competition is important, learning to compete should be the focus, not winning. For best long-term results, 70 percent of the time spent in the sport should be spent in practice, and only 30 percent of the time should be spent competing.

This is an important time to work on flexibility and to develop endurance through games and relays. This is also the time to develop and refine all fundamental movement skills and learn overall sport skills. The brain is nearing adult size and complexity and is capable of very refined skill performance. Late developers (those who enter puberty later than their peers) have an advantage when it comes to learning skills, because the Learn to Train stage lasts longer for them.

Finding the Right Sport

A child's desire to play a particular sport should always be the most important consideration when deciding to enroll him in a program. However, there are ways to find out what sports your child might excel in. SportFit (www.sportfitcanada.com), developed by 2010 Legacies Now and the Government of British Columbia, Canada, is a simple online questionnaire in which children an answer simple sport-related questions and enter the results of some simple physical tests, which can be done at home with very basic equipment (details are available online). The site processes the test results and answers provided and suggests sports that fit well with the child's profile. It often suggests sports that children and their parents have not considered.

Learn to Train Physical Literacy Activities

- Continue to encourage children to engage in unstructured physical play with their friends every day, regardless of the weather.
- Enroll children in minor sport programs each season, and have them try different positions or events. They might find something they are very good at that was unexpected.
- Encourage children to take every opportunity to play different sports at school, during physical education classes, in intramurals, or on school teams, if available.
- Try to have children take part in some land-based, some water-based, and some snow and ice–based activities.
- Keep children working on flexibility, speed, endurance, and strength. For strength activities, they should use their own body weight, Swiss balls, or medicine balls—not heavy weights.
- Keep sport and physical activity fun.

By this stage, children have developed clear ideas about the sports they like and in which they feel they succeed. These ideas should be encouraged. The focus should be on playing at least two sports in different seasons. Focusing on only one sport year-round should be discouraged.

End of Childhood

The Learn to Train stage of development, which marks the last stage in the development of physical literacy, ends with the onset of puberty and the rapid growth that accompanies this important life event. There are some simple ways to track the onset of adolescence, and many parents already have tools and records that can help. Parents often go through the birthday ritual of measuring how tall the child is and have the birthday heights etched on the kitchen doorframe. They can see how much the child has grown since her last birthday to determine how fast she is growing. This is called her height velocity.

During the years from about age 6 until the onset of puberty, children grow at a fairly constant rate—usually about 2 inches (5 cm) per year. An increase in this value indicates that the child is starting the adolescent growth spurt and that puberty is not far behind. Recording and plotting height every three months from about age 8 onward provides an even more accurate picture. (For more details, see the document "The Role of Monitoring Growth in Long-Term Athlete Development" at www.canadiansportforlife.ca.) In general, girls start the adolescent growth spurt at around age 11, about two years earlier than boys, but this varies greatly. Some girls start their adolescent development at age 8 (more common in girls who are overweight or obese), whereas other girls don't start until their early to mid-teens. This means there are early developers, typical developers, and late developers.

Late Developers

Physical literacy needs to be developed before the onset of the adolescent growth spurt. This can provide late developers with some advantages, but the situation is complex. The potential advantage for the late developer is a longer period of time spent in the Learn to Train stage, during which skill development and movement speed can be honed. The longer a child remains in this stage, the more time he has to develop speed and skills. The situation of being an early or late developer is different for males and females.

For males there is both an advantage and a disadvantage to being a late developer. The advantage is that the late-developing male has a longer period in which to hone his sport skills and develop hand and foot speed. The disadvantage is that he plays sport with an immature body while those around him are rapidly become bigger, stronger, and faster as a result of the adolescent changes they are going through. In many sports this increased size and strength gives the more mature males a huge physical advantage, and the physically immature players tend to be overlooked in team selections. Because they are unable to compete, they tend to drop out. This is unfortunate because if the late maturers were to stay in their sport until they too went through their adolescent growth spurt, the extra time they spent in the Learn to Train stage would pay off.

For females the advantage of late development is twofold. Late-developing females have the same longer period in the Learn to Train stage as do late-developing males, and in addition, the less mature female body shape (narrower hips and less developed breasts) is sometimes better suited to sport activities than the body of fully mature females. (To learn more, access "Developing Physical Literacy" at www.canadiansportforlife.ca/resources/physical-literacy-definitions.)

Appropriate Skill Development in Children

The current organization of sport delivery in many parts of the world, and particularly in North America, makes it very difficult for parents and caregivers to ensure that children are exposed to a sufficient range of movement skills to fully develop physical literacy, despite the fact that most national, state or provincial, and local sport organizations offer programs.

Sometimes it is not easy to work out what physical literacy skills a child will learn from programs in a particular sport. Figure 3.5 should help with this. Following are a couple of things to remember when looking at figure 3.5:

- This is not a definitive list because programs change all the time. Use it as a rough guide only.
- Not everyone agrees on which sport programs best develop which physical literacy skills. Our aim is to be roughly right about the big picture, rather than exactly right about any specific skill or sport.

Clearly, the education system must be involved if we are to give all children broad exposure to the skills needed to fully develop physical literacy. In Canada, a number of universities and physical education associations are taking up this challenge, including Physical and Health Education Canada, Canada's leading professional organization in the fields of health-promoting schools and physical and health education.

Making sure that every child has the opportunity to develop physical literacy will be a challenge. It is particularly difficult for children growing up in less-than-optimal circumstances, or those who come from populations that have traditionally been underrepresented in physical activity, recreation, and sport. Those underrepresented groups have typically included the following:

- Aboriginal youth
- Youth with disabilities
- Girls, especially those from ethnic groups that have not traditionally valued physical activity
- Disadvantaged inner-city youth

The challenge of ensuring that children from these disadvantaged groups develop physical literacy will only be met when parents and caregivers demand that schools, preschools, day care centers, community recreation centers, and sport organizations make physical literacy a priority. This means making programs child-development centered, rather than sport centered. It also means that parents and caregivers need to hold the organizations that work with their children accountable for delivering activities and programs that develop fundamental movement and sport skills from birth to the onset of adolescence.

Parents need to support programs and organizations that foster physical literacy and, whenever possible, avoid those that either do not offer sufficient physical activity or offer activities that are far too specialized too early in life. Moreover, programs to develop physical literacy need to be child centered; parent driven; and club, school, and community supported.

There are implications for many sport programs in the move toward developing physical literacy rather than sport-specific skills. Specifically, sport programs need to do the following:

- Incorporate a wide range of fundamental movement skills into warm-ups, drills, and cool-downs.
- Teach fundamental sport skills to all participants regardless of the event or position they might eventually play or compete in.
- Ensure that children and youth have access to a wide range of sports and don't specialize in one sport too early.
- Partner with other similar sports to provide a broad introductory experience. For example, communities could design and offer introduction to aquatics programs that teach children to swim and also introduce them to synchronized swimming, diving, and water polo, sports they might not otherwise get to try. Sports such as soccer, basketball, and volleyball could get together to offer an introduction to team sports program that would run year-round and let youth try out all three sports in a single program.

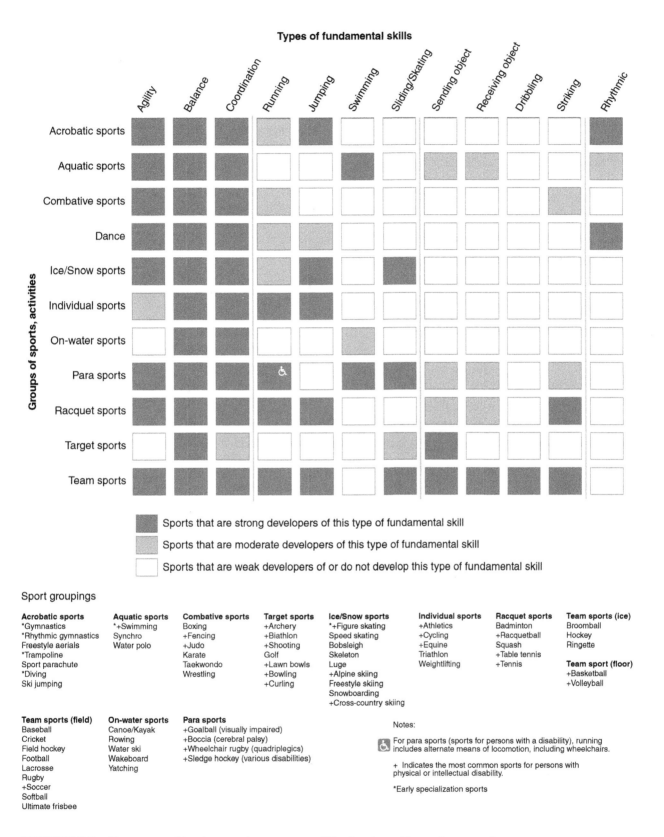

FIGURE 3.5 The types of fundamental movement skills developed by various sports.

Summary

Physical literacy is the development of a range of basic human movements, fundamental movement skills, and foundational sport skills that give people the tools to engage in health-enhancing physical activity for life—to be active for life. Having the physique, talent, skill, and drive to be competent performers allows people to move through the stages of the sport excellence stream—the Train to Train, Train to Compete, and Train to Win stages of LTAD.

Questions for Reflection

- What are the consequences of a child missing out on learning a critical fundamental movement skill such as throwing or catching?

- What could be done in schools to ensure that children become physically literate?

- What needs to be done to keep children from specializing in one sport too early?

- How would you define physical literacy if you wrote your own definition?

- What is the major problem facing a parent or caregiver who wants to ensure that a child develops physical literacy?

References

Balyi, I., Cardinal, C., Higgs, C., Norris, S., & Way, R. (2005). *Canadian sport for life: Long-term athlete development* [Resource paper]. Vancouver, BC: Canadian Sport Centres.

Centers for Disease Control and Prevention. (2011). *Overweight and obesity: Health consequences.* Retrieved from www.cdc.gov/obesity/causes/health.html

Dale, D., & Corbin, C.B. (2000). Physical activity participation of high school graduates following exposure to conceptual or traditional physical education. *Research Quarterly for Exercise and Sport, 71* (1), 61-68.

Dale, D., Corbin, C.B., & Dale, K.S. (2000). Restricting opportunities to be active during school time: Do children compensate by increasing physical activity levels after school? *Research Quarterly for Exercise and Sport, 71* (3), 240-248.

Dishman, R.K., Motl, R.W., Saunders, R., Felton, G., Ward, D.S., Dowda, M., et al. (2004). Self-efficacy partially mediates the effect of a school-based physical-activity intervention among adolescent girls. *Preventive Medicine, 38* (5), 628-636.

Dishman, R.K., Motl, R.W., Saunders, R., Felton, G., Ward, D.S., Dowda, M., et al. (2005). Enjoyment mediates effects of a school-based physical-activity intervention. *Medicine & Science in Sports & Exercise, 37* (3), 478-487.

Dobbing, J., & Sands, J. (1973). Quantitative growth and development of human brain. *Archives of Disease in Childhood, 48* (10), 757-767. doi:10.1136/adc.48.10.757

Emmanouel, C., Zervas, Y., & Vagenas, G. (1992). Effects of four physical education teaching methods on development of motor skill, self concept, and social attitudes of fifth-grade children. *Perceptual Motor Skills, 74* (3 Pt 2), 1151-1167.

Goni, A., & Zulaika, L. (2000). Relationships between physical education classes and the enhancement of fifth grade pupils' self-concept. *Perceptual Motor Skills, 91* (1), 246-250.

Kirk, D. (2005). Physical education, youth sport and lifelong participation: The importance of early learning experiences. *European Physical Education Review, 11* (3), 239-255. doi:10 .1177/1356336X05056648

Le Masurier, G., & Corbin, C.B. (2006). Top 10 reasons for quality physical education. *Journal of Physical Education, Recreation and Dance, 77* (6), 1-58.

McKenzie, T.L., Sallis, J.F., Prochaska, J.J., Conway, T.L., Marshall, S.J., & Rosengard, P. (2004). Evaluation of a two-year middle-school physical education intervention: M-SPAN. *Medicine & Science in Sports & Exercise, 36* (8), 1382-1388.

Pate, R.R., Ward, D.S., Saunders, R.P., Felton, G., Dishman, R.K., & Dowda, M. (2005). Promotion of physical activity among high-school girls: A randomized controlled trial. *American Journal of Public Health, 95* (9), 1582-1587.

Physical and Health Education Canada. (2011). What is physical literacy? www.phecanada.ca/programs/physical-literacy/what-physical-literacy

Prusak, K.A., Treasure, D.C., Darst, P.W., & Pangrazi, R.P. (2004). The effects of choice on the motivation of adolescent girls in physical education. *Journal of Teaching in Physical Education, 23,* 19-29.

Sallis, J.F., McKenzie, T.L., Alcaraz, J.E., Kolody, B., Faucette, N., & Hovell, M.F. (1997). The effects of a 2-year physical education pro- gram (SPARK) on physical activity and fitness in elementary school students. *American Journal of Public Health, 87* (8), 1328-1334.

Trudeau, F., Laurencelle, L., Trembley, J., Rajic, M., & Shephard, R. J. (1998). A long-term follow-up of participants in the Trois-Rivieres semi-longitudinal study of growth and development. *Pediatric Exercise Science, 10,* 366-377.

Twist, P., & Hutton, J. (2008). Sport conditioning for children and youth. *Fitness Business Canada, 9* (4), 40-42.

Whitehead, M. (2001). The concept of physical literacy. *British Journal of Teaching Physical Education*. Retrieved from www.physical-literacy.org.uk/concept.php

Whitehead, M., & Murdoch, E. (2006). *Physical literacy and physical education: Conceptual mapping*. Retrieved from www.physical-literacy.org.uk/conceptualmapping2006.php

To Learn More

Higgs, C., Balyi, I., Way, R., Cardinal, C., Norris, S., & Bluechardt, M. (2007). *Developing physical literacy: A guide for parents of children ages 0 to 12*. Calgary, AB: Canadian Sport Centres.

Higgs, C., Balyi, I., & Way, R. (2008). *Developing physical literacy: A guide for parents of children ages 0 to 12: A supplement to Canadian sport for life*. Vancouver, BC: Canadian Sport Centres.

Mandigo, J., Francis, N., & Lodewyk, K. (2007). *Physical literacy concept paper. Ages 0-12 yrs*. Retrieved from www.cscpacific.ca/Images/Reports/Physical_Literacy_Concept_Paperl_April07.pdf

Discover Physical Literacy: http://activeforlife.ca

Physical & Health Education Canada: www.phecanada.ca

Physical Literacy: www.physical-literacy.org.uk

SportFit: www.sportfitcanada.com

Specialization

Peter and Sarah had a tough decision to make. They had known about long-term athlete development (LTAD) and sport for life for some time and raised their three children following those values and principles. Their kids had all participated in the foundation sports of swimming, running, and gymnastics. Regularly, Peter and Sarah received compliments on the athleticism of their kids, who loved sport and being active.

Over the course of their first 10 years, the kids had all taken dance classes; their son loved hip-hop! The children had developed social skills through team sports and the value of hard work through all the activities they participated in. Their agility, balance, coordination, and speed were impressive.

At 9, 11 and 13, the kids were now moving through the Learn to Train stage and into the Train to Train stage. The pressure for them to specialize in one sport was building. As they were selected for rep teams, the scheduling was making it difficult for Peter and Sarah to keep them in a variety of sports. Now, the select soccer program required training three times a week and travel on weekends; it was the same with field lacrosse, hockey, baseball, and softball. The individual sports were not quite as bad because the kids could miss some meets and not let the team down. It was tough to know what to do now.

For the kids, the experience was mostly positive: they loved to play, so the more the better. However, Peter and Sarah were starting to see fatigue in their oldest child and a greater desire to "chill out" as the growth spurt was obviously taking some energy. Finding the balance seemed harder than ever.

Their 13-year-old was accepted to a soccer "school of excellence," which would mean additional soccer to the tier one league he was now in. What about field lacrosse? And he enjoyed other sports such as badminton, but would he have time to play them?

The 11-year-old had been invited to try out for the travel team in soccer as well. She had been the leading scorer on her top-tier team the year before, so she would likely make the team. But playing at that level would probably eliminate softball, where she was becoming a strong pitcher and loved catching. Plus, it might mean no more hockey, which had been a lot of fun. It would be only her third year, but she would be playing on the top line next year. What to do?

It should have been easier with the 9-year-old, but it wasn't. In soccer last year, she had "played up" against the boys and had been a strong player. Now what? The older soccer girls wanted her to play, but she also played hockey and field hockey and ran track, all of which she excelled in. Would playing too much on one team prevent her from excelling in the long term?

To deal with these tough questions, Peter and Sarah turned back to the long-term development model—specifically, information on specialization—for answers.

This chapter outlines how views regarding specialization have evolved in an attempt to provide better guidance to coaches and program designers. Over a five-year period, the authors of this book had the opportunity to work with more than 100 sport-specific LTAD models. This helped them form new opinions on the topic of specialization. Before the development of LTAD, there was no mention of early or late specialization sports in the sport specialization literature. In 2005 the LTAD model delineated sports into the two categories of early and late specialization. Now, having worked with so many sports, the authors have developed a more comprehensive overview of specialization. Early specialization is now divided into two types, and late specialization is divided into four types. This will help sport program planning design better programs for developing athletes as well as help parents ensure that their children participate in multiple sports before they specialize.

Why is the timing of specialization so important?

- Participants must be ready on many levels (e.g., physically, mentally, emotionally, and cognitively) to specialize in one sport.
- Athleticism must be developed before sport-specific technical, tactical, and physical development.
- Athletes need a wide range of sport abilities that they can transfer from one sport to another.
- Specialization that is correctly timed can prevent burnout, loss of interest, and overuse injuries.

During the past few decades, early specialization in sport has been a leading topic of discussion among coaches, sport scientists, sport administrators, and parents. The salient success of the former Communist countries at international competitions, especially at the Olympic Games, demonstrated the benefits of a fully aligned sport system that focused on early talent identification, early selection, and early specialization. That sport system, which has produced an unusually high number of champions, has been described and analyzed by Schneidman (1978), Riordan (1977), Gilbert (1979), and Brokhin (1978).

It is clear now, since the collapse of Communism, that sport was a major propaganda tool for the Soviet and pro-Soviet leadership in all of the former Communist countries. The institutionalization of sport in those countries was based on the Soviet model. It was responsible for the creation of identical sport systems. The Communist sport system was outstanding in terms of its ability to produce athletes of international acclaim, but in terms of encouraging

participation in sports at the recreational level, it was poor. The Soviet school system provided the vehicle for talent identification and recruitment and catered to talented athletes. Students with lesser talents were eliminated from the elite programs. Few programs were in place to encourage those of average ability to participate in recreational sport.

Special sport schools were created in all of the Communist bloc countries, including Bulgaria, Cuba, Czechoslovakia, East Germany, Hungary, Mongolia, North Korea, Poland, Romania, and, of course, the Soviet Union. Early selection, early specialization, comprehensive sport science input, full medical support, and high-quality coaching were the key components of elite athletic development. The objective of early specialization was to produce and prepare world-class athletes in the shortest possible time, regardless of any negative consequences to their health and development.

Harsanyi (1983) noted that Communist countries that exploited athletes through early specialization developed a practice without any scientific theory to support it. Winning at all costs became the basic principle of training in some of these countries, regardless of the health and well-being of the athletes. Bompa (1995) referred to sport scientists Nagorni of the Soviet Union and Harre of East Germany when he said that early specialization was not efficient at developing the best talent in those countries.

Although the Eastern Europeans developed early specialization in the 1970s and 1980s, it has since become a growing trend in North America and around the world. Many athletes, parents, and coaches believe that early specialization is necessary for reaching elite levels. However, there is much evidence to support the contention that this approach is flawed.

Specialization Defined

Hill (as cited in Hill & Simons, 1989) described specialization as athletes limiting participation to a single sport, which they train for and compete in on a year-round basis. Baker, Cobley, and Fraser-Thomas (2009) used four parameters to define early specialization:

1. Early start age in sport
2. Early involvement in one sport (as opposed to participating in several sports)
3. Early involvement in focused, high-intensity training
4. Early involvement in competitive sport

Balyi, Cardinal, Higgs, Norris, and Way (2005) introduced the notion of early or late specialization sports. Early specialization sports (mostly acrobatic and artistic sports such as diving, figure skating, and gymnastics) are defined as sports in which early sport-specific training (by ages 5 to 7) is necessary for future excellence. In these sports, complex movement and sport skills should be acquired before the onset of the adolescent growth spurt (or peak height velocity, or PHV), which is approximately 12 years of age for females and 14 years of age for males. Because one cannot specialize late in early specialization sports, some of the negative consequences of early specialization are unavoidable, although they are manageable. Late specialization sports are practically all other sports, including team sports, racket sports, combative sports, and gliding sports. Late specialization refers to the idea that early specialization is not warranted, and that specializing early in late specialization sports has its own negative consequences (see the next section).

Côté, Lidor, and Hackfort (2009) argued that early diversification (multisport or multilateral involvement in the LTAD jargon) enhances athlete development, whereas early specialization hinders it. They identified the following seven postulates about youth sport activities:

1. Early diversification (sampling) does not hinder elite participation in sports in which peak performance is reached after maturation.
2. Early diversification is linked to a longer sport career and has positive implications for long-term sport involvement.
3. Early diversification results in participation in a range of contexts that promote positive youth development.
4. A lot of deliberate play during the sampling years promotes intrinsic regulation and builds a solid foundation of intrinsic motivation through involvement in enjoyable activities.
5. A lot of deliberate play during the sampling years establishes a range of motor and cognitive experiences that children can ultimately bring to their principal sports of interest.
6. Around the end of primary school (about age 13), children should have the opportunity either to specialize in their favorite sport or to continue in sport at a recreational level.
7. Late adolescents (around age 16) have developed the physical, cognitive, social, emotional, and motor skills needed for investing their efforts into highly specialized training in one sport.

Negative Consequences of Specializing Too Early

Although focusing on one sport develops the skills, coordination, and sport-specific fitness necessary for doing well in that sport in the short term, it limits or prevents the development of other transferable sport skills (see the chapter 3 opening vignette). Transferable skills allow athletes to participate in a variety of sporting and social situations, which increases the likelihood that they will have a positive and fun experience in sport. Consequently, it is beneficial for young athletes to participate in various sports and to meet and interact with a number of coaches.

Some of the negative consequences of specializing in one sport too early are overuse injuries (DiFiori, 2002) and chronic injuries such as tennis elbow, rotator cuff injuries, stress fractures, and ACL injuries, especially in female athletes (Harber, 2007). Early specialization also contributes to a one-dimensional self-concept as a result of "a constrained set of life-experiences" (Coakley, 2000, as cited in Hill, 2009, p. 133).

To become positive and productive, athletes need to develop the social and mental skills that allow them to adapt to various situations outside of their sporting community. Young athletes may put too much of their selves into one sport and then feel devastated when they fail. They may become obsessed with winning and grow especially frustrated when they do not win. This can lead to an imbalanced lifestyle as they abandon their social lives, spend all of their time training, and deny themselves the opportunity to build the mental and social skills needed for living a successful life away from the playing field (Coakley, as cited in Hill, 2009).

Specialization in one sport contributes to "the progressive loss of freedom in exchange for increased excellence and precision" (Novak, 1976, as cited in Hill, 2009, p. 108). Athletes face not only demands from themselves and their coaches to win, but also intense pressure from their parents.

Consistent training and specialization in a sport can lead to psychological burnout (Gould, Udry, Tuffey, & Loehr, 1996). Among school, sport, and the basic demands of life, athletes' schedules may allow little time for socializing with friends and other recreational activities. When their schedules become too busy, athletes can feel as though they no longer have any control over their lives. Symptoms such as depression, eating disorders, and chronic fatigue may manifest.

Ironically, the initial intention of creating an exceptional athlete can result in hindered development and increase the likelihood of that athlete dropping out as a result of anxiety from the extreme pressure to win.

Positive Effects of Specialization at the Optimal Time

Athletes who experience a relaxed and fun approach emerge more balanced and well rounded than those who do not. This increases their chances of reaching elite levels in their sports. Youth who try a number of sports and specialize at older ages reach higher performance levels than those who specialize early. Such athletes are less likely to burn out and do not develop the perfectionist attitudes that often come with early specialization. They develop better movement patterns and decision-making skills because they are involved in a range of activities that require a variety of cognitive

and physical functions. Being in various sport situations also keeps them mentally fresh and open-minded. The more sports youth practice at young ages, the greater ease they feel when eventually selecting one sport that suits their mental makeup and body composition. If they choose to specialize, they will know the sport in which they will excel.

Participating in a variety of sports also allows athletes to become more athletically diverse and adaptable. For example, a basketball player may be a good center, but if he spends all of his time training for this specific position and fails to win this position on a new team, he is left with limited skills to apply to other positions. This dramatically decreases the chance that he will be able to get a position on the team. Such an experience can be emotionally rough on youth, especially if they have invested a lot of time in the sport. Young athletes may end up dropping sport permanently and settling for a sedentary lifestyle because it is emotionally easier. However, if young athletes have the chance to try a number of sports and experience various positions within those sports, they are more likely to have a positive experience when they choose to specialize. This, in turn, helps ensure that they remain active for life.

When children are between the ages of 6 and 12, parents are responsible for getting them involved in a variety of sports and activities. Côté (1999) refers to this important period as the sampling years. Sampling various sports and activities gives young athletes the opportunity to develop their fundamental movement skills and experience a variety of environments. After this period of diversity and skill development come the specializing years, when the athlete begins to focus on one or two sport activities.

Baker, Côté, and Abernethy's (2003) research further described the importance of sport sampling in youth. Their findings demonstrated a positive correlation between an increase in sports sampled as a youth and the chances of succeeding and becoming an elite athlete. This is most likely because young athletes who sample sports acquire a broader range of movement and decision-making skills, and this contributes to their success later in life. Baker and colleagues' evidence also showed that to reach excellence and elite levels in a sport, single-sport training is not the vital factor in determining success; developing physical literacy and specializing late is. When sport-specific training begins too early, athletes have less success in their sporting careers. Consequently, late specialization is encouraged.

Optimal Time to Specialize

Each sport has an optimal time in which to specialize. Sport-specific profiles can be identified by analyzing international normative data. An analysis of top athletes in a particular sport can identify the age at which they specialized, the age at which they started sampling sports, and the types of sports they were involved in before they specialized. In developing their long-term athlete development models, national sport organizations in Ireland, England, Scotland, Northern Ireland, Wales, Canada, and the United States conducted this type of sport-specific research to identify the optimal time in which to specialize in a variety of sports.

Specialization Groups

Balyi and Way (2010) identified six specialization groups to guide parents, coaches, and administrators in choosing the optimal time for specialization in each sport.

Early Specialization

- Acrobatic
- Highly kinesthetic

Late Specialization

- Early engagement: kinesthetic, team, and visual
- Common (typical timing of specialization)
- Late
- Very late or transfer

Please note: The chronological ages listed are for guidance only; athletes move from stage to stage based on their capabilities. In the LTAD model, developmental age supersedes chronological age.

Early Specialization: Acrobatic

Examples of sports in the acrobatic category are figure skating, gymnastics, and diving. These sports require early specialization based on the following characteristics:

- They are highly acrobatic.
- They require highly precise technique.
- They involve simple decision making.
- They are routine based.
- Specialization in these sports happens at approximately 9 to 13 years of age.
- Females typically specialize approximately two years earlier than males do.

Early Specialization: Kinesthetic

Examples of sports in the kinesthetic category are equestrian, snowboarding (half-pipe), synchronized swimming, and swimming. These sports require early specialization based on the following characteristics:

- They are highly kinesthetic.
  - Feel for snow (half-pipe)
  - Feel for water (swimming and synchronized swimming)
  - Feel for horse (equestrian)
- They require highly precise technique.
- They involve simple decision making.
- They are routine based.
- They are highly acrobatic (half-pipe).
- They require strength to lift and rotate equipment (half-pipe).
- Early engagement in skiing and riding (snowboarding) occurs at approximately age 6, whereas specialization in these sports occurs at approximately age 14. For swimming, specialization (focusing on one sport only) occurs between age 8 and 13.
- Females typically specialize approximately two years earlier than males do.

Kinesthesia Defined

Kinesthesia is defined as a sense mediated by receptors located in muscles, tendons, and joints and stimulated by bodily movements and tensions; *also*: sensory experience derived from this sense (Merriam-Webster, 2012).

Late Specialization: Early Engagement, Kinesthetic

Examples of sports in the early engagement, kinesthetic category are alpine skiing, freestyle skiing, snowboarding (giant slalom and boardercross), cross-country skiing, and luge. Although these are late specialization sports, athletes need to develop a high level of feel for the surface (snow or ice) they are moving on to be successful; therefore, they need to engage early with snow or ice. The characteristics are as follows:

- They are highly kinesthetic, requiring a feel for snow or ice (balance).
- They are athletic and acrobatic.
- They require highly precise technique.
- Equipment must be lifted and moved.
- They require simple decision making (race tactics).
- Early engagement in skiing or sliding occurs at approximately age 6, whereas specialization in these sports occurs at approximately age 14 to 16.
- Females typically specialize approximately one year earlier than males do.

Late Specialization: Early Engagement, Team

Examples of sports in the early engagement, team category are basketball, field hockey, floorball, ice hockey, netball, soccer, and water polo. Although these are late specialization sports, athletes need to develop a high level of feel for the bat or stick with the ball or puck to be successful. Therefore, they need to engage early in these sports. However, because movement skills and general athletic ability are so valuable, early specialization in these sports has a negative impact on the athlete. The characteristics are as follows:

- They involve complex decision making (no routines).
- Multiple skills are required.
- They are kinesthetic, requiring a feel for the ball or puck.
- They are athletic more than acrobatic.
- Technique is important.
- Visual tracking is important.
- Early engagement in these sports occurs from age 6 to 8, and specialization occurs at approximately age 15.
- Females typically specialize approximately one year earlier than males do.

Late Specialization: Early Engagement, Visual

Examples of sports in the early engagement, visual category are badminton, fencing, racquetball, squash, and tennis. Although these are late specialization sports, athletes need to develop acute visual tracking of an object to a handheld implement to be successful in the long term. Therefore, they need to engage early in these sports. However, because movement skills and general athletic ability are so valuable to the athlete, early specialization in these sports can have negative consequences. The characteristics are as follows:

- Visual tracking is very important.
- Opponent-based decision making and tactics are important (no routines).

- They are kinesthetic, requiring a feel for the racket or sword.
- They are athletic more than acrobatic.
- Technique is very important.
- Early engagement occurs from age 6 to 8; specialization occurs at approximately age 16.
- Females typically specialize one or two years earlier than males do.

Common Late Specialization Sports

Examples of sports in the late specialization category are athletics (this varies depending on the event group), baseball (requires early engagement in visual tracking sports), biathlon (requires early engagement in skiing), bowling, boxing, canoeing, cricket, curling, football (large variation depending on position), Gaelic football, judo, karate, lacrosse (requires early engagement in visual tracking sports), orienteering, ringette (requires early engagement in skating), rugby (large variation depending on position), sailing, softball (requires early engagement in visual tracking sports), speedskating (long track and short track; requires early engagement in skating), taekwondo, wheelchair rugby, weightlifting, and wrestling. These sports require specialization around age 15 to 16 for males and 13 to 14 for females.

- Visual tracking is important.
- They involve basic decision making and tactics.
- Kinesthetics is important.
- They are athletic more than acrobatic.
- Technique is important.
- Specialization occurs at approximately age 16.
- Females typically specialize approximately one year earlier than males do.

Late Specialization: Very Late or Transfer

Examples of sports in the very late specialization or transfer category are bobsled (requires power to move sled), cycling (requires power

and endurance to move bike), golf (requires power to hit for distance), rowing (requires power and endurance to move boat), triathlon (requires power and endurance to move bike), volleyball (beach; requires jumping power in relation to net), volleyball (indoor; requires jumping power in relation to net), wakeboard (requires power to maneuver behind boat) and waterskiing (requires power to maneuver behind boat). Although these are late specialization sports, athletes require high power to be successful. Therefore, they need to mature physically to achieve long-term success. Because these sports are in the very late specialization category, athletes can transfer from other sports and succeed. The characteristics are as follows:

- Power is very important (see notes with sports).
- They involve basic decision making and tactics.
- Kinesthetics is important.
- Visual tracking is not too important.
- Technique is important.
- A very high volume of total training is required before entering the Train to Compete stage.
- Specialization ranges from age 18 to 20; bobsled is even later.
- Females typically specialize at approximately the same time as males do.

Exceptions

The previous lists illustrate average specialization ages for the high performers in various sports. Following are some exceptions within sports due to the specific requirement of certain positions:

- Bobsled driver (earlier engagement on ice with speed to develop feel)
- Football quarterback (earlier engagement because of the high skill required and more complex decision making than other positions)
- Rugby halfback (earlier engagement because of the high skill required and more complex decision making than other positions)

- Volleyball setter (indoor; earlier engagement because of the high skill required and more complex decision making)

Sport-Specific Specialization Athlete Development Models

In closing, it is important that we review a few sport-specific specialization models to show the differing patterns of specialization. Two generic (non-sport-specific) sports, four individual sports, and one team sport are described to illustrate the trends of specialization. Three of the four individual sports are athletics, gymnastics, and swimming, which together make up the base for all other sports. Athletics is the base for the run, jump, and throw that occurs in many sports. Gymnastics addresses the ABCs of agility, balance, coordination, and speed. Swimming is the base for all water sports and an important skill from the point of view of water safety.

Sanderson (1989) called for a four-phase athlete development plan and pointed out that training content and implementation have to be flexible enough to allow both early and late developers to progress at their own rate. Instead of using chronological age, this plan identifies the optimum length of the phases. Table 4.1 describes the phases, durations, and developmental stages of Sanderson's athlete development model.

The following models are based on chronological age; developmental age is not considered.

Athletics

Thumm (1987) emphasized the importance of basic training for athletics and remarked that without optimizing general performance capacity, athletes cannot achieve high performance. He identified three phases of athlete development, as illustrated in table 4.2. He also recommended specialization in a discipline (sprinting, long distance running, jumps, throws, or multiple events) to begin at around age 15, and specialization in an event to begin at around age 17 to 18.

Team Sport: Rugby

King (1992) analyzed and described the aspects of LTAD in a team sport. Table 4.3 identifies six stages of development for rugby players. King recommended beginning with basic specialization by age 14 or 15, specialization by age 16 or 17, and advanced specialization by age 18 or 19, including position-specific specialization.

Swimming

Touretski (1993) described the stages of long-term preparation of young swimmers in an Australian Institute of Sport document. He recommended initial specialization to begin between ages 7 and 9 for girls and ages 10 and 11 for boys, and in-depth specialization to begin between ages 12 and 14 and 13 and 15, respectively.

- **Stage 1—preliminary preparation.** The optimum age for girls is 7 to 9 and for boys is 8 to 10. The duration of this stage is approximately two years.
- **Stage 2—initial sport specialization.** At the beginning of this stage, girls are ages 9 to 10 and boys are ages 10 to 11. This stage lasts three to four years.
- **Stage 3—in-depth specialization.** At the beginning of this stage, girls are ages

TABLE 4.1   Long-Term Structure of Training

Phase	Duration	Developmental stage
Initiation	3-4 years	Early school years
Basic training	5-7 years	Prepubescent and during puberty
Build-up training	3-4 years	Postpubescent
Systematic high-level training	6-10+ years	Adulthood

Reprinted from L. Sanderson, 1989, "Growth and development considerations for design of training plans for young athletes" *SPORTS* 10(2).

12 to 14 and boys are ages 13 to 15. The duration of this stage is three to four years.

- **Stage 4—sporting perfection.** At the beginning of this stage, girls are ages 15 to 16 and boys are ages 16 to 19. This stage may last anywhere from two to eight years, depending on the swimmer.

Gymnastics

Belov (1995) provided a remarkable athlete development model for gymnastics. In his 21-page document, he described the basic details of a long-term approach to training, including normative data about age-related physical characteristics, fitness, technical (skill) content, and a recommended number of competitions. He distinguished three periods and five stages of athlete development in gymnastics. Figure 4.1 illustrates the initial, intermediate, and final periods with the distinctions of general preparation, initial technical preparation, specialized perfection, elite (highest level), and end of competitive career. Specialization begins after general preparation, and initial technical preparation occurs at the third stage of the model.

TABLE 4.2 Long-Term Structure of Training in Athletics

Phase	Duration (years)	Age	Goals and characteristics
1. Basic training	4-5	9-14	Making of the general movement experiences; dominance of many-sidedness; general sport motor goals; acquisition of rough structure of many, or all, athletic movements.
2. Build-up training	3-4	15-18	Introduction of the suitable competitive event; improvement of movement techniques; at least rough differentiation into sprint, middle and long distance events, and throwing, jumping, or multiple events.
3. Top-level training	6-10	19	Mastering of the finest technical form in changing situations; realization of the conditional, coordination, and psychological potential.

Reprinted, by permission, from H. P. Thumm, 1987, "The importance of the basic training for the development of performance," *New Studies in Athletics* 1: 47-64.

TABLE 4.3 Multiyear Plan for Rugby

Stage	Chronological age	Training age	Training phase
1	12-13	1-2	Preliminary
2	14-15	3-4	Basic specialization
3	16-17	5-6	Specialization
4	18-19	7-8	Advanced specialization
5	20-21	9-10	Phase of perfection
6	22+	11	High performance

Reprinted, by permissions, from I. King, 1992, *Strength training for rugby.* Paper presented at the New Zealand Sports Medicine Federation Annual Conference.

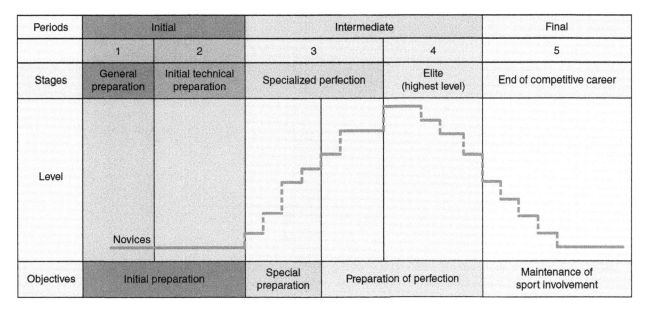

FIGURE 4.1 Long-term athlete development in gymnastics.

Specialized Versus Multilateral Model of Sport Participation

Bompa (1995) identified a two-phase long-term periodization model, including the generalized phase (ages 6 to 14) and specialized phase (ages 15+). Each phase is broken down into two stages. The two stages within the generalized phase are the initiation stage (ages 6 to 10) and the athletic formation stage (ages 11 to 14). The two stages within the specialized phase are referred to as specialization (ages 15 to 18) and high performance (ages 19+). Bompa, like Thumm, also underlined the importance of overall athletic development versus early specialization for young athletes. Figure 4.2 describes the relationship between specialized and multilateral training; specialization increases from 40 to 80 percent, and multilateral training decreases from 60 to 20 percent over time.

Summary

The timing of specialization in a particular sport is a tricky business. For the most part, sports require late specialization for athletes to be successful. In a few sports, however, early specialization is the only way to achieve national and international success, regardless of the negative consequences that stem from a lack of multisport involvement.

Early specialization in late specialization sport has a negative impact on athlete development. In late specialization sports, physical literacy should be acquired early in life through multisport activities to provide the foundation for lifelong physical activity and national and international excellence.

When children try a number of sports and choose to specialize later, they increase their chances of excelling. They develop better movement patterns and decision-making abilities and are less likely to burn out. Sampling also helps athletes become more athletically diverse, which increases the opportunity for participation in a variety of physical activities later in life.

Some sports require early involvement to establish feel, such as snow and ice sports and stick-and-ball sports. Children gain a feel for these activities early on, but do not specialize until much later. Again, multisport participation ensures that children develop the full range of

Long-Term Athlete Development

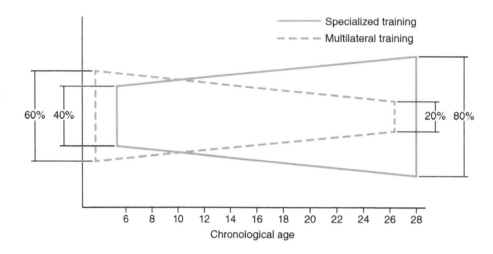

FIGURE 4.2 The relationship between specialized and multilateral training.

Reprinted, by permission, from T. Bompa, 1995, *From childhood to champion athlete* (Toronto, Canada: Veritas Publishing).

skills necessary for choosing a sport when the time comes for specializing.

Questions for Reflection

- What are the early specialization sports?
- What are the late specialization sports?
- What are the consequences of not specializing early in early specialization sports?
- What are the consequences of specializing early in late specialization sports?
- Why is multisport participation important before puberty and during puberty?
- How does a multisport background enhance excellence later in a sport career?
- Why do athletes have to specialize early in certain sports?
- Why do many parents and coaches believe that early specialization is advantageous in all sport?

References

Baker, J., Cobley, S., & Fraser-Thomas, J. (2009). What do we know about early sport specialization? Not much! *High Ability Studies, 20* (1), 77-89. doi: 10.1080/13598130902860507

Baker, J., Côté, J., & Abernethy, B. (2003). Sport-specific training, deliberate practice and the development of expertise in team ball sports. *Journal of Applied Sport Psychology, 15,* 12-25.

Balyi, I., Cardinal, C., Higgs, C., Norris, S., & Way, R. (2005). *Canadian sport for life: Long-term athlete development* [Resource paper]. Vancouver, BC: Canadian Sport Centres.

Balyi, I., & Way, R. (2010, October). *LTAD specialization.* [PowerPoint slides]. Presented at the International Coaching Enrichment Certificate Program, Newark, DE.

Belov, E, (1995). *For those who are starting gymnastics, Long-Term Athlete Development in Gymnastics.* Printed in Spanish; translated by Gymnastics Canada.

Bompa, T. (1995). *From childhood to champion athlete.* Toronto, ON: Veritas.

Brokhin, Y. (1978). *The big red machine.* New York: Random House.

Coakley, J. (2000). *Sport in society: Issues and controversies* (6th ed.). Toronto, ON: Times Mirror/Mosby.

Côté, J. (1999). The influence of the family in the development of talent in sports. *The Sport Psychologist, 13,* 395-417.

Côté, J., Lidor, R., & Hackfort, D. (2009). ISSP position stand: To sample or to specialize? Seven postulates about youth sport activities that lead to continued participation and elite performance. *International Journal of Sport and Exercise Psychology, 9.* 7-17. Retrieved from www.issponline.org/documents/positionstand2009-1.pdf

DiFiori, J.P. (2002). Overuse injuries in young athletes: An overview. *Athletic Therapy Today, 7* (6), 25-29.

Gilbert. D. (1979). *The miracle machine.* New York: Coward, McCann and Geoghegan.

Gould, D., Udry, E., Tuffey, S., & Loehr, J. (1996). Burnout in competitive junior tennis players: I. A quantitative psychological assessment. *The Sport Psychologist, 10*, 322-340.

Harber, V. (2007). *The female athlete perspective: Coach/parent/administrator guide.* Victoria, BC: Canadian Sport Centres. Retrieved from http://canadiansportforlife.ca/sites/default/files/resources/The%20Female%20Athlete%20Perspective.pdf

Harsanyi, L. (1983). A 10-18 eves atletak felkeszitesenek modellje. *Utanpotlasneveles, 10*, (n.p.).

Hill, G. (2009). *Sport specialization: Causes and concerns* [PowerPoint slides]. Presented at the Long-Term Athlete Development Conference of the Utah Athletic Foundation, Salt Lake City, UT.

Hill, G.M., & Simons, J. (1989). A study of the sport specialization on high school athletics. *Journal of Sport & Social Issues, 13* (1), 1-13. doi: 10.1177 /019372358901300101

King, I. (1992). *Strength training for rugby.* Paper presented at the New Zealand Sports Medicine Federation Annual Conference. Wellington, New Zealand.

Merriam-Webster Dictionary. (2012). Retrieved from www.merriam-webster.com/dictionary/kinesthetic

Novak, M. (1976). *The joy of sports.* New York: Basic Books.

Riordan, J. (1977). *Sport in Soviet society: Development of sport and physical education in Russia and the USSR.* Cambridge, UK: Cambridge University Press.

Sanderson, L. (1989). Growth and development considerations for design of training plans for young athletes. *SPORTS, 10* (2).

Schneidman, N.N. (1978). *The Soviet road to Olympus. The Ontario Institute for Studies in Education.* Toronto, ON: OISE.

Thumm, H.P. (1987). The importance of the basic training for the development of performance. *New Studies in Athletics, 1*, 47-64.

Touretski, G. (1993). *Physiological development of the young swimmer. A rational for the long-term preparation of the young swimmer.* Paper presented at the Australian Institute for Sport, Canberra, Australia.

To Learn More

Bloom, B. (1985). *Developing talent in young people.* New York: Ballantine Books.

Bompa, T. (1995). *From childhood to champion athlete.* Toronto, ON: Veritas.

Drabik, J. (1996). *Children and sport training.* Island Pond, VT: Stadion.

Hill, G. (1993). Youth sport participation of professional baseball players. *Sociology of Sport Journal, 10* (1), 107-114.

Age

Mary and Carol were good friends who played on the school volleyball team together. They were roughly the same weight and size and were at a similar skill level in volleyball and other sports. That was before Carol started her growth spurt. In a year she grew 4 inches (10 cm), whereas Mary grew only 2 inches (5 cm). Carol was now 5 pounds (2.7 kg) heavier and 2 inches (5 cm) taller than Mary and dominated the volleyball scene at their school. By now, many of Mary's teammates had also grown taller. She no longer felt comfortable with the team and felt like quitting because of her lack of height. But her coach talked to her and explained that this was only a temporary situation, and that eventually she would catch up with the others. The coach encouraged her to stay on the team and work hard on her fitness, backcourt skills, and overall movement skills, as well as decision making.

In the meantime, Carol neglected her coach's advice to further develop her fitness and movement skills and ignored the warning that she could not rely on height alone. When Mary eventually caught up with Carol, not only did she have her size, but she also demonstrated better technical and movement skills. Now Carol was the one thinking of quitting.

There are both advantages and disadvantages to being either an early or late maturer. With proper intervention through the help of a knowledgeable coach, players can exploit the advantages and minimize the disadvantages.

This chapter describes the various age categories used by sports, such as chronological age, skeletal age, relative age, developmental age, general training age, and sport-specific training age. Although it is often the determinant, chronological age is not a good indicator of an athlete's stage of development. The focus of this chapter is on relative age and developmental age because these two age categories have a significant impact on training, competition, and recovery program design during prepuberty and puberty. Parents and coaches should be aware of the relative age of their athletes. This chapter describes how to monitor growth to identify early- and late-maturing athletes. This will help determine their developmental age, thus allowing for the development of appropriate training plans.

In this chapter you also will learn protocols and tools for measuring growth, as well as why, how, and when to measure. Tables will help you plot standing height, sitting height, and arm span. You will also learn how to use measurements in planning annual training, competition, and recovery programs. (Chapter 6 on trainability provides more detailed information on applications.)

Age Categories

Although growth and development are natural processes, the tempo of the maturation process can vary greatly: "A child with a chronological age of 12 years may possess a biological age between nine and fifteen years" (Borms, 1986, p. 5). The biological differences between a 9-year-old and a 15-year-old are huge, and yet in spite of these biological differences, athletes of the same chronological age are often trained the same way at every age and participate in age group competitions.

When designing a training, competition, and recovery program for an athlete, a coach must take into consideration the age of the athlete. However, other factors that must be taken into consideration require more than just checking the athlete's date of birth. Following are age categories that coaches need to consider when designing sport programs:

- *Chronological age* refers to the number of years and days that have elapsed since birth. Children of the same chronological age can differ by several years in their level of biological maturation.

- *Skeletal age* refers to the maturity of the skeleton, which is determined by the degree of ossification of the bone structure. It takes into consideration how far bones have progressed, in size and density, toward maturity.

- *Relative age* refers to the age variation among children in the same age group, resulting from their different birth dates. Thus, if a grade 1 class is composed of children who will turn 6 years old between September 1 of the school year and August 31 of the following year, then the children with September birth dates will have an approximate one-year relative age advantage over the children born in August of the following year. Conversely, the children with August birth dates will have about a one-year developmental disadvantage relative to their September-born peers. Therefore, the 5 1/2-year-old child going to school with 6 1/2 -year-olds has an 18 percent maturational disadvantage. The relationship of relative age to a variety of performance indicators has been the subject of a number of research reports (Barnsley, Thompson, & Barnsley, 1985; Morris & Nevill, 2006). A participant who is 18 percent smarter, faster, bigger, and stronger than another has a significant advantage in sport.

- *Developmental age* refers to the degree of physical, mental, cognitive, and emotional maturity. Physical developmental age can be determined by skeletal maturity or bone age. Mental, cognitive, and emotional maturity are then considered to determine developmental age.

- *General training age* refers to the number of years the person has spent in training and participating in various sports.

- *Sport-specific training age* refers to the number of years that an athlete has specialized in one particular sport.

With the exception of relative age and developmental age, age definitions and concepts are simple and straightforward. For this reason, this chapter focuses on relative age and developmental age.

Relative Age

The month in which a child is born is important because of the age cutoff dates in sports. The percentages of young athletes who are selected for individual and team sports are 40, 30, 20, and 10 percent for the four quarters of the year after the age cutoff date, respectively. This is called the "relative age effect" (Barnsley et al., 1985).

Relative age plays an important role in coaching decisions. "The relative age effect describes the observation that greater numbers of performers born early in a selection year are over-represented in junior and senior elite squads compared with what might be expected based on national birth rates" (Barnsley, Thompson, & Legault, 1992, p.78). This means that a child born on January 1 may participate in the same programs as a child born on December 31 of the same year, although one is almost a year older than the other. It is well documented that relative age has a great effect in athletic selections. The age group cutoff date for entry into organized youth sport is August 1 in British school sports, and January 1 in most North American sports. The relative age effect is often clearly observable.

Figure 5.1, *a* through *d*, shows birth dates in male squads for athletics, tennis, swimming, and football (soccer) in British sports (Morris & Nevill, 2006). Significantly more athletes born in the first quarter were selected than those born in the fourth quarter, which clearly shows the relative age effect.

Figure 5.2 shows the birth months of players in the Western Hockey League and Ontario Hockey League (Barnsley & Thompson, 1988). The graph clearly shows the relative age effect: 16 percent, 15 percent, and 13 percent of players were selected in the first quarter versus only 4 percent, 3 percent, and 5 percent in the last quarter. The bias against players born in the autumn months is just as striking as the bias against those born in the first quarter of the year in figure 5.1.

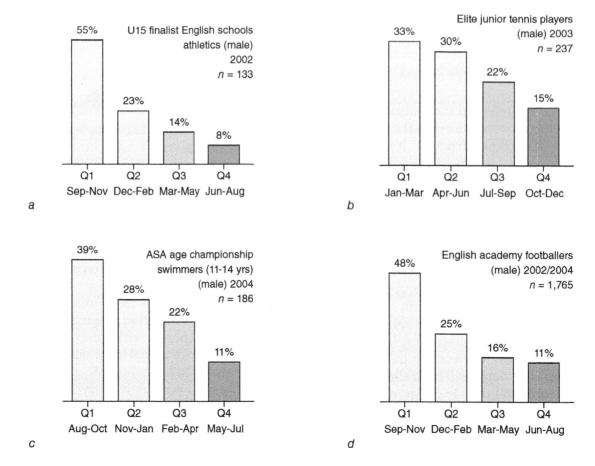

FIGURE 5.1 Birth dates and subsequent relative age effects for *(a)* athletics, *(b)* tennis, *(c)* swimming, and *(d)* football (soccer).

Reprinted, by permission from J.G. Morris and M.E. Nevill, 2006, *A sporting chance-enhancing opportunities for high-level sporting performance: Influence of 'relative age'.* Available: http://www.lboro.ac.uk/microsites/ssehs/youth-sport/downloads/research-archive-downloads/sporting-chance-relative-age-2.pdf.

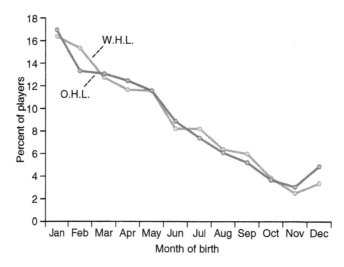

FIGURE 5.2 Distribution of birth months of Western Hockey League and Ontario Hockey League players.

Reprinted, by permission, from R.H. Barnsley and A.H. Thompson, 1988, "Birthdate and success in minor hockey: The key to the N.H.L.," *Canadian Journal of Behavioral Science* 20: 167-176.

When athletes compete all year in the same age groups based on their birth dates, they may always be the oldest or the youngest players, resulting in tremendous advantages or disadvantages. Children who are always the oldest in their age group tend to be larger, stronger, and more skilled than their younger teammates. This often causes coaches to believe that they are overall better players. As a result, they often give them more attention and playing time, which results in their becoming better players. Consider that, in 2007, more than 40 percent of hockey players who played in major junior hockey were born in the first quarter of the year, whereas only 12 percent were born in the last quarter (Gladwell, 2008).

Because there can be almost a 12-month difference between the youngest and oldest children in an age group, talented young athletes are being unfairly rejected in the selection process because of the month in which they were born. For boys the relative age effect is very strong; for girls it is not nearly so obvious, although some effects can be noted. The discrepancies are widely seen in young male athletes in both team sports and noncompetitive activities. It is unfortunate that thousands of children who wish to participate in team sports don't make the cut because of their developmental disadvantage (Morris & Nevill, 2006). This causes them to miss out on social, fitness, and other important life lessons such as strategic decision making and dealing with loss that sport offers.

Renowned sociologist Robert Merton coined the term the Matthew effect (Merton, 1968), which can describe a situation in which kids given early developmental advantages through sport are simultaneously set up for success in other areas. Those seen as "special" are likely to be granted more opportunities, which, in turn, open more doors and essentially create a pathway to further success. Sociologists refer to this snowball effect as accumulated advantage (Gladwell, 2008).

"The professional hockey player started out a little bit better than his peers. And a little difference leads to an opportunity that makes that difference a bit bigger, and that edge in turn leads to another opportunity, which makes the initially small difference bigger still—and on and on until the hockey player is a genuine outlier" (Gladwell, 2008, pp. 30-31). This is the mechanism of relative age effect. Remember the 18 percent advantage given to 6 1/2-year-old entering grade 1? Community sport gives the same advantage to children starting in minor sport leagues.

Coaches, sport administrators, and parents need to work with sport organizations to find ways to reduce the relative age effect. Following are some suggestions:

- Use the actual birth date to determine an athlete's activity year and not an arbitrary cutoff date. Applying this principle is relatively simple in individual sports, but rather complicated in team sports.
- Base age groupings on a period of 9, 18, or 30 months. In each group, the age-advantaged or age-disadvantaged rotate as athletes progress through their careers in youth sport.
- Use capability-based groupings based on athletes' abilities regardless of their chronological age. This is easily done in timed sports in which groups can be determined based on a range of time. In contact sports or sports requiring complex decision making, group selection is more difficult; however, quality coaches with good assessment tools can select athletes appropriately.

If athletes cannot be grouped based on capability, a good approach is to use their age on the date of competition to create competitive fairness. Remember that there is value in both winning and not winning. Athletes who win all the time based on their relative age advantage are not challenged to improve. By using their age based on the date of competition, they will have the opportunity to be the youngest as well as the oldest in their age group.

In capability-based grouping, tiering can ensure that participants are grouped correctly and not cut from the team when their capability is still developing. An option is to establish "current" and "potential" squads based on athletes' current abilities and potential abilities (i.e., proficient in decision making and technical abilities but physically not as well developed as the "current" squad members) (Morris & Nevill, 2006).

Developmental Age

If relative age (a 10- to 12-month difference) can have such a big impact on sport selection, participation, and performance, clearly the issue of early- and late-maturing athletes needs special attention. Developmental age can reveal a four- to five-year spread of maturation differences (Borms, 1986). Thus, understanding the maturation process and its consequences is important for athletes, coaches, parents, teachers, and sport administrators. Figure 5.3 illustrates the differences among early-, average-, and late-maturing females and males, respectively.

Following are some concerns raised about the issue of late and early maturers.

• Early maturers, who have always relied on their advanced developmental age, lose this advantage as average and late maturers catch up. Because of their reliance on their early physical development, some do not develop the necessary skills or fitness. The loss of their physical advantage combined with their lack of skill and fitness can lead to

frustration, which causes many early maturers to leave the sport around the age of 14 or 15 (Lawrence, 1999).

• Because late maturers lack the initial developmental advantage of early maturers, they are seen as less skilled in the sport because of their lack of physical presence. As a result, late maturers are often tiered down and given lower-quality programming and coaching. This diminished opportunity hurts their chances of fully developing their skills. If late maturers can withstand these initial deterring circumstances and remain in the sport, they ultimately have the potential to be the better athletes (Lawrence, 1999).

Balyi and colleagues (2005) described the patterns of growth and development and identified the differences between chronological and developmental age. The terms *growth* and *maturation* are often used together and sometimes synonymously; however, each refers to specific biological activities.

Growth refers to observable step-by-step quantitative and measurable changes in body size, such as height, weight, and fat percentage. *Maturation* refers to qualitative system changes, both structural and functional, in the body's progress toward maturity, such as the change from cartilage to bone in the skeleton.

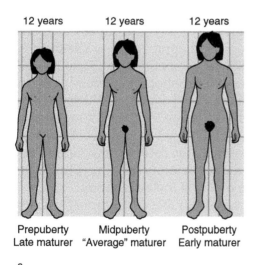

12 years   12 years   12 years

Prepuberty   Midpuberty   Postpuberty
Late maturer   "Average" maturer   Early maturer

a

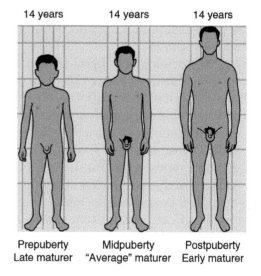

14 years   14 years   14 years

Prepuberty   Midpuberty   Postpuberty
Late maturer   "Average" maturer   Early maturer

b

FIGURE 5.3 Maturation in *(a)* girls and *(b)* boys.
Adapted from Tanner 1973.

Long-term athlete development (LTAD) identifies early, average, and late maturers to facilitate the design of developmentally appropriate training and competition programs to optimize trainability and readiness. The beginning and the peak of the growth spurt (after growth decelerates) are very significant in LTAD applications to training and competition design.

Measuring and Monitoring Growth

Growth measurements are needed for monitoring and identifying the maturity level of athletes, so that training, competition, and recovery programs will be based on developmental age and not chronological age. Identifying early and late maturers and educating them about the advantages and disadvantages of their developmental status is key. Monitoring growth also helps to identify the sensitive periods of accelerated adaptation to training, which will be explained in chapters 5, 6, and 9.

Kinanthropometry is a form of measurement used to determine athletes' structural status (i.e., shape, size, proportion, composition, and maturation), as well as to quantify differential growth and the influences of training (Ross & Marfell-Jones, 1991, p. 2). Comparing

athletes with others of their same sex and age range reveals how typical they are for their age. Longitudinal growth velocity curves (see figure 5.4) can help coaches monitor the growth patterns of athletes to identify their maturity status.

LTAD is based on maturity (i.e. developmental age), not chronological age. Although we all follow the same stages to maturity, the timing, rate, and magnitude of maturity differs among individuals. Programs based on LTAD identify early, late, and average maturers to help coaches design instruction, training, and competition programs based on the readiness of the participants.

During puberty, participants require a training program based on their individual pattern of growth. For this reason, height should be monitored regularly to determine the onset of the growth spurt and the peak height velocity (PHV) curve for each athlete. Peak height velocity is the maximum rate of growth in height during the growth spurt. Figure 5.4 shows a typical growth rate pattern for girls and boys. The highest point of the line is the maximum rate of growth, or PHV. The steep rise in the line immediately before PHV is the growth spurt. These figures also identify secondary sex characteristics with relation to growth.

On average, PHV occurs in girls at about 12 years of age, although the normal sequence of

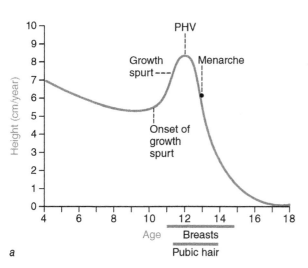

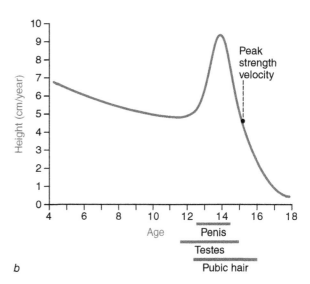

FIGURE 5.4 Growth velocity curves for *(a)* girls and *(b)* boys.

Adapted, by permission, from Canadian Sport for Life 2006; Modified from Ross et al. 1991.

developmental events may take place two or more years earlier or later. The first physical sign of adolescence is usually breast budding, which occurs slightly after the onset of the growth spurt. Shortly thereafter, pubic hair begins to grow. Menarche, or the onset of menstruation, comes rather late in the growth spurt, occurring after PHV is achieved (Ross & Marfell-Jones, 1991).

PHV in boys is more intense than in girls and occurs, on average, about two years later. As with girls, the developmental sequence for male athletes may occur two or more years earlier or later than average. Growth of the testes, pubic hair, and penis are related to the maturation process. Peak strength velocity (PSV) comes a year or so after PHV. Early-maturing boys may have as much as a four-year physiological advantage over their late-maturing peers. Eventually, the late maturers catch up when they experience their growth spurt (Ross & Marfell-Jones, 1991).

Whether an athlete is an early or late maturer is not of issue; the issue is the potential short-term and long-term treatment of the athlete. Appropriate training and competition schedules can be set up to meet the needs of early-, average-, and late-maturing athletes.

Six Phases of Growth

Growth is tracked by collecting data and analyzing it using models and graphs (Balyi & Ross, 2009a, 2009b). Somatic (musculoskeletal) growth follows six phases, as illustrated in figure 5.5.

- **Phase 1: Chronological age—age 0 to 6 (Active Start stage in LTAD).** This phase is characterized by very rapid growth during infancy and very rapid deceleration after age 2. Standing height and weight should be measured every birthday.

- **Phase 2: Age 6 to the onset of the growth spurt (FUNdamentals and Learn to Train stages).** This phase is characterized by steady growth (an average of 5 cm, or 2 in., per year). Standing height, sitting height, and arm span should be measured every birthday. If measurements take place in a club, the first measurement of the year should happen at the beginning of the annual training season. Once the onset of PHV is identified, measurements of standing height, sitting height, and arm span should be done quarterly (every three months). During this phase the sensitive periods for training skill, speed, and suppleness should be identified by chronological age.

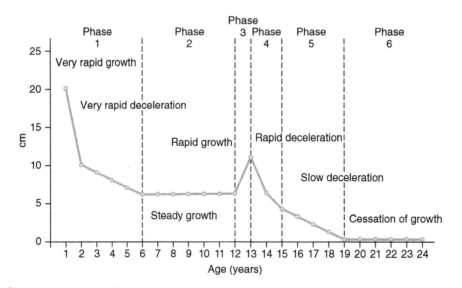

FIGURE 5.5 Six phases of growth.

Adapted, by permission, from I. Balyi and R. Way, 2009, *The role of monitoring growth in long-term athlete development* (Vancouver, Canada: Canadian Sport Centres).

- **Phase 3: From the onset of the growth spurt to peak height velocity (Train to Train stage).** This phase is characterized by rapid growth. During the first year of the spurt, the average growth is about 3 inches (7 cm), and then about 3.5 inches (9 cm) in the second year in boys, and roughly 2.3 inches (6 cm) and 3 inches (8 cm) in girls (Tanner, 1989). Standing height, sitting height, and arm span should be measured and recorded quarterly to monitor which part of the body is growing the fastest. Changes in the center of gravity, leg length, and arm span can help the coach understand a player's loss of coordination and speed as a result of rapid growth. During this phase the aerobic capacity window should be identified by the onset of PHV; and the second sensitive period for speed, by chronological age (for more information, see chapter 5) (Balyi & Ross, 2009a, 2009b; Stafford, 2005).

- **Phase 4: From peak height velocity to slow deceleration (Train to Train stage).** This phase is characterized by rapid deceleration— about 3 inches (7 cm) in boys and 2.3 inches (6 cm) in girls during the first year after the peak, and roughly 1.2 inches (3 cm) the next year for both genders (Tanner, 1989). Standing height, sitting height, and arm span should be measured quarterly to monitor deceleration. During this phase, the sensitive period for aerobic power and strength can be identified after deceleration, as described earlier. That is to say, aerobic power should be trained after PHV, when growth decelerates. For females, strength training can be prioritized immediately after PHV or at the onset of menarche. For males, strength training should be a priority 12 to 18 months after PHV (Anderson & Bernhardt, 1998; Beunen & Thomis, 2000; Ross & Marfell-Jones, 1991).

- **Phase 5: From slow deceleration of growth to cessation of growth (Train to Compete stage).** Slow deceleration starts one to two years after PHV and ends with the cessation of growth (Tanner, 1989). It is recommended that training loads and intensities be determined gradually by diagnostics. Because all systems are now fully trainable, testing can be used to identify individual and team training priorities.

- **Phase 6: Cessation of growth (Train to Win stage).** During this phase it is recommended that individual diagnostics of the strengths and weaknesses of the athlete determine training loads and intensities.

The biological markers of (1) the onset of PHV, (2) PHV, and (3) the onset of menarche enable the coach to optimize training for the prepubescent and pubescent athlete. The coach should also use the opportunity provided by the sensitive periods of accelerated adaptation training (see chapter 6).

Measurement Accuracy

Proper technique must be used when measuring athletes. The more measurement errors there are, the less effective the program design will be. To decrease the likelihood of error, ensure the following:

- The environment is consistent and controlled (same place; same equipment).
- Clothing is consistent and not bulky.
- Feet are bare.
- The athlete is cooperative.
- Standardized and consistent procedures are followed.

Determining the rate of growth requires accurate measurements; therefore, measurements need to be made to the nearest 0.04 inch (0.1 cm). Measurements should be taken twice and should not differ by more than 0.16 inch (0.4 cm). If they do not differ by more than that, the mean of the two measurements should be taken. If they do differ by more than that, a third measurement should be taken, and the median of all three measurements should be calculated (Williams, 2009a).

When measuring a child's height, it is important to pay special attention to technique to ensure accurate results. Ideally, two measurers should be present—one to position the athlete and the other to record the measurement. If a second measurer is not available, it is still possible to get valid results; however, the measurer should pay close attention to technique.

To measure accurately, the position of the athlete's head must be correct. A head tipped forward or backward changes the measurement. Figure 5.6 shows proper head position.

The orbitale (O) is located on the lower or most inferior margin of the eye socket. The tragion (T) is the notch above, or superior to, the tragus, or flap of the ear, at the superior aspect of the zygomatic bone. This position corresponds almost exactly to the visual axis when the subject is looking directly ahead. The person who is conducting the measurement should place the head in the proper position before taking the measurement (Ross & Marfell-Jones, 1991).

Measurement Timing

Coaches or support staff should not become overly focused on measurements. Measuring too often can have the following results:

- Participants may become bored.
- Participants may become preoccupied

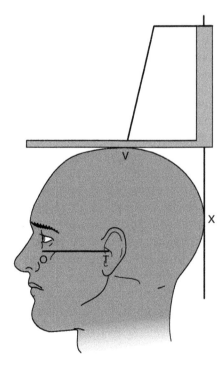

FIGURE 5.6 Proper head position for measurements.

Reprinted from W.D. Ross and M.J. Marfell-Jones, 1991, Kinanthropometry. In *Physiological testing of the high performance athlete*, 2nd ed., edited by J.D. MacDougall, H.A. Wenger, & H.J. Green (Champaign, IL: Human Kinetics), 223-308. By permission of H.J. Green.

with the measurements, particularly if they perceive they are not growing as fast as their peers.

- Intervals between testing periods may not be long enough to allow for substantial growth (Williams, 2009a).

The following measurement guidelines are recommended:

- Take measurements once quarterly.
- Take measurements as close as possible to the same date of the month. Part of a training session should be set aside for measurements.
- Take measurements after a day of rest (this ensures that there are no confounding effects from the previous day's training).
- Take measurements at the beginning of the training session when athletes have not been affected by the training session (stretching, bouncing, and drop jumps can all affect stature) (Williams, 2009a).

Even if the coach believes that an athlete has already started the pubertal growth spurt, quarterly measurements will show whether the athlete is past the stage of PHV. Taking measurements from a young age prior to the growth spurt gives the coach a greater opportunity to adjust the training program according to the athlete's growth rate. It is beneficial to have as many measurement points as possible prior to the age at which PHV occurs (typically at 12 years for females and 14 years for males).

Measuring Peak Height Velocity

The following three measurements are taken to determine PHV (Williams, 2009a, 2009b).

- Standing height
- Sitting height
- Arm span

As previously stated, accuracy is very important when taking measurements. Use equipment that is specially designed for measuring accurately. A freestanding or wall-mounted stadiometer is ideal for measuring standing and sitting height. It should have sliding headboards and a dial or digital screen. The following sections outline how to measure standing height, sitting height, and arm span.

Protocol for Standing Height Measurement

The following steps should be completed to get an accurate standing height measurement (Simmons, 2000):

- The subject stands erect in bare feet with the heels, buttocks, and shoulders pressed against the stadiometer.
- The heels are together with arms hanging freely by the side (palms facing thighs).
- The tester applies gentle upward traction to the subject's skull behind the ears.
- The subject looks straight ahead, takes a deep breath, and stands as tall as possible.
- The tester draws down the measuring bar to the subject's head and records standing height to the nearest 0.039 inch (1 mm).

Figure 5.7 illustrates these steps. Figure 5.8 is an example of monitoring growth for a hypothetical subject. Notice that only annual measurements were taken before age 11, and that four measurements were taken a year after age 11 (every three months). The total growth

FIGURE 5.7   Setup for measuring standing height.

Reprinted, by permission, from I. Balyi and R. Way, 2009, *The role of monitoring growth in long-term athlete development* (Vancouver, Canada: Canadian Sport Centres).

Standing height example

Age	9	10	11				12				13				14			
Growth in cm	5	6	0.9	1.3	3	1	1.9	2.6	3.0	1.1	4.3	3.0	3.4	1.3	1.0	2.1	2.7	1.9
Total growth in cm	5	6	6.2				8.6				12				7.7			

15				16				17				18				19				20			
2.1	1.6	1.3	2.0	1.4	0.7	0.9	1.0	1.1	0.5	0.6	1.0	0.7	0.3	0.5	0.6	0.4	0	0	0.4	0	0	0	0
7.00				4.00				3.2				2.1				0.8				0			

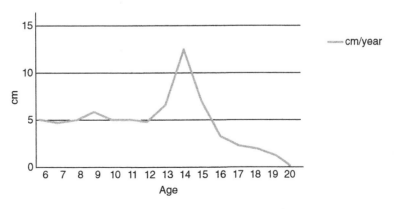

FIGURE 5.8   Sample standing height chart and growth velocity curve graph.

Reprinted, by permission, from I. Balyi and R. Way, 2009, *The role of monitoring growth in long-term athlete development* (Vancouver, Canada: Canadian Sport Centres).

in centimeters for each year is entered on the graph to show the growth velocity curve. To determine the velocity curve, the increase in stature from one measurement time period to the next consecutive measurement time period is subtracted one from the other. On this chart, steady growth occurs from age 6 to age 13, the onset of PHV is at age 13, PHV is at age 14, slow deceleration begins at age 16, and cessation of growth is at age 20. Figure 5.9 is a blank chart and graph for recording measurements.

Protocol for Sitting Height Measurement

The following steps should be completed to get an accurate sitting height measurement (Simmons, 2000):

- The subject sits on the base of the stadiometer with knees slightly bent and hands resting on knees.
- The buttocks and shoulders rest lightly against the stadiometer, which is positioned vertically behind the subject.

There should be no gap between the subject's buttocks and the stadiometer.

- The tester applies gentle upward traction to the skull behind the ears to ensure that the trunk is fully stretched.
- The tester draws down the measuring bar to the subject's head and records sitting height to the nearest 0.039 inch (1 mm).
- Once sitting height is calculated, it can be subtracted from the standing height score to derive leg-length height.

Figure 5.10 illustrates these steps. Figure 5.11 is a blank chart that can be used to plot measurement results.

Protocol for Arm Length Measurement

The following steps should be completed to get an accurate arm length measurement (Simmons, 2000):

- A tape measure is mounted on the wall at about shoulder height of the subject

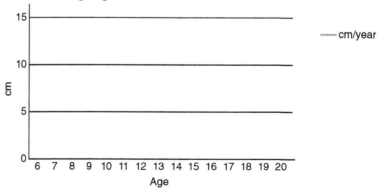

FIGURE 5.9 Blank chart and graph for tracking standing height.

Reprinted, by permission, from I. Balyi and R. Way, 2009, *The role of monitoring growth in long-term athlete development* (Vancouver, Canada: Canadian Sport Centres).

FIGURE 5.10   Setup for measuring sitting height.

Reprinted, by permission, from I. Balyi and R. Way, 2009, *The role of monitoring growth in long-term athlete development* (Vancouver, Canada: Canadian Sport Centres).

being measured. The starting point of the tape measure should be fixed to a corner of a wall. This is where the subject's fingers must be fixed.

- The subject stands erect with abdomen and toes facing the wall, feet together, and head turned to the right.

- The arms are extended laterally at shoulder level (horizontal) with palms facing forward, fingers stretched.

- The tip of the middle finger is aligned with the beginning of the tape measure (corner of wall), and arms are outstretched along the tape measure.

- The tester uses a ruler held vertically to the tape measure to record total arm span to the nearest 0.039 inch (1 mm).

Figure 5.12 illustrates these steps. Figure 5.13 is a blank chart that can be used to plot measurement results.

Using Growth Information

Measuring PHV is a way to track growth. Monitoring growth velocity curves and recognizing the timing and tempo of growth is essential when training adolescent athletes (prepubertal and pubertal). Monitoring growth and plotting the patterns of growth can help coaches decide how to adjust training, competition, and recovery programs

Sitting height

Age	9	10	11	12	13	14
Growth in cm						
Total growth in cm						

15	16	17	18	19	20

Plotting the growth velocity curve for sitting height

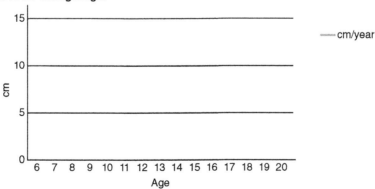

FIGURE 5.11   Blank chart for tracking sitting height measurements.

Reprinted, by permission, from I. Balyi and R. Way, 2009, *The role of monitoring growth in long-term athlete development* (Vancouver, Canada: Canadian Sport Centres).

FIGURE 5.12 Setup for measuring arm length.

Reprinted, by permission, from I. Balyi and R. Way, 2009, *The role of monitoring growth in long-term athlete development* (Vancouver, Canada: Canadian Sport Centres).

according to the velocity of growth (see chapters 6 and 9 for more information).

Measuring standing height, sitting height, and arm span quarterly after the onset of PHV reveals what part of the body is growing and at what velocity (this usually begins with the feet and hands, followed by the legs, then the arms,

and finally the trunk). This gives the coach a better understanding of the impact of growth on skills, speed, and flexibility.

Summary of Growth Measurements

Monitoring growth before, during, and after the adolescent growth spurt is very important for creating an individualized, developmentally appropriate plan to optimize an athlete's development. The following is a summary to guide coaches as they monitor their athletes and develop training, competition, and recovery programs for long-term development:

- Growth measurements are needed to identify early, average, and late maturers.

- The onset of PHV, PHV, and menarche should be determined to adjust training, competition, and recovery programs according to the tempo of growth.

- Plotting growth helps to identify the point at which growth begins to decelerate.

- Average and late maturers can be identified by measuring growth early.

Arm span

Age	9	10	11	12	13	14
Growth in cm						
Total growth in cm						

15	16	17	18	19	20

Plotting the growth velocity curve for arm span

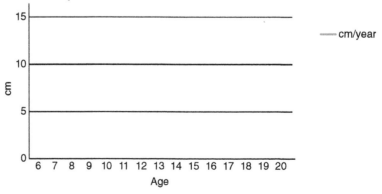

FIGURE 5.13 Blank chart for tracking arm length measurements.

Reprinted, by permission, from I. Balyi and R. Way, 2009, *The role of monitoring growth in long-term athlete development* (Vancouver, Canada: Canadian Sport Centres).

- Because menarche begins about a year after growth decelerates, coaches can estimate the time of onset.
- Before the onset of the growth spurt, standing height should be measured on every birthday, or at the beginning of the annual training cycle in clubs.
- Standing height, sitting height, and arm span should be measured quarterly after the onset of the growth spurt.

Summary

Age, especially relative age and developmental age, have a significant impact on children's participation and achievement in sport and physical activity. Monitoring relative age is essential, because those born early in the active year have initial advantages and those born late have initial disadvantages. Coaches should be able to inform athletes and parents about the consequences of and solutions for relative age disparities.

Chronological age is not a good predictor of developmental age. Identifying early, average, and late maturers during puberty is essential for providing developmentally appropriate training, competition, and recovery programs. Monitoring growth by using standing height, sitting height, and arm span measurements helps coaches identify early, average, and late maturers so they can create developmentally appropriate training and competition programs.

Questions for Reflection

- Why is it important to monitor growth?
- What kinds of measurements should be used to monitor growth?
- Why do measurements have to be reliable?
- How can you identify early-, average-, and late-maturing athletes?
- What are the advantages and disadvantages of being an early or late maturer?
- Should parents tell their children about the relative age effect?

- What is the best way for coaches to let players know that they are aware of their relative age?

References

Anderson, G., & Bernhardt, T. (1998, fall). Coaching children: Growth and maturation considerations. *BC Coaches Perspective*, 14-15.

Balyi, I., Cardinal, C., Higgs, C., Norris, S., & Way, R. (2005). *Canadian sport for life: Long-term athlete development* [Resource paper]. Vancouver, BC: Canadian Sport Centres.

Balyi, I., & Ross, G. (2009a). Optimal trainability for the young developing performer. In I. Balyi & C. Williams (Eds.), *Coaching the young developing performer* (pp.17-38). Leeds, UK: Coachwise.

Balyi, I., & Ross, G. (2009b). Key coaching issues concerning growth and maturation of the young developing performer. In I. Balyi & C. Williams (Eds.), *Coaching the young developing performer* (pp. 39-45). Leeds, UK: Coachwise.

Balyi, I., & Way, R. (2010). *The role of monitoring growth in Long-Term Athlete Development.* Vancouver, BC: Canadian Sport Centers.

Barnsley, R.H., & Thompson A.H. (1988). Birthdate and success in minor hockey: The key to the N.H.L. *Canadian Journal of Behavioral Science, 20*, 167-176.

Barnsley, R.H., Thompson, A.H., & Barnsley, P.E. (1985). Hockey success and birth-date: The relative age effect. *Canadian Association for Health, Physical Education and Recreation, 51*, 23-28.

Barnsley, R.H., Thompson, A.H., & Legault, P. (1992). Family planning: Football style, the relative age effect in football. *International Review for the Sociology of Sport, 27* (1), 77-88.

Beunen, G., & Thomis, M. (2000). Muscle strength development in childhood and adolescence. *Pediatric Exercise, 12*, 174-197.

Borms, J. (1986). The child and exercise: An overview. *Journal of Sport Sciences, 4*, 3-20.

Gladwell, M. (2008). *Outliers*. New York: Little, Brown.

Lawrence, M. (1999). *US swimming sport science summit for young swimmers: Learning about athlete development.*, Colorado Springs, CO: U.S. Olympic Committee.

Merton, R. (1968). The Matthew effect in science. *Science, 159 (3810)* 56-63. Retrieved from www.garfield.library.upenn.edu/merton/matthew1.pdf

Morris, J.G., & Nevill, M.E. (2006). *A sporting chance: Enhancing opportunities for high-level sporting performance: Influence of 'relative age'* [Report]. Retrieved from http://www.lboro.ac.uk/microsites/ssehs/youth-sport/downloads/research-archive-downloads/sporting-chance-relative-age-2.pdf

Ross, W.D., & Marfell-Jones, M.J. (1991). Kinanthropometry. In J.D. MacDougall, H.A. Wenger, & H.J. Green (Eds.), *Physiological testing of the high performance athlete* (2nd ed., pp. 223-308). Champaign, IL: Human Kinetics.

Simmons, D. (2000). *Talent identification of British diving: Physiological and anthropometrical test* [DVD]. British Diving.

Stafford, I. (2005). *Coaching for Long-Term Athlete Development.* Leeds, UK: Coachwise.

Tanner, J.M. (1973). Growing up [Figure]. *Scientific American.*

Tanner, J.M. (1989). *Foetus into man: Physical growth from conception to maturity* (2nd ed.). Hertford, UK: Castlemead Publications.

Williams, C. (2009a). An overview of growth and development: Peak height velocity. In I. Balyi & C. Williams (Eds.), *Coaching the young developing performer* (pp. 6-16). Leeds, UK: Coachwise.

Williams, C. (2009b). Tracking growth and development: How to measure PHV. In I. Balyi & C. Williams (Eds.), *Coaching the young developing performer* (pp. 74-86). Leeds, UK: Coachwise.

To Learn More

Balyi, I., & Way, R. (2009). *The role of monitoring growth in long-term athlete development* [Resource paper]. Vancouver, BC: Canadian Sport Centres.

Balyi, I., & Williams, C. (Eds.). (2009). *Coaching the young developing performer.* Leeds, UK: Coachwise.

Malina, R.M., Bouchard, C., & Bar-Or., O. (2004). *Growth, maturation, and physical activity.* Champaign, IL: Human Kinetics.

Trainability

George's mood was foul as he arrived at the first practice of the year. The fact that the soccer team he coached would have to share the facility with another team this year during some of his practices annoyed him. The worst thing about it was that Jim coached the other team. George felt a bit of disdain toward Jim because he did things differently. For years now, Jim had been running his kids through ladders and doing other different things. A smile came to George's face, though, as he thought of his win–loss record against Jim's team. His team dominated, and he knew it had to be because he outcoached Jim tactically. Jim had his kids all over the place; they never seemed to settle into positions. He didn't run plays the way George did.

George's 13- and 14-year-olds knew the drills well and quickly fell into line. As his kids ran through the next drill, he looked over to see that Jim was up to his odd practices again. He had three groups: the smaller guys were doing speed work, the gangly-looking kids were doing more endurance work, and the beefier kids were doing power work. George shook his head, looking forward to their first game against each other. Unfortunately, they would not meet each other until well into the season.

The season flew by, and George's team was well up in the standings. His team might not have been as dominant as in previous years, but it was still pretty good. What was a bit disconcerting was that Jim's team was doing really well, too. Now that it was game time, George was taken aback. Jim's kids seemed to be much more athletic now. The younger, smaller kids—the ones George would always run plays against—were getting so quick and skilled now. They had no weaknesses! Not only had Jim's players all improved their athleticism, but their movement and decision making seemed to flow better as well. They were making George's team look very static. By the end of the game, Jim's team was commanding the play.

George had a tough decision to make, but didn't like either option. He could either let his ego stop him from trying to learn from Jim, or he could suck it up and talk to his foe. Fortunately, George had a strong desire to do the right thing for his kids, and at the next practice he asked Jim if he had time for a coffee.

During their meeting, Jim explained that he had studied long-term athlete development and learned that there were better times to train various things, referring to the sensitive periods of accelerated adaption to training. He had also discovered that all kids of the same age are not really the same age. George concentrated. He was about to receive a lesson in coaching.

Trainability is the responsiveness of developing individuals to the training stimulus, at various stages of growth and maturation (Malina, Bouchard, & Bar-Or, 2004). For example, at certain periods of time (windows), children can make their reflexes faster by practicing skills that test those reflexes. By focusing on fast feet or quick hand movements during the speed window, children achieve better results than when they practice the same movements outside of the window.

A sensitive period of development refers to the point in the development of a specific capacity at which training has an optimal effect. Current scientific insight confirms the existence of sensitive periods, or broad time frames, during which people can learn new tasks more efficiently and effectively than at other times (Gallahue & Ozmun, 2006).

This chapter discusses the sensitive periods of accelerated adaptation to training, or windows of trainability (Viru et al., 1998). In addition, the optimal trainability of the five Ss—stamina (endurance), strength, speed, skill, and suppleness (flexibility)—are analyzed, and biological markers are introduced to identify the sensitive periods of accelerated adaptation to training during the growth and maturation process.

Trainability is well documented in the coaching and research literature (Arbeit, 1997; Borms 1986; Kobayashi et al., 1978; Rushall, 1998; Viru, 1995; Viru et al., 1998, 1999). However, the concept of accelerated adaptation to training has been criticized (Ford et al., 2011) because some of the information was published in coaching journals as opposed to peer-reviewed scientific journals. The fact is that coaching has always been both an art and a science: in the face of limited research into some theories and practices during puberty, we must still make decisions based on the best information we have. There is reasonable evidence to support the concept of accelerated adaptation to training, or windows of trainability; hence, LTAD proceeds with the assumption of its validity until proven otherwise.

Coaches and parents can use trainability information to identify when a change of emphasis in a training plan for young developmental athletes is necessary. Competition and performance demands should not inter-fere with the optimization of training during puberty (Viru, 1995). Athletes should not miss the opportunity offered by accelerated adaptation to training in the development of their physical capacities and skills.

Rather than offer a comprehensive review of the trainability literature, this chapter synthesizes and generalizes relevant trends in the literature to guide coaches and parents in developing training programs for young athletes.

Sensitive Periods of Trainability

In 1930 Scammon charted the processes of general, neural, and genital (hormonal) development. His chart acts as a road map of trainability, illustrating the quick development of the nervous system; the trends of general development of the skeleton, ligaments, tendons, organs, and muscle mass; and the hormonal predisposition to enhance training adaptations. His graph (see figure 6.1) highlights the sensitive periods in general, neural, and genital (or hormonal) development.

The general curve describes the growth of the body in terms of stature (size) and weight. It includes the growth patterns of various

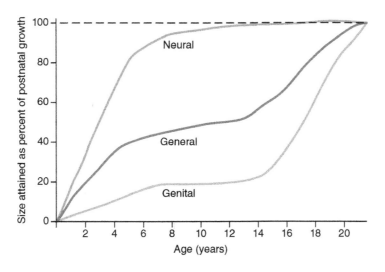

FIGURE 6.1 Various patterns of system growth during childhood.

Adapted from R.E. Scammon, 1930, The measurement of the body childhood. In *The measurement of man*, J.A. Harris (Minneapolis, MN: University of Minnesota Press).

systems of the body, such as muscle mass, the skeleton, lungs, the heart, ligaments, and tendons. The shape of the curve indicates a slow but steady development of the body structure, or stature, between the ages of 5 and 12. In simple terms, this period of life is the best time for skill development. During and after puberty, fitness can be improved as a result of the maturation of the skeletal structures, muscle mass, lungs, and cardiovascular system.

The neural curve describes the growth of the brain and the nervous system. By about 7 years of age, 95 percent of the central nervous system is developed. The shape of the neural curve suggests that children should work on the movement skills of agility, balance, coordination, and speed earlier rather than later. Fundamental movement and sport skills can, and should, be developed during childhood, before the onset of adolescence.

The genital curve shows the patterns of growth of both the primary and secondary sex characteristics. Genital tissue shows slow growth, with a latent period during childhood, before extremely rapid growth and maturation during the adolescent growth spurt. The shape of this curve indicates hormonal maturation, which has a significant positive contribution to fitness development and performance improvement.

Unfortunately, coaches never considered using this road map until the late 1980s. Before that time, watered-down or scaled-down adult training programs were superimposed on young female and male athletes. Even today, many coaches do not recognize or understand the sensitive periods of trainability during the growth of young athletes. When young athletes are biologically ready (that is, in the sensitive period for a specific domain), biological markers can help coaches identify which training components need to be emphasized and which need to be maintained or refined. During sensitive periods, the stimulus must be properly timed to achieve optimum adaptation to improve motor skills, speed, strength, stamina, and suppleness.

The key biological markers are as follows (figure 6.2):

- The onset of the adolescent growth spurt, or peak height velocity (PHV). (PHV is the fastest rate of growth during puberty. The terms *growth spurt* and *PHV* are used interchangeably in this chapter.)
- Peak growth (after which, growth decelerates)
- The onset of menarche (for female athletes)

Coaches who are aware of the key biological markers and can recognize the developmental

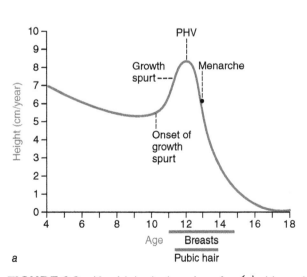

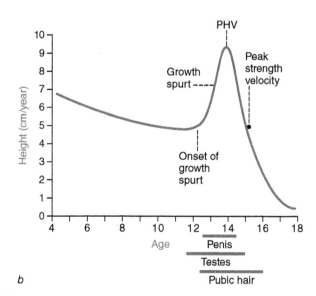

FIGURE 6.2 Key biological markers for *(a)* girls and *(b)* boys.

stage of their athletes can take advantage of the opportunities provided by the sensitive periods of accelerated adaptation to training.

The best way to describe the windows of optimal trainability is to use the five Ss of training and performance:

- Stamina (or endurance)
- Strength
- Speed
- Skill
- Suppleness (or flexibility)

Following are several key issues for coaches and parents to consider in relation to the five Ss:

- Capacities of stamina, strength, speed, skills, and suppleness are always trainable; however, during the sensitive periods, accelerated adaptation will occur if the proper volume, intensity, and frequency are chosen.
- Improvements in various capacities occur during adolescence, without training. For example, $\dot{V}O_2$max (the maximum amount of oxygen a person can consume during exercise, or the measure of aerobic power) increases in boys by about 150 percent and in girls by 80 percent between the ages of 8 and 16 (Armstrong & Welshman, 1997). This increase occurs without structured physical activity, because lung capacity increases with growth.
- Strength increases by two thirds after the growth spurt—again, without structured physical activity, as a result of growth.

Implementing proper endurance and strength training programs during the sensitive periods of trainability enhances adaptation and can contribute significantly to the foundation of aerobic and strength development. Unfortunately, many coaches design long- and short-term training programs, as well as competition and recovery programs, based on the chronological age of their athletes rather than on what individual athletes need; thus, the programs are not developmentally appropriate. In addition, some coaches superimpose scaled-down adult versions of training, competition, and recovery programs on developing athletes, which is not in their best interests.

Ideally, coaches should determine the biological maturity of their athletes and use this information as the foundation for athlete-specific training, competition, and recovery programs. Unfortunately, no reliable, noninvasive procedure exists for identifying biological maturity. The dangers of using other procedures (e.g., X-rays) for assessing biological or skeletal age have already been outlined by experts (Williams, 2009).

Chapter 5 describes and analyzes some solutions to help coaches. One is to use the onset of the growth spurt and the peak of growth (the point at which growth begins to decelerate) as reference points for the design of optimal, individual programs, in relation to sensitive periods of trainability during the maturation process. Prior to the onset of the growth spurt, boys and girls can train together, and chronological age can be used to determine training, competition, and recovery programs.

By using simple measurements, coaches can monitor PHV and prioritize training to take advantage of the sensitive periods of trainability. This approach can enhance the development of short- and long-term individually optimized training, competition, and recovery programs.

Windows of optimal trainability (accelerated adaptation) for stamina (endurance), strength, speed, skill, and suppleness (flexibility) are shown in figure 6.3. The different time frames for females and males are easily recognizable.

The arrows in figure 6.3 indicate moving scales, which depend on growth patterns. Boxes without arrows are based on chronological age. Chronological age is used in figure 6.3 and in program design because all research on speed and flexibility is based on chronological age, whereas research on stamina, strength, and skills is based on developmental age. Note that these windows are fully open during the sensitive periods of accelerated adaptation to training and partially open outside them. Again, a child can train to become faster (speed) outside of the window, but the training would not be as effective or efficient. Also, training speed at this

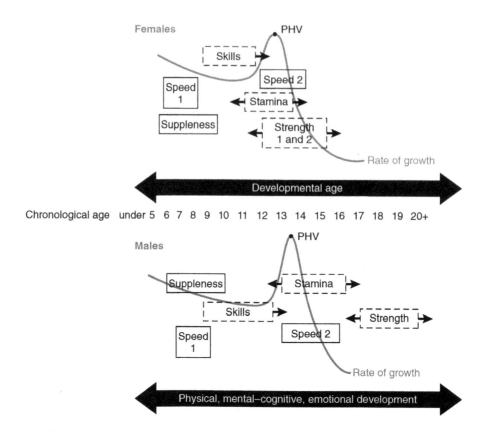

FIGURE 6.3 Windows of accelerated adaptation to training.

Reprinted, by permission, from I. Balyi and R. Way, 2005, *LTAD Summit* (Ottawa, Ontario, Canada); adapted from Canadian Sport for Life.

time might interfere with other training, such as endurance training, for which this might be a sensitive period.

Trainability of Stamina

The onset of the growth spurt indicates that the body is ready for accelerated adaptation of aerobic endurance training, or stamina. Prior to puberty, children mainly build endurance by improving the economy of their movement. This is reflected in a decrease in the oxygen cost of their physical activity, without an increase in $\dot{V}O_2max$. However, young people do increase their $\dot{V}O_2max$ significantly after the onset of the growth spurt, which peaks between ages 12 and 15 for females and 14 and 16 for males.

After the onset of the growth spurt, boys exhibit a spurt in $\dot{V}O_2max$ that often occurs just after the greatest increase in height, corresponding with the advance of male hormone

secretion. The steep rise in $\dot{V}O_2max$ of boys continues until about 16 years of age (Armstrong & Welshman, 1997). After this, a slower rise continues until about age 18.

In girls, $\dot{V}O_2max$ reaches its peak around 14 years of age, with a slow rise continuing until age 16. This increase would also occur without structured training, because it is due to growth. Coaches can achieve an increase in $\dot{V}O_2max$ during this period by implementing and monitoring a properly planned and structured training program. In support of this idea, Kobayashi and colleagues (1978) stated, "Beginning approximately one year prior to PHV and thereafter, training effectively increased aerobic power above the normal increase attributable to age and growth" (p. 666). Many leading coaches have experimented successfully with training programs that emphasize the development of aerobic capacities during this key period of development.

Beginning with the onset of the growth spurt, sports that require a strong aerobic base—that is, most late specialization sports (see chapter 4)—should prioritize aerobic capacity with continuous exercise, such as long slow distance (LSD) aerobic intervals and fartlek (or speed-play) type, training. When the tempo of growth decelerates, aerobic power training should be progressively introduced (see figure 6.4). Sports requiring less of an aerobic base (e.g., gymnastics and diving) should use ultrashort interval training to train the aerobic and anaerobic systems in parallel (Finn, 2001; Rushall, 1998). Aerobic capacity and power indirectly and directly contribute to enhanced quality of training time, help recovery between bouts of exercise or training sessions, and help recovery in general. Aerobic capacity and power also play a significant role in environmental adaptations, such as to altitude and jet lag, and assist with recovery from minor injuries. Thus, the extent of aerobic training should be determined by the demands of the sport—that is, how much endurance is required to train and compete well in that sport.

Aerobic training programs for females between 11 and 15 and males between 12 and 16 should be individualized. Participants in these age ranges should be grouped together based on their state of maturity (early, average, or late maturers) for developmentally appropriate fitness preparation, after the onset of the growth spurt. In principle, early-, average-, and late-maturing training groups should be formed to base fitness and skills training on maturation and not chronological age. Otherwise, under- and overtraining may occur resulting in only a certain number of athletes in each chronological age group being properly trained. In addition, the sensitive period of accelerated adaptation of the aerobic system could be compromised.

In team sports, players should work together for technical and tactical training, but have their own fitness programs based on their maturation levels and unique needs. Keeping young athletes in their age groups as much as possible is a positive approach because of their common emotional development and need for socialization.

Non-weight-bearing aerobic activities reduce the risk of injuries, overuse or otherwise. During the growth spurt, the "growing pains" can be reduced or better controlled by using proper progressions of technical-tactical training and strength training involving weight-bearing activities. Aerobic training at this developmental level should consist of non-weight-bearing and weight-bearing activities (e.g., swimming, rowing, treadmill running, using stair-climber machines, running, and cycling) to prevent overuse injuries during this particularly sensitive period.

Athletes in sports that do not require a high contribution of energy from aerobic sources, such as gymnastics, fencing, table tennis, and diving, need to develop a sport-specific aerobic base. Aerobic capacity and power, however, will not be a high priority at the onset of the growth spurt for these athletes.

Trainability of Strength

Strength gains during preadolescence or before the growth spurt are possible (Blimkie & Bar-Or, 1996). Children appear to be as trainable as adolescents or young adults, although mainly with regard to relative strength (related to body weight) rather than absolute strength. Strength training can be introduced at an early training age using body weight (push-ups, chin-ups), medicine balls, and Swiss ball exercises, which

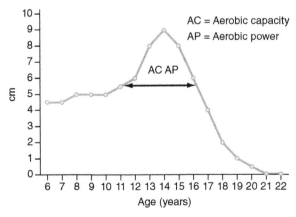

FIGURE 6.4 The trainability of aerobic capacity and aerobic power for late specialization sports.

Reprinted, by permission, from I. Balyi and C. Williams, 2009, *Coaching the young developmental performer* (Leeds, United Kingdom: Coachwise).

will improve basic movement skills and general strength and power development.

Ankle, knee, hip, shoulder, and vertebrae alignment should be evaluated and corrected if necessary from an early training age. Body alignments and optimal sport-specific flexibility ranges should be achieved before structured free weight training is introduced.

Strength gains before puberty will occur through motor learning, improvements in motor coordination, and morphological and neurological adaptations. Exercise and increased muscle activation will also increase strength.

Short-term strength training before puberty does not seem to interfere with endurance activities (Blimkie & Sale, 1998). However, unlike adults, prepubescent athletes cannot maintain strength gains with one session per microcycle (Blimkie & Sale, 1998). Training should take place two or three times per week, and the duration should not exceed 30 minutes. The sensitive periods of accelerated adaptation to strength training occur toward the end of, or immediately after, PHV (International Gymnastics Federation, n.d.) and at the onset of menarche for females, and between 12 and 18 months after PHV for males (Anderson & Bernhardt, 1998; Ross & Marfell-Jones, 1991).

The two windows for strength training in females are immediately after PHV and at the onset of menarche (figure 6.5a). Strength training is emphasized for males at the peak of strength velocity, 12 to 18 months after PHV (figure 6.5b).

Athletes should learn correct weightlifting technique prior to the window of optimal trainability for strength and during the sensitive periods of skill learning, which is prior to the onset of the growth spurt. In sports in which maximum strength plays an important role, Olympic lifting techniques and free weights should be introduced early. Because Olympic lifts are very technical, introducing them before the onset of PHV will prepare athletes for optimal strength training.

Trainability of Speed

Speed development incorporates linear, lateral, multidirectional speed, change of direction, agility, and segmental speed. Following are the windows of accelerated adaptation to speed training (Borms, 1986; Mero, 1998; Viru et al., 1998):

- Females from 6 to 8 and 11 to 13
- Males from 7 to 9 and 13 to 16

The first window for speed training for females and males is not concerned with training the speed energy systems (anaerobic alactic

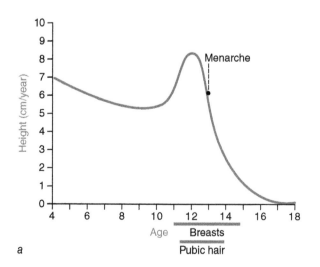

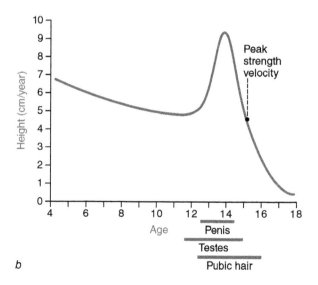

FIGURE 6.5 Windows for strength training in (a) girls and (b) boys.

Reprinted, by permission, from I. Balyi and R. Way, 2005, *LTAD Summit* (Ottawa, Ontario, Canada).

power and capacity) , but rather, with training the central nervous system (CNS). Agility, quickness, change of direction, and segmental speed are controlled by the CNS. The volume of training is very low, the intensity is very high, and the CNS and the anaerobic alactic power system should be challenged. The duration of the exercise should be less than five seconds, and full recovery should occur between sets.

Anaerobic alactic power and anaerobic alactic capacity interval training should only start during the second window of accelerated adaptation to speed training. The duration of the exercise is recommended to be between 5 and 20 seconds, and full recovery should occur between sets. The overall volume of training is low.

Interestingly, Cooper (1995) reported that children were more often engaged in short bursts of intense activity than in long-term activities. The average duration of this high-intensity activity was only six seconds, and the average interval between short-burst activities was about 20 seconds. During growth, this activity pattern seems more natural than long exercise bouts. According to Mero (1988), "The age phase from seven to 12 is a sensitive phase for speed development . . . . Both the development of the nervous system and the increasing skills offer possibilities to improve stride rate and consequently speed" (pp. 261-262).

Following are several key issues regarding the trainability of speed:

- Speed should be trained regularly and frequently (e.g., at every training session after the warm-up).

- Toward the end of the warm-up or immediately after it, there is no central nervous system or metabolic fatigue. This is an optimal time to train speed.

- The volume of training should be low, and full recovery should occur between exercises and sets.

- Acceleration should be over a short distance, with proper posture and correct elbow, knee drive, and head positions.

- Takeoff speed and segmental speed should be trained regularly, outside of the window of optimal trainability for speed.

- In addition to regular parts of the training session being set aside for speed development (such as the end of the warm-up), proper block training should be allocated to speed the periodized annual training program.

- For the second speed window, energy system training and block loading should occur during the general and specific preparatory phases, and sometimes during the precompetitive phase.

- Coaches should pay particular attention to the two speed windows of trainability.

Trainability of Skill

Fundamental movement skills and sport skills are most trainable between the ages of 5 and 12 (Borms, 1986). Figure 6.6 illustrates some of the key fundamental sport skills children should acquire. Coordination and motor skills develop very well in physically active boys and girls during childhood, as does the nervous system (Mero, 1998).

Tittel (1991) noted that children who were biologically about 11 years of age showed better coordination test results than those biologically aged 13 to 14 years. This indicates that coordinative maturity occurs before sexual maturation and is the main reason early specialization sports begin sport-specific training at 5 or 6 years of age. Children in these sports need to acquire the necessary sport-specific and general skills before the onset of the growth spurt. However, in late specialization sports, intense training of specialized skills at an early age can prove detrimental to development. Early sport-specific training contributes to unbalanced fitness, which, together with early training of technical–tactical and sport-specific skills, results in young athletes not developing the broader skill base necessary at later stages.

The accelerated adaptation to motor skills and coordination development, from 8 to 11 years of age for females and 9 to 11 years of age for males, is called peak motor coordination velocity (PMCV). Most experts confirm this sensitive period (Borms 1986; Rushall, 1998). Both coaches and parents need to understand that fundamental movement and basic sport-specific

FIGURE 6.6 Fundamental sport skills.

Reprinted, by permission, from I. Balyi et al., 2005, *Canadian Sport for Life: Long-term athlete development* (Vancouver, Canada: Canadian Sport Centres).

skills need to be acquired before ages 11 and 12, for girls and boys respectively. Specializing early in late specialization sports tends to have negative consequences. A considerable body of evidence shows that early specialization in late specialization sports contributes to burnout and early retirement (Bompa, 1995).

Coaches should realize that, although skills are always trainable, skill trainability gradually declines after 11 to 12 years of age, or, more precisely, after the onset of the growth spurt. That is not to say that improving skills after 12 years of age is impossible; rather, the point is that the foundations for skill learning are laid before age 12. When these foundations are not properly developed, people have more diffi-

culty improving skills later in life. As a result, development may be hindered.

It is recommended that fundamental movement skills, such as the ABCs of athleticism (agility, balance, coordination, and speed) and the RJTs of athletics (run, jump, and throw) be introduced in a child-friendly environment through fun-and-games activities in the early stages of the skills window (usually from 6 years of age). As children become more confident and competent with these basic movement skills, they can progress to a wide variety of fundamental sport skills (i.e., the basic sport skills that are often introduced, using adapted equipment and a mini-game approach). For late specialization sports, children and young people should sample a wide variety of fundamental sport skills. This has been shown to be more conducive to long-term development, once adolescents are specializing in a particular sport (usually between 13 and 15 years of age).

Trainability of Suppleness

Suppleness (or flexibility) is a key training and performance factor. Optimal individual and sport-specific flexibility should be established at an early training age. However, information on how best to develop flexibility and how training flexibility affects children is limited. In principle, training for increased joint mobility should start before the onset of PHV (Armstrong and Welshman, 1997; Mero, 1998). According to Mero (1998), the period from age 9 to 12 (before puberty) is a sensitive phase for flexibility training, a phase in which optimal levels of flexibility can be achieved.

Prior to the onset of the growth spurt, dynamic mobility and static stretching should be emphasized. Athletes should not stretch during rest days in a training cycle. If flexibility is lacking, flexibility training should be undertaken five to six times per week. To maintain current flexibility levels, athletes should have two or three sessions of flexibility training each week, or train every other day.

Static stretching should not be part of the warm-up, because it does not prevent injury. Fitness, on the other hand, does (Shrier, 1999). In principle, static stretching and proprioceptive neuromuscular facilitation (PNF) should be performed two hours prior to or two hours after training or competition.

Training and Competition During Puberty

Viru (1995) noted a crucial factor for coaches to consider when designing programs for young athletes going through the maturation process. If a conflict exists between long-term athlete development and the demands of competition, long-term athlete development must take priority. This is a vital message for coaches. Competition and performance demands should not interfere with the optimization of training processes during puberty. If they do, athletes miss the opportunity offered by windows of accelerated adaptation to training in the development of their physical capacities and skills. When competition activities interfere with training activities, athletes are unlikely to reach their full genetic potential.

Monitoring individual athletes' growth patterns with biological markers helps coaches know when to adapt the training program to make full use of sensitive periods of accelerated adaptation to training. The training gains offered by using the sensitive periods for the five Ss of training and performance ultimately help young athletes reach their full potential. It makes sense, therefore, that periodized training, competition, and recovery programs for developing athletes should be adapted for their particular needs, focusing on their developmental age. Knowing the tempo of growth (acceleration and deceleration) identified by biological markers enables coaches to adjust training when required. Prioritizing, integrating, and sequencing training activities for young athletes in relation to their tempos and patterns of growth are essential to exploit the sensitive periods of accelerated adaptation to training.

The trainability chart shown in figure 6.7 summarizes the windows of optimal trainability and identifies chronological age and developmental age, general training age, and sport-specific training age. The shading on the left and right of the figure identifies prepuberty and postpuberty. During prepuberty, before the onset of the growth spurt, or PHV, simple diagnostic filed tests can determine training priorities. Strengths and weaknesses can be identified by comparing athletes to national or international normative data. Of course, the sensitive periods of accelerated adaptation of training concerning skills, speed, and suppleness should be taken into consideration in program design and implementation.

During puberty (the shading in the middle of the figure), chronological age is not a good indicator for program design, but developmental age is (this is why there are no ages indicated from 11 to 16 on the chronological age

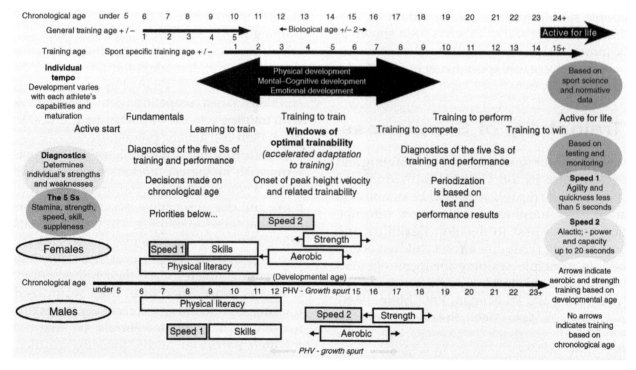

FIGURE 6.7 Optimal trainability. ABCs = agility, balance, coordination, speed; RJT = run, jump, throw; KGBs = kinesthesia, gliding, buoyancy, striking with object; CPKs = catching, passing, kicking, striking with body.

Reprinted, by permission, from I. Balyi et al., 2009, *Karate for life* (Montreal, Canada: Karate Canada), 58.

continuum). The arrows on the boxes indicate moving scales, which are determined by the tempo of growth of the individual athlete (i.e., early- or late-maturing athlete). The biological markers described earlier in this chapter determine training priorities. During puberty, the Train to Train stage, there are three windows for accelerated adaptation to training—for stamina (aerobic endurance), speed, and strength.

In postpuberty all systems are fully trainable; thus diagnostics (field tests, laboratory tests, skills tests, and performance tests) will identify strengths and weaknesses, and short- and long-term training priorities can be established for training, competition, and recovery programs.

Summary

The sensitive periods of accelerated adaptation to training, or windows of opportunity (optimal trainability), outlined in this chapter indicate the priorities for varying capacities within the stages of LTAD. Coaches working with young athletes should do the following:

- Measure and monitor the key reference points of growth from the onset of the growth spurt to adulthood for each athlete.

- Note biological markers to help with the decision-making process (see figure 6.2).

- Respond to biological marker data by monitoring and adjusting training programs according to the tempo of athletes' growth.

- Design an appropriate program for each athlete that takes advantage of the windows of trainability. Each program should be based on individual and sport-specific needs.

- Keep in mind that stamina, strength, speed, skill, and suppleness are always trainable; however, the rate of improvement is influenced by the sensitive periods of trainability and maturation levels.

- Remember that two windows of trainability are based on chronological age: speed and suppleness (all research is based on chronological age).

- Keep in mind that three windows are based on the athlete's tempo of growth and biological maturity: stamina, strength, and skill.

- To monitor growth, use these biological markers: the onset of the growth spurt, peak of growth (after the peak growth decelerates), and the onset of menarche (see figure 6.2).

This chapter identified the complex maturational process in young athletes and described how maturation relates to trainability. The intention is to give coaches and parents information on the development of the five Ss of training and performance at various ages. In addition, biological markers have been used to help coaches decide when a change of emphasis in a training plan for young developmental athletes is necessary.

Questions for Reflection

- What is a biological marker?

- What is accelerated adaptation to training?

- What are the windows of trainability, or windows of opportunity?

- Which trainability factors are based on chronological age?

- Which trainability factors are based on developmental age?

- When are the windows of trainability closed?

References

Anderson, G., & Bernhardt, T. (1998, fall). Coaching children: Growth and maturation considerations. *BC Coaches Perspective*, 14-15.

Arbeit, E. (1997, April 5-6). *Practical training emphases in the first and second decades of development.* Paper presented at the XXth European Athletics Coaches Association (EACA) Conference, Belgrade, Serbia.

Armstrong, N., & Welshman, J. (1997). Children in sport and exercise. *British Journal of Physical Education, 28* (2), 4-6.

Balyi, I., Devlin, K., Lauzière, G., Moore, C., & Way, I. (2009). *Karate for life.* Montreal, Quebec: Karate Canada, p. 58.

Balyi, I., & Way, R. (2005). LTAD summit [PowerPoint presentation]. Ottawa, Ontario, Canada.

Blimkie, C.J.R., & Bar-Or, O. (1996). Trainability of muscle strength, power and endurance during childhood. In O. Bar-Or (Ed.), *The child and adolescent athlete.* London, UK: Blackwell.

Blimkie, C.J.R., & Sale, D.G. (1998). Strength development and trainability during childhood. In E. Van Praagh (Ed.), *Pediatric anaerobic performance* (pp. 193-224). Champaign, IL: Human Kinetics.

Bompa, T. (1995). *From childhood to champion athlete.* Toronto, ON: Veritas.

Borms, J. (1986). The child and exercise: An overview. *Journal of Sport Sciences, 4*, 3-20.

Cooper, D.M. (1995). New horizons in pediatric exercise science research. In J. Blimkie & O. Bar-Or (Eds.), *New horizons in pediatric exercise science.* Leeds, UK: Human Kinetics Europe.

Finn, C. (2001). Effects of high-intensity intermittent training on maximum oxygen uptake and endurance performance. *Sportscience, 5*, 1-3. Retrieved from www.sportsci.org/jour/0101/cf.pdf

Ford, P., Croix, M., Lloyd, R., Meyers, R., Moosavi, M., Oliver, J., Till, K., & Williams, C. (2011). The long-term athlete development model: Physiological evidence and application. *Journal of Sports Sciences*, 1-14.

Gallahue, D.L., & Ozmun, J.C. (2006). *Understanding motor development: Infants, children, adolescents, adults* (6th ed.). Boston: McGraw-Hill

International Gymnastics Federation. (n.d.). *Age group development program* [DVD].

Kobayashi, K., Kitamura, K., Miura, M., Sodeyama, H., Murase, Y., Miyahita, M., & Matsui, H. (1978). Aerobic power as related to body growth and training in Japanese boys: A longitudinal study. *Journal of Applied Physiology, (44)* 5, 666-672.

Malina, R.M., Bouchard, C., & Bar-Or, O. (2004). *Growth, maturation, and physical activity.* Champaign, IL: Human Kinetics.

Mero, A. (1998). Power and speed training during childhood. In E. Van Praagh (Ed.), *Paediatric anaerobic performance.* Champaign, IL: Human Kinetics.

Ross, W.D., & Marfell-Jones, M.J. (1991). Kinanthropometry. In J.D. MacDougall, H.A. Wenger, & H.J. Green (Eds.), *Physiological testing of the high performance athlete* (2nd ed.). Champaign, IL: Human Kinetics.

Rushall, B. (1998, summer). The growth of physical characteristics in male and female children. *Sports Coach, 20*, 25-27.

Scammon, R.E. (1930). The measurement of the body in childhood. In J.A. Harris (Ed.), *The measurement of man.* Minneapolis: University of Minnesota Press.

Shrier, J. (1999). Stretching before exercise does not reduce the risk of local muscle injury. *Clinical Journal of Sport Medicine, 9*, 221-227.

Tittel, K. (1991). Coordination and balance. In A. Dirix, H.G. Knuttgen, & K. Tittel (Eds.), *The Olympic book of sport medicine.* Oxford, UK: Blackwell.

Viru, A. (1995). *Adaptation in sports training*. Boca Raton, FL: CRC Press.

Viru, A., Loko, J., Harro, M., Volver, A., Laaneots, L., & Viru, M. (1999) Critical periods in the development of performance capacities during childhood and adolescence. *Physical Education and Sport Pedagogy, 4* (1), 75-119.

Viru, A., Loko, J., Volver, A., Laaneots, L., Karlesom, K., & Viru, M. (1998). Age periods of accelerated improvements of muscle strength, power, speed and endurance in age interval 6–18 years. *Biology of Sport, 15* (4), 211-227.

Williams, C. (2009). Tracking growth and development: How to Measure PHV. In I. Balyi & C. Williams (Eds.), *Coaching the young developing performer* (pp.74-86). Leeds, UK: Coachwise.

To Learn More

Armstrong, N., & Welshman, J. (1993a). Children's physiological responses to exercise. In M. Lee (Ed.), *Coaching children in sport* (pp. 64-77). London; New York: Spon Press.

Armstrong, N., & Welshman, J. (1993b). Training young athletes. In M. Lee (Ed.), *Coaching children in sport* (pp. 191-203). London; New York: Spon Press.

Balyi, I., & Williams, C. (Eds.). (2009). *Coaching the young developmental performer.* Leeds, UK: Coachwise.

Bar-Or, O. (Ed.). (1995). *The child and the adolescent athlete.* Oxford, UK: Blackwell Scientific.

Bar-Or, O., & Rowland, T. (2004). *Paediatric exercise medicine.* Champaign, IL: Human Kinetics.

Blimkie, C.J.R., & Marion, A. (1994). Resistance training during pre-adolescence: Issues, controversies and recommendations. *Coaches Report, 1* (4), 10-14.

Devlin, K., Bisson, G., Jennings, J., Lauziere, G., Moore, C., & Oliver, P. (2009). *Karate for life.* Ottawa, ON: Karate Canada.

Kenney, L.W., Wilmore, J.H., & Costill, D.L. (2012). *Physiology of sport and exercise* (5th ed.). Champaign, IL: Human Kinetics.

Laaneots, L., & Viru, M. (1999). Critical periods in the development of performance capacity during childhood and adolescence. *Physical Education & Sport Pedagogy, 4,* 75-119.

Lawrence, M. (1999). *US swimming sport science summit for young swimmers: Learning about athlete development.* Colorado Springs, CO: US Swimming.

MacDougall, J.D., Wenger, H.A., & Green, H.J. (Eds.). (1990). *Physiological testing of the high performance athlete* (2nd ed.). Champaign, IL: Human Kinetics.

Malina, R.M., & Bouchard, C. (1991). *Growth, maturation and physical activity.* Champaign, IL: Human Kinetics.

Rushall, B.S. (1999). Ultra-short interval training the best form of competition-specific aerobic adaptation and neuromuscular patterning. *Programming considerations for physical conditioning* (p. 2). Spring Valley, CA: Sports Science Associates. Retrieved from http://coachsci.sdsu.edu/csa/vol71/rushall.htm

Stafford, I. (2005). *Coaching for long-term athlete development.* Leeds, UK: Coachwise.

Van Praagh, E. (Ed.). (1998). *Paediatric anaerobic performance.* Champaign, IL: Human Kinetics.

Intellectual, Emotional, and Moral Development

The soccer coach was puzzled. Mary was big, strong, and fast and had great ball control skills, but she was constantly giving the ball to her opponents because she lost concentration. Not only that, but she also got mad with herself for making bad decisions, which often led her to commit fouls as she tried to undo the damage. The free kicks she was giving up were hurting the team—badly.

In chatting to Mary's mother one day after practice, Coach learned that Mary really enjoyed playing with some of the younger girls in her neighborhood, and that she would play for hours with them, dressing dolls and having pretend tea parties. Then her mother said something that really made Coach think. "You know," she said, "although Mary's a big girl and looks older than she is, she's still a little girl at heart."

Coach then made the connection and realized what a mistake she had made. She knew Mary was physically advanced for her age, appearing to be at least 12 or 13 while everyone else on the Under-11 team looked their age. Because Mary was big, Coach had been expecting her to have the thinking, tactics, strategy, and emotional control of a 13-year-old.

Once Coach realized that not all aspects of a young player develop at the same rate, and that Mary's body was way ahead of her brain in terms of development, Mary's behavior made sense. So Coach changed her coaching accordingly. She began coaching Mary physically in ways that were right for a player going through her adolescent growth spurt, but coached strategy and tactics that were right for Mary's 10-year-old brain.

This chapter addresses how body systems develop at different speeds, and how this can affect an athlete's capacity to train, compete, recover, think, and deal with the strong emotions that are part of the sport experience. The child's level of capability determines when to move from one stage to the next—not chronological age—and it is common for a child to be at one stage in terms of physical development and another in terms of skill, tactics, or emotional development.

The ways athletes learn, and how different learning styles need to be accommodated, are discussed. In addition, this chapter also covers what needs to be done at each long-term athlete development (LTAD) stage in terms of mental training, emotional control, and training the decision-making mechanisms of the brain.

Capacities

Although the LTAD process suggests some ages at which boys and girls reach and leave each stage, these are only rough guides. Develop-ment is a continuous process. Children do not wake up on their birthdays magically ready to move to the next stage. The suggested ages are simply those at which children typically have developed the physical, mental, and emotional capacities associated with that LTAD stage.

What do we mean by *capacity*? In sporting terms it means how well a particular body system responds to a specific type of activity or training. There is strong evidence that sensitive periods exist within human development—periods in the athlete's life when certain systems respond more favorably to training than at other times (Fetters, 2010).

As children grow, their capacity to respond to instruction and training tends to go through the same developmental sequences—but children of the same age do not necessarily progress at the same speed or at the same time (Ulrich, 2007). This is one of the main reasons training programs need to be individualized. If one young athlete has already begun the adolescent growth spurt, that athlete's training needs to be focused on what needs to be done during adolescence even if the rest of the athletes in the program have not begun the growth spurt. This means building the "engine" of the body, or developing fitness and strength, even though the rest of the team might still need to focus more on skill development.

To further complicate matters, the components of a single athlete's body develop at different rates. Figure 7.1 shows the typical development pattern for a child, but keep in mind that there is considerable variation, both in the timing of the development sequence and in the speed of change.

All of this variation addresses only the body's physical growth and development. To work effectively with developing athletes, coaches and parents also need to track their intellectual, emotional, and moral development. To do this, they must keep a close eye on each child and not jump to conclusions. The easiest changes to monitor are physical ones. Parents and coaches can see when children start to rapidly outgrow others in their classes or on their teams. Careful observation will also identify which children are physically behind their peers. The real difficulty comes from trying to determine the levels of children's mental, emotional, and moral development.

Until the growth spurt, no readily observable markers indicate the transition from one stage to the next. This means that we have to rely on chronological age as the dividing line between the Active Start and FUNdamentals stages, and between the FUNdamentals and Learn to Train stages. The line between the Learn to Train and Train to Train stages marks the start of the adolescent growth spurt (see chapter 5), and the end of the Train to Train stage coincides with the end of adolescent growth. The Train to Compete and Train to Win stages are determined predominantly by the athlete's level of competition. Very few athletes ever reach the Train to Win stage because this stage covers athletes who are competitive (meaning that they have a chance to win) at the highest level of performance in their sport: at the Olympic Games, at the Paralympic Games, in world championships, or in professional leagues.

Interplay of Intellectual, Emotional, and Moral Development

The stages of physical development that each person goes through when passing from infancy to childhood to adolescence to adulthood are reasonably easy to see. People become taller and heavier, and their features change in predictable ways as they become sexually mature.

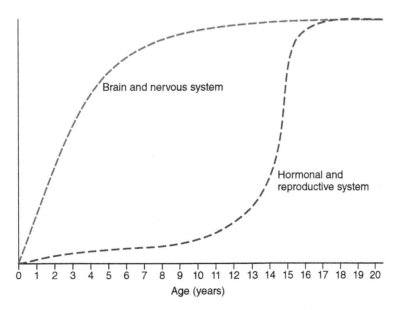

FIGURE 7.1 Different systems in the body develop at different ages and speeds.

The changes in the ways children process information (intellectual development), respond emotionally to what is going on around them (emotional development), and think about what is right or wrong (moral development)—each of which happens at a well-defined stage—are much more difficult to define.

Figure 7.2 shows the relationships among various stages of change in physical, intellectual, emotional, and moral development, as well as the stages of LTAD. Some of the key characteristics of each stage are then described.

Figure 7.2 shows, in simplified form, what the parent or coach working with a young athlete must take into consideration. The child goes through a number of stages in the four areas of physical development, intellectual development, emotional development, and moral development. However, the ages at which children typically move from one stage to the next are not consistent among these areas; even within one area of development, the age at which children move from stage to stage varies considerably.

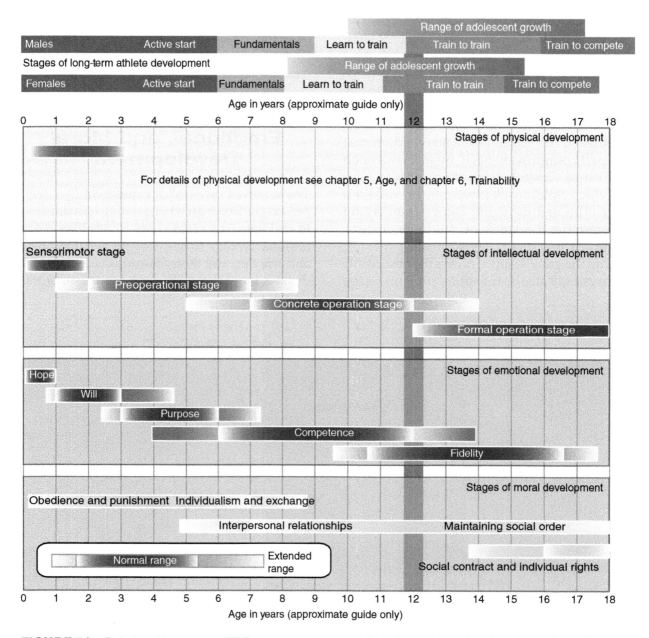

FIGURE 7.2 Relationships among LTAD stages and stages of intellectual, emotional, and moral development.

When we look at an individual child (represented by the gray vertical bar through figure 7.2), we can see that female children will likely be in the Train to Train stage, but that males could be in either the Learn to Train or the Train to Train stage. Physically, they could be prepubertal or going through their adolescent growth spurt, and exactly where they are in that growth spurt would have an impact on the kind of physical training they should be doing.

Intellectually, they could be at the end of the concrete operation stage or at the start of the formal operation stage (these stages are discussed in more detail later in the chapter). Emotionally, they could be at the end of the competence stage or at the start of the transition to the fidelity stage. In the area of moral development, they are probably in the transition from the interpersonal relationships stage to the maintaining social order stage.

Keeping track of where the athlete is in each of the dimensions of development is difficult enough in individual sports; it is exceptionally difficult in team sports in which all players may be at a different stages of development in each of the four domains. Coaches and parents need to remember that the important thing is to be roughly right in the big picture and not believe that they have to be exactly right in every aspect of teaching and coaching.

Physical Development

Details of physical development are covered in chapters 5 and 6 (on age and trainability, respectively) and are not covered again here. The key idea for parents and coaches to remember is that physical maturity is not a reliable indicator of intellectual, emotional, or moral development.

Intellectual Development

Most current thinking on the intellectual development of children is based on the groundbreaking work of Jean Piaget (1954). He broke the intellectual development of children into the following four major stages, with early stages consisting of a number of substages.

- **Sensorimotor stage.** The sensorimotor stage takes place from birth to age 2. During this period, children explore their surroundings through movement and their senses. They are generally unable to perceive or understand the world from any other person's point of view. Through a series of six substages, developing infants gain progressive control over their movements and their surroundings. By the end of their first year of life, they begin to understand the permanence of objects (i.e., that they continue to exist even when out of sight). By around age 2, they are able to both plan and execute movements that will get them what they want (e.g., they are able to move one object to get to something behind it).

- **Preoperational stage.** The preoperational stage occurs between ages 2 and 7. During this stage, language development is rapid. Children in the preoperational stage do not understand logic and cannot mentally manipulate information. They are still unable to understand the point of view of other people and remain self-centered. They develop the ability to use language to represent things that are not present, and understanding that things exist whether they can see them or not.

  Children also become increasingly competent at using symbols in the preoperational stage. This is shown in their enhanced ability to pretend (e.g., pretending a blanket suspended between two chairs is a house in which they, and sometimes their imaginary friends, live). Role-playing also becomes important during this stage; children understand how, and are able, to play at a good number of roles such as mommy, daddy, policeman, and bus driver.

- **Concrete operation stage.** The concrete operation stage begins around age 7 and continues until approximately age 11. During this time children gain a greater understanding of the world and how it operates. They can think reasonably logically about concrete objects and events, but usually have great difficulty understanding concepts or abstractions, such as game plans and team strategy.

  Children at the concrete operation stage are generally good at expanding their thinking from a specific example to a general principle, but have difficulty the other way around; that is, going from a general principle to determine what would happen in a specific event. In sporting terms this means that they understand direct instructions in soccer, such as, "Don't touch the ball with your hands; if you do, the referee will give the ball to the other team for a free kick," but not abstract instructions, such as, "Let's not give away unnecessary fouls."

One additional development at the concrete operation stage is an understanding of the "reversibility" of relationships. This means that a child at this stage of development can usually reverse the order of relationships among various categories of objects. For example, a boy might be able to recognize that kicking the ball in basketball is a foul, and that if he gets five fouls, he will be out of the game. At this stage he should also be able to recognize that there is a "five fouls and out" rule, and that there are different types of fouls, of which kicking the ball is one.

• **Formal operation stage.** The formal operation stage begins at approximately age 12 and remains the dominant stage for the rest of a person's life. During this time, the ability to think about abstract concepts emerges and people are able to use logical thought and deductive reasoning. This is also the stage of development at which systematic planning emerges.

Deductive reasoning requires the ability to use general principles to reach specific conclusions, and involves the ability to think through hypothetical situations to determine probable outcomes. Without this type of reasoning, long-term planning is not possible. In the area of sport, the ability to undertake formal operations is critical to fully understanding the rules of the game, as well as the consequences of one's actions, particularly in such areas as cheating, unethical behavior, and doping.

Emotional Development

Much of our understanding of emotional development comes from the work of Erik Homburger Erikson (1959, 1964), who was born in Denmark, grew up in Germany, and worked most of his life in the United States. Within each of his eight stages of human emotional development he identified what children (or

adults) would gain if parented and taught well, and what their problems would be if they were not. Generally, the first five stages identified by Erikson are important to the coach or parent engaged in LTAD, although all eight stages are described.

• **Hope—basic trust vs. mistrust.** Children who are well cared for and shown affection develop trust in adults. Children who are not become distrustful of adults. This stage covers the first year of life.

• **Will—autonomy vs. shame and doubt.** From the second year of life to age 3, children start to explore the world. They develop autonomy if allowed to explore in a safe and secure environment and if they receive approval for their exploration, but develop shame and doubt if parenting is too smothering or if they are neglected.

• **Purpose—initiative vs. guilt (ages 4 to 6).** With encouragement and support, children develop initiative by learning to plan and doing things on their own, including feeding and dressing themselves. In the absence of opportunity, encouragement, and support, children may feel guilty about making independent decisions, although Erikson believed that this guilt is usually short lived.

• **Competence—industry vs. inferiority (ages 7 to 12).** From about age 6 to the onset of puberty, children judge their own and others' behavior. They compare themselves to others, particularly in sporting and classroom environments. They are able to recognize differences in abilities, and when they judge themselves as inferior to others, they may well withdraw from participation. Interventions to help children develop skills equal to those of their peers help prevent feelings of inferiority.

• **Fidelity—identity vs. role confusion (ages 13 to 19).** The teenage years involve much questioning of self. Teens ask, "Who am I? How do I fit in? Where am I going in life?" Erikson believed that youth of this age should be allowed to explore their own ideas of who they are and how they fit in, and that parental or coach pressure to take on a particular role is a source of role confusion. Parents living vicariously through their children and pushing them to high levels of sport performance against their will are at high risk of leaving their children confused.

Beyond the teenage years, when LTAD is nearing completion, Erikson identified the following three stages:

- **Love (in intimate relationships, work, and family)—intimacy vs. isolation (ages 20 to 34).** This is the period during which long-term romantic relationships are formed and young adults are trying to balance the demands of sport, school, work, and family.

- **Caring—generativity vs. stagnation; the midlife crisis (ages 35 to 54).** This is a time when people start to measure their lifetime accomplishments and failures and ask themselves whether they are satisfied with their lives. Those who are satisfied tend to want to help the younger generation through serious involvement in coaching or sport administration. Those who are dissatisfied with their lives to this point risk feelings of stagnation, of not having done anything to help the next generation.

- **Wisdom—ego integrity vs. despair (old age until death).** Some people handle the approach of death well, having lived long and productive lives during the earlier stages. Others may be unhappy, resentful, or dissatisfied, with a probability of feeling despair.

Moral Development

Much of our understanding of the stages of moral development comes from the work of Lawrence Kohlberg (1973), which are usually considered an adaptation of the theories of Jean Piaget. Kohlberg developed his theories while a graduate student at the University of Chicago, and he continued to work on this theory for much of his life. In all, he identified three levels of moral reasoning, each with two substages. Unlike the areas of physical, mental, and emotional development, there is little evidence that everyone goes through all of the stages of moral development. In fact, in sport, as in life, many people never reach the higher levels of moral development.

- **Level 1 (preconventional moral reasoning).** This stage lasts, generally, until the age of 6 or 7.

  - *Obedience and punishment orientation.* At this earliest stage of moral development, the child asks, "How can I avoid punishment?" For children at this stage, good, bad, right, and wrong are determined by those things for which they are punished. There is no consideration of the rightness or wrongness of any actions outside of whether there is punishment for doing them.

  - *Self-interest orientation.* At this stage of development, the child asks, "What's in it for me?" There may be some consideration of the impact of one's actions on others, but the importance of this is limited, almost entirely, to "I'll scratch your back if you scratch mine."

- **Level 2 (conventional moral reasoning).** This stage starts at about age 7 and may persist into adult life in less morally thoughtful people.

  - *Interpersonal accord and conformity.* At this stage actions are considered in light of what others will think. Will the actions you take be thought of as good, proper, right, or respectful by others, and will you be considered a "good boy" or "good girl" for what you have done? Social approval becomes very important at this stage, and actions are generally taken in accordance with prevailing social norms. The social norms may be those of general society, the family, or the team, and internal conflict is possible if a young player is exposed to social norms on the team that are different from those of the family or society in general. This clash of societal norms may be particularly strong when players on a team come from different ethnic backgrounds.

  - *Authority and social-order-maintaining orientation.* This is often described as law-and-order morality, recognizing that playing by the rules is

99

in everyone's best interest. There is consideration of what would happen if everyone broke the rules. Sport is often contested at this level of moral thought.

• **Level 3 (postconventional moral reasoning).** This is the normal adult level of moral thought.

　○ *Social contract orientation.* At this level of moral reasoning, there is an understanding that following the rules may generate an internal clash with what a person knows to be right. Stealing is wrong, but stealing bread to feed a starving child would be the right thing to do if there were no reasonable alternatives. This stage is marked by thinking about the consequences of one's actions—consequences to the self and to society (others)—and then making a reasoned decision about how to proceed, even when the course of action is not in one's own best interest.

　○ *Universal ethical principles.* In this, the highest level of moral reasoning, decisions are based on abstract reasoning using universal ethical principles. Following the law is only justified when the law itself is right and just, and the person is committed to doing what is right (i.e., has a principled conscience).

Influence of Intellectual, Emotional, and Moral Development on LTAD

The key issue for parents and coaches is to match everything they do to the level of development of the athlete in each of the areas of physical, intellectual, emotional, and moral development. In some ways this issue is at the very core of effective coaching and cannot be covered in-depth in just one chapter of a book. Some examples might be useful, however, so let us consider the areas of tactics, decision making, and cheating (tables 7.1, 7.2, and 7.3).

TABLE 7.1　Influence of Intellectual Development

Stage of development	Teaching	Approach
FUNdamentals	The use of space, width, and depth—not "bunching up" all the players in soccer as they chase the ball around.	Players are in the preoperational stage, with good developing language, but no real grasp of logic or "big picture" ideas. If the purpose of soccer is to kick the ball, then they are going to chase it. And if they are not chasing it, then they are probably not going to be engaged—and will likely end up picking daisies! Toward the end of this stage, some children are developing to the level of concrete operations and are able to cope with the learn to train coaching strategy.
Learn to Train	The use of space, width, and depth—not "bunching up" all the players in soccer as they chase the ball around.	Players are in the concrete operation stage of intellectual development; they are likely to understand general concepts such as "stay spread out." The coach should focus on the concrete and tell the players something like: "Stay at least 5 yards away from your teammates."
Train to Train	The use of space, width, and depth.	Players are now (generally) in the formal operation stage of intellectual development and can deal with abstractions, such as, "stay in open space," "play the ball into space," and "get free."

TABLE 7.2   Influence of Emotional Development

Stage of development	Teaching	Approach
FUNdamentals	Learning to swim	At the beginning of this stage of LTAD, children are generally at the end of the purpose stage or the beginning of the competence stage of emotional development. To develop autonomy (purpose stage), they need opportunities to try things out, encouragement from adults and other children, and support to help them succeed. As they move into the competence stage, they begin to compare themselves to others and will either move toward industry (practicing and getting better) or to inferiority, with the potential for withdrawal from the sport. At this stage of emotional development, children who have lower levels of skill than their peers must be given the extra attention they need to catch up, so that they don't develop feelings of inferiority. If they fall too far behind now, they may never catch up.
Learn to Train	Learning to swim and developing as a swimmer	Athletes at this stage of LTAD are predominantly at the competence stage of emotional development. During this stage they become industrious and practice hard if they see themselves as competent, but develop feelings of inferiority, and likely withdraw, if they see themselves as being significantly less skillful than their peers. Helping children keep up with their peers is the most important thing coaches, parents, and caregivers can do to help them emotionally.
Train to Train	Developing as a swimmer	The Train to Train stage overlaps with the fidelity stage of emotional development, a time when teens are very concerned with developing their individuality and a strong sense of who they are. In sport, this can be a time of conflict and emotional upheaval because parents and coaches may have ideas about how much time athletes should train and in which events they should specialize. Although adult guidance about strengths, weaknesses, and potential is appropriate, trying to force the athlete to do what the coach thinks is best runs a very high risk of driving the athlete from the sport.

Learning Styles

In addition to ensuring that coaching is consistent with the child's stage of physical, intellectual, emotional, and moral development, parents and coaches must also take into account differences in learning styles. Of the following three major learning styles, people generally have a preference for one of them.

• **Visual learners.** As the name suggests, these learners like to see demonstrations, videos, and diagrams and like to watch the coach's face and body language to fully appreciate what is going on. They often think in pictures and have difficulty doing things they cannot internally visualize. They may get bored with explanations and just want to see something done and then be given a chance to try it. For children who are visual learners, the key is to show them and then have them do it.

• **Auditory learners.** These learners benefit through listening and may prefer to look

TABLE 7.3 Influence of Moral Development

Stage of development	Teaching	Approach
FUNdamentals	Following the rules of the game—not picking up the ball in soccer (except for goalkeepers)	At the FUNdamentals stage of LTAD, children are at the end of the obedience and punishment stage or the beginning of the self-interest stage of moral development. The coach should not say, "it's wrong to pick up the ball," but rather, needs to match instructions to the moral development stage of the athlete: "If you run with the ball, you'll have to sit out for one minute," with the focus on the consequences of breaking the rules, on punishment (in the mildest sense of the word), and on "what's in it for me if I follow the rules."
Learn to Train	Trying not to harm opponents when tracking or checking them	Athletes at this stage of LTAD are generally at the stage of conventional moral reasoning. The coach might want to focus on conformity (doing the right thing because other people will think you are a good person), as well as on an authority and social order orientation, with a focus on playing by the rules because it is in everyone's best interest.
Train to Train	Not using performance-enhancing drugs	Many athletes are still at the conventional moral reasoning stage (in fact, many athletes never progress beyond this stage), and so the approach will not be much different from that used at the Learn to Train stage. Athletes with more advanced moral development may have moved on to the social contract orientation, in which they may start giving deep thought to the consequences of their actions both for themselves and for society, and can start challenging coaches about the underlying reasons for rules. They may also start making decisions that may not be in their own best interest, but are in the best interest of the team or society in general.

away from the coach to fully concentrate on what they are hearing. It is therefore important not to assume that they are not paying attention. Generally, auditory learners respond well to rich and detailed verbal instructions and like to ask questions to confirm that they have understood. Even good demonstrations need to be accompanied by verbal descriptions for auditory learners.

• **Kinesthetic (tactile) learners.** These learners adapt by moving, doing, and touching. They may like to have their bodies physically moved by the coach through the movement they are trying to learn. They can then feel the movement and try to replicate the feeling as they try it out.

In real life, few children learn in only one way. For this reason coaches should use multiple channels of communication: demonstrations accompanied by good, but brief, verbal descriptions of the demonstration, and then working one-on-one with children to move their limbs through complex movements if they don't understand after seeing and hearing. Because the amount of information that children can take in at any one time is limited, a good rule of thumb is never to have an athlete concentrate on more than one thing at a time.

Summary

When we consider athletes' readiness, we take into account physical, intellectual, emotional, and moral development. Athletes develop in these areas at varying speeds, which can affect their capacity to deal with the overall sport experience. Their level of capacity determines when to move from one stage to the next. Skills must be not only technically correct but also developmentally appropriate.

Although physical development is generally visible and easy to monitor, the way people process information, respond emotionally, and consider what is right or wrong is much more difficult to ascertain. Also difficult to determine, yet critical for coaches and parents to understand, is whether young athletes are visual, auditory, or kinesthetic learners.

Although athletes tend to go through the same developmental sequence, the speed at which they do so can vary greatly. Because of this, the various components of an athlete's development should be closely monitored, and training programs should be individualized. Coaches should work with athletes to understand (and help them understand) their preferred methods of learning, and to provide instruction to them in the way that helps them the most.

Questions for Reflection

- What is meant by capacity?
- What are the components that determine readiness?
- What are the stages and levels that affect development?
- What are some ways people learn?
- Why is it important that training programs be individualized?

References

Erikson, E. (1959). *Identity and the life cycle: Psychological issues 1*. New York: International Universities Press.

Erikson, E. (1964). *Insight and responsibility: Lectures on the ethical implications of psychoanalytic insight*. New York: W. W. Norton.

Fetters, L. (2010). Perspective on variability in the development of human action. *Physical Therapy, 90* (12), 1860-1867.

Kohlberg, L. (1973). The claim to moral adequacy of a highest stage of moral judgment. *Journal of Philosophy, 70* (18), 630-646.

Piaget, J. (1954). *The construction of reality in the child*. (M. Cook, Trans.). New York: Basic Books. (Original work published 1937)

Ulrich, B. (2007). Motor development: Core curricular concepts. *Quest (00336297), 59* (1), 77-91.

To Learn More

Hyson, M. (2004) *The emotional development of children: Building an emotion centred curriculum*. New York: Teachers College Press, Columbia University.

Jones, C., & McNamee, M. (2003). Moral development and sport. In J. Boxill (Ed.), *Sports ethics* (pp. 40-52). Hoboken, NJ: Wiley-Blackwell.

National Scientific Council on the Developing Child. (2004). *Children's emotional development is built into the architecture of their brains* [Working paper no. 2]. Retrieved from http: //developingchild.harvard.edu/resources/reports_and_working_papers/

Proios, M., Doganis, G., & Athanailidis, I. (2004). Moral development and form of participation, type of sport, and sport experience. *Perceptual Motor Skills, 99* (2), 633-642.

University of Illinois at Chicago's Studies in Social and Moral Development and Education. Featured articles. Retrieved from http: //tigger.uic.edu/~lnucci/MoralEd/articles.html

Excellence Takes Time

Everyone was talking about Tamara's sudden success in tennis. She had just won the junior state championships at age 17 and was being offered tennis scholarships from a half dozen colleges. Out of nowhere she had suddenly emerged as a tennis star, and everyone was mystified. One of her parents' friends commented, "I guess she is just one of those naturally talented athletes." Tamara's parents frequently heard these types of comments and were beginning to tire of explaining the truth. Before long, they decided it was easier to simply reply, "Yes, it is a bit of a surprise."

The truth was that Tamara was not an overnight success. She had started taking an interest in tennis when she was about 9 years old. Her dad had started hitting the ball with her at a local outdoor court with lumpy asphalt when she was just a little girl as a way of getting her active while spending time with her one-on-one. They wouldn't keep score—they were only concerned with keeping the ball moving back and forth and seeing how long they could keep their rallies going.

By the time she was 11, Tamara was pretty good at returning the ball. At that time she had started to want a little more than a simple rally. She and her dad started to keep score. Tamara grew determined in her playing and tried to hit harder shots crosscourt or lobs over the net to try to beat her dad. Her parents registered her for a series of introductory tennis lessons over 12 weeks at the local recreation center. From the very start, Tamara loved her tennis lessons. Her coach knew a lot more about the game than her dad did, and she started teaching Tamara all kinds of techniques, from body movement and positioning to striking the ball for different effects. Her coach explained things clearly; she demonstrated all of the techniques like an expert. She made it clear that Tamara could eventually do all of these amazing things if she just practiced regularly. On top of that, she was nice to Tamara and made her feel capable and even talented. There were other young players in the recreation program, too. Tamara enjoyed playing games with them.

Tamara registered for all of the recreation center tennis programs and did the summer tennis camps as well. After two years she joined the local tennis club and was soon working with a new coach who was even better than the first. Her new coach had played professional tennis for many years and knew how to help Tamara with more specific aspects of her game. All the while, Tamara kept playing baseball and other sports such as volleyball at school. No one outside of her close friends and her parents really knew what she was up to. She wasn't a star tennis player yet, so most of her parents' friends and acquaintances had no idea she even played.

By the time she reached grade 12, Tamara had quietly become a very good player. She had played a lot of tournaments through her tennis club and grown in the game. Since she was 13, she had been playing at least six hours a week during the winter months and had generally played around 15 hours a week during the spring and summer. By the time she won the junior state championship, she figured she had probably played more than 4,000 hours of tennis since those early evenings with her dad when she was 9. Add to that all of the hours she had spent playing baseball, badminton, and volleyball, and she probably had at least 6,000 hours of general sport training and practice under her belt already.

Now she would be training and playing tennis competitively at the college level. Who knew how far she could go? If she trained and competed at that level for the next four years, she would probably put in another 4,000 hours of tennis. By the time she finished college, she imagined she might be good enough to go professional, and she would still be only 22 years old.

No one becomes an elite athlete overnight, and excellence in sport doesn't happen magically. It also takes much more than natural athleticism to win an Olympic gold medal or Wimbledon. Such success is the product of many hours of practice, requiring patience on the part of athletes, parents, and coaches. Of the many factors that influence the development of expert performance, research makes it clear that the greatest predictor of expertise is the number of hours spent in practicing a skill, whether the person is a concert musician, a computer programmer, a surgeon, or a professional athlete.

In the sporting world, swimmer Michael Phelps and basketball star Steve Nash are great examples of athletes who put in the time required to develop excellence. Phelps started swimming at age 7, and it was twelve years later, as a 19-year-old at the Athens Olympics in 2004, that he won an astounding six gold and two bronze medals. (He then bettered his record by winning eight gold medals at Beijing 2008, and he won another four gold and two silver medals at the 2012 London Games.) Notably, Phelps also spent many hours playing baseball, soccer, lacrosse, and golf as a youth (Black Book Partners, 2008).

Nash only started playing basketball at age 12 or 13. However, in addition to practicing and playing with his high school team, he spent countless hours playing on the weekend with his friends, practiced shooting outdoors in all weather, and worked on his dribbling in the family garage. As well, prior to playing basketball, he accumulated hundreds of hours of additional sport training through several years of youth soccer and hockey. His thousands of hours of practice eventually helped him to win a basketball scholarship to Santa Clara University in 1992; he was then drafted to the NBA in 1996 at the age of 22, and he went on to win back-to-back NBA league MVP awards in seasons 2004-2005 and 2005-2006 (Sport Reference, 2011).

Both Phelps and Nash made their breakthroughs to the top ranks of their sports after more than 10 years of sport-specific training, complemented by several years of additional practice and play in other sports. This fits the general pattern of development of the U.S. Olympic athletes described by the USOC in *The Pathway to Excellence* (2002).

The concept that excellence takes time is one of the key concepts of long-term athlete development.

Importance of Practice in Excellence

A popular misconception persists that the world's greatest athletes are great mainly because they were born that way. Certainly, we have all seen children who seem to exhibit natural athleticism at a young age, while many of their peers seem to struggle to develop physical coordination in early sporting activities. Many of these early talents are quickly identified and streamed into select programs with specialized coaching in the hope that they are marked for greatness. Occasionally, they do achieve greatness, which seems to suggest that early talent identification has been rewarded. But these success stories belie much of what really determines excellence and achievement in sport.

Research tells us that simple natural ability or genetic predisposition is not a major determinant of expertise in any field. In the world of sport achievement, genetic potential is increasingly recognized as a relatively small factor (even though it may play a slightly larger role in sports such as basketball and gymnastics, where genetic characteristics such as height are significant). The work of investigators such as Ericsson, Charness, Feltovich, and Hoffman (2006), and research initiated by predecessors such as Benjamin Bloom (1985), has made it clear that the greatest predictor of expertise is the number of hours spent practicing a skill.

In recent years there has been much discussion about precisely how much time is required to develop excellence. Popular books such as *Outliers* by Malcolm Gladwell (2008) have helped to dispel the myth that elite athletes are simply born with talent, highlighting that the greatest determining factor by far is practice. Quoting research by notable specialists in the study of expertise, such as Ericsson, Gladwell has helped bring public awareness to the fact that expertise in any field, including sport, requires extensive hours of dedicated practice over many years. Research by Ericsson and colleagues (1993) firmly established the fact that expertise in any discipline is the product of many hours and years of deliberate practice. Based on research by Ericsson and others, experts suggest that 10,000 hours, or 10 years, of practice are needed to achieve elite status in sport.

These are convenient round numbers, but they do not tell the entire story. In some sports the number of repetitions of an essential skill may be more important than the total hours of practice. Consider the following:

- Athletes training in biathlon may enter the Train to Win stage after 7,500 hours of ski training; however, that does not include the time they have taken to shoot between 300,000 and 380,000 bullets.

- In golf, mastery is measured in quality ball strikes; the most proficient golfers have had between 1.5 and 2 million quality ball strikes. These golfers have spent between 20,000 and 30,000 hours participating in anywhere from 300 to 600 events or more.

- Becoming an international standard archer usually takes at least seven years, but what is most important is the number of quality arrows shot, from a low of 150,000 to a high of more than 600,000.

- Bobsled, skeleton, and luge do not focus on the hours of training, but rather, on the number of runs down a track. Bobsled and skeleton pilots typically have to take 1,000 runs on a variety of tracks before they can be considered masters of the sport. For luge, mastery requires approximately 2,000 runs.

- In sport parachute, athletes must have upwards of 1,000 jumps to step on an international podium. Imagine the flight time required for each jump! This sport's hours spent training are radically changing with the use of vertical wind tunnels; athletes can complete the required numbers of jumps without spending as much time jumping from a plane.

Additional evidence suggests that the time required to develop excellence in a particular sport can vary according to the discipline or activity, as well as the quality of the training and coaching. For example, the U.S. Olympic Committee found that U.S. athletes who competed between 1984 and 1998 trained an average of 12 to 13 years before they were selected to the Olympic team, and medal winners took an average of two to three more years to step onto the podium. Similarly, top coaches in a range of sports around the world have observed that it takes 8 to 12 years, or two or three Olympic quadrennials, to develop an international-caliber athlete.

Clearly, we need to qualify our assumptions about precisely how much time is required to achieve excellence. It is likely sufficient to observe that expertise and excellence require many thousands of hours to develop, and generally in the range of a decade or longer.

The other major qualifier is how training time is used and the quality of coaching throughout. Furthermore, additional research suggests that the hours and years spent in practice need not be devoted entirely to structured and formalized training in the targeted sport: unstructured practice and free play are also beneficial to developing expertise, as are hours spent in other sports.

LTAD encourages the continuation of unstructured play and participation in other sports during the early stages of LTAD. As well, LTAD promotes a training and coaching philosophy that addresses each individual's physical, mental, cognitive, and emotional domains to develop all capacities as athletes put in the required years of training and apprenticeship. Sport organizations and governments play a role in ensuring that athletes receive the support they need to achieve these hours of practice over the span of many years.

Importance of Multisport Participation and Free Play

LTAD maintains that early sport training and competition should not focus entirely on one sport. The anecdotal histories of athletes such as Michael Phelps and Steve Nash strongly suggest that optimum performance in one sport is enhanced by trying a variety of sports during the early years. Participating in a number of sports appears to help elite athletes develop complementary skills that serve their chosen specialization in the long term, while further enhancing capacities that are universal to all sports (e.g., aerobic power and endurance, muscle development, decision making, mental skills, agility, balance, and coordination).

Work by Coté, Baker, and Abernethy (2003) and others has suggested that a certain amount of unstructured practice and experience in the form of deliberate play is beneficial to developing expertise. LTAD expresses this same notion by encouraging unstructured play throughout the early LTAD stages, even as structured training and competition are gradually introduced and begin to assume more prominence in the total hours of participation.

Free play is self-regulated play managed by children themselves with little or no adult intervention (e.g., sandlot baseball, street hockey). Rules are frequently negotiated and adapted by the participants, which results in more creativity, experimentation, decision making, and exploration of skills and techniques than is generally allowed in more formal practice or training sessions led by coaches and other adults.

Hours spent in free play certainly count toward the thousands of training hours athletes need. Even during the early stages of LTAD, hours spent in free play can count toward their total training hours because free play contributes to the development of physical literacy.

Importance of the Physical, Cognitive, and Emotional Domains to Excellence

Athletes need considerable dedication and motivation to complete 8 to 12 years of a constructive training and competition regime. Their parents and coaches also need dedication and patience. LTAD maintains that throughout their long-term training, athletes will develop to their maximum potential if their training experience addresses the physical, mental, cognitive, and emotional domains of their individual learning processes. Although most sport training naturally addresses the psychomotor domain by developing the specific motor skills needed, we cannot assume that the training will automatically address the affective domain (the way people react emotionally and their ability to feel others' pain or joy) and cognitive domain (knowledge, comprehension, and critical thinking).

To complete 8 to 12 years of training, athletes need a training methodology and philosophy that keeps them happily engaged, meaningfully challenged, and appropriately instructed at every stage of their physical, emotional, and mental development. Coaches and program designers need to reflect on the cognitive and emotional domains as much as the physical domain. Does the training program and system of competition develop positive feelings about the sport? Does the training regimen give athletes everything they need to excel, such as information about nutrition, injury prevention, and recovery techniques?

There is more to athlete training than simply practicing physical motor skills, yet it is remarkable how frequently the other learning domains are neglected. The seven-stage LTAD approach to training and competition is designed to achieve this goal, thereby preventing athlete dropout as a result of injury, burnout, or simply lost interest.

Perils of Premature Selection

Given the length of time required for an elite athlete to emerge, coaches and sport organizations need to be wary of streaming athletes too early. Identifying athletic talents at too young an age runs the risk of overlooking other athletes who may have greater genetic potential for excellence, but whose talent will only blossom if nurtured with time and training.

Prior to late adolescence, children who are the oldest in their age cohorts can be markedly more advanced in physical development and motor coordination than their peers, generating the illusion that they are the "natural born" athletes with the greatest athletic potential. Often, these children are streamed early into select teams and training programs, where they receive specialized coaching, more training hours, more competition experience, and better facilities and equipment than their peers. What happens should be no surprise: they develop into skilled athletes more quickly, which seems to confirm the notion they are the better athletic specimens than their peers.

This chronological age factor has startling consequences, given that some players may be better genetically endowed than others but not the oldest in their age cohorts. For example, if you have a baseball program for 8-year-olds who are born in a particular calendar year with a registration cutoff date of December 31, the children who are born in the first three months of the year will usually display superior motor coordination and strength to those who are born in the last three months of the same calendar year. These early-born children may be selected for special training and tournament teams, further exaggerating the differences in abilities. The reason for their superiority is, more than anything, extra training hours.

Meanwhile, a child who was born in November of the same year may, in fact, have superior genetic potential to the early-identified "natural born" talent (e.g., greater height for basketball in the long term). Given time, patience, and equal training opportunities, the November child may eventually realize far greater physical and mental attributes for elite performance in the sport. However, because this late-born child is ignored early in the program, she does not receive the training hours needed to develop that potential, and might therefore drop out of the sport altogether. This is clearly a loss for everyone concerned—the child, the coach, the parents, and the sporting association.

Keys to Achieving the Necessary Training Hours

If we know that thousands of hours of quality training and competition are needed to achieve athletic excellence, how can we best support our athletes in amassing those hours? We know that early streaming and premature talent identification must be avoided. The task, then, is to keep as many athletes as possible engaged in

training and competition for the years needed to accumulate thousands of hours, and provide them with the necessary supports so they can pursue training and competition unhindered by obstacles.

In the early stages of LTAD, young athletes are engaged primarily through an emphasis on fun. During the Active Start and FUNdamentals stages, children have cognitive and emotional needs appropriate to their stages of maturation. If sport programs take away the element of fun that children naturally seek in play at those ages, they lower their level of engagement and subsequently the gains achieved in activity and "training." Even at the Learn to Train stage, fun must have a place in the training program, although its emphasis may be slightly reduced from that of the two earlier stages.

At the stages following Learn to Train, other training factors take far greater prominence. The children have become youth and young adults who have chosen to pursue a route to excellence, and they increasingly understand that the motivation required for elite training and competition needs to be more than simple fun and amusement. In the 2003 report "Reflections on Success" (Gibbons, McConnell, Forster, Tuffey, & Peterson, 2003), the U.S. Olympic Committee (USOC) presented 10 key factors that U.S. Olympic athletes reported as being the most important in supporting their success. In order of ranking, the factors were as follows:

1. Dedication and persistence
2. Support of family and friends
3. Quality of coaches
4. Love of sport
5. Quality of training programs and facilities
6. Natural talent
7. Competitiveness
8. Focus
9. Work ethic
10. Financial support

From these survey responses, it is clear that even athletes consider natural talent a relatively minor factor in their achievement. In keeping with the concept that excellence takes time, dedication and persistence comes out on top, and several of the other top 10 factors can be seen as directly supporting this factor. Focus, work ethic, financial support, quality coaches, and support of family and friends are all factors that further the athlete's primary dedication to and persistence in training and competition.

The USOC report also listed the top 10 obstacles to success as reported by Olympic athletes. These also have a direct bearing on the efficacy of training.

1. Lack of financial support
2. Conflict with roles in life
3. Lack of coaching expertise or support
4. Lack of support from USOC and NGB (national governing body)
5. Mental obstacles
6. Lack of training and competition opportunities
7. Medical problems
8. Lack of social support
9. Physical limitations
10. Failure

Of these 10 obstacles, only the ninth-ranked, physical limitations (and perhaps medical problems), bears any real suggestion of relating to genetic potential. Most of the obstacles relate directly to the athlete's ability to train unhindered by lack—in finances, coaching, facilities, and social supports. The consistent message is that training hours are the most important factor in success.

Support for Training Hours

The road to becoming an elite athlete is long, and as the USOC report "Reflections on Success" indicated, athletes face plenty of challenges in accumulating thousands of training hours. The physical, mental, and emotional demands on the athlete are tremendous, and the costs in time, resources, and finances can be overwhelming. A sport system can help aspiring athletes succeed by addressing the external factors and support structures required for effective and continued long-term training: financial support, facilities, equipment, expert coaching, scientific training, and appropriate competition.

The rise of American and Canadian long track speedskaters in international competition since the late 1990s is perfect testimony to how facilities can help athletes achieve thousands of training hours. Prior to the late 1990s, the United States was not a major competitor in international speedskating, and Canada was virtually nonexistent on the scene. The top medal counts were generally from countries such as Norway, the Netherlands, Germany, and the Soviet Union (Russia). In 1987, in preparation for the 1988 Winter Olympics in Calgary, an indoor long track oval was completed in the city, one of the first in the world. Canadian speedskaters failed to win any medals at the 1988 Games, but they now had a first-class facility as a base for national team training. Eleven years after the opening of the Calgary Olympic Oval, Canadian long track speedskaters took five medals at Nagano 1998—one gold, two silver, and two bronze. They followed this performance with three medals at Salt Lake City 2002, eight medals at Turin 2006, and another five medals at Vancouver 2010.

There could hardly be a better example of the role played by facilities in supporting long-term excellence and the rule that excellence takes time. Suddenly, Canada was a world power in speedskating alongside Germany and the Netherlands while Norway and Russia faded.

As Canadian speedskaters rose in the medal standings, so did the Americans. The American team began training at the Calgary oval not long after the Canadians, and the indoor Utah Olympic Oval became available to them just prior to Salt Lake City 2002. They went from averaging three medals in each Olympics from 1988 to 1998 to suddenly taking home eight medals at Salt Lake City 2002, seven at Turin 2006, and four at Vancouver 2010.

Of course, there was nothing sudden about the success of the American and Canadian skaters. They had access to world-class facilities for quality training, so they were able to train for the thousands of hours and years required to become world-class athletes in their sport. Those facilities also attracted high-level competitions that allowed North American Train to Win athletes to compete at home, and also offered international race exposure to local Train to Compete athletes. The lesson for sport organizations, clubs, recreation departments, health departments, and governments is this: To produce top athletes, they must be prepared to either provide or assist in providing the ancillary supports athletes need to train effectively over the long term.

Excellence Takes Time To-Do List

To support athletes in achieving thousands of training hours, the following activities are recommended for coaches, parents, and sport administrators:

- Practice patience. Reduce the emphasis on winning, which generally focuses on the short term and ignores long-term aspects of training and development. Remember that greatness takes time.
- Encourage children to engage in unstructured physical play with their friends every day, regardless of the weather. Free play at school also contributes to thousands of hours of athlete training.
- Enroll children in minor sport programs each season, and have them try a variety of sports, positions, and events. Be sensitive to their preferences, but avoid premature specialization in one sport.
- Encourage children to play a variety of sports at school for additional hours of "deliberate practice," including in physical education classes, in intramural leagues, and on school teams.
- Keep sport and physical activity fun, especially during the preteen years.

Summary

To achieve expertise in an activity, people require thousands of hours of practice over the span of approximately a decade. The precise amount of time required varies depending on the activity and factors such as the quality of coaching, but natural ability plays much less of a role than once thought. In terms of specific sport expertise, these thousands of hours do not have to be solely dedicated to structured training in that sport; unstructured practice and free play in other activities are also beneficial to developing expertise.

Multisport involvement at a young age helps children become physically literate. Physical literacy, in turn, plays a huge part in reaching the highest levels in sport. By developing a variety of skills over a range of sports and activities, athletes are often better equipped to excel in a single sport later on.

The concept that excellence takes time is a key factor of the LTAD philosophy. LTAD maintains that thousands of hours of training over a decade or longer, can help athletes reach their maximum potential if their physical, mental, cognitive, and emotional capacities are appropriately addressed. Young athletes, particularly those born later in the year, need equal training opportunities and support to remain in sport until they have fully developed. Premature selection deprives some youth of the chance to pursue the thousands of hours they need to achieve excellence.

Taking the time to succeed requires more than just dedication on the part of the athlete, although that is a key component. To amass thousands of hours of training in a given activity, athletes need support—friends and family, good coaches, appropriate equipment and facilities, and financial support. For each athlete who reaches the podium at the Olympics, countless people and organizations have played a role behind the scenes. Nobody can become an expert without enough practice, and nobody can get that practice without support.

Questions for Reflection

- Am I prepared to practice patience to support the long-term development of young athletes? As a coach? As a parent?
- Am I prepared to place less emphasis on short-term winning, and more on long-term training targets?
- Do my athletes associate positive emotions with training and competing? Or

are these activities colored by negative feelings?

- How does premature selection ignore the concept that excellence takes time?
- What factors help athletes reach the thousands of training hours they require?
- Do my athletes have access to ancillary supports to sustain their training, such as finances, good nutrition, and transportation?
- Are my athletes facing obstacles to training, such as social conflicts, medical problems, financial hardships, mental problems, and limited opportunities for training and competition?
- Why is support so important for this process to take place?

References

Black Book Partners. (2008). *Michael Phelps biography.* Retrieved from www.jockbio.com/Bios/Phelps/Phelps_bio.html

Bloom, B. (1985). *Developing talent in young people.* New York: Ballantine Books.

Cote, J., Baker, J., & Abernethy, B. (2003) From play to practice: A developmental framework for acquisition of expertise in team sports. In K.A. Ericsson & J.L. Starkes (Eds.), *Expert performance in sport: Advances in research on sport expertise* (pp. 89-113). Champaign, IL: Human Kinetics.

Ericsson, K.A., Krampe, R.T., & Tesch-Romer, C. (1993). The role of deliberate practice in the acquisition of expert performance. *Psychological Review 100:* 363-406.

Ericsson, K.A., Charness, N., Feltovich, P.J., & Hoffman, R.R. (Eds.). (2006). *The Cambridge handbook of expertise and expert performance.* New York: Cambridge University Press.

Gibbons, T., McConnell, A., Forster, T., Tuffey, S., & Peterson, K. (2003, June). *Reflections on success: U.S. Olympians describe the success factors and obstacles that most influenced their Olympic development. Phase II: Results of the Talent Identification and Development Questionnaire to U.S. Olympians.* Colorado Springs, CO: USOC.

Gladwell, M. (2008). *Outliers.* New York: Little, Brown.

Sport Reference. (2011). *NBA & ABA most valuable player award winners.* Retrieved from www.basketball-reference.com/awards/mvp.html

U.S. Olympic Committee. (2002). *The pathway to excellence.* Retrieved from www.teamusa.org/About-the-USOC/In-the-Community/Partner-Programs/Community-Olympic-Development-Program.aspx

To Learn More

Archambault, R., Ball, A., Boruta, R., Coyne, G., & Lefebvre, D. (2006). *Biathlon Canada LTAD model: Planning for the sporting excellence and well-being of Canadians.* Ottawa, ON: Biathlon Canada.

Baker, J., Horton, S., Robertson-Wilson, J., & Wall, M. (2003). Nurturing sport expertise: Factors influencing the development of elite athletes. *Journal of Sports Science and Medicine, (2),* 1-9.

Barker, P., Bernard, G., Norris, S., Roxburg, D., Sinclair, D., Thompson, J., & Wells, G. (n.d.). *Long-term player development guide for golf in Canada.* Oakville, ON: Royal Canadian Golf Association.

Coyle, D. (2009). *The talent code.* New York: Bantam Book

Coyle, D. (2012). *The little book of talent.* New York: Bantam Books.

Ericsson, K.A., Prietula, M.J., & Cokely, E.T. (2007). The making of an expert. *Harvard Business Review, (85)* 7/8, 114-121.

Farrow, D., Baker, J, & MacMahon, C. (2008) Developing sport expertise: Researchers and coaches put theory into practice. New York: Routledge.

Gibbons, T., Hill, R., McConnell, A., Forster, T., & Moore, J. (2002). *The path to excellence: A comprehensive view of development of U.S. Olympians who competed from 1984-1998. Results of the Talent Identification and Development Questionnaire to U.S. Olympians.* Colorado Springs, CO: USOC.

Salmela, J., & Moraes, L.C. (2003) Development of expertise: The role of coaching, families, and cultural contexts. In KA. Ericsson, & J.L. Starkes (Eds.), *Expert performance in sport: Advances in research on sport expertise* (pp. 275-293). Champaign, IL: Human Kinetics.

Starkes, J.A., & Ericsson, K.A.. (2003). *Expert performance in sport: Recent advances in research on sport expertise.* Champaign, IL: Human Kinetics.

Syed, M. (2010). *Bounce.* New York: Harper-Collins.

Periodization

Lauren and Tom have coached basketball at the same high school for years. For the past few seasons, Lauren's girls' teams have consistently outperformed Tom's boys' teams in their respective league playoffs. Her teams generally seem to perform the same as Tom's teams early in the season, but they always come on strong toward the middle of the schedule. By the playoffs, they're dominating. Tom's teams simply seem to fizzle out. He has noticed this pattern, but he doesn't understand what is happening.

Lauren explains that she follows a periodization plan, a basic training road map for the season, based on when she wants her players to peak in their physical conditioning and when she wants to have them taper their training loads. She also maps different types of skills and tactical training, while building aerobic capacity and anaerobic endurance.

Lauren also uses a monitoring plan to keep track of each player's growth so she can identify early, average, and late maturers. Using a training diary, she makes adjustments to her periodization plan if circumstances prevented her from implementing content from the daily or weekly plan. At the end of the season, she uses the diary to analyze what went wrong and what went well. It gives her feedback on her training, competition, and recovery program. She can then "feed forward" the relevant information into next year's plan (i.e., what to prioritize and what to eliminate), thus optimizing the development of her players.

Simply put, periodization is time management. It is planning for training, performance, and recovery. It organizes the aspects of volume, intensity, and frequency of training through long-term (multiyear) and short-term (annual) training, competition, and recovery programs, so that athletes achieve their peak performances when they need to. As a planning technique, periodization provides the framework for arranging the complex array of training processes (skill development, strength training, and regeneration) into a logical schedule to bring about optimal improvements in performance. Periodization sequences training components into weeks, days, and sessions. The process is situation specific based on priorities and the time available to bring about the required training and competition improvements.

Periodization is also the process of integrating and sequencing sport science and sports medicine with sport-specific technical and tactical activities. In the context of LTAD, periodization links the stage an athlete is currently in to the sport requirements of that stage.

Periodization is practically nonexistent for prepubertal, pubertal, and early postpubertal athletes; most often, scaled-down and watered-down adult programs are superimposed on young, developing athletes. Thus, this chapter describes what periodization is and how it is used to design developmentally appropriate training, competition, and recovery programs for prepubertal and pubertal athletes. The elements of periodization are briefly described and analyzed. Examples of periodized annual plans are presented, and finally, a step-by-step approach for creating an annual plan for prepubertal and pubertal athletes is provided. This chapter also connects the age and trainability chapters (chapters 5 and 6, respectively); this is the "operationalization" of those chapters.

This chapter includes a brief discussion of the structure and flow of periodization as well as a brief explanation of how to periodize, including how to create and quantify annual programs. In addition, appendix B offers a step-by-step procedure for creating an annual training, competition, and recovery program. Consult the To Learn More section at the end of this chapter for more in-depth information on periodization.

Periodization Definitions

This chapter uses many phrases you may not be familiar with. Here is a quick breakdown of those terms.

annual plan–A yearly training program consisting of several phases of training. The objective of the annual, or yearly, training and competition plan is to provide optimum performance(s) at the required time(s) or time series within the year.

frequency of training–The number of training sessions within a given time frame (e.g., a day or a microcycle).

integration–Including and sequencing all factors of training and performance (stamina, strength, speed, skill [technical and tactical], and suppleness–the five Ss of training and performance) to optimize adaptation to training. Integration in a broader sense refers to the integration of sport-specific technical and tactical training programs with sport science and sports medicine support programs.

intensity of training–The qualitative component of training that includes all training activities performed in a given unit of time.

interference–The inhibition of one training component by another, or the negative impact of one training component on another, when the two (or more) are performed simultaneously.

long-term plan–A multiyear plan, usually 8 to 12 years in duration.

maintenance–Retaining already established fitness levels, sport skills, and mental skills through training, versus developing levels further or losing them as a result of undertraining.

mesocycle–A short training period of two, three, four, or five weeks, or microcycles, of progressive overload training, followed by one or two unloading, or restorative, microcycles (or both).

microcycle–A period of three, four, five, or six days of training, using a variety of training sessions followed by a recovery or resting day. The most common microcycle is a 6:1 breakdown: six days of training followed by a rest day.

overstress–A condition resulting from increased training load combined with everyday stress.

overtraining–A condition resulting from inadequate recovery or an increase in training volume or intensity (or both).

periodization–The structuring, or cycling, of short- or long-term training programs (or both) to provide optimum performance(s) when required. *Periodization* is a synonym for planning for athletic training and performance.

periods of an annual plan–There are three periods within an annual plan: preparation, competition, and transition.

phases of an annual plan–In principle there are five phases of training in an annual plan:

- **general preparatory phase (GPP)**–A training phase characterized by high volume and low intensity of training, emphasizing general individual or team-specific fitness and technical or tactical training.
- **specific preparatory phase (SPP)**–A training phase characterized by lower volume and higher intensity of training, emphasizing individual or team-specific sport and event-specific training.

> *continued*

> continued

- **precompetitive phase (PCP)**—A training phase characterized by high intensity and low volume of individual or team-specific training, emphasizing performance-specific training and modeling taper and peak procedures.
- **competitive phase (CP)**—A training phase characterized by competition-specific training, tapering, and peaking for major competitions, tournaments, or league schedules, as well as by the maintenance of established fitness and performance levels.
- **transition phase (TP)**—This training phase is characterized by rest and regeneration, in the form of a short passive and active rest.

quadrennial plan—A four-year plan (or Olympic cycle) to optimize long-term training and performance. During each of the four years, a different component of training and performance is emphasized. The objective is to have relatively good performances in each year, but the ultimate goal is to obtain optimum performance at the end of the fourth, or Olympic, year.

single, double, triple, and multiple periodization—One, two, three, or several distinct competitive phases within an annual cycle.

specificity of training—The content, or "direction," of training performed during a session or a given period of time; the percentage of training content performed with reference to sport-specific training versus overall, or general, training.

taper—A period of reduced training prior to a competitive performance. Peak performance occurs when fitness and fatigue differences are maximized.

training load—The qualitative and quantitative components of training (i.e., volume, intensity, duration, frequency, and specificity).

training session—A unit of training with three components: a warm-up, the actual workout, and a cool-down.

volume of training—The quantitative component of training containing the duration or extent of training.

Periodization and LTAD

Periodization, far from being a single, fixed process or methodology, is in fact a highly flexible tool. When used appropriately in conjunction with sound methodology and ongoing monitoring and evaluation, it is an essential component in optimal sport programming and athlete development at all levels. LTAD addresses this issue by developing periodization models for all stages. It considers the growth, maturation, and trainability principles unique to both the primary development stages (the first two decades of life) and the LTAD stages of athletic performance.

LTAD is typically a 10- to 12-year procedure that optimizes physical, technical, tactical (including decision making), and mental preparation, as well as supporting ancillary capacities. LTAD uses both quadrennial planning (the four-year Olympic and Paralympic cycle of elite athletes) and the annual plan, which is based on identified periods of athletic preparation, competition, and the transition into the next calendar plan.

Periodization models described in the current sport performance literature are designed for the subelite and elite senior, or mature, performers. There is very little information on periodization for children or adolescents, or for athletes with disabilities (see chapter 2). For a mature athlete, it is relatively easy to design short- and long-term training, competition, and recovery programs. By profiling the athlete's strengths and weaknesses, a short-term (one-year) and a long-term (multiyear) program can be plotted to eliminate shortcomings and further develop strengths.

For prepubertal and pubertal athletes, long-term planning is much more complex. The previously described biological markers (onset of peak height velocity [PHV], PHV, and menarche; see chapter 5) will dictate program planning as coaches react to the magnitude and tempo of athletes' growth. This process is called reactive periodization—reacting to the tempo of the growth spurt and adjusting training, competition, and recovery programs accordingly. Of course, this requires the careful monitoring of growth before and during puberty.

Components of Periodization

Periodization is the subdivision of the seasonal program into smaller periods of training cycles (Matveyev, 1983). There are four types of periodization plans: short-term, long-term, annual, and quadrennial. Within each type of plan, there are smaller subsets of time: periods, phases, mesocycles, and microcycles.

Let's look at the components of periodization by examining an annual periodization plan. An annual plan is a training, competition, and recovery sequence that takes place within the 52 weeks of a year. An annual plan strives to prepare athletes so that they peak during key competitions. Within an annual cycle, there are both periods and phases (see the sidebar of terms earlier in this chapter).

Within one annual cycle, there are three periods: preparation, competition, and transition.

- The preparation period is characterized by general and sport-specific training.
- The competition period is the competitive season of the annual plan.

- The transition period consists of rest and recovery and transitioning into the next annual season.

In the preparation period, there are three phases: the general preparatory phase, specific preparatory phase, and precompetitive phase.

- The general preparatory phase (GPP) is a training phase characterized by high volume and low intensity of training, emphasizing general individual or team-specific fitness and technical or tactical training.
- The specific preparatory phase (SPP) is a training phase characterized by lower volume and higher intensity of training, emphasizing individual or team-specific sport and event-specific training.
- The precompetitive phase (PCP) is a training phase characterized by high intensity and low volume of individual or team-specific training, emphasizing performance-specific training and modeling taper and peak procedures.

The three phases of the preparation period, combined with the competition and transition phases, make up five phases within one annual cycle.

- The competitive phase (CP) is characterized by competition-specific training, tapering, and peaking for major competitions, tournaments, or league schedules, as well as by the maintenance of established fitness and performance levels.
- The transition phase (TP) is a training phase characterized by rest and regeneration, in the form of a short passive and active rest.

Within each phase are mesocycles. Within each mesocycle are microcycles. There are also daily cycles (units of training) within microcycles. (Mesocycles, microcycles, and training sessions are discussed later in this section.)

Let's break this down:

Units make up training sessions → training sessions make up microcycles → microcycles make up mesocycles → mesocycles make up phases → phases make up periods → periods make up an annual plan

Figure 9.1 illustrates annual periodization plans (along with the periods and phases) for summer and winter sports. The three periods—preparation, competition, and transition—are listed at the top of the figure. Notice how, for summer sports, an athlete needs to start the preparation period in October! This allows the athlete to peak during the summer competition months of April through August. During the preparation period, the athlete is setting goals, working on strength and endurance training, developing sport-specific fitness, and learning strategies and tactics; this

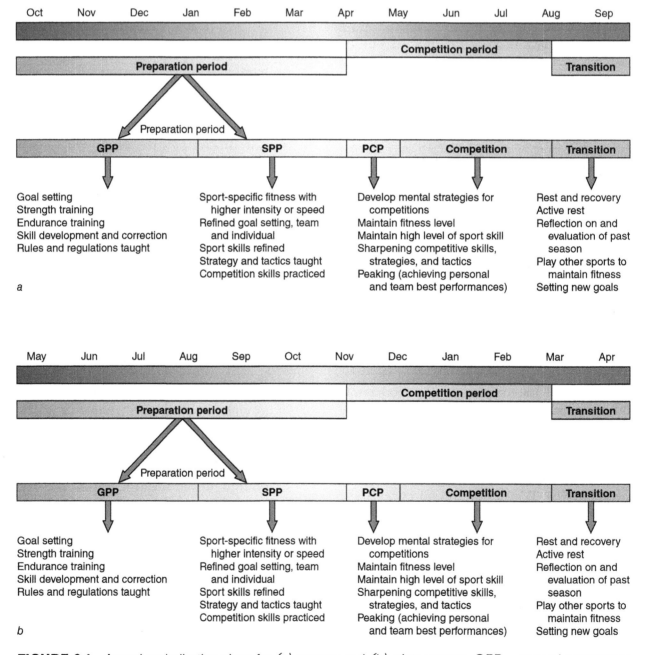

FIGURE 9.1 Annual periodization plans for *(a)* summer and *(b)* winter sports. GPP = general preparatory phase, SPP = specific preparatory phase, PCP = precompetitive phase.

section of the preparation period encompasses the general preparatory phase and the specific preparatory phase.

During the competition period, the athlete is maintaining and sharpening fitness, sport skills, and strategies and tactics.

Finally, during the transition period, the athlete is resting and recovering, reflecting on and evaluating the past season, and setting new goals. The transition period then leads into a new annual periodization plan that prepares the athlete for the next competition season.

An annual periodization plan can be single, double, or triple. A single periodization plan has one competitive phase, as shown in figure 9.2. A double periodization plan has two distinctly separate competitive seasons in the year and includes general, specific, and precompetitive preparation before the first competition cycle and specific and precompetitive preparation between the two competition cycles. (General preparation is not required after the first competition cycle, because it has been accomplished at the beginning of the annual plan.) A triple periodization plan has three distinctly separate competitive periods.

Single periodization is for the beginner athlete, double periodization is for the intermediate athlete, and triple periodization is for the elite athlete. Double periodization consists of more sport-specific training than single periodization does, and obviously, triple periodization consists of more sport-specific training than either single or double periodization does. The more sport-specific training that is done, the better the improvement of athletes' physical, technical, and tactical capacities. However, developing those capacities to be able to undertake higher-quality training and competition takes time. Usually, three or four annual cycles are required to develop the capacity to start double periodization, and two to four years are required to start multiple periodization. The required number of years in single and double periodization is determined by the individual needs of the athletes, and many athletes will never develop the capacity to undertake triple periodization.

Table 9.1 illustrates the phases of an annual plan for single, double, and triple periodization.

Mesocycles

Mesocycles, small blocks of time lasting between two and five weeks, are shorter units,

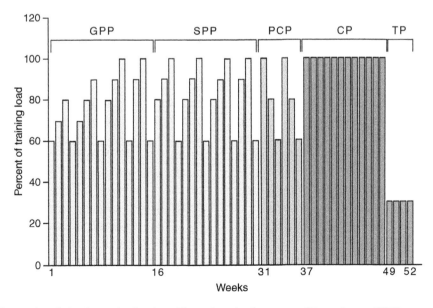

FIGURE 9.2 Example of single periodization. Note the single competition phase. GPP = general preparatory phase; SPP = specific preparatory phase; PCP = precompetitive phase; CP = competitive phase; TP = transition phase.

TABLE 9.1 Phases of an Annual Plan

Five phases of a single periodized annual plan	Eight phases of a double periodized annual plan	Eleven phases of a triple periodized annual plan
General preparatory phase	General preparatory phase	General preparatory phase
Specific preparatory phase	Specific preparatory phase 1	Specific preparatory phase 1
Precompetitive phase	Precompetitive phase 1	Precompetitive phase 1
Competitive phase	Competitive phase 1	Competitive phase 1
Transition phase	Specific preparatory phase 2	Specific preparatory phase 2
	Precompetitive phase 2	Precompetitive phase 2
	Competitive phase 2	Competitive phase 2
	Transition phase	Specific preparatory phase 3
		Precompetitive phase 3
		Competitive phase 3
		Transition period

or cycles, of the phases of training. The phases of training are broken down into smaller units for easier management. Each week of the mesocycle is one microcycle. The first one to four weeks of a mesocycle are called loading weeks, because athletes are progressively increasing the training loads as they apply the physiological principles of progressive overloading. A mesocycle always ends with a recovery microcycle and is characterized by a decreased training load (figure 9.3). The last week of a mesocycle is called the recovery week. The recovery microcycle at the end of the mesocycle is not a rest cycle, but a period of reduced training load to enhance recovery and adaptations. The introduction of a recovery week marks the end of one mesocycle and the start of a new one. Table 9.2 describes the mesocycle types that have been identified in the scientific periodization literature.

The content of the mesocycle is determined by its location—that is, how far or close it is from competition. Figure 9.3 illustrates 4:1, 3:1, 2:1, and 1:1 mesocycles; the longer the mesocycles is, the higher the volume is and the lower the intensity is. Consequently, the shorter the mesocycle is, the lower the volume is and the higher the intensity is. Thus, more frequent recovery is necessary for enhancing adaptation and diminishing fatigue.

Microcycles

The smallest training block is a microcycle; it is usually seven days long—six days of training followed by one day of rest (6:1). A microcycle can have a 5:1, 3:1, or 2:1 training-to-rest ratio. The ratio of a microcycle is determined by its location in relation to competition day. Table 9.3 describes the microcycle types that have been identified in the scientific periodization literature.

The content of a microcycle is determined by the specific need(s) of an individual athlete or team and the location of the cycle in relation to competition. If competition occurs later in the annual cycle (GPP and early SPP phases), introductory, developmental, and shock microcycles facilitate fitness, technical, and tactical improvements. Closer to competition (late SPP and PCP phases), stabilizing, taper, and restorative cycles help the athlete or team prepare for competition. During the competitive phase, competitive microcycles ensure the maintenance of already-established physical capacities and technical and tactical development, always with an optimal recovery program. Restorative microcycles can also be used during the transition phase with transitional, or rest, cycles.

The taper and peak microcycles are designed to eliminate the fatigue produced by training

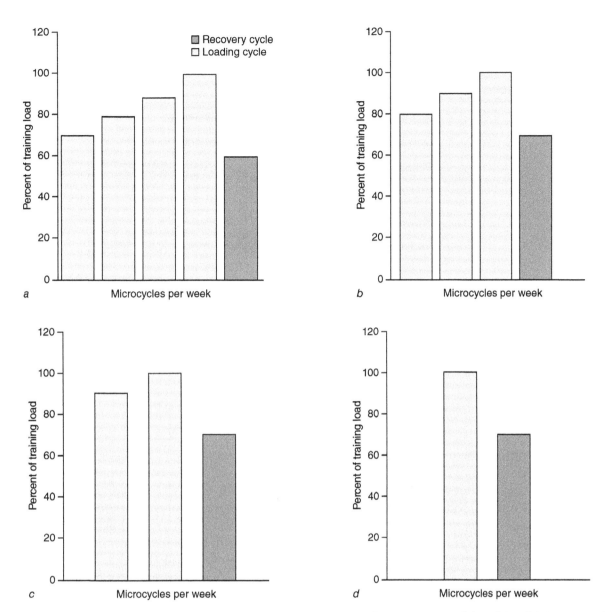

FIGURE 9.3 Traditional mesocycles showing various ratios of loading to recovery: *(a)* traditional 4:1 mesocycle; *(b)* traditional 3:1 mesocycle; *(c)* traditional 2:1 mesocycle; and *(d)* traditional 1:1 mesocycle.

TABLE 9.2 Mesocycle Types

Types of mesocycles	Description
Introductory	Introduce new skill, fitness, or tactical elements
Developmental	Develop new skill, fitness, or tactical elements
Stabilizing	Stabilize skill or fitness elements
Competitive	Mesocycles of the competitive phase determined by the competition calendar
Taper and peak	Reduced volume but high intensity and frequency of training and peaking for competition(s)
Competitive maintenance	Maintaining established skill and fitness levels between competitions
Restorative	Enhanced recovery after a series of competitions
Transition	Passive and active rest

TABLE 9.3 Microcycle Types

Types of microcycles	Description
Introductory	Introduce new skill, fitness, or tactical elements
Developmental	Develop new skill, fitness, or tactical elements
Shock	Pushing the athlete to the limit but avoiding overtraining
Stabilizing	Stabilizing skill or fitness elements
Competitive	Microcycles of the competitive phase
Taper	Reduced volume but high intensity and frequency of training
Peak	Peaking for competition
Modeling	Mimicking certain aspects or conditions of the upcoming event
Competitive maintenance	Maintaining established skill and fitness levels
Restorative	Enhancing recovery after a series of competitions
Transition	Passive and active rest

prior to competition. The volume of training is significantly cut down, whereas the intensity and frequency of training remain high. Tapering is the least-understood process in athletic preparation. Tapering is not detraining. Many coaches do a poor job on taper planning and implementation, and the biggest mistake of many coaches is not significantly decreasing the volume of training before competition. It is well documented in the scientific literature on tapering that a high intensity and high frequency of training with reduced volume will maintain established physical and technical capacities (Mujika, 2009). In a well-trained athlete, these capacities cannot be improved during the few weeks before competition because of the delayed nature of the training effect. Of course, tactics and decision-making skills can be improved during the last days before the competition, but endurance, strength, speed, and skill cannot!

Let's look at some examples of microcycles. (For further information on microcycle planning and sequencing, see Balyi and Hamilton, 1998 and 1999.) Figure 9.4 is an example of an introductory microcycle inducing metabolic or aerobic adaptations. Note the differences in volume and intensity between figure 9.4 and figure 9.5. In figure 9.4 the volume of training is high (100, 80, 100, 60, 90 and 100), whereas the intensity is steady at 70 percent (this means that an athlete with a maximal heart rate of 200 beats per minute will do continuous, uninterrupted training at 140 bpm).

Figure 9.5 is an example of an introductory or developmental microcycle inducing skill or speed adaptations. Again, note the differences in volume and intensity between figures 9.4 and 9.5. In figure 9.5 the volume of training is low, because skill and speed cannot be developed in a tired state. The volume of training is 30, 40, 30, 40, 30 and 20 percent; whereas the intensity of training is 100, 90, 100, 80, 100, and 100 percent.

Figure 9.6 is an example of a mixed skill, technique, and metabolic adaptation microcycle. Here, skill (or speed) is emphasized during the first three days of the cycle. A high intensity and low volume of training characterizes these first three days. Because of cumulative fatigue from the first three days, a lower quality of metabolic (endurance) training takes over to produce the optimal training effect during days 4, 5 and 6. Days 4, 5, and 6 are characterized by lower-intensity and

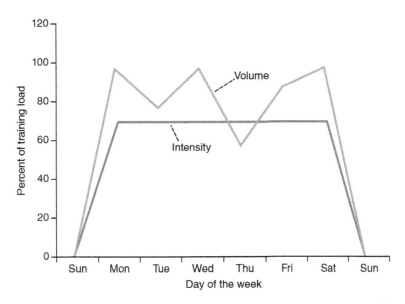

FIGURE 9.4 Introductory, developmental, or stabilizing microcycle showing an endurance emphasis.

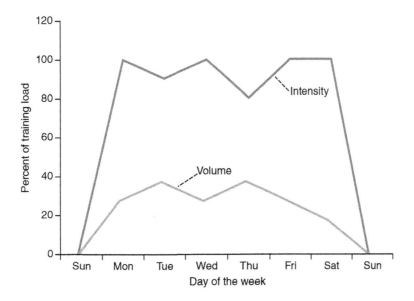

FIGURE 9.5 Introductory or developmental microcycle showing a skill or speed emphasis.

higher-volume training. The volume of training is 40, 35, 30, 90, 100, and 100 percent, and the intensity of training is 100, 90, 100, 70, 70, and 70 percent.

Training Sessions and Units

The number of training sessions within a microcycle is determined by the needs of the athlete or team. The more advanced an athlete is, the higher the number of required training sessions will be. For beginners, two or three training sessions per microcycle is ideal, in addition to participation in other sports.

The most common microcycle has a 6:1 ratio—six sessions per week with one rest day. This ratio is practical and convenient, because it follows a weekly schedule. Athletes

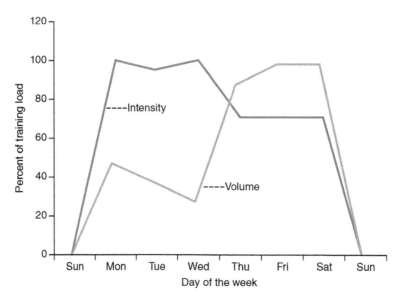

FIGURE 9.6 Introductory or developmental microcycle showing a mixed skill emphasis.

train during the week and compete on the weekend. As they progress in their selected sports, the progression evolves to nine sessions and, eventually, 12 sessions per week. Elite athletes in many sports train 12 to 15 times per microcycle.

A training session consists of the warm-up, the main part of the session, the complementary or secondary activity, followed by the cool-down procedure, regeneration, and rest. A training session also consists of units of training: skill training, speed training, power training, strength training, and endurance training. Some of these components cannot be executed in a single session because they interfere with each other.

The sidebar Structure of a Tennis Training Session shows an actual training session. The term *rotation* refers to the movement of the group of athletes to different tasks. Units are the activities within the various rotations (i.e., fitness, agility, balance, speed, or power, etc.).

10-Step Approach to Creating an Annual Plan

Following are the 10 steps used to create an annual plan. Planning an annual cycle is done backward, starting from the first competition.

Step 1: Identifying the first competition of the annual cycle. In individual sports, coaches or athletes can select the competition(s) best suited for the athletes. Team sports are dictated by competition schedules. Exhibition games and friendly matches offer more choices.

Step 2: Identifying the last competition of the season. This, along with step 1, determines the competitive period of the overall annual cycle.

Step 3: Determining the length of the transition period. Traditionally, it is three or four weeks long, including some passive rest and active rest. During the transition period, athletes should be active after a brief rest. Participating in complementary sports (i.e., those that use the same energy systems) provides mental recovery and helps them avoid detraining. If the transition period is too long, detraining will take place. Steps 1 through 3 are illustrated in figure 9.7.

Step 4: Determining the length of the precompetitive phase. The purpose of this phase is to get athletes into competitive shape. The precompetitive phase is traditionally three to five weeks, or microcycles, long. This period includes the taper for the selected competition.

Step 5: Determining the length of the specific preparatory phase. For beginner athletes, this phase is shorter, and for intermediate and elite

Structure of a Tennis Training Session

Time	Rotation	Court
1:30-3:00	Drilling	14
3:00-4:30	IPI	Dome
4:30-6:00	Match-play	21
6:00-6:20	Cool down	Pool

Note: On Mondays each student will have 45 minutes of mental conditioning. On Thursday a mental conditioning staff member will observe each student on the courts.

Rotation 1: Drilling

Time: 1:30-3:00

Objective: Match simulation drills

1.	Warm-up: Mini Tennis	10 min
2.	Defend baseline crosscourt	15 min
3.	Attack baseline D-T-L	15 min
4.	Control center and close in	15 min
5.	Change of direction	15 min
6.	Depth and consistency	10 min
7.	Cool-down: Stretch and hydrate	10 min
Total		90 min

Rotation 2: Fitness, International Performance Institute, Dome

Time: 3:00-4:30

Objective: Download before competition

1.	Warm-up	10 min
2.	Agility	10 min
3.	Balance	10 min
4.	Speed	10 min
5.	Rest	10 min
6.	Strength	10 min
7.	Power	10 min
8.	Pre-habilitation*	10 min
9.	Regeneration	10 min
Total		90 min

Rotation 3: Match Play

Time: 4:30-6:00

Objective: Practice set

Rotation 4: Cool-down (pool)

Time: 6:00-6:20

1. Swimming (lactate removal; reduce core temperature after exercise)

* Prehabilitation, or prehab, refers to injury prevention exercises.

Adapted from Bollettieri Tennis Academy 2000.

athletes, it is longer. Doing more sport-specific work can improve capacities and performance, but because beginners do not have the capacity to do so, they need more general preparation.

Step 6: Determining the length of the general preparatory phase. Because beginners have more specific need of this phase, it is longer for them and shorter for intermediate and elite athletes. Steps 3 through 6 are illustrated in figure 9.8.

Step 7: Plotting the volume of training (figure 9.9). Progressive overloading of the volume of training happens during GPP. After entering SPP, the volume progressively decreases (because of the increasing specificity and intensity of training); it enters maintenance mode during PCP and CP.

Step 8: Plotting the intensity of training. As illustrated in figure 9.10, a very stable intensity is plotted during GPP. This is due to the

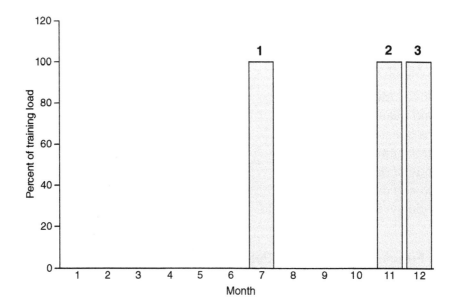

FIGURE 9.7 Steps 1-3: determining the competition and transition periods of the annual plan.

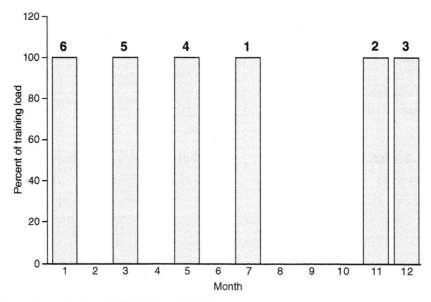

FIGURE 9.8 Steps 4-6: plotting PCP, SPP and GPP.

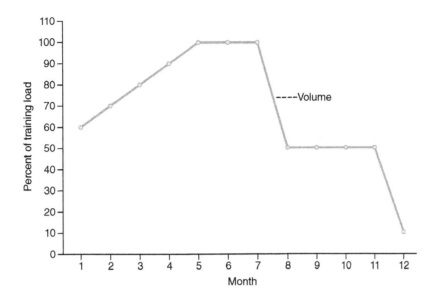

FIGURE 9.9 Step 7: plotting the volume of training.

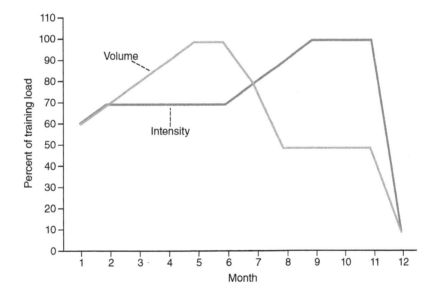

FIGURE 9.10 Step 8: plotting the intensity of training.

progressive increase in the volume of training; volume and intensity cannot be increased at the same time. When athletes enter SPP the intensity of training increases gradually, while the volume of training decreases. PCP and CP are characterized by high intensity and relatively low (maintenance) volume. Major and minor peaks can be identified during CP, if necessary.

Step 9: Finalizing mesocycle and microcycle distribution (figure 9.11). This is done by planning backward from the beginning of CP, and considering physiological and empirical coaching guidelines (see appendix A). During GPP, because of general workload, high-volume and low-intensity 4:1 and 3:1 mesocycles are recommended. During SPP, 3:1

and 2:1 mesocycles are recommended. Because specific training places higher demands on the body, more recovery microcycles are planned. During PCP, mostly 2:1 and 1:1 mesocycles are implemented to provide better recovery, lessen fatigue, and create better performances. After the mesocycles are identified, a careful overview is warranted to identify the Christmas season, exams, school breaks, and other holidays to ensure that the plan is optimized.

Step 10: The quantification process is based on individual test and performance records and normative data. Using the five Ss of training, the proportions of emphasis, or priority of training, can be determined (figure 9.12). For example, a 50 percent emphasis on stamina would be called for if test results revealed the need for a major improvement in endurance. But if endurance were well established, stamina could receive a 20 percent allocation and strength could receive a 50 percent allocation.

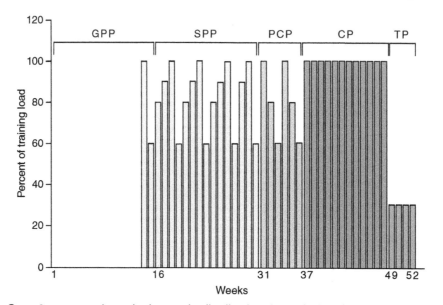

FIGURE 9.11   Step 9: mesocycle and microcycle distribution through the phases.

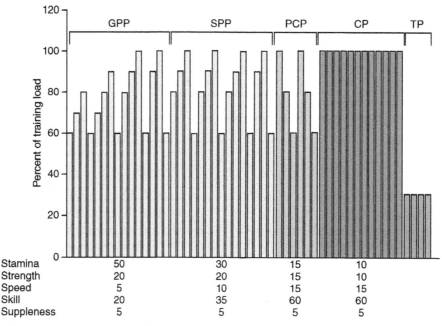

	GPP	SPP	PCP	CP
Stamina	50	30	15	10
Strength	20	20	15	10
Speed	5	10	15	15
Skill	20	35	60	60
Suppleness	5	5	5	5

FIGURE 9.12   Step 10: quantification of the training load using the five Ss of training and performance.

The percentages can also be distributed among the other Ss based on the needs of the athlete. So, during GPP, the distribution of the workload should be 50 percent stamina, 20 percent strength, 5 percent speed, 20 percent skills, and 5 percent suppleness (flexibility).

During SPP, stamina is reduced to 30 percent, strength is maintained at 20 percent, speed is increased to 10 percent, skills are increased to 35 percent, and suppleness is maintained at 5 percent.

During PCP and CP, stamina and strength are maintained at 10 percent, whereas speed increases to 15 percent and skills increase to 60 percent; suppleness remains at 5 percent.

Implementing the 10 Steps of an Annual Cycle

This section presents a condensed version of the step-by-step process of creating an annual plan. See appendix B for a detailed outline.

Step 1: Evaluating (Feedback and Feedforward)

The first step of periodization is evaluating the process and laying the foundation for the rest of the plan. With a strong understanding of the athletes and their developmental ages, you can begin to develop appropriate programs based on the strengths and weaknesses of the previous years' programs. A layout of the year to come can also be developed.

- Profile the athlete or team
  - Identify developmental ages.
  - Identify strengths and weaknesses.
- Evaluate training, competition, and recovery programs from the previous years.
- Identify the strengths of the previous annual program.
- Identify the weaknesses of the previous annual program.
- Develop a program for the upcoming year.

Step 2: Drafting a Plan

The second step of periodization is to draft a plan for the upcoming year. This process involves working backward from the main competitive event of the season. The draft should include the competitive, precompetitive, specific preparatory, and general preparatory phases of the plan, as well as a preliminary chart of the volume and intensity of training during the plan.

- Categorize selected competitions.
  - Individual sports (selected competitions)
  - Team sports (dictated competitions)
- Determine the competitive period(s) of the annual plan.
- Determine the precompetitive phase(s) of the plan.
- Determine the specific preparatory phase(s) of the plan.
- Determine the general preparatory phase(s) of the plan.
- Calculate the optimum volume and intensity of the annual plan (training and competition load).
- Plot preliminary volumes and intensities of training on the yearly training plan (see appendix A).

Step 3: Planning Mesocycles and Microcycles

Once the draft has been conceptualized, you can begin to structure the mesocycles and microcycles of the plan. Use a top-down method by keeping the athlete's larger and broader goals in mind when structuring each cycle.

- Working backward from the beginning of the competitive period, design and expand mesocycles and microcycles of the annual plan.
- Reevaluate mesocycle and microcycle distribution, taking into consideration exam periods, holidays, training, competition, and rest.
- Finalize the mesocycle and microcycle distribution, based on the objectives of

the annual plan. Identify the content of training within microcycles.

- Based on the established mesocycle and microcycle values, record final volumes and intensities on the yearly training plan (appendix A). Ensure that the training and competition loads cover the technical, tactical, physical, mental, and recovery and regeneration components.

Step 4: Quantifying Training Loads, Volumes, and Intensities

Following the creation of the mesocycles and microcycles, the critical aspects of training loads, volumes, and intensities must be addressed. The five Ss of training are key features to keep in mind while progressing through the fourth step.

- Quantify the percentage contributions of the five Ss of training and performance for each phase of the annual plan.
  - Stamina (endurance)
  - Strength
  - Speed
  - Skill
  - Suppleness (flexibility)
- Quantify the percentage of distribution of the five Ss of training and performance only for the microcycles of the first mesocycle of the annual plan. (The annual plan is a skeleton identifying all key elements, but is impractical for quantifying microcycles eight or nine months ahead. It needs to be flexible; if short-term goals are not accomplished, change is necessary for ensuring that peak performance happens when required.)
- Determine the number of weekly and daily training sessions in the microcycles of the first mesocycle, and sequence those sessions to provide optimum adaptation to training, as well as to optimize recovery and regeneration.
- Quantify the daily and weekly volume of training.

- Identify the taper procedure to achieve peak performance.

Step 5: Monitoring and Evaluating

Monitoring and evaluating the implementation of the plan and the adaptation (improvement) processes are very important. Regular field, laboratory, and performance tests should be performed, including medical and psychological monitoring and tests. Monitor the adaptation processes regularly to ensure that the planned training effects are accomplished.

Summary

Periodization integrates sport science and sports medicine with sport-specific technical and tactical programs. This chapter described the various cycles of an annual periodized training, competition, and recovery program, including annual plans, periods, phases, and meso- and microcycles.

In periodization, the planning occurs backward beginning with the first competition of the season. Single, double, and triple periodized annual plans were presented, together with mesocycle and microcycle examples. A step-by-step approach is needed for creating an annual plan (see appendix B).

Questions for Reflection

- What is periodization?
- What is an annual plan?
- What is the duration of a mesocycle?
- What is the duration of a microcycle?
- What are the three key factors in periodization?
- What is a quadrennial plan?

References

Balyi, I., & Hamilton, E. (1998). Microcycles and microcycle planning of the annual training and competition cycle. *BC Coaches Perspective, 3*, (2), 6-18.

Balyi, I., & Hamilton, E. (1999). Microcycles and micro-cycle planning of the annual training and competition cycle. *BC Coaches Perspective, 2* (4), 6-17.

Matveyev, L.P. (1983). *Aspects fondamentaux de l'lentraine-ment.* Paris: Vigot.

Mujika, I. (2009). *Tapering and peaking for optimal perfor-mance.* Champaign, IL: Human Kinetics.

To Learn More

Balyi, I. (1992). Beyond Barcelona: A contemporary critic of the theory of periodization. In *Beyond Barcelona, 4th Elite Coaches Seminar* (pp. 13-17). Canberra: Australian Coaching Council.

Balyi, I. (1999). Long-term planning of athlete develop-ment, multiple periodization, modelling and normative data. *FHS, The UK's Quarterly Coaching Magazine, 4,* 7-9.

Blimkie, C.J.R., & Bar-Or, O. (1996). Trainability of muscle strength, power and endurance during childhood. In O. Bar-Or (Ed.), *The child and adolescent athlete.* London: Blackwell Scientific Publications.

Blimkie, C.J.R., & Marion, A. (1994). Resistance training during preadolescence: Issues, controversies and rec-ommendations. *Coaches Report, 1* (4), 10-14.Bompa, T. (1985). *The theory and methodology of training.* Dubuque, IA: Kendall Hunt.

Bompa, T. (1995). *From childhood to champion athlete.* Toronto, ON: Veritas.

Bompa, T.O., & Haff, G.G. (2009). *Periodization: Theory and methodology of training.* Champaign, IL: Human Kinetics.

Dick, F. (1997). *Sport training principles.* London: A & C Black.

Harre, D. (1980). *Principles of sport training.* Berlin: Sport-verlag.

Issurin, V.B. (2010). New horizons for the methodology and physiology of training periodization. *Sports Medi-cine, 40* (3), 189-206.

Kellmann, M. (Ed.). (2002). *Enhancing recovery.* Cham-paign, IL: Human Kinetics.

Mujika, I. (1998). The influence of training characteris-tics and tapering on the adaptation in highly trained individuals. *International Journal of Sports Medicine, 19,* 439-446.

Nadori, L. (1986). *Az edzes elmelete es modszertana.* Buda-pest: Sport.

Nadori, L. (1989). *Theoretical and methodological basis of training planning with specific considerations within a micro-cycle.* Lincoln, NE: National Strength and Conditioning Association.

Norris, S.R., & Smith, D.J. (2002). Planning, periodiza-tion, and sequencing of training and competition: The rational for a competently planned, optimally executed training and competition program, supported by a multidisciplinary team. In M. Kellman (Ed.), *Enhancing recovery: Preventing underperformance in athletes* (pp.121-141). Champaign, IL: Human Kinetics.

Platonov, V.N. (1988). *L'entrainement sportif: Theorie et methode.* Paris: Ed.EPS.

Smith, D. (2000). A framework for understanding the training process leading to elite performance. *Sports Medicine, 33* (15), 1103-1126.

Competition

Special thanks to Carolyn Trono, Douglas Duncan, Andre Lachance, Mike McKay, and Sylvie Beliveau for reviewing this chapter and contributing their thoughts on advancing competition.

Henry strode toward the ball. He was a little tired, because he had just played a full game and then overtime. His mom, dad, brother, and grandparents were a short distance away, encouraging him to score. His purposeful walk belied the fact he was really nervous. Although his team had yet to score, he knew that all of his teammates expected him to because he was slightly older, slightly stronger, and more mature than they were; as a result, all of the boys looked up to him. So here, in the tournament final for the U10 Boys Championship, he *must* score, *now*, in the shootout. He struck the ball. . . . It curled just inside the post . . . YES, they were ahead.

As Thomas, from the other team, collected the ball, he thought, "Oh my gosh, this is a nightmare." He was the last shooter; it was up to him to score or his team would lose. The parents and supporters inched closer; they were yelling at the top of their lungs only a few feet from the nervous 9-year-old. Thomas' coach rushed forward to encourage him: "Don't be nervous; I know you can do it!"

Thomas thought, *Don't be nervous? Are you crazy? How can I not be nervous?* He wondered, *How does he know I can do it? I don't even know if I can do it.* He checked to make sure the ball was not in a hole, positioning it for his shot. He backed up. The yelling continued, but not from his mother, who was now covering her eyes. Thomas shot. . . . The ball sailed inches wide. He dropped to his knees, his eyes flooding with tears. Those tears were matched by those of a number of his teammates. Others on the team showed signs of anger because they thought *they* should have shot; they knew they would have scored.

Henry was now on his coach's shoulders, a hero by the narrowest of margins. His teammates squealed with delight as parents congratulated each other on the superiority of their 9-year-old boys.

Thomas' coach tried to console him with futile comments such as, "It's OK; you tried your best." Thomas knew otherwise. What happened was *not* OK; it was devastating. Many of his teammates were crying and their parents were sad, trying to console them. Thomas thought, *I am never going to play again!*

Back at home, Thomas' computer games beckoned. They were always ready to offer support and a second chance. He would be safe there with no one to disappoint and no one to yell at him.

The preceding scene plays out across our fields, rinks, and floors all the time. But why? Although it feels good to win, it can also be demoralizing to lose—especially in such high-pressure situations. So who benefits from having a U10 shootout? Is it the players? The parents? The administration?

The argument that such scenarios build character is often used to defend them. But it is interesting to wonder how the 9-year-old boys would respond if both teams were deemed champions. Because both teams won many games to reach the finals, by calling it a draw perhaps everyone involved would feel positive from the experience—not just the winners. This might, in turn, encourage more young players to remain in the game for longer periods of time. Remember, they are only 9 years old.

As it stands, more children are now playing computer games, as participation in organized sport declines. Is this because they do not want to play anymore? Or is it because the pressure to win has replaced the opportunity to simply have fun and develop skills?

This chapter identifies types of competition as well as the interaction between development and winning. It outlines how to create the most effective competition based on long-term athlete development (LTAD). Competition issues such as point chasing, tiering, ranking, and standings are discussed in light of their effects on the quality of competition design.

At all stages of athlete development, optimal competition calendar planning is critical. Skill development is the key component at early stages. At certain times, developing the physical capacities takes precedence over competition. Once athletes have developed their skills and capacities by the later stages, they can focus on competing well.

Competition and LTAD

One of the overarching shortcomings of the sport system is adult competition superimposed on youth. This issue was identified a number of decades ago, long before Canadian Sport for Life (CS4L) came to the scene in the mid-2000s. More than 20 years ago, mini-soccer upset traditionalists by modifying competition formats to make them appropriate for children at various developmental stages and ages. "This is supported by academic research from around the world on the value of small sided games for improving technique and skills" (The Football Association, 2012, p. 4).

Big Changes in Competition

When those in positions of authority are challenged with the idea of changing competition, they often respond by saying that it cannot be changed. Their argument is that it is important to deliver sport as it has traditionally been delivered. They make a case that changing competition cannot be done because it has not been done. The following are a few examples of how sport at high levels has changed significantly, demonstrating that sport at any level can be altered. Keep in mind that these examples do not suggest that these changes are appropriate for all stages of development; they simply highlight that changes can be made even at the highest level, where the added complexity of business considerations is the greatest.

- Olympic and Commonwealth Games: Youth games that include modified events were added.
- Baseball: One of the top two leagues in the world eliminated the need for the pitcher to hit and added a designated hitter.
- Basketball: A shot clock was added to make teams shoot within a specific time, and 3 points were awarded for longer shots.
- Cross-country skiing: The length of races was reduced and the lap distances were shortened.
- Hockey: The top league in the world eliminated tie games by adding a shootout and changed the point structure in league standings. Goalies were restricted to particular areas in which they could touch the puck.
- Soccer: The top leagues in the world changed to award 3 points for a win after a century of awarding 2 points for a win in the league standings.
- Volleyball: The scoring system was changed from points being awarded only when the serving team grounded a ball on the other team's court to points being awarded to the appropriate team for every serve, including side-outs. A specialized player (libero) also was added, which was limited to only some of the positions.

Yet, after decades of many youth sport organizers doing the right thing at the right time, there are still challenges to address. As a result of the way youth sport operates in Canada, new parents are recruited annually to volunteer at the local minor level. These parents generally have good intentions but little experience with or understanding of sport. The understanding they do have is often from their own experiences or from watching sport on television.

Continual LTAD education is needed for ensuring that new parent volunteers have the right foundation from which to make decisions. Following are some important guidelines:

- Recognize that coaches train athletes based on the format of competition.
- Ensure that competition is meaningful.
- Understand training-to-competition ratios.
- Optimize training-to-competition ratios for each stage.
- Recognize the pressure to program adult-style competition for youth.
- Use LTAD to maximize facility usage.
- Recognize that the role of winning is different at each stage.
- Understand the difference between development and winning.
- Recognize the need for more coaches and fewer game managers.
- Have coaches shake hands *before* the competition.
- Ensure that sport is more than just sport.

High-performance coaches, experienced youth sport organizers, and professional athletes are critical to the implementation of LTAD. Whether they realize it or not, they are leaders in their sports and within their communities. They can make a difference by understanding the impact of competition on the long-term development of sport participants. As a result, they can take on leadership roles and encourage coaches, parents, and especially administrators, whether one-on-one or in a large group, to properly develop athletes. They can help them consider the key factors in the design of competition structures, as outlined in the following sections.

Let's take a closer look at each of the previous bulleted points.

Recognizing That Coaches Train Athletes Based on the Format of Competition

At the core of competition is victory and defeat, and coaches train to whatever measure is created. If the competition is skill based, coaches will train skills; if bonus points are awarded for fair play, coaches will encourage fair play. This is why setting up an appropriate system of competition is so critical at all stages of LTAD. As Orjan Madsen, a Norwegian sport physiologist, said, "In a democratic society the only way to make a change is to modify the competitive structure to change behaviour" (Sport Manitoba, 2007, p. 2). Therefore, the trick is to create a competition format that develops athletes' abilities according to the stage they are in.

Ensuring That Competition Is Meaningful

The word *meaningful* implies a chance to succeed and even win (Rowing Canada LTAD Work Group, 2007; Speed Skating Canada LTAD Work Group, 2009). This requires that the results—the score—must be uncertain to breed a feeling of excitement. Competition is *not* meaningful when who wins or how athletes place is predictable most of the time. Meaningful competition, in some cases, may be having the chance to improve; in other cases, it may be having the chance to win. For example, in individual timed sports, when finish times are spread out (i.e., there is a large time difference among athletes), athletes are essentially racing alone. Athletes in these races know their result in advance, which makes these races neither fun nor worthwhile from a competitive perspective. They provide limited challenge and minimal learning. Similarly, in team sports in which the result is a foregone conclusion, competition has a limited developmental purpose and is detrimental in many ways to both teams.

Sport development, excitement, and enjoyment result from the uncertainty of the outcome.

Understanding Training-to-Competition Ratios

When determining training-to-competition ratios, coaches and sport administrators should consider a variety of factors related to both training and competition. A more detailed ratio should include off-field training (physical, mental, educational), on-field training (technique, tactics), competition simulation (strategy), and actual competition. Although more complicated than a traditional training-to-competition ratio, a ratio that considers all of these factors is a better guide for planning and periodization and results in a better program for athletes. Coaches, parents, and administrators should check their sport's LTAD plan to find the right training-to-competition ratios for each development stage. (To find their sport's LTAD, do a web search with the sport's name along with LTAD.)

Optimizing Training-to-Competition Ratios for Each Stage

Generally, in North America, there is a low training-to-competition ratio in team sports, whereas the opposite is often true in individual sports:

Low training-to-competition ratio	High training-to-competition ratio
Soccer	Figure skating
Hockey	Dance
Baseball	Athletics
Softball	Gymnastics

An analysis of sports reveals a high correlation between sports with a low training-to-competition ratio and volunteer coaches, and between sports with high training-to-competition ratios and paid coaches at the early stages. This is not surprising because sports with paid coaches often have financial structures that generate money from training, not competition, whereas the opposite is true of sports with vol-unteer coaches. Therefore, regardless of what is good for the development of the player, we must consider the financial model if we want to change the training-to-competition ratio (Balyi, Cardinal, Higgs, Norris, & Way, 2005).

First, low-competition sports cannot rely on generating revenue from tournaments. Second, coaches need to be trained to deliver fun, interesting practices—a considerable undertaking if the coach's only skill is in managing the game. Further, this is a large challenge, because substantial time is needed to be valued for one's work as a coach in training and practice. Because high-participation team sports need so many quality coaches, creative solutions are needed for developing coaches in these sports.

Recognizing the Pressure to Program Adult-Style Competition

The competition calendar is set by parent volunteers at the early stages of LTAD and by international federations at the later stages. As noted, parent volunteers are not experts in planning competition to facilitate development. This is because they often have the thought of televised sport in their minds and enjoy watching their children compete. They are often influenced by "event entrepreneurs," who generate revenue through the promise to expose athletes to scouts and colleges by way of additional tournaments and travel, or by the facility manager, who generates revenue by hosting events. In comparison, the later LTAD stages are directed by international organizations that generate revenue through the hosting of global events. Because fame and fortune are created in events and competitions, training and, thus, proper LTAD often suffers.

Using LTAD to Maximize Facility Usage

The backdrop of every playing experience is the playing surface itself. The availability of facilities affects the access to programs for athletes of all ages and in all sports. Often, facilities do not create schedules that share time equally among sports, age groups, and tiers. The best facilities are often offered to elite teams and older age group teams. Poor facilities are offered to child and youth programs and house league teams. Equitable scheduling of facility use among age groups and tiers is critical (Canadian Lacrosse Association LTAD Work Group, 2011).

Recognizing That the Role of Winning Is Different at Each Stage

Winning and being competitive are two very different things. Winning focuses on the result of the competition, whereas being competitive means trying hard to do one's best during competition. The importance of winning should be determined by individual sports for each of their specific LTAD stages. A common expression is *Winning is everything.* Although this might be true for athletes in the Train to Win stage, it is not appropriate for children in early stages of development. Research shows that children in sport rate fun, love of the game, and social connections well ahead of winning, yet coaches, parents, and league organizers repeatedly ignore such information in their design of competition formats and rules by modeling professional sport. Do 9-year-old girls have to go to a shootout to determine the tournament winner? Couldn't both teams be awarded winner status? In many cases professional sports have taken ties out of the game to boost the entertainment value of their products. That doesn't necessarily make it right for youth sport.

Understanding the Difference Between Development and Winning

Winning the next game, or as the saying goes, *Peaking by Friday,* often drives coaches' decisions. Obviously, the roles of winning and development are different at different stages. Using the *Peaking by Friday* approach to make decisions often compromises development. Some examples follow:

Development	Winning (short-term)
Use substitutes.	Limit substitutes.
Play many positions.	Specialize in a position.
Let players make decisions.	Run plays.
Practice skills.	Yell instructions.
Work on athleticism.	Practice strategies.
Don't use tactical systems.	Work on tactics.
Play everyone.	Use tactical systems (e.g., zone defense).
Distribute the ball.	Play only the best players.
Practice.	Focus on early talent.
Play big kids everywhere.	Play games.
Pride yourself on fun and development.	Limit the positioning of big kids.
Limit physical stress (e.g., pitch counts).	Pride yourself on your win–loss record.
Monitor retention rates.	Disregard physical stress.
	Disregard retention rates.

This is not to say that winning is bad; however, compromising the quality of sport programming for the sake of winning is shortsighted and does not help athletes develop to their full potential.

Recognizing the Need for More Coaches and Fewer Game Managers

Recognizing the difference between coaches and game managers is crucial. Coaches are well trained and, as a result, have the ability to run a great practice in which athletes have fun and learn and develop technical and life skills. Coaches enjoy practices; they typically want more practice time so they can develop the capabilities of their charges. In contrast, game managers are often volunteer "coaches" who prefer games to practices because they enjoy organizing substitutes and hollering at players more than running well-organized practices. Further, game managers tend to use the majority of the practice to scrimmage. Because the mentality of a game manager is less prevalent in individual (versus team) sports, there are often more trained (and paid) coaches in individual sports.

Shaking Hands Before the Competition

Every Sunday we see pro coaches on TV shaking hands after the game. This is mimicked in youth sport and is a prime example of a classic adult activity being superimposed onto children. North American coaches who coach at developmental stages of LTAD seem to believe that it is *their* team and that *they* are competing against the other coach. This then spills over to the parents, who believe *they* are competing with the other parents and that they are better parents if their children are victorious.

Detrimental to development is the "team first" mentality that allows coaches to insulate the team or group from the club. This attitude inhibits collaborative development for both players and coaches. For example, top-tier teams with more highly trained coaches do not invite players or coaches from lower tiers to practice with them, because they fear it will negatively affect *their* team. The solution to this problem is to work together by supporting, mentoring, and building small practice communities in which teams and coaches can share and learn together with the common goal of delivering higher-quality sport.

What if youth coaches were to shake hands before competitions? Would they be more respectful in their approach to the competition and the opposition? Some coaches do make a point of saying hello and chatting to the opposition coach prior to the game. Their goal is to break the façade that they are competing with each other, communicating instead that they are partners in managing a quality sporting experience for the kids. They make it personal, in a positive way.

Ensuring That Sport Is More Than Just Sport

Children participate in sport for many reasons. Some love to play the game and test their athletic abilities, whereas others are involved to gain social acceptance. Coaches must consider the many reasons why the players they are coaching are involved in sport before planning their training and competition. The many skills that are needed for them to develop as participants and people need to be identified and then designed into training sessions to ensure interest from all—including learning the game and having fun. Further, what participants take from sport also differs; a select few derive a living from sport, and others have their college paid for. Most, however, use sport to maintain a healthy lifestyle while gaining valuable life lessons, enabling them to become good decision makers in education, business, and family life.

Leaders in sport must recognize that they have an important role in delivering quality sport at all stages of LTAD. The success of athletes at the Train to Compete and Train to Win stages is often predicated on the quality of the programs they received at earlier stages. The quality of talent development depends on its progression in a sport environment, which is often controlled by parents whose expertise is not in sport. To develop more quality athletes, and to have more athletes develop the capabilities outlined by sports at the Train to Compete stage, leaders need to encourage proper competition at all LTAD stages.

The success of sport programs is often determined by the number of registered participants. Because competition is often a primary experience in sport, coaches need to encourage proper competition at all LTAD stages.

Issues in Competition

A variety of controversial issues exist regarding competition. This section focuses on three of these issues—point chasing, ranking, and tiering—and the unintended outcomes of each.

Point Chasing

Consider an organization that decided to select athletes based on their rankings in a series of races. They had seen this model used in many sports based on the World Cup and other events. What the organization failed to realize was the following unintended outcomes to this decision:

- Athletes with more financial resources have an advantage over those with less, because they are able to travel to more of the competitions that award ranking points.
- Athletes limit their development as they minimize their risk taking or creativity in competition to keep from being eliminated early, resulting in a lower number of ranking points from that competition.
- Event organizers seek to be sanctioned as a ranked race to encourage participation in their event.
- Athletes participate in as many events as possible to keep their ranking. This results in overcompeting.
- Event organizers pressure coordinating organizations to increase the number of ranking events required for athletes to be selected or funded, to increase participation in their events so their revenues increase.
- Athletes living farther from the ranked competitions are at a disadvantage compared to those living closer.

As a result of the preceding, the best athletes are not always selected; those who have the funds to participate in more events have the advantage. However, to be selected, these athletes must overcompete, compromising their development.

Ranking

Imagine a league that wanted an increase in media coverage. To accomplish this, league leaders decided to provide the media with a weekly ranking of teams across a number of divisions, even if those divisions didn't play

each other. Further, to create value in this ranking, the league invited a wild card team based on ranking to the championships. The media caught on and, to get the readers engaged, started the rankings at the start of the exhibition season. The league failed to take into account the following unintended outcomes to this decision:

- Because every game counted, coaches wanted to win, even during the exhibition season.
- Substitutions were used minimally to ensure wins.
- Winning big was rewarded because it was reflected in the subjective ranking.
- Risk taking was eliminated because it could cause turnovers.
- Coaches wanted to control all games because each had a high value.

Tiering

Appropriate tiering groups children of similar ability to provide the best sport experience possible for every athlete. Teams should be tiered based on their performance and should be allowed to "play up" if they desire. Athletes should be tiered through an open and transparent evaluation process (i.e., via a third party, not parents or coaches) and should not be permanently typecast to particular tiers.

To tier or not to tier? That is the question. If the decision is to tier, how many tiers are needed? All youth league organizers should be aware of the benefits and problems associated with tiering athletes at young ages. Although little research exists on the effects of tiering on performance and participation, studies at the University of Alberta have shown that tiering in youth hockey creates a relative age bias (Barnsley, Thompson, & Barnsley, 1985). Simply put, older kids get placed in the higher tiers based on the belief that because they are older, they are better. Studies from the Texas Christian University show that a coach's expectations often become reality, regardless of whether they are valid (Solomon, 2010). If the coach believes a player is good, that player will become good, and vice versa.

Does tiering result in sending the message to younger, less able players that they are not as good as others? We have to assume this is the case, especially if they are receiving poor coaching and less practice and game time. Once tiers are created, advantages arise for those in higher tiers: they receive more playing time and better coaches, facilities, officials, equipment, and uniforms. It is no surprise that higher-tiered athletes end up performing better than lower-tiered athletes. Everything is structured for them to be better.

The underlying problem is that athletes are categorized based on their chronological age, and then adult-style competition formats are imposed on them. Categorizing athletes based on their capability is a much more effective strategy. This, in fact, is done to some extent when athletes "play up." It should also be done with those who "play down." Playing up is a form of tiering in that a few athletes with greater capabilities are selected to play at the next level. This strategy is misused when talented players play up without having all the capacities to do so. For example, a highly technically skilled athlete who is selected to play up may not be physically or mentally ready to do so. This athlete then develops coping skills, which result in bad habits (e.g., passing too quickly for fear of being hit). Further, creating four or five tiers at the FUNdamentals or Learn to Train stage hardly makes sense because there is no research to prove its value.

As discussed, there are pros and cons to tiering as well as various levels of tiering. One option is to remove tiering but create liberal playing-up and playing-down policies. In this situation, having the knowledge to make the correct decision becomes the challenge.

The cons of tiering can be mitigated by not tiering teams for practice. This requires a cultural shift because young coaches often focus

Strengths and Weaknesses of Tiering

Strengths

- Meaningful competition
- Better experience for some athletes
- Safer
- More opportunities to succeed
- Increased retention
- More competitive atmosphere
- Increased recruitment
- Creates a pathway to excellence

Weaknesses

- Athletes labeled and believe they cannot move up
- Less experienced coaches at lower tiers
- Fewer resources at lower tiers
- Biased player evaluations (coaches' kids and their friends get preference)
- Players cut too often
- Tough on psyche to "drop" levels
- Not enough participants at lowest levels
- Not enough competition or events at lower levels
- Children separated from friends
- Lower-tiered players never getting a chance to play more talented players
- Bias in the assessment process

on their own teams to the exclusion of others. This attitude needs to change, and it certainly can with innovative competition formats. For example, an association with a large age group of athletes with a wide variety of abilities can create two tiers for competition but link the teams in practice, structure, and standings (i.e., combine the standings of the teams in the two tiers). When league standings are kept in this format, coaches (and players) on the top-tier teams have an investment in the lower-tier teams. Such an innovative competition format minimizes the negative impact of tiering.

Keep in mind that each sport needs to be considered differently in terms of tiering. Football, lacrosse, and ringette are games in which a skilled young player can control the object very easily because of the equipment and rules (i.e., players can hold the ball in their hands in football, carry the ball in their nets in lacrosse, or secure the ring with their stick in ringette). In other sports such as hockey, soccer, baseball, volleyball, and basketball, equipment and rules do not allow for complete control of the object (i.e., balls can hit the stick, bat, feet, and hands, but can rarely be completely secured or controlled as with the sports above). Players who can control the ball easily (in sports such as football and lacrosse) can dominate play to a greater degree (i.e., once they have possession, they retain possession). In this situation, tiering is beneficial to ensure that top players are challenged and experience more meaningful competition.

Following are some examples of tiering models:

- **Pure tiering.** Every team in a club is placed in a different tier.
- **Combined house league and representative system.** All players compete on balanced teams in a house league system and then play in tiered teams for tournaments or state championships.
- **Separate house league and representative system.** Players on rep teams do not participate in the house league.
- **House league only.** All players compete in a parity house league system. There may or may not be tournaments and provincials.
- **Mixed bag.** All players are put into a house league system but are grouped differently at different times (i.e., grouped or balanced based on such factors as ability, month of birth [age], height, weight, speed). Therefore, teams are formed and reformed based on different criteria. (*Note:* This is particularly applicable to the Active Start and FUNdamentals stages, in which skills are the primary focus because reforming teams reduces the coach's ability to focus on tactics and strategy.)

Making Good Decisions

The design and review of competition are complex processes. Many decisions have to be made to create the right form of competition for various sport situations. To make good decisions when designing or reviewing competition structures, coaches and other sport leaders should answer the following questions, which are discussed in detail in the following sections:

- What is the purpose of the competition (i.e., the big picture)?
- What is the LTAD stage?
- What are the types of competition?
- Who has the authority to change the competition?
- Who can influence those in authority?
- What is the developmental emphasis for the competitors?
- What parameters are set for the competition?
- What are the cost considerations?
- What format will make for a great competition?
- What rewards and titles are appropriate for the competition?

Answering these questions will result in a great competition structure, one that helps

Competition Checklist

This checklist will help you design competition structures, formats, and rules that ensure a high-quality sport that is complex and challenging. The following list of questions can be discussed and answered, and the results can determine what course of action is best for the athletes for whom the competition is designed.

Is Competition Fair?

- Does the athlete or team have a chance to win?
- Is the competition accessible and affordable for those who should be there?
- Do athletes born earlier in the year have an advantage?
- Do early maturers get advantages in competition over late maturers?
- In individual sports, is the ranking or seeding appropriate, so that all of the fastest or most skilled athletes advance to the next round?
- Are teams balanced evenly within tiers?
- Do athletes living in certain parts of the country have an advantage because of climate and geography?

Is Competition Meaningful?

- Does the competition system deliberately consider the ability of the participants to ensure that they experience close competition, and provide maximum opportunities for each athlete?
- Is there an opportunity for self-improvement?
- Is there a chance to win?
- Do officials and umpires have the appropriate training and attitudes to provide the right support to the athletes during competition?

Does the Competition Make Sense?

- Does the competition emphasize the objectives for the LTAD stage of development of the athletes?
- Does the system of progression within the competition and to the next competition show a clear pathway for the team or athlete? Do athletes, coaches, parents, and administrators understand how athletes can qualify for the next competition or team (including selection procedures)?
- Do all elements of the competition type, schedule, and format align well with club, school, regional, provincial, national, international, and multisport events?
- Does the system of competition set up the correct ratio of training to competition based on the priorities of the LTAD stage?
- Do the rewards match the stage and level of competition?

administrators understand why they are doing what they are doing!

What Is the Purpose of the Competition (the Big Picture)?

The first question sport leaders must ask is: What are the primary, secondary, and tertiary priorities for the competition? It is critical that the people and organizations working together to create the competition format share the same priorities. Following are some examples of competition priorities:

- Nation building
- Entertainment
- Business
- Lifelong health
- Athlete development
- Athlete selection
- Winning a prize

Because competitions often have multiple purposes, most have more than one of the preceding priorities. However, to determine the best competition format, those who control the competition should articulate its primary purpose so that everyone involved has a clear understanding.

What Is the LTAD Stage?

The LTAD stage of the participants in the competition must be identified. If the objectives for that stage do not match the priority of the competition, that priority may need to change. The other LTAD considerations are addressed in the stages section of this book (see chapters 13 through 19). They need to be clear to determine the competition format that best suits the athletes.

What Are the Types of Competition?

Competition can be divided into four types; each fits differently within a coach's annual plan. The first type is scrimmages, in which training within the team simulates competition. The second is preparatory, or controlled,

competitions, in which the competition against other teams is considered training and used to practice specific skills or to test the state of athletes' preparation. Third is performance-oriented competition, for which athletes are specifically prepared and aim for overall success. Fourth is decisive competitions, which are the main, or peak, events that represent the culmination of months or years of preparation.

Who Has the Authority to Change the Competition?

It is important to determine who actually has the authority to change the competition format, as well as the process for creating change. Who makes the decisions within each organization? Lastly, it is important to understand the culture of the organization. Is the organization sensitive to the technical development of athletes? Are the people within the organization focused on running events and remaining financially sustainable, or are they purely in it to generate the largest profit possible?

Who Can Influence Those in Authority?

In addition to knowing who has the authority to make change, sport leaders need to know who can influence those in positions of authority. Ultimately, change occurs when people in positions of authority are convinced by "influencers." An influencer might present information about LTAD to the person in authority and help that person make the change. Depending on the situation, a variety of people in a number of positions can influence change. Currently, in youth sports, parents have a tremendous influence on the authorities. Unfortunately, they are often the least informed stakeholders, which can be a challenge in creating quality competition.

What Is the Developmental Emphasis for the Competitors?

With the possible exception of gold medal matches and major finals, competition always has a developmental emphasis, because athletes and teams are always trying to improve their performance. During different stages, the developmental emphasis changes to improve participants' ability over the long term. Competition should be structured to reward the developmental emphasis, which is appropriate to the stage of the athlete. Following are descriptions of various developmental emphases for competition:

- **Physical.** The physical developmental emphasis based on the stage of the participants must be considered in the design of any competition. The following aspects all need to be built into the competition to a greater or lesser degree: agility, balance, coordination, stamina, strength, speed, and flexibility.

- **Fundamentals.** Fundamentals are the foundational skills or principles that every player must learn. In learning the fundamentals, players are educated in the "how to" and "why to" basics of their sports. For example, basketball players who know how and why to dribble have acquired the basic fundamental skill of dribbling. Keep in mind that there are layers of complexity for the simplest of skills. The simple skill of passing a soccer ball, for instance, has multiple variations. What part of the body is used to pass it (head, chest, knee, foot)? What area of that part is used (which foot—and inside, outside, top, toe, or heel)? What distance and weight does the pass need to be? The complexity and importance of fundamental skills is why they must be trained at all stages.

- **Technical.** Technical skills are more specific than fundamental skills and involve decision making. Technique focuses on when to execute a skill instead of how. Lots of repetition is required for learning technical skills. For example, when a player changes direction to avoid a defender, that player has the technical skill of a change-of-direction dribble. Further, the skill of passing a soccer ball involves many technical decisions such as choosing one's speed and direction in relation to the teammate, deciding where the ball should go based on the movement of that teammate, and sending the ball so the teammate will receive it in the best position to perform the next move. Because they are so varied, technical skills require many years to develop and refine.

- **Strategy.** The strategy is the long-term plan. Here, the learning takes place through exposure to gamelike conditions. The team player learns what to do in creating the team's style of play, and the athlete in an individual sport determines with the help of the coach how to compete (e.g., run a race). To take part in their teams' offensive strategy, players learn a simple pattern or are given roles or concepts to use to attack the defense in a specific way.

- **Tactics.** Tactics are the short-term adjustments that are made to the long-term strategy. Tactics are very specific and are used in preparation for, or within, particular games. For example, the day before a game, a team works on forcing the opposition to attack from the left side because scouting reports have shown that the opposition has succeeded when attacking from the right. In individual sports, the coach and athlete adjust to the opposition by doing such things as changing the approach in the middle of the race if the opponent is pushing the pace.

- **Mental.** The components of mental techniques (or fitness), such as concentration, relaxation, visualization, and goal setting, must be considered in the delivery of any competition. In the early stages of LTAD, competition should be fun. Later, fun should remain while the athlete's ability to perform under pressure develops. These aspects are addressed in the chapters of this book that address LTAD.

- **Personal.** Competition can be designed for personal development in areas ranging from fair play to etiquette, enjoyment, or thriving in a team environment. For example, a single-location tournament, in which the team travels somewhere new but then stays in that location to train and compete for a period of time, can help athletes learn to work in a team environment.

- **Lifestyle.** Competition can also be designed to challenge the athlete to develop basic lifestyle skills in areas such as time management, nutrition, hydration, rest, and recovery. The design of the competition can test these skills to lesser or greater degrees as coaches and athletes are required to plan ahead and self-monitor. For example, consider a competition in a remote area. In such a situation, coaches and athletes need to plan their nutrition and fluid replacement well before the competition to ensure that their needs are met.

What Parameters Are Set for the Competition?

Very few organizers of competitions have carte blanche to dictate exactly how the competition will be delivered. In most cases, the competition must fit within a series of parameters.

- **Time.** How long and over what period of time is the competition (e.g., over how many days)?
- **Facility.** When is the facility available, and what amenities and equipment does it offer?
- **Human resources.** Are there qualified coaches, officials, event organizers, and volunteers? All have to be considered in competition design.
- **Modified rules.** Rules for each stage are outlined in sport-specific LTAD models. Using these modified rules in competition is critical, because they are often created to help athletes develop. As we know, the structure of the competition also affects the development of athletes. For example, a U11 soccer team should have a 7v7 game format, a squad size of 9 (and a maximum of 12), two games of 25 minutes each, and a ball size of 4. The field size should be 30 to 36 meters wide and 40 to 55 meters long, and the goal size should be no larger than 1.83 by 4.88 meters (6 feet by 16 feet) (Canadian Soccer Association LTPD Work Group, 2009). The modified U11 soccer rules provide guidelines for the time, facilities, equipment, and human resources needed for hosting a competition.

What Are the Cost Considerations?

The cost of a competition has two angles: the cost of hosting or delivering the competition to the participants and the cost of the competition to the participants. In many countries, national governments are passing the cost of operating facilities on to the users. The increase in cost of both training and competition results in narrowing the range of those who can participate by eliminating those who do not have the means. Some sports, such as alpine skiing, equestrian, and yachting, have competition structures that eliminate a large percentage of the population because of the high cost of participating.

In some traditionally low-cost sports, such as soccer and basketball, expensive and exclusionary competition structures have been created, which reduce the numbers of participants. This is why the basic financial costs must be considered when designing competition. This is done by simply adding up all of the expenses associated with the competition. In addition, the time cost must also be addressed.

For children in the early stages of development, the return on investment for driving hours to a competition is minimal. Instead, the time could be used for training, resulting in a lower-cost program that is more inclusive. Parents need to take a long look at the benefits of travel teams in the first three stages of LTAD. Athletes who overcompete often do not have the time to balance life and sport and, as a result, lack a healthy social life. Further, without balance, burnout can occur, which results in athletes leaving the sport early without having fulfilled their potential.

Competition design and planning can address the issue of life balance by, for example, building social activities into the competition program. For this to occur, event planners need to go beyond the typical offerings of a dance or banquet at the end of the season and include educational activities throughout the season, such as trips to local museums.

What Format Will Make for a Great Competition?

The area of competition format is where the art of design builds on the science of sport. There is no standard design—no easy answer—because there are so many situations and so many solutions. The intent is to design a competition that considers the principles of successful tiering while putting children's enjoyment of sport

Our Carbon Footprint

A carbon footprint is the total amount of greenhouse gas emissions caused directly or indirectly by an individual, organization, event, or product (Carbon Trust, 2011). All sectors of society, including sport, need to have a heightened awareness of their carbon footprint because of the vast effect these emissions have on our environment. Competition is one of the most impactful aspects of sport in terms of the carbon footprint. Consider the following scenario:

In the small town of Boswell outside of a midsized U.S. town, the U9 soccer team prepared for another season. The team played in a regional league to get the best competition possible for the top 8-year-olds in the town. Because Boswell was in a rural area, the team averaged a 45-minute drive to get to the other teams in their league. Over the course of eight road games in the 16-game season, this team would drive a total of 12 hours! Including carpooling, total travel adds up to 400 hours of driving for 8-year-olds to play in a competitive league. Is this really needed?

No!

These children should be riding their bikes to their neighborhood park and playing and practicing in small-sided games, which are a lot of fun. The cars produce a significant amount of emissions, which is a detriment to the environment, and the time spent traveling is a huge waste of time for the parent and child. The solution for parents and children who are keen on the sport is to start a skill training academy in their community with quality coaching so participants can develop the skills appropriate to their level of capability through practice, not games. The skill training academy should have a curriculum that includes a wide range of movement and sport skill development. Those 12 hours of travel time could be used for thousands of ball touches to develop the basic skills they need to be successful and enjoy the sport later in life. Certainly, parents are in a rush for their children to be in competitive situations, but they need to be patient! The time will come when they will need to travel to get appropriate levels of competition. Parents who are club executives must take the lead to ensure that leagues follow proper LTAD-based rules and formats.

first. Creating the right competition format is critical because we know that those who stop enjoying a sport stop participating and lose out on future improvement and long-lasting health benefits.

The first challenge in competition design involves the grouping of the participants. Typically, this is done based on chronological age because it is the easiest option from an administrator's perspective. However, such groupings create large disparities because of the various rates at which children develop. As discussed earlier in the chapter, meaningful competition can be achieved by creating groups that are tiered based on skills. This allows some athletes

to play up and, in sophisticated programs, to play down.

Among the weaknesses in grouping based on chronological age is the fact that experience is not considered (e.g., of two 9-year-old soccer players, one may have seven years of experience; the other, two years). Further, this sort of grouping creates a fixed cutoff date resulting in the relative age effect (see chapter 5). In individual sport, the relative age effect can be addressed by basing competition on athletes' age on the date of the competition (e.g., all the 9-year-olds race against each other instead of all the kids born in 2005 racing against each other). Then, instead of having a cutoff date such as January 1, all of the children of a particular birth year compete against each other regardless of the date. By using athletes' age on a particular date, kids compete against others of their age at the time of the competition. In this way, kids can be the oldest or the youngest, depending on the time of the year. For team sports, an option is to have 18-month age groups. Similarly, over a three-year period, kids have the opportunity to be the oldest and youngest and in the middle of the age grouping, thus eliminating the birth-month bias where kids are either always the oldest, middle, or youngest depending on their birthday.

League and meet formats can vary tremendously. All decisions should be based on what is best for the athlete at the particular stage. League seasons in early stages should be short, allowing for participants to play multiple sports; however, as athletes move well into the Train to Train stage, seasons can be longer as athletes focus on a limited number of sports. Similarly, meets for individual sports such as athletics and speedskating in the early stages should occur over the course of hours, not days. Only in later stages should multiday competitions be considered. Modifying the formats of leagues and meets must be done at all stages to ensure that they are stage appropriate and enjoyable for the participants.

Tournaments, multisport games, and play-offs are exciting competitions for many participants. The way the competition is structured will affect the way games are coached (see table 10.1).

How the competition is scored also affects the coaching strategy. Remember, coaches coach to the required measure, and many parents determine success by the score only. There are many ways to keep score and times to stop keeping score (e.g., the mercy rule in baseball). Generally, there is no need to keep score in the FUNdamentals stage. Even in early Learn to Train competitions, organizers do not have to keep official score, because the participants and their parents will anyway. Although this is the stage when scoring can be introduced, if one side is dramatically beating the other, the best thing is to display the score to a maximum number. For example, when leading by five goals, no more goals go on the scoreboard until the losing team scores a point. The score can be recorded on a score sheet and not the scoreboard, unless mercy rules are in place.

Innovative scoring also affects the competition. In a Québec regional soccer league, points awarded in games are 3 points for a win, 2 for a tie, 1 for a loss, 1 for fair play, plus 1 for administrative compliance (i.e., the scores are reported to the region correctly and on time). In a lacrosse tournament in British Columbia, points are awarded for winning each period, but points are taken away if there are too many penalties. In many rugby leagues, extra points are awarded for scoring a certain number of tries. Again, adult scoring does not have to be superimposed on sport at all stages.

TABLE 10.1 Coaching for Various Tournament Formats

Format	Coaches' action
Knockout	Must play top players every game.
Round-robin	Have more opportunity to use subs depending on tiebreakers.
Guaranteed number of games	Have more opportunity to involve the whole team.
All teams make the playoffs	Focus less on winning in the regular season and so have more opportunity for development.
Few teams make the playoffs	Focus intensely on winning at the cost of development for contending teams; results in less meaningful games for those out of contention.

What Rewards and Titles Are Appropriate for the Competition?

World champion at the age of 11! Olympic (youth) champion at 14 years old! What is left? What mountain is bigger? Why would such an athlete want to work for 10 years just to become world champion again? Clearly, rewards and titles should be appropriate to each stage.

The way athletes and parents think of a reward or title has a lot to do with the name of the event at which it is won. Because a prestigious-sounding event will have prestigious-sounding rewards and draw more ambitious athletes, organizers often choose longer, fancier-sounding event names for promotional reasons. However, although most parents would rather see their children win a national championship over a state, provincial, or local title, they must not be tricked by labels and hype, especially at the earlier stages. Although traveling across the continent sounds exotic and exciting, the cost is high; often, a nearby event is equally good for development, just as much fun, and far less expensive.

National organizations can also control the hype created by how events are named. The challenge in countries such as the United States, Russia, China, and Canada is that they are enormous in size; therefore, single national championships are expensive because of travel and accommodations. This limits participation. One solution is to have more than one national championship. For example, the American BMX Association has five national championships in Canada spread across the country. As a for-profit organization, American BMX saw the value in branding an event as "national" to attract racers. This fulfills parents' pride needs by having their children participate in the top-notch event, but at a lower expense.

Awards and recognition are great for everyone. A well placed "well done" never goes wrong when effort has been expended. The challenge is to ensure that rewards and recognitions are stage appropriate. When should there be a podium or medals for top placing? When should everyone get a ribbon or medal?

Following is an example of an event that *almost* has it right.

A cross country running race series in a small town successfully connected with a number of elementary schools, which resulted in about 80 runners per category participating in the first event, but that diminished over the series. These kids are of all levels of fitness. They are proud of their participation. These races give ribbons to the top 40 finishers! This ensures that lots of participants are rewarded with a token for their performance. However, it is the kids finishing from 40th to 80th place that society wants to encourage to continue to participate!

What encouragement should these finishers be given? They are not as good as the top 40, but it is great that they are putting themselves and their self-esteem on the line by running in the races. As mentioned, to get the awards and recognition right, organizers should match them with the objective of the particular stage. If the stage is Train to Win and the objective is to determine Olympic champions, then three medals are appropriate. If the stage is Learn to Train and the objective is to develop skills and increase participation, then rewarding everyone would seem appropriate. Prizes such as gifts, contracts, cash, and scholarships should be stage appropriate, thus matching the objective of the stage and allowing for progression. The same can be said for recognition by peers, parents, and the media.

Based on all of the preceding decisions, coaches and administrators can construct great competition to ensure quality sport experiences for all. From there, proper periodized plans can be put in place (see chapter 9).

Training-to-Competition Ratios Through the Stages

The following training-to-competition ratios are broad generalizations that will change depending on the emphasis of the phase of an annual plan. Table 10.2 outlines the general recommendations for the ratio of general and sport-specific training to competition and competition-specific training. Consider how the quantity and quality of the training and

TABLE 10.2 **Training-to-Competition Ratios**

Stage	RECOMMENDED RATIOS	
	General training and sport training	**Competition and competition-specific training**
Active Start	No formal competition, so no specific training ratios	
FUNdamentals	All activity is fun based	
Learn to Train	70%	30%
Train to Train	60%	40%
Train to Compete	40%	60%
Train to Win	25%	75%
Active for Life	Based on individual's desire	

competition program changes as the long-term plans progress.

Summary

It is time to reconsider the way competition is structured and administered at the various stages of development. Children do not require the same type of competition layout as high-performance adults. Exposing children to high-pressure competition situations before they have had a chance to develop the skills and capacities necessary for coping could have a negative effect on their outlook of sport and cause early dropout. The pressure may come from the child, but it often originates from parents or coaches who measure success based on wins and losses, not the whole development of the child.

For children and youth, sport should not be all about winning. They are competitive enough without having a scoreboard flashing the results. Importance should rest on development, inclusion, and positive experiences. That is not to say that competition should be removed entirely from children's sport; however, a number of formats can be used so that adult competition is not superimposed on youth. This includes everything from the facilities, to the scoring system in individual games, to the league structure of an entire sport, and even to tiebreakers! Many facets of

competition must be considered and modified if children are to develop properly and *want* to remain in the game.

But just as competition should be modified to suit children and youth, care must also be taken to avoid overcompetition. During the Learn to Train and Train to Train stages, overcompetition will result in decreased fitness and a lack of basic skills. Adequate training is critical at this time because training is where youth learn most of their skills and establish the base fitness levels that will help them make it through the later stages in LTAD. Appropriate competition enhances technical, tactical, and mental development.

The following are points to consider when modifying competition for children and youth:

- Optimal sport-specific competition ratios are required for all stages of LTAD.
- The level and length of the competitive season should be aligned with the changing needs of the athlete progressing through LTAD.
- Overcompeting and undertraining at the Learn to Train and Train to Train stages result in a lack of basic skills and fitness.
- The appropriate level of competition is critical to technical, tactical, and mental development at all stages.
- Schedules are often set for team sports by leagues and organizations and not by

the coach and athlete, making optimal training based on periodization difficult. In individual sports, the coach and athlete can select the competition schedule based on the athlete's developmental needs.

- Many current systems of competition are based on tradition. They should be changed to enhance training and performance based on athletes' LTAD stages.

- Competitions must be created and scheduled considering strategic planning, and with due regard for the optimal performance of an athlete and tapering and peaking requirements.

- Optimal training-to-competition ratios for individual sports vary greatly and must be determined on a sport-specific basis.

- Although international and national calendars are usually well integrated, a systematic review of all competition needs to be undertaken. This is one of the biggest challenges for team sports and a significant challenge for individual sports that are implementing LTAD.

One way to avoid overcompetition and to ensure that proper competition formats are delivered is to use appropriate training-to-competition ratios. Not all sports require the same ratios, and as athletes move through the stages, training-to-competition rations will alter as well. Generally speaking, the higher the stage, the higher the amount of competition should be. During the first few stages, emphasis should be on training, with very little time spent on competition. Again, this approach will help children build the skill and fitness bases necessary for later involvement in sport while still keeping activities fun.

Questions for Reflection

- In the big picture, what is the priority of the competition?

- Where did the competition come from; who decided on the current format?

- What should be considered in choosing the best competition format?

- What LTAD stage is the competition for?

- What are the types of competition?

- Who has authority to organize the competition?

- Who influences those in authority?

- What is the developmental emphasis of the competition?

- What constraints affect the delivery of the competition?

- What financial considerations are there?

- Is the competition format ideal?

- Are the rewards given during the competition appropriate?

- How has major competition changed? Give examples.

- Is the competition meaningful and fair, and does it make sense?

References

Balyi, I., Cardinal, C., Higgs, C., Norris, S., & Way, R. (2005). *Canadian sport for life: Long-term athlete development* [Resource paper]. Calgary, AB: Canadian Sport Centres.

Barnsley, R.H., Thompson, A.H., & Barnsley, P.E. (1985). Hockey success and birth-date: The relative age effect. *Canadian Association for Health, Physical Education and Recreation, 51*, 23-28.

Canadian Lacrosse Association LTAD Work Group. (2011). *Lacrosse for life: Competition review.* (p. 20). Canadian Lacrosse Association. Retrieved from http://cla.pointstreaksites.com/files/uploaded_documents/357/LTAD_competition_review_-_December_2011.pdf

Canadian Soccer Association LTPD Work Group. (2009). *Wellness to world cup: Canadian soccer association long-term player development.* Canadian Soccer Association. Retrieved from www.canadasoccer.com/files/CSA_2009_W2WC_Brochure_EN.pdf

Carbon Trust. (2011). *Carbon footprinting.* Retrieved from www.carbontrust.co.uk/cut-carbon-reduce-costs/calculate/carbon-footprinting/Pages/carbon-footprinting.aspx

The Football Association. (2012). *U7/U8: Their game* (p. 25). Retrieved from www.thefa.com/~/media/my-football-resources/youth-dev-review/u7-and-u8-ydr-booklet.ashx

Rowing Canada LTAD Work Group. (2007). *LTAD competition review* (p. 5). Rowing Canada. Retrieved from www.rowingcanada.org/sites/rowingcanada/files/rowing_ltad_comp_eng_singles.pdf

Speed Skating Canada LTAD Work Group. (2009) *Racing on skates towards developmentally appropriate programs for speed skaters of all ages* (p. 17). Speed Skating Canada. Retrieved from www.scribd.com/doc/100306957/SSC-Racing-on-Skates

Solomon, G.B. (2010). The influence of coach expectations on athlete development. *Journal of Sport Psychology in Action, 1* (2), 76-85.

Sport Manitoba. (2007). *Quebec swimming producing staggering results! Why?* Retrieved from www.sportmanitoba.ca/programs/LTAD_Quebec_example.pdf

To Learn More

Baba, J., Bowes, M., Brousseau, R., Crowther, B., DePena, M., Dickson, J., et al. (2009, May 30). *Recommendation on Baseball Canada competition structure* [Report]. Ottawa, ON: Baseball Canada.

Basketball Canada Competition Review. Ottawa, Canada: Unpublished working paper.

Béliveau, S., Clark, R., Celebrini, R., Findlay, M., Fleming, S., Hart, S., et al. (2011) *Wellness to World Cup: Long-term player development* (2nd vol.). Ottawa, ON: Soccer Canada.

Canadian Lacrosse Association. (2009). *LTAD work group competition* [Report]. Ottawa, ON: Unpublished working paper.

German Football Association with Sports University of Cologne. (2005). *Soccer for 6-11 year olds: What game format and development model is best?* PowerPoint presentation.

Gilday, D., Harris, S., Ireland, S., Lemay, D., McClements, J., & Slot, N. (2009). *Racing on skates* [Report]. Ottawa, ON: Speed Skating Canada.

Morrow, A., Taylor, B., McFarlane, I., Balyi, I., Nolte, V., Way, R., & Trono, C. (2007). *Rowing LTAD competition review* [Report]. Victoria, BC: Rowing Canada.

Softball Ontario. (2011). *LTPD implementation plan.* Retrieved from www.softballontario.ca/content/view/427/166

Way, R., & Balyi, I. (2007). *Competition is good servant, but a poor master* [Report]. Victoria, BC: Canadian Sport Centres.

Sport System
Alignment and
Integration

Mom couldn't believe it. She couldn't figure out how to make it work. She had to laugh, it was so ridiculous! By day, she was a high-paid executive making complex decisions; by night, a mother of three who could not figure out how to get everyone registered and to their community sports on time. She was proud that she had active kids who loved playing sports, and certainly didn't want to disappoint them, but being new in town and without a support system, she could barely figure out how to do it all. Why did she have to choose one of two specific dates and times to register her kids for the soccer club at the community center when there were staff members on duty registering for swimming lessons and other programs all the time? Why couldn't she just register through the community center itself? She could use her credit card and not her checkbook, and she could go at a time that was convenient for her. Why didn't the recreation department work with sport clubs?

Then there was the school and club puzzle. How was she going to get her daughter home after school basketball practice and have her eat something before her night league game? She had tried to get her daughter to play one or the other, but one of the programs was very short and her daughter loved basketball; so for now, they would overlap. Why couldn't the coaches sort it out better for their players? After all, all of the kids seemed to be in the same situation.

That wasn't even the worst of her issues. Her oldest son had made the traveling team. Not only was the travel demand ridiculous, but the coach didn't seem to realize that the kids might be involved in other sports as well. He said practices were mandatory, demanding that her son attend them all. He said "No exceptions" before she could even finish explaining that her son was in the playoffs of another sport, which was more important than his preseason practice. Now what to do? This system was crazy—logic did not apply!

This mother, as a bright executive, asked the simple question: Why can't these organizations get together to arrange things so it's easier to participate in all of these activities?

This chapter looks at system alignment from an individual's perspective and provides questions for parents and athletes to consider as they progress through the long-term athlete development (LTAD) pathway. LTAD is an athlete-centered approach designed around the needs of athletes and implemented through policy and program changes in sport governing bodies, recreation organizations, education programs, and health agencies. The alignment of systems is considered from an organizational perspective and looks at how these four key sectors of health, education, recreation, and sport interact.

Beyond their focus on athletes, LTAD programs are coach driven and administra- tion, sport science, and sponsor supported. Long-term athlete or participant development is the core business of sport organizations, regardless of whether they are community or internationally based. Within the LTAD framework, organizations can define how they contribute to sports, thus allowing them to better understand how they can complement other organizations.

In addition to having a strong impact on coaches' and officials' education curricula, LTAD also addresses the need to fully integrate the activities of schools, communities, and clubs, as well as national, state or provincial, and county sport organizations. This chapter reaffirms why this model should serve as the basis for sport policy, and concludes with implications for the development of an LTAD policy.

System Alignment From an Individual Perspective

Being involved in sport and physical activity exposes participants to a variety of settings and situations, which can collectively be defined as a system. Within a single system, various elements work in harmony to achieve and maintain the integrity of that system. Adjustments are made when needed to maintain a state of balance and increase the efficiency of the system, which allows for a continuous improvement to take place. Our society functions through the interactions of various systems. Although congruency is found in a single system, creating efficiency among systems can be challenging.

This section is a guide along the pathway of LTAD to help coaches, sport leaders, and parents make better decisions about developing athletes, administering sport and physical activity, and remaining active for life themselves. LTAD addresses the needs of individual athletes as they travel through their personal sport and physical activity experiences. Sport organizations need to align their visions, missions, mandates, and policies to the LTAD framework. By doing so, they can engage in partnerships with other sectors such as recreation, education, and health agencies. Each sector plays an important role in keeping people healthy and active. Figure 11.1 shows a number of people and places that support parents in children's early years. Hopefully, all of them contribute to developing physical literacy. Through the use of the LTAD pathway, sport for life (S4L) has emerged as a framework and philosophy for promoting lifelong engagement in sport and physical activity, and encouraging the ethical pursuit of sport excellence. These are common interests and objectives that health, education, recreation, and sport organizations share.

Most parents buy books with titles such as *Baby's First Year*, which teach them what to expect during this time. These books offer helpful tips from the first week with a new baby to the end of the first year; advice on what to do and when and how to do it is laid out across the pages. Once the baby turns 2, parents need to start to thinking about developing physical literacy.

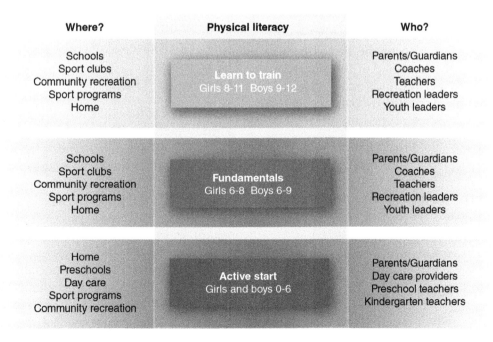

Where?	Physical literacy	Who?
Schools Sport clubs Community recreation Sport programs Home	**Learn to train** Girls 8-11 Boys 9-12	Parents/Guardians Coaches Teachers Recreation leaders Youth leaders
Schools Sport clubs Community recreation Sport programs Home	**Fundamentals** Girls 6-8 Boys 6-9	Parents/Guardians Coaches Teachers Recreation leaders Youth leaders
Home Preschools Day care Sport programs Community recreation	**Active start** Girls and boys 0-6	Parents/Guardians Day care providers Preschool teachers Kindergarten teachers

FIGURE 11.1 The who and where of LTAD's physical literacy stages.

Active Start

During the first year, babies engage in few systems—usually only the system of the home and sometimes the health system. Although the first year can be a lot of work for parents, with little sleep, it remains relatively straightforward for children. When they turn 2, or in some cases earlier, many are introduced to a new system: child care. Then, early childhood education is added. Swimming lessons at the community center are introductions to the recreation system. Then gymnastics, soccer, and other sports incorporate the sport system. At the beginning of the Active Start stage, these little athletes live in a single system, but by the time they are finished with the stage, they are interacting with multiple systems.

During the Active Start stage, although the various systems are largely independent, they do not compete against each other. A baby, toddler, and then child is likely to have experienced environments that focused on fun with minimum skill development.

Questions to Consider

- **In the home:** Do you encourage moving, growing, and exploring? Do you play with your children? Do you limit screen time?
- **In health:** Do you ensure that your children are active to the limits of their ability?
- **In early childhood education:** Does the environment inspire the development of physical literacy? Are the providers trained to get the kids moving? How much time in the day do children spend moving? Is screen time limited?
- **In recreation:** Are the leaders trained? Does the program develop fundamental movement skills?
- **In sport:** Are the coaches trained? Does the program develop a wide range of fundamental movement skills?
- **In all cases:** Are the children having fun?

FUNdamentals

How time flies—the little ones are now off to elementary school, where, hopefully, they are getting good regular physical education in the school system. The recreation system, with its local community center, is even more involved in children's lives because they are involved in swimming lessons, after-school programs, and summer camps. Depending on the season, a plethora of sport clubs are soliciting parents and their children to participate. Play in the home is still very important as the child becomes increasingly affected by the parents as role models.

Questions to Consider

- **In elementary education:** Is quality daily physical education taught by a physical education (PE) teacher? Are kids encouraged to get moving on breaks? How much time in the day do they spend moving? Is screen time limited?
- **In recreation:** Are the leaders trained? Does the program develop fundamental movement skills? Are children developing a wide range of movements?
- **In the home:** Are you a good role model of an active lifestyle? When you play with your children, can you help them move properly? Do you limit screen time? Are children eating properly?
- **In organized sport:** Are the kids in a variety of sports? Are the coaches trained? Does the program develop a wide range of fundamental movement skills?
- **In all cases:** Are children having fun?

Learn to Train

Uh oh, some of the children are starting to put on a little weight, and if they are not good at sports, they tend to shy away from physical activity, preferring inactive screen time. Meanwhile, naturally athletic kids who have always been active are starting to excel. The education system now engages children in physical education and school sports. Sport clubs continue to offer a variety of options; however, coaches are beginning to pressure kids into specializing in their sport. Now the sport entrepreneur has entered the game with a business system of camps, academies, and programs that they guarantee will turn specially talented children into stars. Recreation is still providing a variety of activities as well. Hopefully, the home is still prominent in providing play as well as outdoor experiences. The neighborhood is also now activated as kids can go a little farther afield to meet friends to play in the park. Regardless of their children's ability, parents must exercise their diminishing influence to find physical activities that attract their children. If they do not, and children become inactive, research shows that they will be condemned to a lifetime of sedentary behavior that leads to poor health (Dalton, 2004).

Questions to Consider

- **In elementary education:** Is quality daily physical education taught by a physical education teacher? Are kids encouraged to get moving during their breaks? How much time in the day do they spend moving? Is screen time limited?

- **In elementary school sport:** Are the games following recognized LTAD recommendations? Is the training developmentally appropriate? Are the players grouped for meaningful competition?

- **In organized sport:** Are the kids playing at least three sports (dance included)? Are the coaches trained? Does the program develop fundamental sport and decision-making skills? Do the kids have equal playing time and practice a variety of positions? Is the emphasis on development over winning? Do the programs train speed and allow for creativity? What are the organization's values?

- **In the home:** Are you good role models of an active lifestyle? Do you get the kids out into nature? When attending sport competitions, are you supporting instead of yelling instructions? Do you limit screen time? Are children eating properly?

- **In sport business:** Are the instructors highly qualified? Are they teaching a wide variety of movements, not just those specific to one sport? Do they train speed and allow for creativity?

- **In recreation:** Are the leaders trained? Is the instruction correctly incorporating the principles of LTAD?

- **In the neighborhood:** Are children safe? Do they have the opportunity for free play?

- **In all cases:** Are children having fun?

Train to Train

Now, as the growth spurt starts, there is a junction in the pathway. One path is geared toward excellence, whereas the other path is Active for Life, which includes competitive for life and fit for life. Additionally, this time offers the opportunity to become a sport and physical activity leader.

At the start of the excellence pathway, in the Train to Train stage, many systems interfere with each other. However, as athletes progress through the stage, the systems streamline. Similar to figure 11.1, figure 11.2 shows a number of people and places that influence athletes in the excellence stages of LTAD. Some of these service providers are more advanced divisions of earlier organizations, whereas others are unique to the excellence stages.

Systems in this stage are often not connected, pulling the developing athlete in a number of directions. This results in parents having to make tough decisions with very little knowledge of the sport system. At this point athletes' technique, decision-making abilities, athleticism, and attitude have resulted in their being chosen for select teams. (*Note:* If they were not in an early specialization sport and on a select team before puberty, they may have been overspecializing!) After being involved in many sports and various clubs and teams, the challenge of narrowing participation to develop and refine skills is difficult. This is especially true for children who are really good at a number of sports. When they enjoy focusing on more than one sport, coaches at this stage should try to accommodate them by encouraging their continued participation, especially in complementary sports. However, some coaches look for a greater commitment, sometimes unhealthily seeking an absolute dedication to one team in one sport. Even athletes who are doing one sport very well experience the confusion of various teams, academies, schools, and coaches competing for

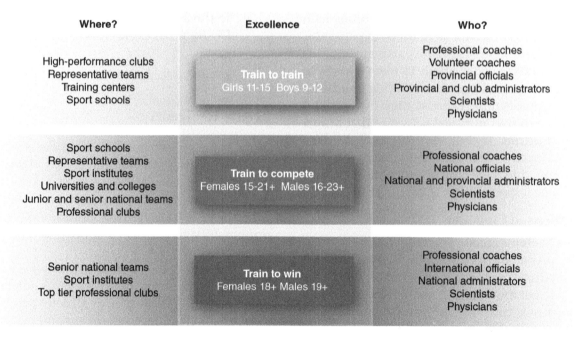

Where?	Excellence	Who?
High-performance clubs Representative teams Training centers Sport schools	**Train to train** Girls 11-15 Boys 9-12	Professional coaches Volunteer coaches Provincial officials Provincial and club administrators Scientists Physicians
Sport schools Representative teams Sport institutes Universities and colleges Junior and senior national teams Professional clubs	**Train to compete** Females 15-21+ Males 16-23+	Professional coaches National officials National and provincial administrators Scientists Physicians
Senior national teams Sport institutes Top tier professional clubs	**Train to win** Females 18+ Males 19+	Professional coaches International officials National administrators Scientists Physicians

FIGURE 11.2   The who and where of LTAD's excellence stages.

their involvement. These are tough decisions. Finding the balance while entering this stage, and addressing the evolving commitments throughout the stage, is difficult. Good guidance from parents is required.

Questions to Consider

- Does the representative team work with the club coach to create unique periodized plans for each athlete?
- Does the high-performance club or team have highly qualified coaches whose primary goal is the development of athletes? Are they willing to build a plan that includes other sports?
- Is the training center tracking growth to ensure that the proper energy systems are being focused on at the appropriate times?
- Has the sport academy connected with club and rep team coaches to assess athletes' strengths and weaknesses, as well as to build their training in a periodized plan?
- Is the school acting as a coordinating agent to ensure that all athletic and academic requirements are being met to give

the student-athlete a variety of options in and out of sport?
- In all cases, are young athletes building their character to be able to contribute to society?

Train to Compete

Athletes in the Train to Compete stage are approaching adulthood. They are obviously strong in their sport and are now traveling extensively. They are recruited, which means they must make life-altering decisions. Again, tough choices are required to ensure that they are in the best possible environment. The opportunity for athletes to improve performance to successfully compete at the international level is increasingly based on advanced sport science and medicine support services and a properly periodized competition calendar that allows the top-quality coach to facilitate development.

Questions to Consider

- Do school sports ensure a balance between academics and athletics, while considering any additional training or competition requirements the athlete may have?

- Does the team have the best possible coach who has a properly periodized plan specific to the needs of each athlete?
- Does the sport institute provide access to world-class facilities, as well as sport scientists, and is it tracking support services to ensure that no chronic injuries are being created?
- Does the university or college provide an optimum training environment along with a coach who has a track record of being a great developer of talent, rather than just a great recruiter of talent?
- Does the junior or senior national team provide individualized information that guides the athlete's improvement with a clear understanding of what constitutes a podium performer, as well as what incremental steps are needed to progress to that level?
- Does the professional club provide the playing opportunities for athletes to develop to the next level? Is the level of play right for athletes at their respective stages of development?
- Is the athlete giving back to the club or community?

Train to Win

People at the Train to Win stage are adults and winning at the highest levels in the world. Their realistic short-term goal is to stand on the podium and stay there. Standing among the world's best and maintaining that ranking is a different challenge than striving to reach the podium. Relationships with the national team, sport institutes, and pro clubs, if applicable, have been developed and established through the Train to Compete stage. The integrated support team provides Train to Win athletes with support that must be managed to be maximized.

Although the systems in the preceding Train to Compete stage generally remain the same, the new pressures of media and business come into play in this stage. Train to Win athletes, because of their international success and achievements in the professional sport environment, are challenged to incorporate the demands of the media and sponsor relations. As well, managing an income derived from performance provides new psychological challenges. At this time, knowledgeable guidance is most imperative. Of course, success brings many who are willing to offer support; thus, Train to Win athletes must understand the new systems to ensure that their success in sport transfers beyond their athletic careers.

Questions to Consider

- Does the sport institute have world-class scientists and physicians available?
- Does the sport institute offer career services to facilitate athletic retirement and transition to the athlete's next career?
- Is the senior national team supporting the athlete's continued development as well as recognizing that maintaining a level of international excellence may be different from striving for it?
- Does the top-tier professional club or team support national team representation?
- Are the business interests and sponsors aware of, understanding of, and able to work around the training demands necessary for continued success?
- Are the media's demands affecting performance?
- As role models, are athletes using their status to contribute to society?

Active for Life: Youth 12 to 20

Sooner or later, athletes transition from the excellence pathway to the Active for Life pathway. They may have started down the Active for Life pathway upon reaching puberty after they developed physical literacy. Generally, not as many systems are involved in this pathway; however, athletes must still understand the landscape to ensure that sport and physical activity remain enjoyable and that participation continues. In Active for Life, there are two streams, competitive for life and fit for life. Some people prefer to play lots of sports to enjoy the competitive experience, recognition, and social aspects. Others choose healthy noncompetitive physical activities that contribute to their health and wellness. Although there are two physically active streams, as shown in figure 11.3, there is also a leaders stream. This provides an opportunity for active and healthy people to be active for life through professional or volunteer leadership positions.

Some teenagers are very talented, but choose to participate in many sports instead of specializing in one. In this case a number of systems are involved as they balance school sport with club play. Others express their athleticism through noncompetitive physical activity. Participation becomes simple for these athletes because they spend less time on competition.

Questions to Consider

Competitive for Life

- Are qualified coaches promoting a holistic high school sport experience?
- Does the club sport complement school sport and ensure that sport is enjoyable with levels of competition that challenge the participant appropriately?
- Are parents continuing to celebrate and support their children's participation?

Fit for Life

- Does the community, recreation center, or private business offer programs with qualified instructors?
- Are parents continuing to celebrate and support their children's participation in healthy physical activity?

Active for Life: Young Adult 21 to 35

The move into adulthood corresponds with moving from educational institutions and into the workforce, both of which are systems that affect participation. People at this stage are at a critical time in their quest to be active for life as their parents' support diminishes. Social groups affect activity along with the new challenge of self-directed school or work.

Questions to Consider

Competitive for Life

- Is there a link between the youth sport club and the adult club, allowing for a place to play?

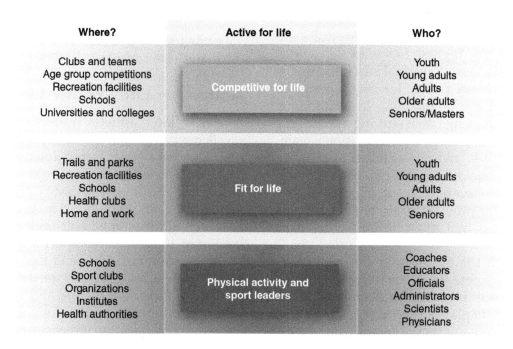

Where?	Active for life	Who?
Clubs and teams Age group competitions Recreation facilities Schools Universities and colleges	Competitive for life	Youth Young adults Adults Older adults Seniors/Masters
Trails and parks Recreation facilities Schools Health clubs Home and work	Fit for life	Youth Young adults Adults Older adults Seniors
Schools Sport clubs Organizations Institutes Health authorities	Physical activity and sport leaders	Coaches Educators Officials Administrators Scientists Physicians

FIGURE 11.3 The who and where of LTAD's Active for Life stage.

- Is there an opportunity to balance education and work with competitive schedules?
- Are there vibrant sport and intramural programs at the college or university?
- Does the peer group support participation?

Fit for Life

- Is there an opportunity to balance education and work with physical activity programs?
- Have peers built physical activity into their lifestyles?

Active for Life: Adult 30 to 55

At this point, most people focus on work and building a life that may include a family; all of these things make demands on their time. Starting a family intensifies time pressures, and education and work are minimized by the attention needed by partners and possibly children. Sport and physical activity during this stage can be an important social glue.

Questions to Consider

Competitive for Life

- Does the club have masters divisions to provide continued participation in appropriate competition?
- Is there an opportunity to balance work with competitive schedules?
- Are there ways to balance family responsibilities and continued participation?

Fit for Life

- Is there an opportunity to balance work with physical activity programs?
- Do the fitness programs provide child care?
- Are there ways to balance family and continued participation?

Active for Life: Older Adult 50 to 70

Work pressures alleviate during this phase of life; children become more independent and leave home; and the body slows down, but still needs physical activity. As the body's ability to recover slows down, health has to be monitored more regularly. Encouragement to be active from a spouse and peers continues to be important.

Questions to Consider

Competitive for Life

- Are older adults checking with their physicians regularly to ensure that any health issues are identified early to allow continued participation?
- Are rules modified to facilitate safe, enjoyable sport?
- Is there an opportunity to balance work with competitive schedules?
- Are spouses and friends supportive of continued participation?

Fit for Life

- Are older adults checking with their physicians regularly to ensure that any health issues are identified early to allow continued participation?
- Have peer groups built physical activity into their lifestyles?

Active for Life: Seniors 65+

In the later years, sport and physical activity become even more important for injury prevention, improved quality of life, and social interaction. With retirement taking away work as place of a social interaction, physical activity and sport become healthy social pursuits to keep the mind and body active . . . for life!

Questions to Consider

Competitive for Life

- Are seniors checking with their physicians regularly to ensure that any health issues are identified early to allow continued participation?
- Are rules modified to facilitate participation in safe, enjoyable sport?

Fit for Life

- Are seniors checking with their physicians regularly to ensure that any health issues are identified early to allow continued participation?

- Are fitness programs designed for seniors?
- Have peers built physical activity into their lifestyles?

System Alignment From a Sport Organization Perspective

The core activity of any sport organization is to deliver quality sport. The core business is sustainable long-term athlete development. Organizations often identify other missions such as member services and event management; however, quality sport is always at the core. Challenges occur when that focus is lost, particularly when a lack of system integration with multiple stakeholders and members occurs. It is not surprising that organizations' missions can get diverted from the simple purpose of delivering quality sport at all LTAD stages when, as shown in figure 11.4, there are multiple pressures by both internal and external organizations to service different mandates. Those pressures often are due to an organization's need to generate revenue, mean-

ing they are forced to seek funds and deliver programs that are not central to their stated organization mission and mandate. Note that the organization's placement in a quadrant may change from country to country. For example, in some countries, professional teams do not contribute funds to national sport governing bodies, whereas in other countries, pro teams are huge revenue sources.

To align with other systems, such as health, education, and recreation organizations, sport organizations need first to rationalize the roles and relationships of the various organizations within their sport. Relationships are defined by mandates. For any sport to operate effectively, the organizations within that sport must determine and agree on their respective mandates. Each organization's mandate defines its roles and responsibilities with respect to its core business—LTAD.

The sidebar Sport Mandate Template shows four organizational levels: national, state (provincial or county), local, and club. The responsibilities of the four levels are outlined to clarify the accountability for the broad-based activities surrounding the delivery of programs and services, administration of the sport, development of policy, hosting of competitions, and governance of the sport.

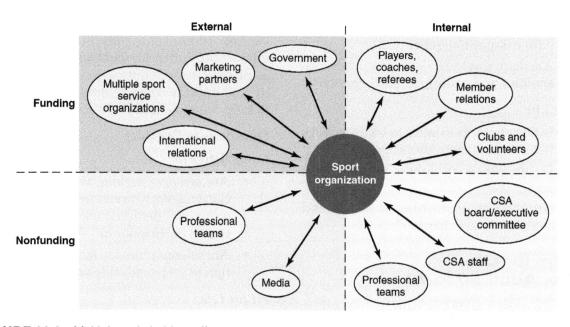

FIGURE 11.4 Multiple stakeholders affect sport organizations.

Adapted, by permission, from P. Montopoli, 2009, *CSA strategic plan* (Ottawa, ON: Canadian Soccer Association).

Sport Mandate Template

National Sport Governing Body (National Sport Organization–NSO) Mandate

- Represent the national sport governing body internationally.
- Provide an LTAD model for the sport in the nation.
- Provide training and competition opportunities for Train to Compete and Train to Win athletes.
- Facilitate communications and relationship building among state, provincial, or county sport governing bodies (SSGB).
- Develop player, coach, official, and volunteer programs for implementation by state, provincial, or county jurisdictions.
- Develop, regulate, and review playing rules, equipment standards, and codes of ethics.
- Sanction and provide national competitions.
- Monitor and abide by the policies and financial requirements of federal institutions.
- Provide exposure and resources to facilitate the growth and development of the sport nationwide.

State, Provincial, or County Sport Governing Body (SSGB) Mandate

- Govern and sanction the sport within the jurisdiction.
- Represent the jurisdictions nationally.
- Deliver relevant national programs.
- Provide training and competition opportunities for Train to Train and early Train to Compete athletes.
- Administer the organization democratically.
- Develop, promote, and deliver programs within the jurisdiction.
- Ensure the communication of, and compliance with, the NSO playing rules and equipment standards.
- Represent the SSGB at the NSO and in any NSO programs.
- Provide LTAD-based programs to players, coaches, and officials.
- Plan and sanction championships within the jurisdiction.
- Adhere to the policies and financial requirements of the NSO.
- Develop and support new local governing bodies and clubs where no local governing body exists.
- Assist in the development of existing local governing bodies.
- Develop and nurture strategies and programs to facilitate communication within the jurisdiction and externally.

Local Sport Governing Body (LSGB) Mandate

- Organize the game competition locally.
- Represent local clubs at provincial events and meetings.
- Assist and implement the LTAD model at the club level.

> continued

> *continued*

- Assist and implement player, coach, official, and volunteer programs.
- Ensure the communication of, and compliance with, the NSO playing rules and equipment standards as well as the rules and regulations of the SSGB and the local governing body.
- Adhere to the policies and financial requirements of the SSGB of state or provincial and municipal government and their agencies.
- Develop and nurture strategies and programs to facilitate communication by its clubs with the SSGB and other local governing bodies and clubs within the jurisdiction.
- Provide volunteers to contribute to the work of the SSGB.

Club Mandate

- Govern the sport within its jurisdiction.
- Implement and deliver the LTAD model at the club level.
- Organize teams in accordance with the rules and regulations within the proper jurisdiction.
- Recruit and retain players, coaches, and referees.
- Provide training and competition opportunities for FUNdamentals, Learn to Train, and Active for Life athletes.
- Ensure compliance with the rules, regulations, policies, and financial requirements of the local governing body.
- Ensure communication and compliance with the NSO and SSGB playing rules and equipment standards as well as the rules and regulations of the local governing body.
- Implement and deliver programs for players, coaches, officials, and volunteers.
- Develop responsible administrative, business, and financial practices and procedures to operate the organization in compliance with local laws.
- Develop and nurture strategies and programs to facilitate communication within its membership and with the state or regional governing body.
- Provide representation at meetings of the local governing body and appropriate meetings of the SSGB.

Once the mandates are identified and agreed on, a sport can align major responsibilities as indicated in figure 11.5. The mandates of the sport should be listed in the columns; and the LTAD stages, in the rows. Optimally, organizations at all levels of sport would work together to determine where each of them has responsibility and at what stage. Then, further details for LTAD implementation can be determined as outlined in figure 11.6. Using both figure 11.5 and 11.6 creates a clear delineation of responsibilities among the national (NSO), state or provincial (SSGB), local (LSGB), and club levels. This permits organizations to fulfill roles such as leadership, education, management, and coordination in the development and delivery of programs and services. When this work is done by organizations, the sport can then align with other systems.

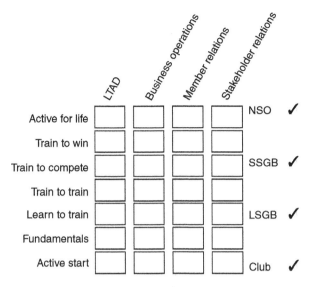

FIGURE 11.5 Checklist of organizations' responsibilities.

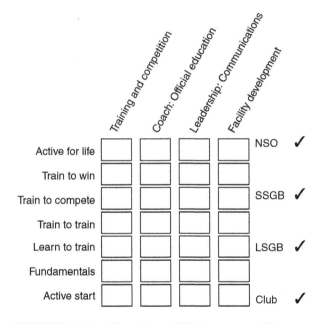

FIGURE 11.6 Checklist of LTAD responsibilities.

System Alignment From a Sector Perspective

Health, education, recreation, and sport share common interests and objectives. All sectors are engaged in the delivery of opportunities for health and wellness with the objective of helping people reach their potential. All are providers of programming and facilities, many of which can be used for sport and physical activity. Although these sectors have common objectives, they have traditionally operated, for the most part, independently from one another. Yet all have much to gain from a closer alignment of values and mission, and a better coordination of roles and responsibilities.

Sport for life (S4L), using the LTAD pathway, has recently emerged as a framework and philosophy for promoting lifelong engagement in sport and physical activity, and encouraging the ethical pursuit of sport excellence. From its origins in national sport policy, S4L has grown to become a movement of like-minded people and organizations committed to improving the quality of sport globally. The core values and foundational principles of S4L go far beyond those traditionally associated with sport and athleticism; proponents look to create collaboration where none existed previously.

When collaboration occurs, partnerships are forged, resulting in higher levels of health and fitness and significantly improved performance in daily living, in the workplace, and in every facet of life.

The health, education, recreation, and sport sectors are complex, coexisting on a broad continuum and spanning from national to local community interests (figure 11.7). Governments at all levels, along with nongovernmental agencies and nonprofits, are active in all sectors, as are businesses. Equally important is the informal involvement of individuals and small groups at the local level. All sectors intersect at the individual participant, regardless of whether linkages exist between sectors through a myriad of organizational, policy, and funding relationships. Although each sector ranges from addressing local to international interests, they vary in characteristics.

The health sector differs depending on the country. Some countries manage health nationally with direct support from and relationships with local authorities. Others decentralize control to state or provincial jurisdictions, allowing for a variety of delivery options depending on regional needs. Still others have localized management and delivery of health services,

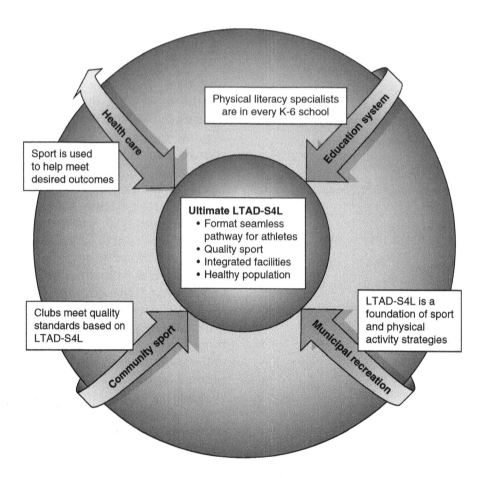

FIGURE 11.7 Four sectors coming together.

with limited support and guidance from senior governments. Globally, support for health services ranges tremendously. The level of government support for health services affects the degree to which the government encourages people to engage in sport and physical activity. Obviously, when senior governments fund health, they are motivated to support quality sport and physical activity because of the well-researched fiscal benefits of participation in those activities.

Healthy body, healthy mind has been a multigenerational mantra. Educational institutions have built gymnasiums and fields for a century. Similar to health, education receives a wide range of support depending on the nation and the specific jurisdiction within it. Compounding this is the complexity of issues local education administrators must address in delivering quality programs in a climate of diminishing resources and increasing parental demands.

From a public policy perspective, the key characteristic of recreation is that municipalities (i.e., governments closest to the community level) are the lead providers. Cities and towns make enormous investments in public recreation infrastructure in the form of community centers, arenas, pools, gymnasiums, playing fields, and many other facilities. These facilities are typically programmed to provide all forms of leisure activity, not just sport. With the objective of promoting healthy living among the population at large, the services provided are oriented to achieve the broadest possible participation.

In contrast to recreation, senior governments and national organizations take a much more prominent role with sport, as well as with multisport bodies such as Olympic committees and sport commissions. In this formal context, there is a high degree of vertical organization and consistency in standards; activity is structured around local, state or provincial, national, and international competition and training for these events.

Given the variety of characteristics of the four sectors, integrating programs and services may be challenging. However, those programs and services intersect at the individual participant, and being athlete centered allows for efficient alignment and integration. Figure 11.8 shows the three levels of organizations (from the top down: federal, provincial or state, and community) and the four sectors (from left to right: health, education, recreation, and sport) who directly affect the parent and the athlete.

The following list identifies actions that the four sectors can take to address their common interests and objectives. The question to ask is, are these actions happening in your community or country?

Creating Networking Opportunities

- The Sport Matters Group in Canada has brought together nine government departments that are now working together to see how each can use sport to further the objective of its area of government. For example, sport has been identified as the second most powerful connection newcomers to the nation have after family and ahead of religion (Mulhollan, 2008). By recognizing this, the immigration department is looking at ways to use sport to assist newcomers.

- The City of Vancouver has created VACNet (n.d.), an organization made up of people in the city who are concerned about the health and well-being of the

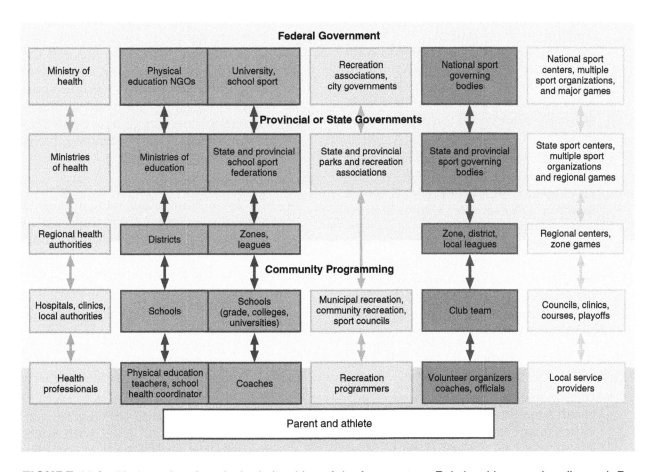

FIGURE 11.8 Horizontal and vertical relationships of the four sectors. Relationships are also diagonal. For example, stage and provincial sport organizations also work with regional sport centers, zone games, recreation departments, schools, and so on.

Reprinted, by permission, from V. Greebe and R. Way, 2011, *Multi channel* (Victoria, Canada).

population. They are from a wide variety of organizations and institutions and get together to identify common issues and then work together to find and implement solutions.

- Sport councils at the local level are a way different sports can sit at the same table to address common issues. From an LTAD perspective, sport councils should not limit themselves to lobbying local government for facilities, but should also provide a forum for working together in the best interest of athletes.

Integrating Strategic Planning

- Because of the structure of the sport system, organizations are usually established with independent governance, and planning is typically done independently, or alone. From an LTAD system integration perspective, joint vertical planning would be a logical evolution that would enable national, state or provincial, and local organizations to work together to create an integrated strategic plan based on figures 11.5 and 11.6.

- Similar to vertical planning, horizontal planning would choose a level in figure 11.8 at which organizations could work together. For example, a sport council composed of clubs, a recreation department, a school board, and a local health authority could identify a challenge or opportunity it could address to improve the quality of sport and physical activity in the community, resulting in improved health and wellness.

Building Infrastructure to Integrate All Four Sectors

- In many communities throughout North America, schools have been built independent from recreation facilities. When sport facilities are built, they too are separate. Hospitals and health clinics are built somewhere else. Based on the concept of system integration, those agencies could have a collabora-

tive approach to facilities development (planning, access, operations).

- Years ago, businesses recognized that working together was significantly more effective than working separately. As a result, malls exist all over North America. This mentality is slowly taking hold in the public sector. Based on system integration, eventually facilities for schools, recreation centers, clubs, and health authorities could be built in the same location offering integrated programs and services.

Delivering Integrated Programming

- The S4L concept allows health, education, and sport to provide programs that develop physical literacy. In delivering such programming, all sectors benefit from healthy physical development.

- In North America, community sport clubs are generally single sport. This is not the case in Europe, nor is it the case with private clubs. From a system integration perspective, single-sport community clubs can build alliances with complementary clubs to create programming efficiency and more athlete-centered sport.

Delivering Integrated Services

- Many youths are much more interested in pursuing sport than they are in education or attending a health clinic. However, combining sport and education can have many benefits. Global examples, such as grassroots soccer (FIFA, 2007), illustrate how sports can effectively be incorporated into educational systems. On a more local level, schools are offering sport programs and academies with the goal of keeping kids in school.

- Another opportunity to integrate services is at the local level with sport club registration; rather than compete with each other for players and athletes, coaches at various clubs connect to offer complementary services. Getting together at the local level using an athlete-centered approach rather than a sport- or institute-centered approach will result in different decisions, ultimately making the mom in the opening vignette much happier!

LTAD and S4L Implications for Policy Development

Organizations are governed by laws and policies that articulate how they act toward achieving their vision, mission, and mandate. S4L can be used as a guide to form and shape policy, which builds system integration. S4L is a framework individuals, organizations, governments, and sectors can work within to find places to link, to integrate. The first column in figure 11.9 is based on the three key actions of LTAD, which have been explained throughout the previous chapters. From those actions the primary output is increased quality of sport and physical activity, resulting in the following initial outcomes:

- More participation across all LTAD stages, which includes Active Start through the Train to Win and Active for Life stages

- Greater sustainability, including the following:
  - Enhanced capacity: human, infrastructure, financial, and technological
  - Enhanced interaction: philosophy, values, communication, and governance
- More frequent strategic use of sport and physical activity for community development

These three outcomes lead to a country or community improving the sport performance of its citizens and ultimately the health and well-being of the nation. For a country or community to achieve these desired outcomes, LTAD must be implemented in a comprehensive manner, as follows:

Increased Quality of Sport and Physical Activity

- Pathways for athlete and participant development are built within every sport and physical activity.
- Resources are made available to all sectors to improve quality.
- Programs for children strive to develop physical literacy first.

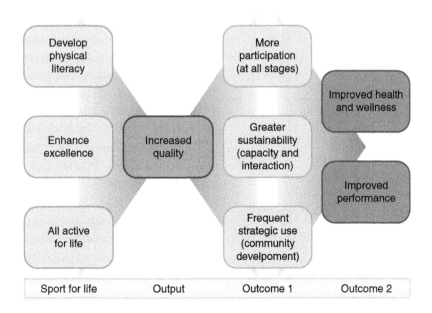

FIGURE 11.9 The how-to of policy development using S4L.

- Programs are based on capability.
- Competition is reviewed and reconstructed based on LTAD.
- Coaching, officiating, governance, and facilities consider LTAD in their design and execution.
- Periodization of athlete training, competition, and recovery programs are developed according to maturation and individual capability, not chronological age.
- Retention strategies are built into competitive and recreational programs.
- Programs and services for developing athletic talent are based on LTAD.
- Success is achieved through scientific and informed methods of training, competition, and recovery.
- S4L training and resources are developed to support people who deliver athletic and physical activity programming (coaches, instructors, administrators).
- Programs and services available for end users (athletes, parents) are modified using LTAD factors.
- Health authorities and educators who can influence programming use LTAD to review and improve what is offered.
- Following LTAD implementation, measurements are in place to determine the effectiveness of the changes in delivering quality sport and physical activity.

More Participation in Sport and Physical Activity

- Increased physical literacy occurs among children and youth.
- Quality daily physical education in schools is delivered by specifically trained educators.
- More children, youth, and adults register for sport and physical activity programs.
- Physically active people with fundamental skills remain active for life.
- Fewer youth drop out of sport and physical activity.
- More people remain active into adulthood and beyond.

- People with all levels of interest, regardless of ability or disability, are included in sport and physical activity.
- People with all levels of interest, regardless of physical, intellectual, or sensory abilities, participate in sport and physical activity.
- LTAD-based programs develop more athletes who are achieving excellence at the national and international levels.
- There is an increased understanding of the role sport and recreation play in serving larger societal needs.

More Sustainable Sport and Physical Activity

- Values-based leadership underpins programs and services.
- Investment is based on S4L values and principles.
- Human resource capacity is built through increased system integration.
- Facilities and the programs in them are designed with LTAD in mind.
- Multiple sectors recognize the value of sport and physical activity, fostering the diversification of financial resources.
- Technology is used to create efficiencies and support that are appropriate to each LTAD stage.
- Policies and practices adopted by sporting organizations at all levels and others who deliver athletic programming (schools, recreation departments, health organizations) are based on S4L, allowing for alignment and sequencing of programs that result in building on the strengths of each sector.
- S4L philosophies are embraced, allowing the LTAD framework to build synergies for success.
- Using the LTAD framework, organizations recognize their roles and responsibilities regarding individual and organizational development.
- Communication is clear and consistent, based on developing physical literacy, enhancing excellence, and ensuring an active life for all.

- Governance structures promote collaboration, striving to improve performance as well as health and wellness.

- Human resources and finances are used to produce maximum results.

- Sport and sectors such as health, recreation, and education move away from a "silo" mentality and independent strategic plans to increased collaboration and integrated strategic approaches.

- The entire system commits to long-term outcomes via short-term gains, accepting that achieving long-term outcomes may or may not deliver short-term rewards.

- S4L peer networks are established to share knowledge and innovation.

- Policies that are adopted by all levels of government (federal, state or provincial, municipal) in all departments that influence sport and physical activity programming (e.g., recreation, sport, health, education) are based on S4L.

- Revised versions of government sport policies are based on S4L.

**Frequent Strategic Use
of Sport and Physical Activity**

- Attendance and attention are improved at school through the use of sport and physical activity programming.

- New immigrants engage in community activities through sport and physical activity programming.

- Sport is developed to promote social inclusion, and social development is promoted through sport.

- Youths are inspired through athlete role model programs.

- Sport and physical activity are used to drive health outcomes.

- Sport and physical activity are used as platforms from which to deliver information to those at risk of diseases.

- Teenage pregnancy is reduced through participation in sport (Sabo, Miller, Farrell, Melnick, & Barnes, 1999).

- Environments "in which people can come together to work towards the same goal, show respect for others and share space and equipment" are created (International Platform on Sport and Development, 2011).

- Psychosocial support to people affected by disaster is provided through sport participation: "Sport and physical activity can provide a cooperative and supportive environment to build resiliency and social cohesion" (International Council of Sport Science and Physical Education, 2009).

- "Girls and women who participate in sport and physical activity . . . demonstrate higher self-esteem as well as improved self-perception, self-worth, self-efficacy, and so on" (International Platform on Sport and Development, 2009, p. 5). (This can occur in both developed and developing communities and countries.)

- The employability of youth is enhanced through involvement in sport programs.

Summary

Effective implementation of LTAD depends heavily on collaboration and system alignment. Because LTAD cannot be fully achieved without the health, recreation, sport, and education sectors working in tandem, it is imperative that they recognize their roles and make the changes necessary for improving the quality of sport and physical activity.

However, change doesn't begin at the organizational level. It requires the dedication and vision of individuals encouraging and driving it forward. At each LTAD stage, people in various positions are needed to perform services and support those who are working through the stages. These people must understand the value of their positions and try to connect with other elements of the system.

From the sport organization and sector perspectives individuals again must take the first steps toward alignment, but these organizations should have the capacity to make fundamental changes when necessary. Networking as well as establishing integrated strategic planning, infrastructure, programming, and services are the keys to system alignment.

System alignment leads to increased quality in sport and physical activity, which encourages more participation, which in turn creates more sustainable activity. Not only do the sectors themselves benefit from this collaboration, but their involvement also makes it possible for everyone to become physically active and remain that way for life.

Questions for Reflection

- Looking at your own role within the sport system, how are you connected to other elements of the system such as sport associations, clubs, recreation departments, schools, government departments, and health professionals? How might you promote more collaboration among these groups?

- If you are a sport club coach or administrator, has your club officially adopted LTAD principles? Does your regional or national governing body have guidelines for LTAD available?

- If you are a health professional who works with athletes, do you communicate with coaches to discuss athlete health needs and general practices for reducing and avoiding injuries?

- If you are involved in creating sport, recreation, and health policy at the municipal, state, provincial, or federal level of government, have LTAD principles been incorporated into the policies that influence sport development and athlete health in your jurisdiction?

- If you are a school teacher, school coach, or school administrator, do you know whether your school or district has built linkages with local sport clubs and recreation groups to promote a collaborative relationship in delivering sport programs to youth? Does your school or district have copies of LTAD guidelines?

References

Dalton, S. (2004). *Our overweight children. What parents, schools, and communities can do to control the fatness epidemic.* Berkley and Los Angeles, CA: University of California Press.

FIFA (2007, November 19). Grassroot soccer: Football's fight against aids. Retrieved from www.fifa.com/aboutfifa/socialresponsibility/news/newsid=640480/index.html

International Council of Sport Science and Physical Education. (2009). Recreation sport and social change in sustainable community development [Bulletin]. Retrieved from http://www.icsspe.org/content/no-55-cd-rom

International Platform on Sport and Development. (2009). *Thematic profile: Sport and gender.* Retrieved from http://assets.sportanddev.org/downloads/090615_sport_and_gender_thematic_profile_for_print.pdf

International Platform on Sport and Development. (2011). The role of sport in peace-building. Retrieved from www.sportanddev.org/en/learnmore/sport_and_peace_building/the_role_of_sport_in_peace_building/

Montopoli, P. (2009). *Canadian Soccer Association strategic plan 2009-2014* [Figure] (p.16) Ottawa, ON: Canadian Soccer Association.

Mulhollan, E. (2008). What sport can do: The true sport report. Retrieved from www.cces.ca/files/pdfs/TS_report_EN_webdownload.pdf

Sabo, D., Miller, K., Farrell, M., Melnick, M., & Barnes, G. (1999). High school athletic participation, sexual behavior and adolescent pregnancy: A regional study. *Journal of Adolescent Health, 25* (3), 207-216.

VACNet partners. (n.d.). Retrieved from www.canadiansportforlife.ca/resources/vancouver-sport-strategy

To Learn More

Balyi, I., Way, R., Norris, S., Cardinal, C., & Higgs, C. (2005). *Canadian sport for life: Long-Term Athlete Development.* Vancouver, BC: Canadian Sport Centres.

Bahrain Sport for Life [in Arabic]. (2010). Manama, Bahrian.

Corbett, R., & Findlay, H.A. (1999). *Good policies, good governance: A guide for sport organizations.* Ottawa, ON: Centre for Sport and Law

Duffy, P., Balyi, I., Aboud, S., Gregg, R., Daly, P., Harbison, L, et al. (2003). *Building pathways in Irish sport: Towards a plan for the sporting health and well-being of the nation.* Limerick, Ireland: National Coaching and Training Centre.

Hughes, A-M., Keane, S., Lyons, D., Quinn, S., & MacPhail, A. (2005). *Lifelong involvement in sport and physical activity: The LISPA model* [Consultation paper]. Retrieved from www.coachingireland.com/files/The%20LIPSA%20Model.pdf

Montopoli, P. (2009). *Canadian Soccer Association strategic plan 2009-2014* [Figure] (p.16) Ottawa, ON: Canadian Soccer Association.

Continuous Improvement

Graham, the local minor baseball association's president, and Charles, the vice president, had just returned from a regional baseball meeting, where two "sport experts" had given a presentation about how minor leagues can improve. Even though the two men were longtime buddies and had been involved in baseball together for years, they didn't share the same reaction to the meeting.

"How dare they?" Graham fumed. "I've been running this league for 20 years, and I do it the way it was done when I was a kid—the right way." Jim and Andy, the two presenters, had pointed out a number of trends in minor baseball: registration is decreasing, more kids are being injured, and parents are yelling during games. Using examples of leagues they had worked with and strategies they had used in the past, they recommended that leagues replace their T-ball programs with the skill development-based Rally Cap program; that coaches monitor pitch counts more closely; and that organizations raise their overall standards.

"What a bunch of nonsense," Graham continued. "I don't need two hotshots from the city telling me how to run this league." Charles saw things differently. He thought the presentation was interesting and that it actually brought up some good points. Registration *was* going down, and kids *were* getting injured too often. He also hated how so many kids were staying at home playing video games nowadays instead of coming to the ballpark. But it was all for naught: Graham was a traditionalist, and Charles knew that as long as he remained president, the league would not be addressing any of these issues. Charles waited for Graham to cool down and then changed the subject.

For Jim and Andy, this was par for the course. They knew there were many leagues out there run by traditionalists like Graham, to whom they'd never be able to sell change no matter how hard they tried. The truth was that some leagues would say no to change until their Grahams had moved on. Charles, however, was someone they could work with. Even though resisting change comes naturally to everyone, people like Charles were willing to listen. These people were eventually able to understand that with these changes came the help and resources needed for continually improving the quality of their sports.

The concept of continuous improvement, a founding principle of LTAD, is drawn from the respected Japanese industrial philosophy known as kaizen (Catalyst for Change, 2008). Change is happening around the world at an increasingly rapid pace. Almost daily we are introduced to new advances in technology and changes in our social, political, and economic realities. Change challenges us to move forward, adapt, and modify our behaviors and institutions as we integrate these changes into our lives.

Sport is no different. At the highest stage of LTAD, Train to Win, international coaches and sport scientists continuously work to make athletes faster, smarter, and stronger. In the meantime the human race gets taller and bigger (Harris, 1997). Training and competition for international-caliber athletes change with regularity as international sport federations partner with both the media and sponsors to modify their sports to capture larger markets. Juxtaposed against this international sport arena are the early LTAD stages, where delivery agencies face changes in support from government, requiring them to place more emphasis on return on investment. Clubs and community centers face the challenge of diminishing financial resources, aging volunteers, and increasing demands of parents, which create a constant pressure to change.

In the meantime the aggressive advancement of sedentary technologies is changing children's behavior as a multibillion-dollar industry seeks to transfix our children to digital screens: televisions, computers, electronic play stations, handheld devices, smartphones, and others as yet unimagined.

Sport and physical activity must change quickly to remain relevant in this ever-changing world of global digital technology. In light of the unprecedented advances in sedentary technologies, sport and physical activity require continuous improvement and change, or they risk becoming irrelevant. Ongoing changes in our technology, social behavior, and political and economic realities challenge these existing sport and physical activity paradigms. Change ultimately confronts personal beliefs and practices, which can be challenging for many people. However, action that results in improvement has to start with individuals who can ignite change within their spheres of influence. Working from this premise, this chapter shows how to continuously improve sport and the physical activity experience.

Three continuous improvement themes permeate LTAD:

- LTAD responds and reacts to scientific and sport-specific innovations and new observations and is subject to continuous research in all its aspects.

- LTAD, as a continuously evolving vehicle for change, reflects the emerging trends of physical education, sport, recreation, and health to ensure the systematic and logical delivery of programs to participants at all stages and of all ages.

- LTAD promotes the ongoing education and sensitization of federal, provincial or state, and local governments; the mass media; business leaders; sport and recreation administrators; coaches; sport scientists; parents; and educators regarding the interlocking relationships in the areas of physical education, school sport, community recreation, healthy living, lifelong physical activity, and high-performance sport.

Technology Changes

Many have said (e.g., Moore, 1965) that we live in the period of the most rapid technological changes in history. This has far-reaching impacts on all elements of our society, from politics to social mores, economics, education, travel, family structures, and physical activity and sport.

The nature and speed of technological change has dramatic implications for our institutions, our social behavior, and our personal well-being. Although advances in medical technology extend life spans and promise remedies to many debilitating illnesses and conditions, technological innovations in other spheres of human activity threaten to undo these advances in human health, frequently working at cross purposes (albeit unintentionally) by making us more sedentary and less engaged in physical activity. If we turn a blind eye to the power of technology and its implications for change, we risk allowing it to control us. If we are careful to monitor advances in technology and leverage these advances for positive effect within our political, social, educational, and health institutions, we can create opportunities to improve sport and our physical health.

Technological change surrounds us. Today, billions of people surf the World Wide Web and exchange media content and ideas on a daily, and even minute-to-minute, basis, whereas the Internet was essentially nonexistent prior to the early 1990s (World Bank, 2010). Within a very few years—less than the blink of an eye in human history—we have made a leap in global communications akin to the invention of the printing press, radio, or television. Technological advances in medicine have made heart transplants almost commonplace, and new biotechnologies are delivering other startling advances in longevity.

Technological and scientific advances in the realm of sport and physical activity promise to have similar profound effects. Advances in athlete conditioning, nutrition, and other training factors are already producing athletes who are bigger, faster, and stronger and jumping higher than ever before. World record times, heights, and distances for events such as the 100-meter sprint (table 12.1), the pole vault, and the shot put reveal steady improvements and regular record-breaking performances, suggesting that we may never see an end to increases in human sport performance. Much of these records are the result of scientific innovations in training, including the application of new technologies.

TABLE 12.1 Men's 100-Meter World Record Progressions (IAAF ratified)

Year	Time in seconds
1964	10.06
1968	10.03
1968	10.02
1968	9.95
1983	9.93
1987	9.83
1987	9.93
1988	9.92
1988	9.92
1991	9.9
1991	9.86
1994	9.85
1996	9.84
1999	9.79
2002	9.78
2005	9.77
2006	9.77
2006	9.77
2006	9.77
2007	9.74
2008	9.72
2008	9.69
2009	9.58

Data from Butler 2009.

On the other hand, the unrelenting appeal and proliferation of video games and virtual media that simulate real life are drawing unprecedented numbers of people into sedentary behavior, threatening the well-being of sport, human health, and longevity, and the viability of our health care systems. This trend is a primary example of how change and technology can work *against* athlete development and physical activity, and human well-being in general. Those working in the areas of sport, physical activity, and health must take these forces of change into account if they are to advance sport through the principle of continuous improvement.

What are the implications of technological change and associated behavioral shifts for the sport system? New trends and innovations force us to consider changing how we promote and deliver sport programs, and this need for change forces us to confront the paradigms that gave shape to our sporting institutions and practices in the first place.

Paradigm Changes

Whatever the source of change, technological or otherwise, we can expect that the paradigms in our thinking and our approach to sport delivery will be challenged. Following are some of the paradigms that we can expect to be challenged as LTAD interacts with ongoing changes in our technologies, social behavior, and political and economic realities:

- From exclusion to inclusion
- From age to stage
- From quantity to quality
- From independence to integration
- From results based to values based
- From goals for self to goals for society
- From short-term to long-term goals
- From random success to planned success
- From single sport to physical literacy
- Relative age: from age cutoffs to age on date
- From guessing to tracking growth to make use of sensitive periods of accelerated adaptation to training
- From adult to junior periodization
- From adult training to using sensitive periods of adaptation
- From a focus on win–loss records to meaningful competition

From Exclusion to Inclusion

The sport system has many hidden barriers that effectively exclude large segments of society from accessing and participating in sport and physical activity. Whether because of the cost of community hockey registration, social stigmas around sport as an "elitist" pursuit, geographical isolation, or lack of programs adapted for people with disabilities, many people do not pursue sport. Our sport organizations and supporting agencies need to address a broad range of factors so that more people can be included.

This includes moving away from the notion of "cutting" participants. The goal of long-term athlete development (LTAD) is to engage people to play; yet traditional sport approaches involve making player cuts when selecting teams. When sport takes an inclusive approach, no one would have to be cut; rather, every participant would have the opportunity to experience either the same sport program or one that is better suited to their abilities. SportFit, which helps connect children and youth to the activities that are right for them (SportFit Canada, 2009), is an example of a tool for inclusion.

From Age to Stage

The traditional approach to athlete development has looked only at the chronological age of participants, rather than their stage of biological maturation. This fixation on chronological age disregards athletes' capabilities. Shifting to stage- or capability-based structures would dramatically improve the balance and value of competition, increase safety, and address the unique training requirements of individuals. An approach more appropriate than the one we follow today would be to group athletes for training and competition according to their capabilities instead of using arbitrary age cutoff dates (see chapter 5).

From Quantity to Quality

Are we delivering sport and recreation programs that address generalized needs for a generalized audience? Or are we being attentive to the range of needs stretching between recreational participants and elite performers? One size does not fit all here. Athletes require quality coaching and competitions and facilities appropriate to their needs at each stage of their development.

Often, the reward system—the funding provided from sponsors or government—is based on the number of participants involved in a program, not the quality of the program itself. LTAD is about improving the quality of the programs delivered so that the right one is offered to the right person at the right time.

From Independence to Integration

The sport system is composed of sporting organizations, recreation departments, educational institutions, health care professionals, and supporting government agencies at the local, state or provincial, and federal levels. Because these groups often work independently of one another, athletes suffer in their training and development as a result of a lack of efficiency and accountability in the coordination of necessary support services and personnel.

In North America, sports seek to be independent of each other and compete on every level for funding, athletes, facilities, and the like. Independence is taken to the extreme in the United States, where there are often multiple national associations in the same sport. At the other end of the spectrum is the European multisport club, where the integration of activities at the local level allows for athletes to easily transfer among sports to find one that matches their abilities.

From Results Based to Values Based

Because the traditional approach in sports is to win at all costs from an early age, athlete training and competition are frequently biased toward achieving short-term results. Most often, the process required to achieve a short-term result does not support long-term engagement and performance in the sport. Short-term thinking is reflected in coaches who force athletes to specialize prematurely, parents who yell abuse at officials, and athletes who turn to banned substances for performance enhancement. An athlete-centered, values-based approach to training and competition would shift our thinking toward an appreciation of fun and fitness as well as the pursuit of excellence.

From Goals for Self to Goals for Society

Leaders in sport need to consider how sport can contribute to better health and wellness in communities. Sport organizations, which have primarily focused on short-term performance results, need to widen their scope to consider how their programs can help keep people active and healthy for the long term. Such a shift would contribute to society by enhancing social, economic, and environmental sustainability by improving the health of the population.

From Short-Term to Long-Term Goals

Parents often live in the moment, along with their children, by determining success based on the win or loss of Friday's game. That pressure is transferred to the coach, who structures training and competition to lead to immediate success. This often compromises the achievement of longer-term goals. For example, high school coaches often plant their tall players under the basket and implore them not to let the ball hit the floor. This strategy may help win games in the short term, but it never develops the tall players' ball-handling abilities. At some point those tall player will be among other tall players, and the most skilled players will be the ones who succeed. As tall players try out for higher-level teams, no one will care about their win–loss record in high school if they cannot handle the ball! Parents' and coaches' focus on short-term success has ultimately excluded players from long-term success. This situation occurs across many sports, especially those in which decision making is a key component. Coaches and parents who make decisions for their players (e.g., by shouting instructions from the sideline) impede the players' ability

to make split-second decisions in the course of a game.

From Random Success to Planned Success

Sport organizations occasionally have the chance to celebrate the special success of one athlete or team, or perhaps the overall performance of a cohort of athletes in a program. The question is whether this success was the result of a logical and repeatable process of training and competition, or simply the isolated result of a particular group of skilled coaches, the random arrival of a few genetically endowed athletes, or the effective direction of one sport administrator who may or may not be involved in the long term. Sport organizations need to plan for success by ensuring consistent processes in athlete training, talent identification, coach education, officiating, sport administration, funding, and facilities development.

From Single Sport to Physical Literacy

Young athletes are often channeled into single sports and forced to specialize prematurely as a result of zealous coaches or parents who believe they have recognized a special talent or competitive advantage in that athlete. Athletes who emphasize a single sport develop only a limited range of sport and physical movement skills, whereas those who participate in a variety of sports and physical activities during childhood acquire a wider range of skills. All parents need to encourage the development of physical literacy, because it is conducive to greater levels of achievement and engagement in sport over the full span of the athlete's life.

Relative Age: From Age Cutoffs to Age on Date

Using cutoff dates to determine age groupings immediately creates advantages and disadvantages within the group. (Good luck to the November- and December-born babies in sport!) Research has shown a bias toward participants born in the early months immediately following an age cutoff, which is described as an older relative age (Morris & Nevill, 2006). So-called talent identification often only identifies children who are bigger, stronger, and faster because they are older—not those who are actually more talented. In individual sports, relative age is easily addressed by changing to an "age on date" system of competition (i.e., athletes are chosen based on their age on the date of the competition), thus rotating the relative age. A solution to the age dilemma is more difficult in team sports. One alternative is to use an 18-month age grouping instead of an annual or biannual grouping, which results in each participant, over the course of a three-year period, spending one year in the older third of the age group, one year in the younger third, and one year in the middle third.

From Guessing to Tracking Growth to Make Use of Sensitive Periods of Accelerated Adaption to Training

Training programs for younger children are often based on chronological age with no consideration for their developmental age. To address this issue, methodologies to accurately measure athletes' biological markers (e.g., onset of peak height velocity) are needed. Once these are in place, coaches can develop training programs that capitalize on the sensitive periods of accelerated adaption to training.

From Adult to Junior Periodization

Adult periodization planning has been in place for more than 50 years. Single-sport periodization is now applied to younger athletes who are often in multisport environments. When this happens, one coach's periodized plan often conflicts with the plans of the three or four other coaches of the same athlete, which may result in overtraining and burnout. Correct junior periodization considers the Train to Train athletes who are in multiple sport situations.

From a Focus on Win–Loss Records to Meaningful Competition

The structure and purpose of competition often fail to support the long-term needs of developing athletes. All too frequently, the primary driver of competition is to determine a winner or deliver a championship title. The drive to win at all costs, again, may compromise the training of the athlete for long-term gains, or it may result in unreasonable competition costs or compromising the educational needs of the athlete.

Influencing Change

In sport and physical activity, as in life, we all have four options when faced with change:

1. Change the things within our control.
2. Influence others to change if change itself is not within our control.
3. Do nothing.
4. Work to inhibit change.

Action 1 involves changing whatever is within our control. Because change usually affects others as well, awareness, education, planning, and leadership are required. However, the change is ultimately made and action is taken.

Action 2 involves convincing others within our sphere of influence to make the needed change. This action is much more complex than action 1. It requires awareness, education, planning, and leadership in a variety of settings and sectors in multiple collaborative partnerships that have a plethora of visions and missions. Organizations and individuals who seek to influence change in others must first change what they can to ensure credibility.

Following are examples of things individuals and organizations may control and what they can influence.

Athlete Training

- Control: Programs can be designed based on the developmental age of each athlete.

- Influence: Others can be encouraged to ensure that training is developmentally appropriate.

Coaching

- Control: Coaches can consider relative and developmental age in their training of athletes.
- Influence: Coaches can educate parents regarding the time required to succeed and other LTAD factors.

Competition

- Control: Sport leaders can change regional sport leagues, competition rules, and formats to better serve the developmental needs of athletes (e.g., adopt LTAD-based rules in a league; see chapter 10).
- Influence: Sport leaders can share strategies for changing competition formats with neighboring leagues and other sport organizations to encourage further change.

Leadership

- Control: Those in senior roles at sport organizations can drive the development of administrative procedures and guidelines through LTAD and True Sport (www.truesportpur.ca) values-based management.
- Influence: Organizations can share their success stories and methodologies with other sport organizations to promote values-based management.

Facilities

- Control: Managers of existing sport and recreation facilities can review how their facilities are being used and by whom, and make changes to improve accessibility for athletes and sport user groups.
- Influence: Sport user groups can approach facility managers to raise concerns regarding accessibility. Governments at the federal, provincial or state, and municipal levels that fund facilities development can stipulate accessibility requirements.

Equipment

- Control: Sport organizations can establish equipment libraries and sponsor equipment swap meets to reduce equipment costs to athletes, improving accessibility to sport and increasing participation numbers.
- Influence: Sport equipment suppliers can partner with sport organizations and offer incentives to establish equipment libraries and swap meets.

Officials

- Control: When working with athletes in the Learn to Train and Train to Train stages, officials can recognize that they are learning and not treat them as adults.
- Influence: Sport leaders can encourage officiating organizations to embrace LTAD-based rule changes made by governing bodies.

Communications

- Control: Everyone in sport can be positive about changes and communicate reasons for such changes.
- Influence: Everyone in sport can encourage others to support changes and communicate reasons for such changes.

Clubs

- Control: Sport environment designers can redesign training environments to facilitate implementing sport-specific LTAD-based changes.
- Influence: Sport leaders can present best practice to others at league and governing body meetings to encourage an increased quality of delivered sport.

National Governing Bodies

- Control: NGB leaders can modify the competition rules and formats of their sanctioned events.
- Influence: Sport leaders can recommend that NGBs change their competition rules and formats and offer to support them in doing so.

State or Provincial Organizations

- **Control:** State or provincial organizations can modify the competition rules and formats of their sanctioned events.
- **Influence:** Sport leaders can provide support for state or provincial organizations to change their competition rules and formats.

Governments

- **Control:** Governments can base their funding and accountability on LTAD-based programming.
- **Influence:** Government organizations can share information with other jurisdictions to help them implement LTAD.

Sport in Schools

- **Control:** School administrators and teachers can ensure that all students participate in developmentally appropriate sport and physical activity. For example, they can stop having them play dodgeball and instead teach them a range of fundamental movement skills.
- **Influence:** Parents and community leaders can recommend to school boards that they embed LTAD values and principles in their policies and guidelines.

Municipal Recreation

- **Control:** Municipal recreation leaders can review their developmental programs to ensure that they contribute to developing physical literacy.
- **Influence:** Municipal recreation leaders can encourage facility user groups, including sport clubs, to deliver LTAD-based programs.

Health

- **Control:** Parents, coaches, and others who are in role-model positions can control their lifestyles to ensure that they are healthy. Eating right, maintaining personal fitness, and managing stress are critical for those in leadership positions. People need to challenge themselves to change their behaviors to ensure that they are positive role models.
- **Influence:** Sport leaders should research and share information with athletes so they understand healthy options when participating in sport and life.

Actions for Continuous Improvement

Change is a process undertaken to achieve a new vision. It requires shifts in personal habits and organizational cultures. The period of greatest risk, from a people perspective, is during transitions. There is a tremendous amount of theory and discussion on creating, initiating, and managing change. The general consensus is that change takes place when a strong case for it has been made and effective leadership and clear communication show exactly how the change can be achieved. With this in mind, consider the following eight LTAD actions for continuous improvement.

1. **Pull the stick out of the mud.** Change is challenging for many people. Parents believe that their children should train and compete the way the adult athletes they worship on TV do. Coaches have adopted habits in their thinking and practice over the years. Change is hard for them. They are the proverbial sticks in the mud. Both must be approached with a strong, well-researched case. Like Graham in the opening vignette, some people simply cannot or will not change, and they must be left behind.

2. **Fuel the fire.** Sport organizations need to recognize and support their champions and encourage them onward. Recognition can take a multitude of forms, from featuring them at conferences, workshops, club quality assurance standards, Internet best practice sites, or recognition awards. Organizations also fuel the fire by providing resources to their champions. Often, champions are very self-motivated, so a little support can go a long way. As in the opening vignette, champions such as Jim and Andy need to be supported, and then they can take best practices from other local sport organizations to show Charles how he can ignite change in his association.

3. **Bubble up.** We don't have to wait for our government officials or the leaders of our sport organizations to initiate the changes we want to see in sport. Parents, coaches, and clubs can initiate positive change from the grassroots level and drive it upward through the sport system. Again, considering the opening vignette, if parents become aware of and educated about the benefits of the new programs suggested by Jim and Andy, they can collectively encourage (pressure) the association to implement changes.

4. **Spread the word.** When the change results in positive outcomes in performance and participation, sport organizations need to spread the good news and encourage other groups to pursue similar efforts. They can share these stories of success by documenting them with media releases, newsletter articles, magazine features, and community cable television shows, or simply by sharing them at sport seminars, workshops, and association meetings. Through their presentations to local baseball associations, Jim and Andy were making people aware that change was happening with positive results. They were sharing information.

5. **Walk the talk.** Organizations control and deliver programs and services. The first action in creating large-scale change is to make LTAD-based modifications to the things the organization controls. Then, having demonstrated a commitment to change, the organization is better able to influence change in other organizations. Often, when the commitment to change—to improve—is made, people who struggle with change protest. It is important, at a certain point, to just do it and not waiver! Indecisiveness usually creates more problems than had originally existed. Jim and Andy could speak confidently at the local baseball association meeting because they had already implemented pitch counts and coaching standards in all the programs they controlled. When skeptical associations said it could not be done, Jim and Andy could always counter with their own stories of success.

6. **Tools, not rules.** LTAD is a set of guidelines to help organizations deliver quality programs; it is not a mandate. It is a framework in which individuals and organizations can collectively provide and share tools to facilitate continuous improvement. When Graham, as president of the local association, chose not to implement the recommended changes, sanctions were not brought against the association because Jim and Andy knew that would not benefit the game or the kids. At that point, LTAD implementation was not a requirement or a rule. First, they would provide all the supporting resources to encourage change. Then, they would monitor the situation to determine whether remaining under Graham's guidance actually hurt the association more than losing a longtime volunteer who was a stick in the mud.

7. **Celebrate.** Change is hard. Often a lot of work is involved to continuously improve. So, when progress is happening—celebrate! Share the joy that the quality of sport and physical activity has improved for children, youth, and adults of all ages. For example, when a national organization embarks on making changes, they should also create a program that recognizes and celebrates those who have the courage and conviction to implement the new programs to improve sport in their local communities. Organizations need to recognize and celebrate quality.

8. **Together forever.** Relationships within sport and the sport system are often framed as an "us versus them" proposition. In many instances, this is an especially destructive paradigm. Often, when sport groups adopt a knee-jerk defensive posture toward one another, they deny themselves the advantages and the progress that could be realized by developing synergistic relationships. When individuals and groups within the sport system can change *versus* to *and* (i.e., "us *and* them"), they create win–win situations for both parties. Unfortunately, Graham immediately viewed Jim and Andy from a "versus" perspective, not realizing that they wanted to contribute to the success of the local association. They understand that local quality programs are the foundation of national success; plus, having active kids learning skills improves the health and wellness of society. If Graham could have seen the world through an "and" lens, he might have had an open mind and found ways to work with Jim and Andy.

Summary

The principle of continuous improvement benefits any area of life. As the world changes and evolves, continuous improvement is required just to keep up. The sport sector is a prime example. The fact that records are constantly being broken and athletes are growing ever faster and stronger is an indication that sport theory and technology continue to develop.

Improvement cannot occur without change: change leads to improvement, and improvement encourages further change. This pattern affects existing paradigms within the sport world. LTAD, in its effort to alter the structure of athlete development, challenges many of sport's paradigms. As LTAD takes hold, these old ways of thinking begin to adapt.

Rule structure is one of the main areas of sport that needs to change for LTAD to be realized. Coaches need to worry less about strategizing with young players and more about the overall development of each athlete. Rules encouraging less-result-oriented approaches should be incorporated. Sometimes all it takes is the effort of one or two people to make these changes happen.

When faced with change, people have the choice to embrace and encourage change directly, to try to influence change indirectly by focusing on the people who control the situation, to simply do nothing, or to actually resist the change. When it comes to the many facets of the sport industry, change can either be accepted or rejected by those at every level.

Questions for Reflection

- What changes have you seen in your favorite sport?
- Of the paradigms listed, which three are most applicable to your situation?
- What rules, in the sport you participate in, encourage coaches to strategize with young players (Learn to Train stage), and what rules allow for the overall development of athletes?
- What things can you control, and what things can you influence with respect to your involvement in sport?
- What are the eight steps to continuous improvement in sport and physical activity?

References

Butler, M. (Ed.). (2009). *12th IAAF World Championships in athletics: IAAF statistics handbook.* Monte Carlo: International Association of Athletics Federations.

Catalyst for Change. (2008). *Kaizen culture: What is Kaizen?* [PowerPoint presentation]. Retrieved from www.c4c.ltd.uk/docs/Lean_Presentations/1.2-Kaizen-Culture.pdf

Harris, B. (1997). Growing taller, living longer? Anthropometric history and the future of old age. *Ageing and Society, 17* (5), 491-512. doi: 10.1017/S0144686X97006594

Morris, J., & Nevill, M. (2006). *Sportnation: A sporting chance: Enhancing opportunities for high-level sporting performance: Influence of 'relative age'.* Leicestershire, UK: Loughborough University.

Moore, G. (1965). Cramming more components onto integrated circuits. *Electronics 38* (8). Retrieved from ftp://download.intel.com/museum/Moores_Law/Articles-Press_Releases/Gordon_Moore_1965_Article.pdf

SportFit Canada. (2009). *See SportFit in action.* Retrieved from www.sportfitcanada.com/?challenge=7&section=2

World Bank. (2010). *World development indicators.* Retrieved from www.google.ca/publicdata/explore?ds=d5bncppjof8f9_&met_y=it_net_user_p2&tdim=true&dl=en&hl=en&q=global+internet+usage+graph#ctype=l&strail=false&nselm=h&met_y=it_net_user_p2&scale_y=lin&ind_y=false&rdim=country&idim=country:CAN&ifdim=country&tdim=true&hl=en&dl=en

To Learn More

James, K., & Posner, B. (2002*). Leadership the challenge: The most trusted source on becoming a better leader.* San Francisco: Jossey-Bass.

Heath, C., & Heath, D. (2008). *Made to stick: Why some ideas survive and others die.* New York: Random House.

Heath, C., & Heath, D. (2010). *Switch: How to change things when change is hard.* New York: Broadway Books.

Gladwell, M. (2008). *Outliers: The story of success.* New York: Little, Brown.

Roberts, W. (1987). *Leadership secrets of Attila the Hun.* New York: Warner Books.

True Sport. (2011). *CCES congratulates True Sport members for embracing values-based sport.* Retrieved from www.cces.ca/en/news-156-cces-congratulates-true-sport-members-for

Part III

Stages of Long-Term Athlete Development

Part III provides detailed information about each stage of LTAD. Key information about each stage is provided including things that parents and coaches should be aware of and details about what programs should focus on.

To implement the LTAD model, people must fully understand the seven stages. Administrators, coaches, and parents should also remember that moving from one stage to another is based on the athlete's development and not just chronological age; however, chronological age can be used as a guide. Some stages also identify a developmental age. For example, the beginning of the growth spurt identifies a specific developmental age, which occurs at widely varying chronological ages. Males and females develop at different rates, and their ages differ through the stages. LTAD, therefore, requires the identification of early, average, and late maturers to design training and competition programs that match athletes' trainability and readiness.

The number of stages changes slightly between early specialization and late specialization sports, and early specialization sports have unique requirements that affect the definition of their LTAD stages. The basic seven-stage LTAD pathway is covered in this part of the book.

1. **Active Start**. Until age 6, it is all about play and mastering basic movement skills! Children should be able to have fun with physical activity through both structured and unstructured free play that incorporates a variety of body movements. An early active start enhances the development of brain function, coordination, social skills, gross motor skills, emotions, and imagination. It also helps children build confidence, develop posture and balance, build strong bones and muscles, achieve a healthy weight, reduce stress, sleep well, move skillfully, and enjoy being active.

2. **FUNdamentals**. From ages 6 to 9 in boys and 6 to 8 in girls, children should participate in a variety of well-structured activities that develop fundamental movement skills and overall motor skills including agility, balance, and coordination. However, activities and programs must maintain a focus on fun, and formal competition should be only minimally introduced.

3. **Learn to Train**. From ages 8 to 11 in girls and 9 to 12 in boys, or until the onset of the growth spurt, children are ready to begin developing foundational sport skills. The emphasis should be on acquiring a wide range of skills necessary for a number of sporting activities. Although it is often tempting to overdevelop "talent" at this age through excessive single-sport training and competition (as well as early positioning in team sports), this can have a negative effect on later stages of development if the child pursues a late specialization sport. This early specialization promotes

one-sided physical, technical, and tactical development and increases the likelihood of injury and burnout.

4. **Train to Train**. The ages that define this stage for boys and girls are based on the onset and duration of the growth spurt, which is generally from ages 11 to 15 for girls and 12 to 16 for boys. This is the stage at which people are physiologically responsive to stimuli and training; in other words, the time to start "building the engine" and exploiting the sensitive periods of accelerated adaptation to training (see chapter 6). Children should establish an aerobic base, develop speed and strength toward the end of the stage, and further consolidate their basic sport-specific skills and tactics. These youths may play and do their best to win, but they still need to spend more time on skill training and physical development and less on trying to win (process vs. outcome). Concentrating on the process as opposed to the result of a competition leads to better development. This approach is critical to developing top performers and maintaining activity in the long term, so parents should check with their national organizations to ensure that their children's programs have the correct training-to-competition ratio.

5. **Train to Compete**. This stage is about optimizing the engine and teaching participants how to compete. They can either choose to specialize in one sport and pursue a competitive stream, or continue participating at a recreational level and thereby enter the Active for Life stage. In the competitive stream, high-volume and high-intensity training begins to occur year-round.

6. **Train to Win**. Elite athletes with identified talent enter this stage to pursue the most intense training suitable for international winning performances. Athletes with disabilities and able-bodied athletes alike require world-class training methods, equipment, and facilities that meet their personal demands and the demands of the sport.

7. **Active for Life**. Young athletes can enter this stage at essentially any age following the acquisition of physical literacy. If children have been correctly introduced to activity and sport throughout the Active Start, FUNdamentals, and Learn to Train stages, they will have the necessary motor skills and confidence to remain active for life in virtually any sport they choose. For high-performance athletes, this stage represents the transition from a competitive career to lifelong physical activity. They may decide to continue playing sport, thus being competitive for life, or they may become involved in the sport as game officials or coaches. They might also try new sports and activities (e.g., a hockey player taking up golf or a tennis player starting to cycle), thus being fit for life.

Limitations of LTAD

Although LTAD is presented as a stage-based development program, in reality, development is a continuous process. This process has been broken down into stages to better help administrators, coaches, and parents understand that different things are important at different stages of development. It also teaches them how to organize sport and physical activity and run programs for children and youth at various times in their development.

Ages mentioned for any of the stages are approximations and vary from person to person. Unfortunately, there are easily identified visual markers for only one stage, Train to Train, which is marked at the lower end by the onset of the adolescent growth spurt, and at the upper end by the cessation of rapid growth. Although birth is the obvious starting point for Active Start, there is no visible marker for the transition to the FUNdamentals stage, nor for the transition between FUNdamentals and Learn to Train. The end point for Learn to Train is the previously mentioned onset of the adolescent growth spurt. Train to Compete and Train to Win are marked by the sport performance of the athlete.

Moreover, there is no sudden jump from one stage to the next. A child does not go to bed one night in the FUNdamentals stage and wake up in Learn to Train. The shift from one stage to the next is gradual, and there will always be considerable overlap between the upper boundary of one stage and the lower boundary of the next. Therefore, programs (or coaches) should be careful not to fall into the trap of making sudden switches in training regimes or competition formats, especially if such changes are made on the basis of age and not stage of development.

Adjusting training and competition to meet the developmental demands of the athlete is very much easier in individual sports than it is in team sports. In team sports it can be difficult to match the training to the developmental demands of individual athletes; training subgroups of athletes of approximately the same developmental age is probably the best coaches can do.

13

Active Start

Jean dropped off her 3-year-old son, Aidan, at preschool and headed down to the gym for her workout. Unfortunately, there was a burst water main near the gym and the building was closed. With nothing else to do, she headed back to the preschool to wait for her son and had a chance to watch him. Aidan was drawing and playing with building bricks. Then he did some painting, sat in a circle with his friends to sing songs, and got ready to go home.

Aidan wouldn't sit still in the car on the drive and wouldn't settle down when he got home. Jean was getting a bit frazzled. Talking to herself, Jean said, "I sure missed my workout today." A few minutes later, while trying once again to get Aidan to quiet down, she thought, "Perhaps he needed his running and playing time today as well." That got Jean thinking about whether Aidan had the right amount and type of physical activity at his preschool. This made Jean realize that she really didn't know what constituted "good" physical activity for young kids. It was time for her to find out.

This chapter explains why physical activity is so important during Active Start (the first six years of life) and what types of activity are most important. It also describes the important changes that take place in the child's brain during this period and how physical activity can facilitate the brain's optimal development. This is a time of rapid physical and mental change, a time when a love of physical activity can be instilled and when habits of daily activity are developed. Because so much of what children do, or do not do, at this stage is controlled by parents and caregivers—and because they have relatively little independence in terms of how they spend their time—they need physically active role models.

Active Start Importance

Active Start, the first of seven stages of long-term athlete development (LTAD), covers the period from birth to age 6 in both boys and girls. The major objective of this stage of development is to learn fundamental movements and link them together in play. It is also a time when a love of physical activity can be instilled and habits of daily activity developed. During this stage, young children need to see and play with physically active older role models, particularly adult caregivers with whom they spend a great deal of time.

Physical activity is essential for healthy development throughout childhood, but particularly during the first six years. Among its other benefits, physical activity at this stage does the following:

- Enhances the development of brain function, coordination, social skills, gross motor skills, emotions, leadership, and imagination.
- Helps children build confidence and positive self-esteem.
- Helps to build strong bones and muscles, improves flexibility, develops good posture and balance, improves fitness, reduces stress, and improves sleep.
- Promotes healthy weight.
- Helps children learn to move skillfully and to enjoy being active.

Physical activity should be a fun, regular part of the child's daily life—not something that is structured, required, or forced on the child. Active play in a stimulating environment is the best way for young children to be physically active. During this stage children need at least 60 minutes of physical activity every day. This activity time should not be continuous, but broken down into many short periods of active play.

Opportunities for physical activity and active play during Active Start are particularly important for the healthy development of children with disabilities if they are to acquire habits of lifelong activity. Children with disabilities often require specialized equipment, such as wheelchairs or prostheses, to be active. Because this is a period when children with disabilities rapidly outgrow their mobility aids, communities need to find effective ways (e.g., equipment swaps or rentals) to ensure that all children have access to the appropriately sized equipment they need to be active.

Childhood obesity and rising inactivity among children threatens the future health of people in developed countries around the world. This problem needs to be addressed now to prevent a generation of children from growing up with chronic health problems.

To be physically active later in life, people need to feel confident in activity settings. That confidence, as an adult, most often comes from having learned fundamental movement and sport skills as a child.

To create an active and healthy population, we need to give *all* children a sound foundation of movement and sport skills to build on later in life. The first building block of this foundation is to give the child an *active start*.

Physical Activity and the Brain

Giving children an active start is all about building a better brain during the critical first six years of life. The phrase that sums up current thinking about brain development is *Cells that fire together wire together.* In any activity (mental or physical), when a movement or thought occurs, some brain and nerve cells "fire" together to make the thought happen or the movement take place. The more the thought occurs, or the more the action happens, the more the cells involved in the thought or action are linked and the easier it is for the thought or action to transpire again. This linking of the cells occurs because of changes at the place where the two cells meet (called a synapse). When physical and chemical changes take place at the synapse, an electrochemical signal jumps from one cell to the next. This is important because during the first six years of life,

the brain produces millions of new brain cells, and billions of synapses between those brain cells are created. After the age of 6, unused connections between brain cells are "pruned," and only those that are used remain.

The recent discovery of mirror neurons has shed some light on why role models are so important. Neurons are brain cells that occur in many different types. Some types have been known for decades, but new types are still being discovered. Consider mirror neurons, which were discovered only within the last decade. When a child sees someone perform an action and understands the purpose of that action, cells in the child's brain fire in essentially the same pattern as those in the brain of the person performing the action. And we know that cells that fire together, wire together. Mirror neurons therefore explain the mechanism of learning by watching. The firing of mirror neurons is one of the reasons watching a demonstration of a skill is so important for learning, and also why physically active role models are so important for young children. This has huge implications for day care and preschool operations, where, unfortunately, too many caregivers use the time set aside for children's active play to socialize with their coworkers. Children see this nonactivity and model their own play after it.

The purpose of play during Active Start is to create as many physical activity-controlling brain connections as possible so that the brain learns to control the many kinds of movement that make up the building blocks of physical activity and sport later in life.

Critical and Sensitive Periods

Brain development during Active Start is a complex and incompletely understood process. Parts of the brain develop at different times and at different rates. As a result, the brain is best able to learn different skills at different times.

There are well-known milestones in children's physical skill development: sitting up unaided, crawling, standing, taking first steps, running, jumping, catching, and throwing.

There are also ages at which, if the child has not reached the milestone, there is cause for concern. We know that, with good instruction, most children who miss milestones can learn the skill in question. But is there a point beyond which it is too late to learn?

There is some evidence that under conditions of extreme deprivation (see the story of Genie in Rymer, 1993), children may be unable to acquire certain movement skills. Of course, we will never, and should never, conduct experiments that would permit us to say with certainty that critical periods do or do not exist for the learning of activity skills.

There is much more agreement that sensitive periods in childhood development exist, periods in which certain skills are most easily mastered. Figure 13.1 shows some of the best-known sensitive periods for learning during childhood.

We know that the period from birth to about age 5 is a sensitive period for the development of gross motor skills, and that whole-body skills such as walking, running, jumping, catching, throwing, and kicking have sensitive periods for their complete development. For example, the period from 10 to 18 months old appears to be a sensitive period for learning to walk. Because the body and brain are in a sensitive period for leaning basic (gross motor) movement skills that use the body's large muscles, we need to make sure children have the opportunity to learn as many skills as possible, as well as possible, during Active Start.

In the social world of the young child, not being able to perform a basic skill can have serious long-term implications. Take, for example, the skill of learning to ride a bike—the two-wheeled, no-training-wheels skill of riding. This skill is usually learned toward the end of the Active Start stage (often by age 5), and for many children it marks the start of independence. If a group of playmates (in a safe environment) can ride their bikes and explore their neighborhood, they will do so, and a boy who can't ride will be left out. In addition, the children who can ride independently will practice their riding skills and get better at riding. The boy who cannot will be unable to join in and get the practice he really needs. As a result, the difference in skill level between those who can ride and the boy who cannot will get greater and greater, and it will become increasingly difficult for the boy who cannot ride to catch up to his peers. This can lead to his being left out, both physically and socially. The same inability to play with peers and to get more practice can also happen to a child who cannot throw, kick, or catch, and who gets left out of spontaneous neighborhood games.

Maturity and Body Movements

Babies are born almost completely helpless, with little or no voluntary control over any of their movements. During the first few years

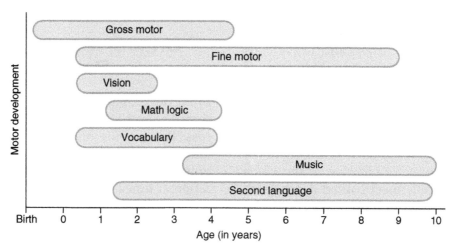

FIGURE 13.1 Sensitive periods in childhood development.

of life, there is a well-established pattern of developing movements: sitting; then crawling; pulling themselves up on furniture; balancing on two feet; taking those precious first steps; and eventually learning to run, jump, kick, catch, hit, throw, and perform all of the normal activities of a healthy 5- or 6-year-old.

Two things need to happen for children to learn all of these basic skills. Their bodies need to mature, and they need opportunities to practice.

Components of Maturity

During the Active Start phase of growth, the body matures in several ways, all of which contribute to the growing physical skill of the child.

- **Strength of bones and muscle.** As children develop, the stress they put on their bones and muscles triggers a strengthening of both. At birth, the lower limbs are less developed than the arms, and it takes a while for the strength of the bones and muscles in the leg to grow. Until the limbs are strong enough to support the weight of the body, there is no possibility that the child can learn to stand or walk.

- **Myelination (nerve development).** For any movement to take place, a message must be sent from the part of the brain that controls the movement to the muscles that produce the movement. At birth, a large number of the long nerves that send messages to the muscles to control movement are unmyelinated. This means that they are a little like a bundle of electrical wires with no insulation around them. A message sent through one nerve will, like the shorted-out wires in an uninsulated bundle of wires, spread to all the other nerves. Myelin is like an insulating sleeve that grows along the length of the nerve. Once it has covered the whole length of the nerve, a message can be sent down that nerve cell, and that nerve alone, allowing for much greater control of the muscles connected to, and controlled by, that nerve. This process is usually complete by around the second birthday, and it shows in the more controlled movements that are possible by this age.

- **Brain development.** The Active Start stage is a time of massive brain development. This development happens in many ways.

The brain is primed and ready to learn, and there are different times when it learns different things best (see chapter 6). The biggest change in the brain during this period is the increased number of brain cells produced and the increased number of connections made between them.

- **Improved senses.** The myelination of nerves results in constant improvement of the child's senses. This is particularly true of the senses of sight, balance, and kinesthesia (the ability to know where one's limbs are without being able to see them).

Need for Practice

We often hear that practice makes perfect, but that is incorrect. Because cells that fire together in practice, wire together through repetition, practice does not make perfect—it makes permanent. The way we learn basic skills remains with us throughout life. What is important at the Active Start stage is *not* to have young children practice their skills in a structured and systematic way, but rather to create the conditions under which young children willingly and eagerly engage in exploratory play that gives them the opportunity for fun, unstructured practice. The learning progression for young children is as follows (see also figure 13.2):

- **Too young to learn.** If the body has not matured sufficiently for the child to be able to perform the activity, no amount of instruction is going to help. In fact, evidence suggests that instruction at this stage might even hinder later learning of the activity as a result of frustration.

- **Ready to learn.** As the body strengthens, the brain develops, and myelination of the nerves takes place. The body becomes physically able to perform the activity, and the child is ready to learn. Instruction at this stage can be effective.

- **Optimum learning.** At a certain stage of development of the body, brain, and nervous system, the child is at a stage of optimal readiness to learn. Instruction at this stage is most effective.

- **Remediation.** Children who have not mastered basic movement skills by the time all of their peers have are in need of remediation. This is best done by a well-trained professional.

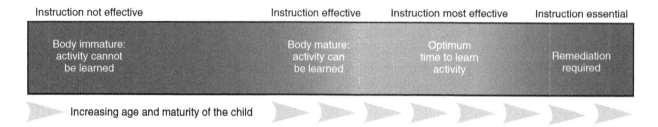

Instruction not effective   Instruction effective   Instruction most effective   Instruction essential

| Body immature: activity cannot be learned | Body mature: activity can be learned | Optimum time to learn activity | Remediation required |

Increasing age and maturity of the child

FIGURE 13.2 Development and learning activity skills.

Appropriate Activities and Programs

Parents and caregivers often ask which activities and skills children should be learning during Active Start. A better question is, What kinds of activities should they be engaged in? Although activities can be divided up in many ways, one of the most common is as follows:

- **Locomotor skills.** Locomotor skills are those children use to move from one place to another and include crawling, walking, running, jumping, hopping, skipping, slithering, rolling, and many more on-land ways of getting around. They also include swimming for those in a water environment as well as sliding and skating for those who spend time on ice or snow.

- **Body control skills.** Body control skills include balance, coordination, and knowing where body parts such as arms and legs are (kinesthesis), even when the body is upside down.

- **Sending and receiving skills.** Sending and receiving skills include pulling and pushing, throwing and catching, kicking and receiving, and striking (hitting something with a bat or other implement).

Children need to learn the basics of all skills during Active Start. In addition, they need to be involved in activities that will do the following:

- Strengthen their growing bodies through activities that make them support their own body weight on their legs, such as jumping, and with their arms through hanging and swinging activities. These upper body-strengthening activities are particularly good for young North

American girls, who typically have less upper body strength than girls from other parts of the world.

- Develop coordination and agility by making different body shapes; playing and climbing on varying sizes and shapes of objects (both natural and synthetic); playing chasing games; and playing with various sizes and weights of bats, balls, and other small equipment.

- Develop body orientation skills and place the body in a wide variety of orientations (upside down, rolling, tumbling) so that the brain can learn to orient itself (know which way is up or down) and can learn to control the movements of body parts even when the body is in an unusual position.

The following sections describe activities and programs that are ideal for children at various ages in the Active Start stage.

Very Young (First Six Months)

Activities need to start in the home soon after birth, although these activities will be very, very basic. Children of this age need to have bright objects in their line of sight so that they see them. If possible, the bright objects need to move. Something as simple as a bright ball of aluminum foil hanging from the ceiling and moving in the breeze is all it takes. Babies will see the bright objects and start the process of learning to track the movements with their eyes. Putting light, clean objects in their hands so they can try to put them in their mouths starts the process of learning to control the arms; helping them stand (supporting their weight) starts to strengthen the legs. Children should be placed on their abdomens and helped to roll around and grab for toys. Most of all, however, this is a time for the child and caregiver to bond. If the caregiver is active and takes the child for walks, the earliest habits of being active start to develop.

Once They Can Crawl (6 to 12 Months)

Playing with objects too large to pose a danger if put in their mouths helps children develop coordination. Putting children on all fours and placing favorite toys just beyond their reach encourages both reaching and crawling. Reaching develops balance and body control, and crawling for the toy develops locomotor skills. This can be a fun game for both caregiver and child. Moving favorite soft toys and other bright objects into and out of children's line of vision, toward them and away from them, and up and down continues to develop their important eye-tracking skills as will rolling balls to them and having them roll them back.

Children this age often like to crawl under tables and into other enclosed spaces that seem to give them a sense of security. Doing this with a caregiver adds to their enjoyment, as does crawling over and around a caregiver who is lying on the floor.

Toward the end of the first year, children start trying to pull themselves up on furniture or pull up on caregivers who are holding their hands. During this stage they show an increasing desire to be on their feet, which should be encouraged. To help them develop their language and social skills, caregivers need to talk to them, describing what they are both doing.

Once They Can Walk (Toddlers; Approximately 1 to 2 Years of Age)

There is no value in trying to get children to walk early. When they are ready, walking comes naturally; however, once they can walk, they need plenty of practice. In the beginning it is easier for children to start walking than it is for them to stop; walking on a carpet or other soft surface can make the bumps of unplanned stops easier. Marking straight and squiggly lines on the floor with chalk or masking tape and having children walk along the line encourages body control, and children find it fun. Walking barefoot on various surfaces helps children develop balance and the ability to feel what is underfoot. Standing face to face and holding hands and moving to music (or just rhythmically) helps children develop a sense of timing and the ability to coordinate their movements to those of another person.

This is a great age for children to explore various ways of moving; pretending to be, and moving like, a variety of animals is an effective way to develop both coordination and imagination. Toward the end of the second year, children are ready to improve balance, which can be done by having them walk on a thin line or try to stand on one foot. Coordination can be developed by having them walk forward, backward, and sideways; body control can be enhanced by playing games that require them to stop and start quickly. Learning to climb stairs under close safety supervision is also important—and children almost always find it easier to go up than to come down.

This is also a time when children learn to run and generally enjoy the exhilaration of speed. For safety, this needs to be done in open spaces to minimize the risk of collision.

From 2 to 4 Years

Ages 2 to 4 is a time of rapid improvement of physical skills. Running improves quickly, and children have the physical capacity to throw small objects, although initially without a great deal of control over where they go. Throwing stones into water is particularly satisfying at this age and provides much throwing practice.

Children can learn to catch large, soft balls by making a basket with their arms and having someone throw the ball gently into the basket. Around this stage of development, they can use lightweight objects such as plastic bats to hit balls, although balls will initially need to be stationary on the ground. It may take several swings to make contact. Hitting ability can be improved by having them try hitting a ball rolling gently in the direction of the swing, and then a ball rolling gently toward them. Only near the end of this stage are children able to hit large balls, such as

197

beach balls, when they are thrown slowly toward them. Even then, the thrower has to make sure to throw the ball directly at the bat. Children at this stage can learn to kick a ball, although once again, using balls that are bright and lightweight makes this a more enjoyable activity.

Hopping, jumping, and other locomotor skills such as riding a tricycle are also developing rapidly between the ages of 2 and 4. Children can start to jump over objects and down from low elevations, run around obstacles, and climb on climbing frames. What they need more than anything else at this stage of development is the opportunity to try new things in safe and stimulating environments. They need to see other children being active, and they need to see good adult role models doing and enjoying activities.

With help (mostly to get skates on and off), children can begin to take to the ice or start to learn to slide on skis at this age. Playing in shallow paddling pools under close supervision begins the process of making them comfortable in and developing a feel for water. Some children are ready to learn to swim, although for most this skill is still a few years away. This is also a time when children have the capacity to tumble, spin, and roll, and doing so helps their brains develop the ability to keep track of their bodies' orientation, learning which way is up and which way is down regardless of which way the body is facing.

Ages 4 to 6

The ages of 4 to 6 is a period of refining and extending many of the skills already learned. Running becomes smooth and fluid; throwing and kicking begin to be controlled; and catching is developing fast. Because throwing is not very accurate at this stage, children do not get much practice at catching when they practice together as the ball is often being thrown too far away from their partner to give him or her any chance of catching it. Faster progress in learning to catch is usually made when an adult throws the ball to the child.

Balance is sufficient at this age for children to learn to ride a bicycle, and they are moving fast enough to make wearing a helmet mandatory.

General Information

Children need space in which to play, role models to emulate, opportunities to be active, encouragement to try and practice new skills, and a safe and supportive physical and psychological environment. When these things are all in place, they have the greatest chance of having a successful active start. The following checklists can help parents, caregivers, and concerned professionals evaluate the physical activity environments of young children.

Questions to Ask Preschool and Day Care Programs: Parent Lobbying Kit

Parents and caregivers should encourage preschools, schools, community recreation organizations, and sport organizations to offer quality physical activity programs. One way to do this is by asking appropriate questions. Although not exhaustive, the following list of questions should provide a good starting point for discussions.

Building, Facility, and Grounds

1. Is there sufficient outdoor space for children to safely run and play vigorously, including ball-kicking and throwing games?   Yes   No

2. Is there sufficient indoor space for children to safely run and play vigorously, including ball-kicking and throwing games?   Yes   No

3. Are the spaces available only at restricted times for organized activities, or are they available both for organized activities and for free play?   Yes   No

4. Is there climbing equipment on which children can climb, hang by their arms, hang upside-down, and otherwise explore?　　　　Yes　No

Equipment

5. Is there enough equipment for all the children to be able to play at the same time?　　　　Yes　No
6. Do they have and use balls of different colors, sizes, and textures?　　　　Yes　No
7. Do they have and use scoops, hoops, and appropriately sized bats?　　　　Yes　No
8. Do they have and use mats to roll and tumble on?　　　　Yes　No
9. Do they have and use scooters and other wheeled toys?　　　　Yes　No
10. Is equipment always available for free play?　　　　Yes　No
11. Is the equipment brightly colored, safe, and in good condition?　　　　Yes　No

Programs and Personnel

12. Do pretoddlers have at least 30 minutes per day, every day, set aside for active play?　　　　Yes　No
13. Do toddlers and older children have at least 60 minutes per day, every day, set aside for active play?　　　　Yes　No
14. Are children encouraged to explore various movements, play with various kinds of equipment, and play both alone and with others?　　　　Yes　No
15. Are program leaders trained in helping children develop fundamental movement and sport skills?　　　　Yes　No
16. Are children encouraged to engage in vigorous physical play during unstructured play times?　　　　Yes　No
17. Are children given the opportunity to complete small challenges that expand their range of movement skills (e.g., jumping onto a soft mat from slightly higher than their comfort zone)?　　　　Yes　No
18. Do the caregivers engage in physical activities with the children to model the importance of being active?　　　　Yes　No
19. Are girls encouraged to be as physically active as boys?　　　　Yes　No
20. Are children with disabilities (if present) included in all physical activities?　　　　Yes　No

Count the number of yes answers. This number indicates how activity friendly the program is, as follows:

- **17-20 yes answers:** This program encourages the maximum development of physical literacy. Stay with the program and encourage other parents to sign up their children.

- **13-16 yes answers:** This is a good program that needs a little help to make it great. Talk to the organizers about what they can do to improve the program. They are likely to be responsive because they obviously care about physical literacy.

- **9-12 yes answers:** This is not a good program for the development of physical literacy, but at least it offers some opportunity for physical activity. You need to have a serious

> continued

> continued

talk with the program organizers to help them improve their program. If they are not willing to make changes, start looking at alternative programs.

- **Fewer than 9 yes answers:** If there are other programs available in your community, run, don't walk to them, check them out, and sign up your child for a program that does more to develop physical literacy.

Checklists for Parents

Checking out preschools and day care programs is important, but as a parent or caregiver, *you* are the most important role model in your child's life. Therefore, you need to ask yourself the following questions:

- Do you play with your child to make physical activity a fun part of the day?
- Does your child have daily opportunities for vigorous play?
- Does your child break up sedentary activity by engaging in active play at least once every hour?
- Does your child have access to simple toys (e.g., balls, bats, scooters) on a regular basis?
- Does your child see active adult role models every day?

Active Start To-Do List

- Provide opportunities for children to learn through play.
- Provide a bright, stimulating environment for play activities
- Make sure children have a wide range of equipment (e.g., balls, beanbags, bats, trikes) to play with, but don't put them all out at once. Regularly rotate the equipment children play with.
- Allow unstructured (child-led) play while keeping an eye on children for safety, as well as more structured (adult-led) play.
- Emphasize the development of the ABCs of agility, balance, coordination, and speed.
- Ensure that equipment is size, weight, and design appropriate for the children.
- Make sure that children get 60 minutes of activity per day, every day.
- Limit screen time and avoid it for children under the age of 2.
- Remember that children master basic movements at different ages. Be concerned only if a child is well behind her peers in a wide range of physical skills. If that is the case, talk the situation over with a health care provider.

Summary

The Active Start stage of LTAD, encompassing the first six years of a child's life, is critical for establishing physical activity in a fun environment and encouraging the first steps toward physical literacy. Important changes take place in the child's brain at this point as well, and physical activity helps the brain develop. Because children are so dependent at this age, it is up to parents and caregivers to ensure that they are physically active and developing appropriate movement skills.

For children to learn basic physical skills, their bodies need to mature and they need opportunities to practice. However, practice should not take place in structured and systematic ways, but should instead occur under the conditions that encourage children to willingly play and explore. If the body has not matured enough for a child to perform a skill, nothing can be done to teach the skill until sufficient maturation has taken place. In fact, persistent instruction can lead to frustration for the child, which can in turn hinder later learning.

As their bodies grow and strengthen and their brains develop, children become physically able to perform activities. At certain stages, children reach an optimum readiness to learn, at which point instruction is most effective. Before children can learn more complex skills, however, their bodies have to be ready to do so, and they often have to learn the preceding skills first.

Knowing how to perform basic skills can also be paramount in the social lives of young children. When children can perform a skill independently, they are more likely to perform that skill with other children, without a parent's or caregiver's help. Also, when alone, they can practice the skill and get better at it. Children who are missing out on a particular skill will be left out when other kids are playing. And, because they cannot practice on their own, they will not improve as rapidly as the other kids, which will hinder their chances of participation later in life. The three most important types of skills for children to learn at this stage are locomotor, body control, and sending and receiving.

Questions for Reflection

- Why is it not a good idea to try to speed up a child's learning to walk and run?
- In what ways do children need to mature before they are able to learn a new skill such as catching a ball?
- Why is it important for a young child to be able to perform age-appropriate physical skills such as throwing or kicking a ball?
- What are the three major types of movement skills that need to be learned during Active Start?

Reference

Rymer, R. (1993). *Genie: A scientific tragedy.* New York: Harper Perennial

To Learn More

Brown, S., & Vaughan, C., (2009) *Play: How it shapes the brain, opens the imagination, and invigorates the soul.* New York: Penguin Group

Canadian Sport Centres. (2007). *Developing physical literacy: A guide for parents of children ages 0 to 12.* Calgary, AB: Canadian Sport Centres

Doman, G., Doman, D., & Hagy, B. (1988). *How to teach your baby to be physically superb: Birth to age six.* Philadelphia: The Institutes Press.

Centre for Child Well-Being at Mount Royal. (2009). *A hop, skip, and a jump: Enhancing physical literacy.* Calgary, AB: Mount Royal College.

Fundamental movement skills: Active start & FUNdamentals stage—A handbook for generalists and physical education teachers, as well as others tasked with teaching motor skill development. (2008). Ottawa, ON: Physical & Health Education Canada.

Fundamental movement skills: Active start and FUNdamental stages—For children with developmental and/or behavioural disabilities. (2010). Ottawa, ON: Physical & Health Education Canada.

Fundamental movement skills: Active start and FUNdamentals stages—For children with physical disabilities. (2009). Ottawa, ON: Physical & Health Education Canada.

Higgs, C., Balyi, I., Way, R., Cardinal, C., Norris, S., & Bluechardt, M. (2007). *Developing physical literacy: A guide for parents of children ages 0 to 12.* Retrieved from www.canadiansportforlife.ca/resources/ltad-resource-papers

Mandigo, J., Francis, N. & Lodewyk, K. (2007). *Physical literacy concept paper.* Retrieved from www.canadiansportforlife.ca/resources/ltad-resource-papers

Watkinson, J. (2010). *Let's play! Promoting active playgrounds.* Champaign, IL: Human Kinetics.

14

FUNdamentals

The ski team was nearing the end of the season—with the year's most important races coming up—and Coach was worried. She had two athletes injured from falls and couldn't afford to lose any more. She thought the issue was that team members, although skiing well, were not protecting themselves during the inevitable falls and spills.

That afternoon in the gymnasium, she rolled out a long gymnastics mat so the skiers could practice running and faking falls, and then rolling on the mat to absorb the impact of those falls. Figuring that she would start them off easily, she asked them to do forward rolls. She was shocked when two of the skiers told her they didn't know how. Another vaguely knew what to do, but was scared to try it.

Somewhat dismayed, Coach spent the first 20 minutes teaching the skiers to do forward rolls, something she thought they would have all learned in elementary school. Being good athletes, they quickly learned and were soon running, falling, and rolling on the mat, protecting themselves and having a good time.

After showering, they all headed out for a meal. During dinner they talked about how they had managed to reach 20 years of age without learning to do a forward roll. Kathy, one of the younger skiers on the team, thought about it and came to this conclusion: "All we've ever done is ski, right from an early age, and no one does a forward roll on the slopes—so I guess we never learned."

"Yeah," said the coach, "I guess you never learned the fundamentals!"

This chapter explains the importance of learning fundamental movement skills, and in particular, of developing a range of locomotor, body control, and sending and receiving skills, as well as the critical ABCs of athleticism: agility, balance, coordination, and speed.

Building on the basic movements developed during Active Start, the years 6 to 8 (for girls) and 6 to 9 (for boys) are critical to building a repertoire of skills that can be adapted and expanded to become fundamental sport skills in the Learn to Train stage of long-term athlete development (LTAD).

Evolution of Skills

As the human body develops and matures, and has opportunities to practice movement skills in a safe and stimulating environment, there is a gradual evolution in the range and quality of skills the child can perform. In Active

Start, children develop the basic movements of sitting, standing, walking, and running; by the time they reach the FUNdamentals stage, most children are competent at these and other basic skills.

The fundamental movement skills that children master at this stage become building blocks for the later learning of sport-specific skills. Without a solid base of well-executed fundamental movement skills, learning sport skills becomes increasingly difficult.

Figure 14.1 shows how basic human movements evolve into fundamental movement skills, and how those fundamental movement skills are related to the fundamental sport skills that children should develop in the Learn to Train stage. As an example, consider the basic movement of pushing an object away from the body.

The basic skill of pushing an object away is usually learned by the end of the first year of life. During Active Start, this usually evolves

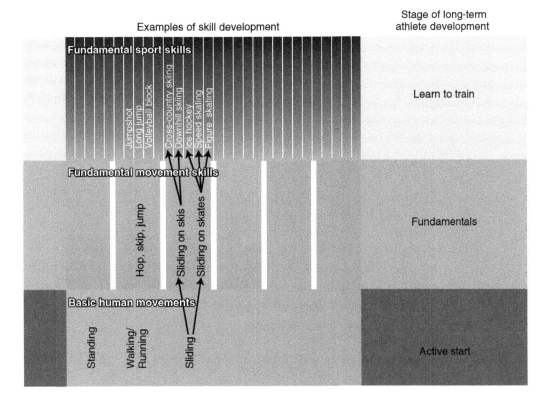

Examples of skill development

Stage of long-term athlete development

Fundamental sport skills

Jumpshot
Long jump
Volleyball block
Cross-country skiing
Downhill skiing
Ice hockey
Speed skating
Figure skating

Learn to train

Fundamental movement skills

Hop, skip, jump
Sliding on skis
Sliding on skates

Fundamentals

Basic human movements

Standing
Walking/Running
Sliding

Active start

FIGURE 14.1 From movement to sport skills.

into a very basic throwing action. With encouragement and the opportunity to practice, children can develop a basic overhand throw early in the FUNdamentals stage. By the time they are ready to enter the Learn to Train stage, they should be able to throw with a mature throwing pattern. In the Learn to Train stage, the fundamental skill of the overhand throw can be used as the basis for teaching pitching in baseball, throwing the javelin in track and field, passing in American football, and even the smash in badminton.

If the fundamental skill of throwing is not well established, the child will have a much more difficult time learning any of the sport-specific skills that use the throwing pattern. For each fundamental movement skill missed, a large number of sport-specific skills will be harder to learn. For this reason, developing a wide range of fundamental movement skills is critical.

Fundamental Movement Skills

Unfortunately, there is no single established and well-recognized list of important fundamental movement skills, although many authors have laid out their opinions about the ones people need to develop. A review by Mandigo, Nancy-Francis, & Lodewyk (2007), undertaken for Canadian Sport for Life (CS4L), explored the wide range of reported fundamental movement skills and grouped them under the headings of body stability and control, locomotor skills, and manipulative skills (table 14.1).

In addition to the specific fundamental skills identified earlier, children need to learn important nonspecific fundamental skills during this stage of development. The three most important are the ABCs of agility, balance, coordination, and speed. In general, these interrelated

TABLE 14.1   Fundamental Movement Skills

Skills	Definitions	Number of references in Mandigo et al. 2007 that include the activity as a fundamental movement skill
Stability and body control skills		
Body rolling	Body moves through space around its own axis while momentarily inverted (Gallahue & Ozmun, 2003, p. 426).	3
Dodging	Fundamental stability pattern that combines the locomotor movements of sliding with rapid changes in direction (Gallahue & Ozmun, 1998, p. 218).	6
Balancing	Keeping the body's center of gravity above its base of support (Hastie & Martin, 2006, p. 224).	7
Bending	Flexing any or all body parts (Kovar et al., 2004, p. 55).	4
Stretching	Extending body parts (Kovar et al., 2004, p. 55).	6
Twisting	Rotating body parts in opposite directions (Kovar et al., 2004, p. 55).	6
Turning	Rotating the body around an axis (Kovar Combs, Campbell, Napper-Owen, & Worrell, 2004, p. 55).	5
Swinging	Keeping the axis of support above moving body parts (Kovar et al., 2004, p. 56).	4
Stopping	Body comes to rest in a balanced and stable position.	2
Rocking	Center of gravity is fluidly transferred from one body part to another (Pangrazi, 2001).	2
Pushing	Directing a force or object away from the base of support (Kovar et al., 2004, p. 56).	2
Pulling	Directing a force or object toward the body (Kovar et al., 2004, p. 56).	2
Rising or stretching	Moving the body or any parts of it to a high level (Kovar et al., 2004, p. 56).	1
Collapsing	Gradually relaxing the body or any parts of it in a controlled way while moving to a lower level (Kovar et al., 2004, p. 56).	1
Swaying	Keeping the axis of support below the moving parts (Kovar et al., 2004, p. 56).	1
Spinning	Rotating the body (on one body part on the spot) (Kovar et al., 2004, p. 56).	1
Shaking	Moving with vibration (Kovar et al., 2004, p. 56).	1
Locomotor skills		
Walking	A period of double support (when both feet are on the ground) followed by a period of single support (Haywood & Getchell, 2001, p. 121).	12
Running	A period of single support followed by a period of flight (limbs off the ground) (Haywood & Getchell, 2001, p. 125).	12
Jumping (vertical and horizontal)	Propelling oneself off the ground with one or two feet; then landing on two feet (Haywood & Getchell, 2001, 129).	12

Skills	Definitions	Number of references in Mandigo et al. 2007 that include the activity as a fundamental movement skill
Hopping	Propelling oneself off the ground with one foot and landing on the same foot (Haywood & Getchell, 2001, 129).	12
Galloping	Forward step followed by a leap onto the trailing foot (Payne & Isaacs, 2002, p. 319).	12
Sliding	Sideways step on one foot and a leap on the other (Haywood & Getchell, 2001, p. 139).	12
Skipping	Alternating step-hops on one foot, then the other (Haywood & Getchell, 2001, p. 139).	12
Leaping	Transferring weight from one foot to the other, but the loss of contact with the surface is sustained, with greater elevation and distance covered in the run (Gallahue & Ozmun, 1998, p. 232).	10
Chasing	Traveling quickly to overtake or tag a fleeing person (Hastie & Martin, 2006, p. 205).	4
Climbing	Ascending and descending using hands and feet (Gabbard, 2000, p. 285).	3
Fleeing	Traveling quickly away from a pursuing person or object (Hastie & Martin, 2006, p. 205).	3
Manipulative skills		
Underhand throwing or rolling	Using an underarm action to project an object.	7
Overhand throwing	Using an overarm action to project an object.	12
Catching	Bringing an airborne object under control by using the hands and arms (Payne & Isaacs, 2002, p. 340).	12
Kicking	A form of striking in which the foot is used to give impetus to a ball (Payne & Isaacs, 2002, p. 352).	12
Striking	Using a designated body part or some implement to project an object (Payne & Isaacs, 2002, p. 349).	11
Punting	Kicking an airborne ball with the foot (Payne & Isaacs, 2002, p. 356).	7
Dribbling with feet	Maintaining possession of a ball with the feet.	7
Dribbling with hands	Sustained bouncing of a ball with one hand.	8
Volleying	Intercepting a downward-moving object with the hands and imparting force to that object in a manner that moves it onward in the desired direction (Gallahue & Ozmun, 2003, p. 532).	6
Trapping	Stopping a ball without using the hands or arms (Gallahue & Ozmun, 1998, p. 244).	2

Adapted, by permission, from J. Mandigo, N. Nancy-Francis, and K. Lodewyk 2007, *Physical literacy concept paper.* Sources: 1. C.A. Buschner, 1994, *Teaching children movement concepts and skills* (Champaign, IL: Human Kinetics). 2. V.G. Payne and L.D. Isaacs, 2002, *Human motor development,* 5th ed. (Boston: McGraw Hill). 3. D.L. Gallahue and J.C. Ozmun, 1998, *Understanding motor development,* 4th ed. (Boston, McGraw Hill). 4. C.P. Gabbard, 2000, *Lifelong motor development,* 3rd ed. (Boston: Allyn and Bacon). 5. D.L. Gallahue and F.C. Ozmun, 2003, *Developmental physical education for all children,* 4th ed. (Champaign, IL: Human Kinetics). 6. P. Hastie and E. Martin, 2006, *Teaching elementary physical education* (San Francisco: Pearson). 7. J. Wall and N. Murray, 1994, *Children and movement,* 2nd ed. (Madison, WI: WCB Brown and Benchmark). 8. S.K. Kovar et al., 2004, *Elementary classroom teachers as movement educators* (Boston: McGraw Hill). 9. G. Kirchner and G.J. Fishburne, 1995, *Physical education for elementary school children,* 9th ed. (Madison, WI: WCB Brown and Benchmark). 10. R.P. Pangrazi, 2001, *Physical education for elementary school children,* 13th ed. (Boston: Allyn & Bacon). 11. K.M. Haywood and N. Getchell, 2001, *Lifespan motor development,* 3rd ed. (Champaign, IL: Human Kinetics). 12. G. Graham, S.A. Holt/Hale, and M. Parker, 2004, Children moving, 6th ed. (New York: McGraw Hill).

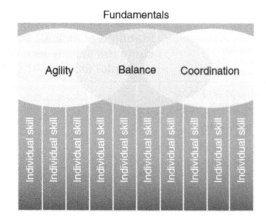

Fundamentals

Agility   Balance   Coordination

FIGURE 14.2 Building agility, balance, and coordination.

meta-skills are learned as combinations of individual fundamental movement skills; this process is shown in figure 14.2

Locomotor Skills in Varied Environments

The extensive list of locomotor skills reported by Mandigo and colleagues (2007) are restricted to land-based activities. For fundamental movement skills to provide a sound foundation for all sports, additional skills in other environments need to be considered. LTAD recognizes four environments in which children should develop fundamental movement skill competence:

- **On land.** This has already been covered.
- **In water.** The fundamental movement skills that need to be developed in water are floating, moving safely through the water (swimming), entering the water feet- and headfirst (jumping and diving), and swimming on the surface of the water and then, without outside assistance, making the body go underwater. These fundamental water-based movement skills open up opportunities for competitive swimming, diving, synchronized swimming, and if the child has developed the land-based skills of catching and throwing, water polo. Children who have developed

water-based skills are also in a better position to more safely take up activities such as sailing, rowing, canoeing, and kayaking.

- **On ice or snow.** The fundamental movement skill on ice and snow is sliding. Children who learn sliding skills have a foundation for ice hockey, figure skating, speedskating, cross-country skiing, downhill skiing, snowboarding, and even curling (curlers slide along the ice surface to deliver their rocks).
- **In the air.** This is perhaps the most difficult environment in which to develop fundamental movement skills. The skills to be developed are related to the ability to orient the body in three-dimensional space—to have one's bearings when upside down or when twisting in the air. Although not strictly an in-air skill, absorbing the impact of landing in a wide variety of circumstances is exceptionally important for avoiding or lessening injury during the inevitable falls and crashes of in-air sport participation. Gymnastics is one sport activity in which children have the opportunity to safely learn fundamental movement skills in the air.

Attaining All of the Fundamental Movement Skills

Traditionally, children have learned fundamental movement skills in the home, in school, and in the community. With more restrictive play environments in modern homes, concern about the safety of playing outside unsupervised, and the diminished role of physical education in schools, ensuring that a child is exposed to a wide range of skills can be difficult. A new approach needs to be developed.

Role of the School

School physical education is the only environment in which all children have the opportunity to develop fundamental movement skills. In too many jurisdictions, generalist classroom teachers with little or no training in physical education are the ones teaching children in the

FUNdamentals stage. Parents who are concerned that their children are missing out on learning fundamental movement skills at school have to look to the community for solutions.

Traditional Approach

It is not easy for parents and caregivers to ensure that children learn the whole range of fundamental movement skills. Children often specialize too early and miss out on developing the full range of these skills. In North America many physical activity opportunities are organized by sport-specific organizations, such as minor soccer or mini-basketball, and too often the focus of those programs is also sport specific. There are two problems with this system: first, the focus is on early success in the sport, rather than on the long-term development of the athlete; and second, sport organizations are reluctant to encourage athletes to leave a program to try a sport for which they might be better suited—after all, by staying with the organization and continuing to pay dues or membership fees, athletes keep adding to the organization's bottom line.

For parents, ensuring that a child is exposed to a wide range of fundamental movement skills can be both difficult and expensive. Consider that a child might need gymnastics to develop body orientation and control skills along with balance, minor soccer to develop foot–eye coordination and the ability to kick, minor baseball to learn to throw and hit and catch, and swimming to develop water-based skills.

A New Approach

Some communities and organizations have started to address this issue and have developed a new approach to ensuring that children get broad exposure to fundamental movement skills. At the community level, children are given the opportunity to enroll in fundamental movement skills programs or year-round programs that let them sample many activities and minor games designed to develop their repertoire of skills. Some programs are also run by sport-specific organizations that deliver skill-learning opportunities, although none, alone, cover all the fundamental skills in each of the four environments (ground, water, ice and snow, and air).

- **Up Down All Around.** Gymnastics Canada has developed the Up Down All Around program for children ages 5 to 11 to encourage both locomotor skills and body orientation skill development.

- **Introduction to Aquatics.** Rather than focusing solely on learning to swim, the Introduction to Aquatics program introduces children to fundamental movement skills such as diving, underwater acrobatics, and ball games in the water, leading to potential involvement in competitive swimming, synchronized swimming, diving, or water polo.

- **Fundamental Skills School (Utah Olympic Oval).** The Fundamental Skills school is a Utah Sport for Life program intended to teach children ages 4 to 7 fundamental movement skills such as coordination, balance, jumping, kicking, and striking to prepare them for activity later in their lives.

- **Run, Jump, Throw.** The Run, Jump, Throw program, developed by Athletics Canada, introduces children to the mechanics of running, jumping, and throwing, teaching them basic techniques used in a multitude of sports. Delivery is primarily through elementary schools, but also through recreation centers and local sport clubs.

- **Blind Sports—Early Intervention Program.** The Blind Sports program serves parents and their preschool children who have blindness or visual impairment as part of their physical condition. The program introduces families to the importance of providing blind children with opportunities for early motor skill development, play, early recreation, and physical activity, and provides resources and support for the transition to school and community physical activity programs.

- **XploreSportz.** XploreSportz is a British Columbia program designed to attract a large participation base of children to sport through an innovative multisport skill development approach.

Learning and Teaching Fundamental Movement Skills

This section is reprinted, by permission, from C. Higgs, I. Balyi et al., 2008, *Developing physical literacy: A guide for parents of children ages 0-12* (Vancouver, Canada: Canadian Sport Centres).

Although children mature and learn at different rates, almost all children learn their fundamental movement skills in the same sequence and go through the same phases.

• **When a child can learn a skill.** As a child grows and develops (matures), nerve cells make more connections, while the muscles of the body get stronger. Until the brain is mature enough, and the muscles strong enough, the child simply cannot learn the skill, and trying to teach the child does little good. What is important at this time is providing the child with as many opportunities to explore all possible movements in a rich environment—which means that the child's environment needs to be both safe and challenging.

• **The child is ready to learn the skill.** At a certain point in maturation, all the hardware—the muscles and nerves—have developed enough that the child has the potential to perform a particular skill (the readiness factor). Now they have to learn it. As the skill begins to emerge naturally, learning can be dramatically improved through opportunities for fun practice using lots of different equipment and materials. Giving the child some simple instruction and lots of practice can help them develop confidence that stays with them for life—although this may not speed up the learning process.

• **The optimum time to learn the skill.** For every emerging skill there is a "best" time for the child to learn. At this time, helping the child though simple instruction and practice can improve learning and pay great dividends. While the "best" time to teach a particular skill to an individual child varies, there is great consistency in the sequence in which children learn skills.

• **Time for remedial work.** If the child goes too long without learning a skill, then learning it may become more difficult. However, the sooner the child starts to overcome the learning deficit the easier it will be for them to catch up—and develop the skill and confidence needed to be fully active with their friends and peers.

The following are three phases in the development of fundamental movement skills and fundamental sport skills.

Initial "Novice" Phase

• Introduce clear, simple, short verbal explanations, cues and visual demonstrations of the skill.

• Allow individual practice time that encourages exploration and self-discovery of the general principles of the skill.

• Facilitate cognitive understanding of the general idea of the skill by focusing on a few key parts of each skill.

• If possible, compare the skill to another similar and familiar skill.

• Provide immediate, precise, and appropriately positive feedback about the skill.

• Focus on the process (understanding of form) and not as much on product (i.e., accuracy, speed, or distance).

• Use practices and simple, cooperative, fun and low-organization games with few required participants and few rules.

Intermediate "Practice" Phase

• Provide numerous short, appropriately paced practices with frequent breaks that stress quality (correct form) while increasing demands on performance objectives (i.e., speed and accuracy).

• As much as possible, focus on the whole rather than the various parts of the skill. The whole method is usually superior to the part method used in teaching specialized skills; however, if the skill is highly complex, it is likely best to divide it into parts. Generally, the method of instruction depends on the readiness of the learner, complexity of the skill, and the rate and amount of learning required (Coker, 2004).

• Reinforce appropriate cues and hints in a supportive and constructive environment.

• Gradually refine the skill and increase the rate of the practice activities to get to the speed and intensity of the skill for the actual competitive setting.

- Use small-group game-like activities that stimulate maximum participation.
- Consider and allow for individual differences and provide choice to enable individuals to accommodate for them.

Advanced "Automatic" Phase

- Practice form, style, and accuracy in a variety of situations.
- Conduct practices that are structured to promote intensity, enthusiasm and applications of skills in varying contexts.
- Teach using methods of personal autonomy support (e.g., useful positive feedback, choices).
- Teach more specific technical aspects of the skills along with strategies and tactics.
- Utilize direct (traditional) and indirect (e.g., Teaching Games for Understanding [TGfU] and inquiry-based) instructional models to promote critical-thinking and self-regulatory capabilities in learners for application of skills according to context (e.g., competition, recreation).
- Consider and train optimal self-regulation of psychological aspects of performance (e.g., mental imagery, arousal, attention, meta-cognition, goal-setting, self-efficacy, attributions, outcome expectations, mastery versus performance achievement orientations).
- To facilitate continual improvement, know and adjust for each individual's needs while encouraging creativity and adjustments (i.e., pace) especially when learners plateau.

Key Training and Performance Characteristics

The years 6 to 8 (for girls) and 6 to 9 (for boys) are critical to building a repertoire of skills that can be adapted and expanded to become fundamental sport skills in the Learn to Train stage of LTAD. Activities at this stage of development should focus on building each child's capabilities in the following areas.

Skill Development

As emphasized throughout this chapter, the development of the basic movement skills is very important at the FUNdamentals stage. During most of every practice, coaches should be working on those skills. Of course, this must be done in a *fun* environment. A certain percentage of the time can be committed to fundamental sport skills or "technical" skills. However, there is no need to commit time to strategies or tactics at this stage because they slow down practices (not fun!) and overspecify roles or positions, creating weaknesses by developing one-sidedness and limiting decision-making opportunities. At this stage, coaches should use small-sided games to teach athletes how to play sports, develop their games sense, and help them problem solve (Thorpe, Bunker, & Almond, 1986). They should use the 80:20 rule for training and competition (if possible). Eighty percent (or more) of the training time should be spent playing adapted small-sided games. The remaining 20 percent can be used for warming up, instruction, and other fun non-sport-specific games that develop multilateral coordination (Fenoglio, 2007). Individual sports are similar, in that a large percentage of time should be focused on fundamental skills development.

Psychology

Although this stage is too early to introduce mental or psychological training in any formal way, children are capable of vivid imaginations; therefore, coaches or program coordinators can stimulate their imaginations with fun, engaging environments. Creative imaginary activities can be used to prepare players for some basic mental skills, which will be introduced more formally at the next stage. Small-sided games such as pirates capturing the flag (or ball) include basic tactics (finding free space, working as a team) and mental skills (goal setting, motivation, communication). Creative games ensure that children have fun while respecting their opponents and learning the rules of play.

Simple methods of measuring how much children enjoy activities (see figure 14.3) can be used to guide program development. It takes only a few seconds at the end of an activity or practice to have participants place a check mark or sticker under the face that best represents how much they enjoyed the activity. Using simple devices like this with young children indicates that coaches or program leaders value their opinion, and provides a starting point for more detailed evaluation processes during later stages of development.

Recovery and Regeneration

At the FUNdamentals stage, smiley faces are a useful tool for monitoring simple things such as how much children enjoy different activities (figure 14.3; Calder, 2007). As children become older, the range of questions asked can be increased to include their perceptions of fatigue, life at school, life at home, and the like. The other critical variable to teach young children to monitor is their hydration. Because the bodies of prepubescent children are inefficient at dissipating excess heat, they can dehydrate and overheat very quickly. Children at this stage are less inhibited than they are at puberty, so if they are taught to check the color of their urine and reminded to do so, they quickly become quite proficient hydrators.

To manage recovery, coaches should end each training practice with a fun activity

How much did you enjoy today's practice?

Put a ✓ in the box under the face that shows how you feel.

FIGURE 14.3 Simple evaluation of how much participants enjoyed a practice or activity.

followed by a few light active stretches of the major muscles used. The session is completed by rehydrating and refueling with some water or fruit juice and a light snack such as a muffin, sandwich, piece of fruit, or yogurt. Children should be encouraged to have a shower or bath when they get home to help their muscles relax.

This is a critical time to begin educating parents about the importance of recovery strategies, given that they are often the ones preparing postsession drinks and food. Parents can help by observing their children's responses postsession and assist the recovery process by reinforcing the importance of a shower or bath and massaging tired legs and backs when tucking their children into bed at night.

Following are the key recovery and regeneration points of this stage:

- Showing children how to check the color of their urine
- Introducing refueling and rehydration strategies
- Introducing light stretching after exercise
- Encouraging a shower or bath after exercise

Character

At this stage, children are beginning to collaborate with others and move from an egocentric mode to one that is more respectful of others (East, 2010). However, children's main focus is still on what they can get out of a situation. A self-centered focus is still prevalent, and children often quit an activity because they are not getting what they want. Children decide to quit because of a wide range of issues, including simply missing a session or not being in the same group as their friends.

More than anything else, children at this stage want to have fun and need to keep having fun to continue to participate. As they develop cognitively through this stage, they will begin to understand the purpose of various activities. Because the attention span of these children is short, the coach should always give instructions in a clear, concise, and fun manner. This is the perfect time to use creativity to achieve developmental outcomes.

During this stage children begin to understand the world around them and to seek fairness in their own ways (e.g., believing that everyone should have a ball). They also want to be acknowledged and appreciated. Coaches should pay special attention to ensuring that all children are treated equally and that they understand the basic concepts of respect for others (other children and coaches). At this stage coaches have an important role to play in teaching the basic rules of a given sport.

Following are the key points of this stage:

- Having fun
- Building the foundation of the basic values of fairness and respect
- Teaching the basic rules of the game

Females

Children are continuing to develop physical literacy skills in the FUNdamentals stage. For the young female, an introduction to the correct technical execution of lower-body movements (e.g., running, jumping, throwing, and performing weight-bearing skills on hands and feet) should be included since they are more prone to lower limb injuries (Harber, 2007). Early exposure combined with regular opportunities to practice new skills is essential.

Proper nutrition is vital for good health and optimal sport performance at any age. For this reason, it is important to start implementing positive eating habits as early as possible. During the FUNdamentals stage, young girls can learn the importance of matching energy intake to energy expenditure. Coaches and others can explain that they need sufficient energy to support the demands of their growth in addition to meeting the energetic requirements of training. Girls at this age can also start to identify the best food sources of each macronutrient (carbohydrate, protein, fat) and key micronutrients (iron, calcium). Parents play a vital role in setting an example and supporting positive eating habits.

Following are the key points of this stage:

- Providing a wide range of exposure to all fundamental movement skills in various environments

- Introducing the correct technical execution of lower-body movements
- Teaching positive eating habits
- Modeling positive eating habits (parents)

Competition

The emphasis at this stage should be on fun, participation, and skill development. Festivals and jamborees are great introductory forms of competition because they promote all three of these qualities, and an emphasis on improving skills, rather than simply winning, can be built in. Competition during the FUNdamentals stage should be an evaluation of how the child is progressing in overall movement skills and general, overall development, such as the ABCs of athleticism (agility, balance, coordination, and speed), while introducing how the sport is played. Because children have different physical and mental abilities than adult athletes, modified games (e.g., small-sided games) are necessary for ensuring that they develop the desired skills for the long term.

There is no recommended training-to-competition ratio at this stage; instead, all activities must be fun based. Children should not be traveling for any sort of competition, because it is not worth the time or the expense. A better use of time would be fun play in their communities.

Following are the key points of this stage:

- Making sure activities are fun
- Remembering that children are *not* mini-adults; designing competition formats and rules to ensure that they are developing the necessary fundamental skills
- Hosting jamborees and festivals

Role of Parents

Parents play a very active role at this stage by immersing their children in various sports and activities. They must assume responsibility for introducing their children to sports, essentially paving the path toward lifelong activity. When parents neglect to do so, children are likely to lead sedentary lives. Parents must educate themselves about local sport programs and opportunities and decide which ones would

FUNdamentals To-Do List

- Keep it fun!
- Ensure that children participate in many sports and activities to ensure optimal development and future success.
- If possible, enroll children in programs or activities that offer a wide variety of activities.
- Have children practice and master fundamental movement skills before introducing sport-specific skills.
- Emphasize the development of the ABCs of athleticism: agility, balance, coordination, and speed.
- Use games to develop strength, endurance, and flexibility.
- Develop strength through body weight exercises and activities.
- Introduce the basic rules and ethics of sports.
- Ensure that equipment is size, weight, and design appropriate for children.
- Don't be concerned with the score; focus on learning and fun!
- Don't get caught in the specialization trap. Developing all-around athletes at this age is far better!

be best for their children. During this stage, participating in many sports (see chapter 4) is vital to the development of the fundamental movement and motor skills, and introduces children to a variety of activities.

Parents should enroll children in three or four sports that they participate in on a regular basis—activities that develop basic strength and flexibility while building the ABCs of athleticism: agility, balance, coordination, and speed. Parents need to encourage the development of physical literacy by creating and choosing environments for their children that focus on fun, fitness, and fundamentals. Children's social skills are also fostered through immersion in the positive environments that activities and sports provide. Parents must also provide the time and settings that allow for unstructured free play with friends or siblings. Screen time is the easy out, whereas physical activity keeps children busy and expending energy.

Providing healthy meals and snacks instills good eating habits in children. Good food not only builds strong bodies, but also develops a habit that children carry into adulthood. Packing balanced meals, including school lunches, providing a nutritious breakfast, and bringing

along healthy snacks to sporting events and games prevents kids from going to the vending machine or clamoring for a quick fast-food option. Parents should measure their children's height four times a year, starting at the age of 10. During the summer months and winter holidays, they should consider signing children up for multisport camp in which they play a number of sports.

Following are the key points of this stage:

- Limiting screen time
- Encouraging and modeling healthy eating habits (for proper nutrition)
- Ensuring a good amount and quality of sleep
- Providing opportunities for physical activity

Summary

The FUNdamentals stage is when children develop a range of movement and sport skills as well as the ABCs of athleticism. As indicated by the stage's name, fun is a key component of development. The more fun children have learning a skill, the more likely they are to want to continue doing sport and physical activity. Because fundamental movement skills are the building blocks for learning sport-specific skills later on, children should have the opportunity to develop and master a wide range of them. Because a solid base of learned skills opens the door to an array of physical activities, children should get a feel for activities on land, in the water, in the air, and on snow and ice.

Because children develop over time, they are not able to perform a skill the same way an adult does when they are first learning it. They learn the skill gradually, getting more proficient as they practice more and grow stronger. It is important that games be modified for children to allow for this developmental period. If an activity suits a child's developmental level, meaning that the child is able to succeed regardless of skill capability, then that child will grow in confidence and continue practicing.

Although parents and caregivers are often the ones teaching young children skills, once those children get into schools and recreation, community, and sport programs, it is paramount that these outlets also teach fundamental movement skills. The only way a child can master the full range of fundamental movement skills is through constant exposure to activities and the chance to practice consistently. If children don't learn the range of skills, their later involvement might be hindered; but if they do master these skills at a young age, their abilities will transcend a single sport or activity and make it possible for them to be involved in all sorts of physical activities. This is the key to successful sport specialization later in life.

Questions for Reflection

- How much fun are children having?
- Why is it important that children take part in a wide range of activities?
- Why should adult games and sports be modified for children?
- Are children learning the necessary fundamental movement skills? How?
- Are children experiencing activities in all four modalities (on land, in water, on ice

or snow, and in the air)? How can children get exposure to these experiences?
- What modifications can be made in children's sport to make it age appropriate?
- What are the consequences in later stages of not mastering fundamental movement skills? What benefits can athletes gain by mastering fundamental movement skills?

References

Calder, A. (2007). *Recovery and regeneration for long-term athlete development.* Vancouver, BC: Canadian Sport Centres.

Coker, C.A. (2004). *Motor learning and control for practitioners.* New York: McGraw-Hill.

East, J. (2010). LTAD-based character development. Unpublished manuscript.

Fenoglio, R. (2007, November). *A neuro-physiological basis for developing future skilful players.* Retrieved from www.footy4kids.co.uk/developing_skilful_players.htm

Gabbard, C.P. (2000). *Lifelong motor development* (3rd ed.). Boston: Allyn & Bacon.

Gallahue, D.L., & Ozmun, J.C. (1998). *Understanding motor development* (4th ed.). Boston: McGraw Hill.

Gallahue, D.L., & Ozmun, F.C. (2003). *Developmental physical education for all children* (4th ed.). Champaign, IL: Human Kinetics.

Harber, V. (2007). *Female athlete perspective: Coach/parent/administrator guide.* Victoria, BC: Canadian Sport Centres.

Hastie, P., & Martin, E. (2006). *Teaching elementary physical education.* San Francisco: Pearson.

Haywood, K.M., & Getchell, N. (2001). *Lifespan motor development* (3rd ed.). Champaign, IL: Human Kinetics.

Higgs, C., Balyi, I., Way, R., Cardinal, C., Norris, S., & Bluechardt, M. (2008). *Developing physical literacy: A guide for parents of children ages 0-12.* Vancouver, BC: Canadian Sport Centres.

Kovar, S.K., Combs, C.A., Campbell, K., Napper-Owen, G., & Worrell, V.J. (2004). *Elementary classroom teachers as movement educators.* Boston: McGraw-Hill.

Mandigo, J., Nancy-Francis, N. & Lodewyk, K. (2007, April 3). *Physical literacy concept paper.* Retrieved from http://canadiansportforlife.ca/sites/default/files/resources/Physical%20Literacy%20Concept%20Paper.pdf

Pangrazi, R.P. (2001). *Physical education for elementary school children* (13th ed.). Boston: Allyn & Bacon.

Payne, V.G., & Isaacs, L.D. (2002). *Human motor development* (5th ed.). Boston: McGraw-Hill.

Thorpe, R., Bunker, D., & Almond, L. (Eds.). (1986). *Rethinking games teaching.* Loughborough, UK: University of Technology.

To Learn More

Buschner, C.A. (1994). *Teaching children movement concepts and skills*. Champaign, IL: Human Kinetics.

Coaching Association of Canada—National Coaching Certification Program. *Fundamental movement skills*. Retrieved from www.coach.ca/fundamental-movement-skills-s12520

Fundamental movement skills: Active start & FUNdamentals stage—A handbook for generalists and physical education teachers, as well as others tasked with teaching motor skill development. (2008). Ottawa, ON: Physical & Health Education Canada.

Fundamental movement skills: Active Start and FUNdamentals stages. (2008). Ottawa, ON: Physical & Health Education Canada.

Fundamental movement skills: Active start and FUNdamentals stages—For children with developmental and/or behavioural disabilities. (2010). Ottawa, ON: Physical & Health Education Canada.

Fundamental movement skills: Active start and FUNdamentals stages—For children with physical disabilities. (2009). Ottawa, ON: Physical & Health Education Canada.

Graham, G., Holt/Hale, S.A., & Parker, M. (2004). *Children moving* (6th ed.). New York: McGraw-Hill.

Kirchner, G., & Fishburne, G. J. (1995). *Physical education for elementary school children* (9th ed.). Madison, WI: WCB Brown and Benchmark.

Wall, J., & Murray, N. (1994). *Children and movement* (2nd ed.). Madison, WI: WCB Brown and Benchmark.

Learn to Train

15

Dad had been so proud of Eddie last year. His club's 11-and-under junior development track and field team had finished the season with wins at all the major meets, and it was largely due to his son's stellar running. The coach made sure he was sprinting only in the major meets, plus anchoring the boys' relay team, which always placed first in the heats and finals. Even though Eddie had only started his growth spurt, his dad was confident he'd develop into an all-star sprinter and receive a number of college scholarship offers.

But this year was different. The team had a new coach. She had all the kids, including Eddie, competing in a variety of athletic events. How were javelin and high jump supposed to help his son earn a college scholarship, when his future was clearly in sprinting? And he wasn't just upset about Eddie's future suddenly being jeopardized; he hated seeing the team not win because the slower kids brought down its average placing. "Let the fast kids do the running and the strong kids do the throwing and stuff," he kept telling the other parents in the bleachers.

Not only that, but this new coach was also encouraging the kids to play other sports. Eddie had always talked about wanting to play basketball and soccer, but Dad kept telling him just to focus on his running, stay committed to his track team and not worry about playing other sports. He was having trouble keeping Eddie focused. It's no wonder the team wasn't placing so well in meets—the kids were trying too many things such as swimming and football instead of staying dedicated to track and field.

Every time Dad tried to voice his concerns with the coach, she'd tell him that the kids were too young to be specialized in any one event, or even in any one sport. She told him that she wanted to develop as many of their skills as possible while they were at this stage, that she was trying to build athletes, not specialists. She also explained that doing multiple events and sports up to the age of 14 developed better athletes in the long term. Eddie's dad didn't understand. His son's future was slipping away, and he didn't know what to do.

This chapter explains why the development of skills is so crucial during the Learn to Train stage—the three to four years before puberty. It also outlines the objectives of this stage and the key issues. Also, parents' roles, along with what to monitor as the child advances through the stage, are explored. Examples show how competition can be modified to bring LTAD to life.

Learn to Train Basics

One of the most important periods of skill development for children is between the ages of 9 and 12. This window of accelerated adaptation for fundamental movement and sport skills can best be described as the skill hungry year or "a golden age period to learn all kinds of movement patterns, certain of which become automatic" (Borms, 1986, p. 11). At this stage, children are developmentally ready to acquire the general sport skills that are the cornerstones of all athletic development. From age 8 in girls and 9 in boys, to the onset of the growth spurt (usually around the ages of 12 for girls and 14 for boys), children are ready to begin training according to more formalized methods. However, the emphasis should still be on general sport skills suitable to a number of activities rather than excessive single-sport training and competition. By this age, children are developing clear ideas about the sports they like and in which they feel they have success (success can range from having fun to mastering a new skill to winning); parents should continue to encourage this development. The focus should be on playing at least three sports in different seasons. Focusing on only one sport year-round should be discouraged. Figure 15.1 shows six examples of how to use LTAD to modify a variety of sports in the Learn to Train stage.

At this stage the nervous system is well developed and the athlete is capable of performing refined technical skills. Now is the time to develop and advance fundamental movement skills and learn overall sport skills (see chapter 4). Late developers (those who enter puberty later than their peers) have an advantage when it comes to learning skills, because the Learn to Train stage lasts longer for them. The Learn to Train stage of development ends with the onset of puberty and the rapid growth that accompanies this important life event (see chapter 5).

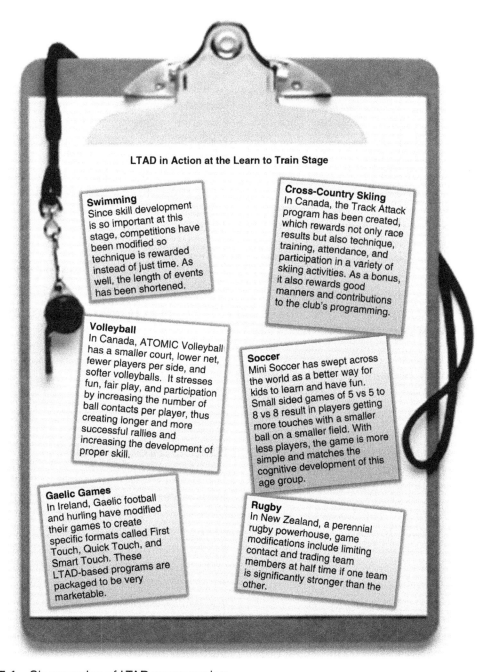

LTAD in Action at the Learn to Train Stage

Swimming
Since skill development is so important at this stage, competitions have been modified so technique is rewarded instead of just time. As well, the length of events has been shortened.

Cross-Country Skiing
In Canada, the Track Attack program has been created, which rewards not only race results but also technique, training, attendance, and participation in a variety of skiing activities. As a bonus, it also rewards good manners and contributions to the club's programming.

Volleyball
In Canada, ATOMIC Volleyball has a smaller court, lower net, fewer players per side, and softer volleyballs. It stresses fun, fair play, and participation by increasing the number of ball contacts per player, thus creating longer and more successful rallies and increasing the development of proper skill.

Soccer
Mini Soccer has swept across the world as a better way for kids to learn and have fun. Small sided games of 5 vs 5 to 8 vs 8 result in players getting more touches with a smaller ball on a smaller field. With less players, the game is more simple and matches the cognitive development of this age group.

Gaelic Games
In Ireland, Gaelic football and hurling have modified their games to create specific formats called First Touch, Quick Touch, and Smart Touch. These LTAD-based programs are packaged to be very marketable.

Rugby
In New Zealand, a perennial rugby powerhouse, game modifications include limiting contact and trading team members at half time if one team is significantly stronger than the other.

FIGURE 15.1 Six examples of LTAD programming.

Some parents get off track when they see their children do well during the Learn to Train stage. With visions of college, professional, or Olympic glory, they can fall into the "more is better" trap, ushering their children into single sports on representative or traveling teams. This focus on one sport is then augmented by special camps during Christmas, spring, and summer breaks. In these years, children are enthusiastic about single-sport participation because they are rewarded by their success and parental attention. However, there is no guarantee this enthusiasm will continue into their teenage years; often, it leads to burnout and a move to other, less active pastimes.

Children in the Learn to Train stage should focus on developing athleticism, which will result in long-term success. Coaches should encourage children to play all positions or do many events (e.g., shot put, 60-meter dash, and high jump) to better understand the sport. Sometimes this takes them outside their comfort zones, which enhances their decision-making skills. Further, parents should not yell instructions from the sidelines; it keeps children from developing decision-making skills. Children who are always listening for direction from the sidelines are not focusing on play or determining the next steps for themselves.

Parents must avoid the trap of believing the following:

- Their children are winning and so they are winning.
- Their children are special and they are special.
- Their children should win, and if they do not, it is the fault of others: the coach, the league, or some unknown conspirators.

Parents of children in the Learn to Train stage need to step back to allow some space for their children to grow through the great lessons sport can teach, while ensuring that their children are participating in a safe, fun environment.

This is also the stage in which "winning" coaches lead their young charges to lopsided victories in undefeated seasons. These coaches recruit players to ensure that the best ones are on their teams, and then devise strategies and tactics to minimize the players' weaknesses and maximize their strengths. This ensures that the players avoid risk taking and follow the systems prescribed by their coaches, believing that winning is paramount. Unfortunately, parents encourage this type of coach because they also revel in the winning. They do not realize that their children are learning a limited range of skills within the specific positions or roles they are assigned. Typically, these coaches put players in the same positions, do not encourage them to take chances or experiment, and are noticeably agitated when the players are not winning. Such coaches limit players' decision-making opportunities and their ability to read the activity from multiple perspectives. Coaches' systems and directions, combined with parents' sideline instructions, result in limited cognitive development. At this stage, creativity should be encouraged. Although being innovative often results in mistakes, parents and coaches must take care that learning is not sacrificed for the sake of winning.

Key Training and Performance Characteristics

The Learn to Train stage is often called the golden age of learning. This means that skill development should be the overall emphasis; however, other characteristics of the young athlete also need to be further developed.

Skill Development

The development of fundamental movement skills is very important at this stage; however, there is an increased emphasis on the fundamental sport skills or technical skills. Simple developmentally appropriate strategies can be used to allow the young athlete to play the game or compete in the event with a growing understanding of the sport's formations. Training or practice can focus on applying the fundamental skills to small-sided games or modified events. Decision-making skills are also developed, because young athletes must decide when to use fundamental skills and how to apply the technical skills.

In team sports, strategies revolve around basic offense and defense, with an emphasis on proper spacing (width and depth) and understanding team play. In individual sports, strategies relate to how the event is contested or the sport is played. At this stage, athletes do not need to engage in tactics to adjust to opponents' strategies. Addressing tactics would not be a good use of training time. Enjoyment (fun) remains a major focus to develop a passion for physical activity and sport. The young participant may become more serious about winning and doing well, but fun still has to be the motivation during these years.

Following are the key points of this stage:

- Further developing fundamental movement skills
- Having an increased emphasis on fundamental sport skills
- Applying fundamental skills to small-sided games
- Developing decision-making skills
- Igniting a passion for physical activity and sport (fun)

Psychology

The psychological goal at this stage is to introduce athletes to the basic skills of relaxation, imagery, goal setting, concentration, communication, and motivation. Coaches and parents must recognize that when children do not perform skills properly, it may be because they are not cognitively ready to do so.

Goal setting can be introduced at this age because most young athletes have goals, some large and some small. When athletes have targets to aim for, they have a direction and purpose for training and competing. Explaining the differences among long-, medium-, and short-term goals helps them gain perspective on their own goals for the sport. Long-term goals may be unrealistic and far-fetched; parents can talk to their children about their dreams without assessing how realistic they may be. Talking about short-term goals can

help young athletes decide to add or change the skills they are learning.

Similarly, the use of imagery at this stage allows athletes to use all of their senses to recreate a situation or imagine a new situation. This increases concentration and motivation and produces a sense of relaxation.

As a result of the enjoyment that comes from increased fitness and improving their skills, youngsters start to develop a passion for sport. This passion underpins their motivation to participate. Further, they are motivated to learn to train so they can experience the good feelings they attribute to doing sport well. This self-motivation is the foundation for their determination to succeed in sport, as well as in life, as they progress through the later stages.

The basic concepts of communication can also be introduced at this stage. Athletes must be able to both understand instructions from coaches and communicate that understanding back to their coaches. Communication is also important in relation to teammates. Whether on the field of play in team sports or off the field of play in all sports, young athletes at this stage need to communicate effectively to advance to the next stage of ability.

Following are the key points of this stage:

- Setting goals
- Using imagery
- Being relaxed and focused
- Focusing on motivation
- Practicing good communication

Recovery and Regeneration

As mentioned in the earlier chapters, coaches need to maximize athletes' adaptation by balancing training with appropriate recovery strategies. Athletes can learn to monitor their recovery (i.e., listen to their bodies) and manage that recovery (i.e., look after themselves) (Calder, 2007).

At practices coaches can ask athletes to rate their fatigue or enjoyment using smiley faces or numbers (from 1 to 3, or from 1 to 10) as a quick gauge of their capability of handling the training both physically and mentally. Fatigue, self-esteem, quality of sleep, illness, and injury are all variables athletes can rate. At this stage the number of variables monitored increases as the child's cognitive abilities increase.

During the Learn to Train stage, the recovery routine should involve some short, active recovery exercises and some light stretching. Athletes should be encouraged to shower as soon as possible after training (to bring their core temperatures back to normal) and to eat within two hours of the end of the session. Long-held stretches (30 to 60 seconds) can be introduced as a prebedtime habit. Hobbies and other sports should be encouraged because they offer young athletes different ways to relax emotionally.

Experts recommend 8 to 10 hours of sleep for this age group (Samuels and Alexander, 2012). Maintaining a regular sleep schedule and an optimal sleeping environment is very important for young athletes, especially as training and competitive volumes are gradually increased or the onset of the growth spurt becomes an issue.

Following are the key points of this stage:

- Using smiley faces or a rating scale after training to monitor fatigue, self-esteem, quality of sleep, illness, and injury
- Using active recovery exercises such as light jogging and easy stretching

Character

Children at this stage are already able to distinguish between right and wrong (East, 2010). They have a strong sense of justice and a huge sensitivity to fairness, but their definition of *fair* varies as they acquire more knowledge. They already know what they like and what they do not like, and this becomes the fertile ground in which their set of values will grow over time. As they become more open to their environments, their social lives expand quickly. Thus, their character is more intensively shaped, both internally and externally, by the behaviors of their peers and the adults around them.

This stage is crucial for teaching strong moral values, such as respect (of teammates, opponents, coaches, and officials), fairness, trust, a competitive spirit, leadership, perseverance,

and citizenship. Maintaining fun as a central focus during this stage facilitates the teaching of these values and slowly integrating them into athletes' lives. Children learn that activity is fun when good behavior occurs. Knowing what each athlete likes about a given sport or activity (i.e., what is fun) is a great asset for coaches, because the reasons vary. The challenge for coaches is to find a balance between letting the players have fun and fostering the competitive spirit that some players already have at this age. It is hard for competitive children to understand that losing can be fun, especially when they have just given the best they have. Coaches need to reinforce that losing is part of everyone's skill and character development. They need to remember that in 10 years' time, the children will not recall their season record, but the skills they learned and the fun they had with their friends will stay with them. Good losers eventually become great winners!

Following are the key points of this stage:

- Having fun individually, in a group, or both
- Learning through good times and bad times
- Respecting others who are essential for playing the game (teammates, opponents, coaches, and officials)

Females

Learn to Train is the last stage of physical literacy. Children are still encouraged to participate in a wide range of activities and sports at this stage. Young girls may have preferred sports, but they should still participate in other sports and activities until they enter the Train to Train stage. They can begin to combine fundamental movement skills with fundamental sport skills and apply diverse skills to various sporting challenges through accelerated learning. To avoid injury, girls need good instruction and training in the technically correct ways to execute lower-body and shoulder movements. Young athletes in this stage are now able to control their bodies to a greater degree and should pay particular attention to correct technique. Correct technique to prevent anterior cruciate ligament (ACL) and patellofemoral joint (PFJ) injury can be introduced to athletes and reinforced by coaches (Harber, 2007).

At the Learn to Train stage, special emphasis should be paid to reinforcing positive eating habits and teaching positive refueling practices before, during, and after training. Specific micronutrients such as calcium and iron are particularly important. The connection between energy intake and positive growth and development can be discussed. Young girls should start to understand the importance of proper refueling for physical activity and training. An imbalance between dietary energy intake and the energy expended in training may lead to poor recovery and less-than-optimal growth. Low dietary energy intake is often associated with low calcium intake, and calcium is an essential mineral for healthy bone deposition and strength. The combination of low energy intake and low calcium intake can lead to reduced muscle growth and strength.

Females at this stage should begin to understand and anticipate the changes that occur with the onset of puberty. These physical changes mark critical periods of increased strength, endurance, and training capacity. The menstrual cycle, which occurs later during puberty, requires energy to function properly—another reason girls should understand the importance of energy intake. The years before peak height velocity (i.e., the Learn to Train stage as well as the Train to Train stage) are critical periods for maximizing bone mass. Menstrual cycle history is also a strong determinant of bone mineral density. With delayed menarche or an increased number of missed menstrual cycles, bone mineral density drops, which has long-term negative effects on female health.

Following are the key points of this stage:

- Teaching correct technical executions of shoulder and lower-body movements and skills
- Providing more thorough instructions about the technical requirements for safe movement
- Introducing, watching for, and correcting high-risk maneuvers associated with ACL and PFJ injuries

- Reinforcing positive eating habits and refueling habits
- Explaining the connections among energy intake, positive growth and development, menstrual function, and bone mineral health

Competition

Competition at this stage continues to be about athlete development, not results. Results are just one indicator of performance, and at this stage, not the most important one. Competition during Learn to Train is an assessment of how the athlete is progressing in overall athleticism including movement skills, sport skills, and in-the-moment decision making in sport contexts. Children have different physical and mental abilities than adult athletes have, and modified games help them develop desired attributes for the long term. As identified in chapter 10, competition occurs naturally among children at this age, especially among boys, because this is part of their enjoyment of sport. Girls place a higher value on the social aspect of sport. Coaches and parents must recognize this and not be put off by a perceived lack of seriousness in players, and make sure to build social opportunities into the sport season. Letting kids be kids while participating in sport and celebrating as they develop in all aspects of the sport are critical at this stage. Fun contests that emphasize particular skills give children a chance to showcase those skills, work to improve them, and measure their improvement. Emphasis at competitions should be on personal bests, challenging oneself, and having fun.

Children at the Learn to Train stage need the proper training-to-competition ratio. For the best long-term results in team sports, generally 70 percent of time should be spent in training or practice, and only 30 percent in competition during this stage. The 30 percent includes competition and competition-specific training (e.g., scrimmaging against an opposition). These percentages vary according to the sport and individual athletes' needs, especially in individual sports. Associations, clubs, leagues, event organizers, and coaches should research the recommended training-to-competition ratio from their sports' national sport organizations (NSOs). Athletes who practice more than they compete are better prepared for competition, in both the short and long term, than those who compete more than recommended by LTAD or NSOs. It is important to note that overcompetition and undertraining at this stage, as well as in the next stage, results in a lack of basic skills and fitness.

Following are the key points of this stage:

- Focusing on skill-based competition and contests
- Explaining to parents the training-to-competition ratio

Role of Parents

Parents must keep their children involved in a variety of sports and activities so they continue to develop basic strength and flexibility, refine their ABCs, and discover new sports and activities to enjoy. At the Learn to Train stage, faster games should be encouraged to develop power and endurance, because this is a time of accelerated adaptation to motor coordination training. Parents should dialogue with their children and listen to them to identify their sport preferences. They should avoid early specialization in late specialization sports because it can be detrimental to children's success. Over time, they can help their children narrow their focus and involvement to three sports. Toward the end of this stage, parents can help their children determine their strengths and weaknesses as well as the sports they enjoy most so they have a better idea of what they might want to specialize in during the next year or so.

As the number of games begins to increase, parents should cheer for their children and the whole team and model good sporting behavior by cheering good plays by the opposition; however, they should not instruct (or yell) from the sidelines! Parents must also see to it that their growing children have ample recovery time and are not enrolled in too many activities that involve extensive strain of the same muscle groups, to avoid overuse and injury. Parents can help their children balance schoolwork with involvement in other nonsporting and sporting activities. Children should be educated about important elements in athlete development, such as proper nutrition, hydration, and recovery time.

Learn to Train To-Do List

- Continue to encourage children to engage in unstructured physical play with their friends every day, regardless of the weather. Active play with friends during recess and lunch at school is great.
- Enroll children in minor sport programs each season, and have them try different positions or events. They might find something surprising that they are very good at.
- Encourage children to take every opportunity to play different sports at school, during physical education classes, in intramurals, or on school teams if their school has them.
- Offer children the opportunity to take part in a range of land-based, water-based, and snow- or ice-based activities as well as movement-to-music activities.
- Keep children working on stamina (endurance), strength, speed, skill, and suppleness (flexibility). Strength activities should involve their own body weight, Swiss balls, or medicine balls—not heavy weights.
- Keep sport and physical activity fun.
- Further develop all fundamental movement skills and teach general, overall sport skills. If this does not occur, a significant window of opportunity is lost, which compromises

the athlete's ability to reach his full potential. Basic movement skills can be reinforced by incorporating them into skill development. For example, the crossover step—a fundamental movement in many sports—can be developed and reinforced by practicing the crossover dribble in basketball.

- Introduce hopping and bounding exercises or routines (or wheeling up gradients for athletes in wheelchairs) to aid in strength development. Hopping and bounding can be found in jump shots, diving to make a save, and a multitude of other skills.
- Further develop endurance through games and relays. Kids run, skate, ski, or swim harder when they are pursuing a ball, puck, or buddy.
- Structure competitions to address differences in training ages and abilities.
- Identify sports the children enjoy and may have a predisposition toward. Narrow the focus from many sports at the start of the stage to three sports at the end.
- Introduce single periodization, noting that some sports such as swimming and tennis need to use double periodization to adequately address the sport's unique needs.
- Encourage unstructured play. Repetitive unstructured practice perfects skills. For example, during unstructured play a hockey player may take thousands of shots for the pure enjoyment of connecting with the puck; a soccer player may develop her touch on the ball through hours of independent ball juggling, and a basketball player may learn how to dribble with either hand all around his body from playing on the streets.

Following are the key points of this stage:

- Involving children in a variety of sports and activities
- Encouraging skill development
- Avoiding early specialization in late specialization sports
- Avoiding instructing from the sidelines
- Balancing schoolwork and extracurricular activities
- Measuring height every three months to determine the onset of the growth spurt

Summary

The three or four years before puberty are crucial for children's development. This stage, roughly between the ages of 9 and 12, is when children are most adaptive to fundamental movement and sport skills—those that provide the foundation for all athletic development. But, for children to *want* to engage in the activities that teach them these skills, activities need to be fun.

Children should focus on building their athleticism by participating in three or four sports—even if they show a proficiency or fondness for one in particular. To ensure full development, they should try each position or event within the sports they play. This might take them out of their comfort zone, but that's good for developing decision-making skills and for building up ancillary capacities.

Winning is not the most important thing at this stage, and neither is strategizing—skill development is. That, and a fun environment that keeps children wanting more of the activity. Positive experiences lead them to want to play and practice on their own as well. This should be encouraged, because both unstructured and deliberate play are essential for skill building.

It is all right for young athletes to make mistakes. This is part of the learning process. Children should be permitted to make and learn from their mistakes without parents or coaches yelling out a bunch of instructions. Guidance is good, but so is a bit of self-discovery.

Questions for Reflection

- Is the child having enough fun that she will continue to take part in the sport or activity?
- What are some examples of how children develop their fundamental athletic skills such as stamina (endurance), strength, speed, skill, and suppleness (flexibility)?
- Is skill development a priority over strategizing to win?
- Do you encourage children to practice or play on their own? Do they?
- Are you, as a parent or coach, shouting too many instructions at players?
- Do you allow children to make and learn from their mistakes?

References

Borms, J. (1986). The child and exercise: an overview. *Journal of Sports Sciences 4*, 3-20.

Calder, A. (2007). *Recovery and regeneration for long-term athlete development.* Vancouver, BC: Canadian Sport Centres.

East, J. (2010). LTAD-based character development. Unpublished manuscript.

Harber, V. (2007). *The female athlete perspective: Coach/parent/administrator guide.* Victoria, BC: Canadian Sport Centres.

Rushall, B. (1998) The growth of physical characteristics in male and female children. *Sports Coach, 20,* 25-27.

Samuels, C.H., and Alexander, B.N. (2012). *Sleep, recovery, and human performance.* Victoria, Canada: Canadian Sport Institute.

Viru, A. (1995). *Adaptation in sports training.* Boca Raton, FL: CRC Press.

To Learn More

Balyi, I., Way, R., Norris, S., Cardinal, C. & Higgs, C. (2005). *Canadian sport for life: Long-term athlete development.* Vancouver, BC: Canadian Sport Centres.

Dick, F.W. (1985). *Sports training principles.* London: Lepus Books.

Docherty, D. (1985). *Trainability and performance of the young athlete.* Victoria, BC: University of Victoria.

Fundamental movement skills: Beyond the fundamentals—a games approach. (2010). Ottawa, ON: Physical & Health Education Canada.

Higgs, C., Balyi, I., Way, R., Cardinal, C., Norris, S., & Bluechardt, M. (2007). *Developing physical literacy: A guide for parents of children ages 1 to 12.* Retrieved from www.canadiansportforlife.ca/resources/ltad-resource-papers

Mujika, I. (2009). *Tapering and peaking for optimal performance.* Champaign, IL: Human Kinetics.

Schmidt, R. (2008). *Motor learning and performance: A situation-based learning approach.* Champaign, IL: Human Kinetics.

US Soccer. (2006). *Best practices for coaching soccer in the United States.* Chicago, IL: United States Soccer Federation.

Train to Train

16

Rick was coaching his son's U14 basketball team in the Smith County Night League. The U14 age division spanned two age years, including boys who were 12 and 13 years old, in grades 7 and 8. In the case of Rick's team, most of the boys happened to be 12 years old and in grade 7, so they were smaller than the boys on many of the other teams, who were mostly in grade 8. Rick's team was struggling in the league standings.

The mother of one of the players on Rick's team was getting frustrated with the weak results. Terri had played a lot of basketball in high school, and then later in her university intramural league, and she knew they could get more wins if they started coaching more tactics and specializing the players in positions. She was busting to talk to Rick and make him understand.

"Look at Anthony," Terri finally said to Rick one evening as the boys were scrimmaging, dramatically pointing at the boy and waving her hand to underscore her frustration. "He's the tallest player on the team—he should be playing center for us and scoring the baskets, but you keep moving him around! He's wasted as a point guard!"

She went through the entire list of players, telling Rick what positions each boy should play. She also said they should be playing a zone defense and pressing. Rick breathed softly all the while, preparing himself to explain. He had met this type of parent while coaching previous teams, and he knew they were well intentioned, so he wanted to take time to explain the purpose and intent of his training regimen and his philosophy about playing different positions.

"These guys are young and they're all at different levels of physical development," said Rick. "This is still the most important age for developing playing skills such as dribbling, shooting, and passing, together with basic principles of court movement and support," he explained. "In another few years, we will start to emphasize different tactics, including zonal defending, but right now we want to develop all-round basketball players, not positional players."

Terri was shaking her hands. "But what about the division title? Two more losses, and we'll be out of the playoffs for sure! It's just so frustrating—we could be challenging for the trophy if we just played the players where they should be playing!"

Rick nodded. "You're right. We could be challenging," he said, "but we'd be selling these players short on the skill development that will help them be successful at the college level."

Now it was Rick's turn to go through the roster. "You see Jacob? He's probably the shortest boy on the team right now, but if you consider the fact that his mother is 6 feet (183 cm) tall and his dad is 6 feet 5 (196 cm), there's a good likelihood that he will be well over 6 feet tall, and probably even taller than his dad. That's a pretty big guy. He's only short now because he's a late maturer. By the time he's in grade 11, he'll probably be the tallest player on our squad and our best choice for center.

"Anthony, on the other hand, is a perfect example of an early maturer. He's the tallest now, but if you look at how short his parents are, I'd just about bet my house that he tops out no taller than maybe 5 feet 10 or 11 (178-180 cm). His best chance of continuing in the sport might be as a point guard, so we owe it to him to make sure he knows how to pass, dribble, and carry the ball, or his playing career could be over at age 15."

Terri was shaking her head in dismay. She couldn't believe what she was hearing. She could feel the league title slipping away, and it pained her.

"Don't get me wrong," said Rick. "I'd love to win the league title. I'm a very competitive-minded guy. But if you gave me the choice of winning a title at U14 or a bunch of these kids playing varsity in university, I'll take varsity ball players. When these guys really start to emerge with their full potential as players, we'll be specializing them in their positions. I'll bet they will be challenging for the title at U16. They'll probably be either winning or challenging for the title every year afterward, too, because their bodies will have pretty much finished growing, they'll have specialized at the right time, and they'll have all the skills they need to continue succeeding in the sport."

Terri held herself silent for what remained of the season, but she still felt frustrated by Rick's approach. When it came time to register the following year, she switched her son to another team that had narrowly lost in the league final the previous year.

She was delighted when her son's new U14 team won a place in the championship final. But she was devastated when they lost to the opponent: Rick's team. She was even more upset by how it happened. The game was decided with a brilliant 3-pointer from a tall guard in the last 15 seconds of the game—Anthony.

Terri tried to show some grace with a humorous quip to Rick after the trophy presentation: "I thought you said you didn't want to win the titles!"

Rick scratched his head. "Yeah, they are a bit ahead of the plan," he said, "but really, I'm just pleased that I have a point guard who knows how to shoot!"

This chapter analyses and describes the Train to Train stage. Although all stages are important, this stage is possibly the most important. It is complex and challenging from the biological, physiological, sociological, mental, and emotional points of view because most boys and girls go through puberty during this stage. Before puberty and postpuberty, simple diagnostics can identify the strengths and weaknesses of the athlete or team, and programs can be developed based on those diagnostics. During puberty a large number of other factors have to be taken into consideration.

Train to Train Basics

During this stage, athletes begin to refine their focus to two sports in different seasons so the sports don't conflict with each. Year-round competition in one sport is not recommended. At this age many teenagers pick a winter sport and a summer sport; toward the end of this stage, many become focused on a single sport.

The goals for athletes at this stage are to strengthen and refine basic skills in the sports they play as well as to develop alternatives to these basic skills while acquiring new ones. Athletes are consolidating and refining basic practical tactical knowledge, and coaches are tailoring new tactical knowledge to match the performance of each athlete. Decision-making skills continue to develop, and athletes are developing solid general physical foundations of speed, strength, endurance, and flexibility.

A number of the key issues for Train to Train athletes have been described in the chapters on age (chapter 5), trainability (chapter 6), and periodization (chapter 9). Objectives at this stage are to build a strong aerobic base, further develop speed and strength toward the end of the stage, and continue building and refining sport-specific technical and tactical skills.

As presented in chapter 6, young athletes during the Train to Train stage consolidate their basic sport-specific skills and tactics. There are three sensitive periods of accelerated adaptation to training: aerobic, speed, and strength. Optimal aerobic trainability begins with the onset of peak height velocity (PHV), the major growth spurt during maturation.

Because of complex biological, physiological, sociological, mental, and emotional processes during puberty, coaches must have good knowledge of the growth and maturation processes. During sudden growth, the body is vulnerable to injury. This can be an issue following the onset of the growth spurt and continuing after PHV. Certain bones and cartilage are more susceptible to injury, which is another reason that training and competition ratios generally follow a 60:40 percent split.

Monitoring body alignment (i.e., ankles, knees, hips, shoulders, and vertebrae), muscle balance (triceps and biceps, quadriceps and hamstrings), and flexibility is essential during this stage. This monitoring should be done during quarterly measurements. At this stage parents and coaches should be looking for any body alignment, muscle imbalance, or flexibility problems, and consult trained professional practitioners if they discover any. If practitioners confirm that problems exist, rehabilitation should take priority over training and competition.

The Train to Train stage is often identified as "building the engine," referring to the body's readiness to improve physiological functions during puberty. Regarding this potential opportunity, Arbeit (1997) determined that programs to develop children for and through sport must capitalize on the most important development phases: prepuberty, puberty, and early postpuberty. The heart and the lungs are rapidly growing; blood volume expands; estrogen and testosterone production increases; and muscle mass and fat mass rapidly increase with the onset of peak weight velocity and peak bone velocity about a year after PHV. The timing of peak weight velocity and peak bone velocity coincides with peak strength velocity. It is well documented in the literature that weight-bearing exercise enhances bone growth (Doyle-Baker, 2009).

The term *adolescent maintenance* (Diving Canada, 2007) refers to the process of managing athlete programs through the growth spurt. Reduced competition schedules, reduced training loads, and optimized recovery help to ease the "growing pains" of adolescence. This is important, because many young athletes across a variety of sports are not trained properly during the growth spurt, as a result of coaches or parents (or both) who are too eager to have them win and neglect to use developmentally appropriate programs. The key message of this stage is that performance is secondary to overall preparation (Viru, 1995). When performance is the focus of the Train to Train stage, athletes are less likely to establish long-term goals and objectives for themselves.

During this stage, general, overall sport skills should be further developed, and sport-specific technical skills should be consolidated before the end of the stage. At the beginning of the stage, athletes play all offensive and defensive positions in team sports and train for all events in individual sports. Toward the end of the stage in team sports, specialization narrows to offensive or defensive positions. In individual sports, the discipline is selected but not the event. In athletics, for example, event groups are identified, but the particular event is not. With jumping, potential events are identified (i.e., long jump, triple jump, high jump, or pole vaulting), but the specific event is not. Position- and event-specific specialization may occur only with early-maturing athletes before the end of this stage.

Key Training and Performance Characteristics

Although the Train to Train stage focuses on "building the engine" as a major emphasis, other characteristics of the young athlete need to be further developed.

Skill Development

At this stage, significant training of fundamental movement skills and technical sport skills continues. However, now strategies evolve as the young athlete starts to compete with adult rules, equipment, and facilities. Coaches are introducing athletes to tactics to adjust to the opposition's approach. These tactics support the intuition, or game sense, already developed through small-side games. Athletes are now working to further develop their skills and to understand all the elements of correct execution. To do this, they must repeatedly practice the skill so that execution becomes reliable. Many hours of formal training are required, along with opportunities to apply the skills in practices and competitive settings. Qualified coaches must lead skill-training sessions so athletes can receive appropriate feedback and correction. Skills are then applied in game situations, which reinforces good skills and exposes weaker ones as needing improvement.

Following are the key points of this stage:

- Strengthening and refining basic skills
- Developing alternatives to basic skills while acquiring new ones
- Consolidating and refining basic practical tactical knowledge
- Tailoring new tactical knowledge to match the performance
- Continuing to develop decision-making skills
- Developing a solid general foundation of speed, strength, endurance, and flexibility

Psychology

During this stage the basic skills introduced in the Learn to Train stage are further developed: relaxation, imagery, goal setting, concentration, communication, and motivation. Additionally, self-talk, thought stopping, and, toward the end of the stage, awareness of personal strengths and weaknesses should be addressed.

Recording feelings and thoughts later evolves into pre-competition and competition planning, to gain a better understanding not only of what works from a nutritional, rest, and recovery perspective, but also of the state of mind that results in the best performance.

Goal setting at this stage evolves to include short-, medium-, and long-term goals. As the stage progresses, the long term can become longer. For example, long term to a 12-year-old may be the end of current season, whereas long term to a 16-year-old may be a career. Goal setting can also become more specific to practice and competition as well as to working on a specific skill at each practice.

Relaxation techniques such as progressive muscle relaxation, breathing to control nerves, or self-suggestion should be used by Train to Train athletes to give create a more relaxed stage when needed.

Self-talk and thought stopping work together to create a positive state of mind for athletes to ensure their best performance and enjoyment of sport. If athletes, after competition, jot down what they were thinking during the competition, they will start to understand how they talk to themselves during competition. With this knowledge, they can ensure that their self-talk is, "I can do it!" rather than "I can't do it!" Whereas self-talk is internal communication with oneself, thought stopping refers to the external situation, such as thoughts about opponents and the environment. At this stage, athletes should be practicing stopping negative thoughts and changing them to positive self-talk—for example, from, "This hill is really long and steep!" to "I am strong on hills; this is going to hurt my competition more than me!"

As this stage progresses, more factors are introduced that can affect concentration. Spectators, opponent interactions, pressure to perform on demand, as well as self-talk can disrupt concentration. Simulating various situations builds athletes' ability to maintain concentration on the day of the event. Using cue words to create focus and to refocus is an effective way to maintain concentration.

Working on the vividness and detail of the imagery should further refine the mental picture, which makes it more useful in competition. The imagery should bring into play the previous skills of positive self-talk and the use of cue words.

Through journaling, athletes can now start to understand the basic skills they are good at and those they need to work on. This self-awareness helps them to develop a complete skill set as they seek to move into the next stage of LTAD.

Following are the key points of this stage:

- Using more specific goal setting
- Using relaxation techniques
- Using positive self-talk and thought stopping
- Maintaining concentration and refocusing with cue words
- Refining imagery
- Understanding personal skills

Recovery and Regeneration

Techniques learned during the Train to Train stage can have a long-lasting effect on an athlete's future in sport and health. Although athletes at this stage are experiencing rapid physical changes, they are also being exposed to increased workloads. Increased growth, especially of muscle, bone, and connective tissues, and hormonal changes coupled with an increase in mechanical loading require careful management (Calder, 2007).

Athletes at this stage have the highest chance of experiencing overtraining, overuse, and burnout. As a result, it is important that they keep records of their training loads, performances, and responses to stress. Other data such as resting heart rate, quality of sleep, and fatigue levels should also be recorded daily, as well as self-esteem, soreness, appetite, stresses, illness or injury, and for females, the onset of each menstrual cycle. By monitoring all of the variables discussed, athletes learn to listen to their bodies.

As workloads increase and their bodies are developing, athletes in the Train to Train stage require more recovery strategies than they did in previous stages. These include daily contrast showers, stretching prior to bedtime, a weekly hot tub with short (30- to 60-second) cold immersion plunges, and weekly massages.

Train to Train athletes need to address nutritional requirements before, during, and after training and competition situations. At this stage they need specific carbohydrates, proteins, and electrolytes, as well as information about the unique metabolic requirements at their particular maturational stage.

Following are the key points of this stage:

- Keeping records of training loads, performances, responses to stress, resting heart rate, quality of sleep, fatigue, self-esteem, soreness, appetite, stresses, illness or injury, and for females, the onset of each menstrual cycle
- Increasing the use of recovery strategies
- Seeking nutritional advice

Character

At this stage, coaches must balance the restrictive aspects of the sport's requirements and rules with teenagers' need for freedom. Young teens (girls 12 to 13 and boys 15 to 17) often have unpredictable behaviors and oppose the established order (e.g., questioning the justification of a given sport rule). They often break rules for the fun of it as they confuse what is right with what peers want them to do, because they want to be loved and respected. They are also very concerned about what people think of them (East, 2010).

This stage continues to focus on sport as a fun experience. Athletes are given more autonomy to help them learn new skills as well as to maintain the discipline needed for continuing to develop as athletes. They are mature enough to take responsibility for their commitment and have respect for their sport. At this age, athletes have a good understanding of their responsibilities to, and their appreciation of, their team, coach, and sport support system. Issues of ethics and fairness become more concrete, especially with participation in higher-stakes competitions. Coaches should also begin teaching about the importance of determination and commitment in achieving training results.

Following are the key points of this stage:

- Providing more autonomy as trust builds
- Acknowledging athletes' increased sense of responsibility to teammates and respect for themselves and their sport

Competition

At this stage, travel demands often increase as athletes travel for competition. In the minds of the athlete, coach, and parents, the stakes of competition are higher, particularly when travel is involved. However, long-distance travel takes away from training time, which continues to be crucial for optimal development at this stage. Competition gives athletes a chance to learn how to overcome adversity or disappointment. Meaningful competition (see chapter 10) can provide a high degree of challenge and serve as proof of the benefits of practice and hard work. Meaningful competition also introduces physical and mental challenges that prepare athletes for future competitions. Fun social activities should be included at competitions at this stage.

At the Train to Train stage, significant differences begin to appear between athletes who train year-round and those who train seasonally. Coaches need to carefully monitor competition volume to ensure that athletes get enough training and recovery time even as many are requesting more opportunities to compete.

Appropriate training-to-competition ratios need to be observed, too. For the best long-term results in team sports during this stage, generally 60 percent of time in the sport should be spent in training or practice, and only 40 percent in competition. The 40 percent includes competition and competition-specific training (e.g., scrimmaging against an opposition). These percentages vary according to the sport and individual athletes' needs, especially in individual sports.

Following are the key points of this stage:

- Recognizing that traveling more or farther does not guarantee higher-quality competition
- Providing meaningful competition to motivate athletes

Females

Because most females at this stage are reaching the onset of PHV, they can realize the benefits of training aerobic capacity and strength capacity. An emphasis on correct technique for the fundamental and sport-specific skills should continue. Functional training and resistance training should be regular components of programs for females (Harber, 2007).

Because girls can experience rapid physical changes during this stage, they and their coaches should note any changes in movement patterns, agility, balance, and coordination and continue to check for the correct execution of lower-body and shoulder movements. Coaches and female athletes should be familiar with the high-risk movements associated with anterior cruciate ligament (ACL) and patellofemoral joint (PFJ) injuries during deceleration combined with a cut or change in direction, or when landing from a jump. Reinforcing proper technique during these movements may reduce nonimpact injury rates.

Coaches of female athletes should continue to reinforce positive eating habits and refueling practices before, during, and after training, keeping in mind that some athletes may not have learned about these practices during earlier stages. Because many young girls begin menstruating during this stage, they need information about supporting their reproductive functions nutritionally and about healthy bone development.

Poor or inadequate energy intake may lead to delayed menarche and other menstrual irregularities. Depending on the duration and severity of the energy insufficiency, various hormonal disturbances may occur and result in irregular periods (oligomenorrhea) or periods stopping altogether (amenorrhea). A decrease in estrogen may result in weakened bones, reduced peak bone mass, increased susceptibility to stress fractures, and premature osteoporosis. Stress fractures may occur and limit participation in training and competition for long periods of time. Stress fractures occur more frequently in active women with menstrual irregularities; amenorrheic athletes are two to four times more likely to suffer stress fractures compared to normally menstruating athletes. Missing an occasional menstrual period is normal; however, missing several periods without explanation should be discussed with a physician to ensure that reproductive maturation milestones are achieved.

Following are the key points of this stage:

- Understanding the factors that lead to ACL and PFJ injuries
- Adding strength training and functional training

- Reinforcing, or introducing, positive eating and refueling habits
- Watching for hormonal disturbances—in particular, lower estrogen levels
- Referring athletes who have not begun menstruating by the age of 16 to a physician
- Reiterating, or introducing, the connections among menstrual function, energy intake, and bone mineral health

Role of Parents

Parents must continuously monitor and track their children's growth so they know when the growth spurt begins. Communication between parent and child should increase as they continue to discuss various sporting options and begin setting long-term goals. Parents can help their children choose a sport in which to specialize by offering their input and suggestions.

Information about early and late developers (see chapter 5) must be shared with athletes, ensuring that they understand the consequences or benefits of their own maturation process and how they might use it to their advantage. Late developers should be encouraged not to drop out of sport.

At this time, extracurricular activities are often cut as athletes a focus on a few preferred activities. School workloads also increase and students become more immersed and interested in their studies. Training time and game time also increase, and as athletes become more involved in their clubs, so do their parents. Parents who want to volunteer at events or within the club organizations must be prepared to sacrifice a significant amount of their free time. They should continue to demonstrate interest in and enthusiasm for the sport, and they may even choose to learn more about the sport by taking an officials course.

Communication among parents, coaches, and athletes continues as parents organize their children's schedules—keeping track of competition times, tournaments, and other important dates while minding the dates of important final exams and other commitments. Parents should also trust the coach, intervening only when necessary. Planning ahead by

scheduling transportation and budgeting for the increased costs of training and competition can reduce the stress caused by these factors. Also, while athletes are going through a growth spurt, their parents should accommodate their changing body size by providing appropriate equipment, shoes, and clothing.

As best they can, parents should ensure that their children get plenty of rest and regeneration time given their sporting activities and the increasing demands of their social lives. During the growth spurt in particular, they should make sure their children do not overtrain, because growing bodies are more susceptible to injury. Stretching is important because the rapid growth rate comes at the expense of flexibility. The teen years are awkward and trying for everyone, even athletes, so parents need to demonstrate patience and understanding. Periods of rapid growth may cause some skill regression, which can be upsetting to athletes. They need to understand that this is normal, and that they should not drop out! The emotional and social impact of the growth spurt can be frustrating. Adding fluctuating hormone levels to the mix can begin to create friction and confusion within young teens.

Emotional development can be different for males and females. Parents must watch for girls who are now more susceptible to low moods, which can lead to depression, eating disorders, and low self-esteem. Being involved in sports and on teams can offset these issues by fostering a positive body image and boosting self-confidence.

Parents of athletes at this stage should monitor the following:

- Fitness levels
- Body alignment and symmetrical development
- Social skills
- Cognitive abilities
- Emotions and behaviors
- Physical and technical abilities
- Iron levels in female athletes
- Emotional development (girls are at an increased risk for low moods, which can

Train to Train To-Do List

- Make aerobic training a priority after the onset of the growth spurt while maintaining or further developing skill, speed, strength, and flexibility.
- Emphasize flexibility training given the rapid growth of bones, tendons, ligaments, and muscles.
- Consider the two windows of accelerated adaptation to strength training for females: the first occurs immediately after PHV, and the second begins with menarche. For males, there is one window, and it begins 12 to 18 months after PHV.
- Note that both aerobic and strength trainability depend on the maturation levels of the athlete.
- Understand the relative age effect and the implications it can have on talent recruitment and development.
- Training emphases based on whether participants are early, average, or late maturers.
- Understand the sport-specific technical skills required to compete at the next stage of development. Build technical skills into training and have athletes further practice them in competition.
- Identify and teach the strategies and positional tactics required to compete at the next stage of development. Use a wide variety of tactics in training so athletes can use them in competition.
- Understand the physical and mental challenges of competition.
- Introduce athletes with disabilities to sport-specific equipment such as wheelchairs and athletic prostheses. For all athletes, the use of body-size-appropriate and skill-level-appropriate equipment remains important.
- Optimize training and competition ratios. Too much competition wastes valuable training time; conversely, not enough competition inhibits the practice of technical, tactical, and decision-making skills.
- Use talent identification to help athletes focus on two sports at the beginning of the stage.
- Use single and double periodization.
- Train participants in daily competitive situations in the form of practice matches or competitive games and drills.

The Learn to Train and Train to Train stages are the most important for athletic preparation.

increase the risk of depression, eating disorders, and low self-esteem)
- Doping (athletes should be educated about doping at the end of this stage)
- Measurements (watch for PHV)
- Menarche
- Schoolwork
- Social life

Summary

The Train to Train stage is possibly the most important and most challenging in terms of development, because most children go through puberty at this stage. Athletes begin focusing on two sports in alternating season and without year-round competition. Coaches should help athletes refine basic sport-specific skills while acquiring new ones.

Three sensitive periods of accelerated adaptation to training take place during this stage: aerobic, speed, and strength. Optimal aerobic trainability begins with the onset of PHV. The onset of peak weight velocity and peak bone velocity occur about a year after PHV to coincide with peak strength velocity, which makes this the prime time to train for strength.

Because the body is vulnerable to injury after the onset of the growth spurt and during PHV, training-to-competition (and competition-related training) ratios should follow the 60:40 split. Monitoring body alignment is key at this time. If issues arise, rehabilitation should take priority over all else. To help keep athletes healthy and interested in sport during this time, maturation patterns should be addressed. Although the body is ready to improve physiological functions, performance must remain secondary to overall preparation.

Questions for Reflection

- How can a coach or parent determine when an athlete should be focusing on aerobic, speed, or strength training?

- What is the training-to-competition ratio for Train to Train?

- How can coaches and parents support athletes to remain in sport as they progress through puberty?

- What do coaches and trainers have to be particularly careful of while building the engine?

References

Arbeit, E. (1997, April 5-6) Practical training emphases in the first and second decades of development. Paper presented at the XXth European Athletics Coaches Association (EACA) Conference, Belgrade, Serbia.

Calder, A. (2007). *Recovery and regeneration for long-term athlete development.* Vancouver, BC: Canadian Sport Centres.

Doyle-Baker, T. (2009). Effects of weight-bearing activities & calcium intake on bone development. *Fitness Informer,* 24-25.

Diving Canada. (2007). *Foundations of excellence: Diving Canada long-term athlete development model.* Calgary, AB: Canadian Sport Centres.

East, J. (2010). LTAD-based character development. Unpublished manuscript.

Harber, V. (2007). *The female athlete perspective: Coach/parent/administrator guide.* Victoria, BC: Canadian Sport Centres. Retrieved from www.canadiansportforlife.ca

Viru, A. (1995). *Adaptation in sports training.* Boca Raton, FL: CRC Press.

To Learn More

Balyi, I. (1998, September). Long-term planning of athlete development: The training to train phase. *The UK's Quarterly Coaching Magazine, 1,* 8-11.

Balyi, I., & Hamilton, A. (2001). Key to success: Long-term athlete development. The training to train stage. Part 1. *Sports Coach, 24* (2), 30-31.

Balyi, I., & Way, R. (1995). Long-term planning of athlete development. The training to train phase. *B.C. Coach,* 2-10.

Belov, E. (1995). *For those starting artistic gymnastics.* Ottawa, ON: Canadian Gymnastics Federation.

Blimkie, C.J.R. (1992). Resistance training during pre- and early puberty: Efficacy, trainability, mechanism, and persistence. *Canadian Journal of Sport Sciences, 17* (4), 264-279.

Blimkie, C.J.R., & Marion, A. (1994). Resistance training during preadolescence: Issues, controversies, and recommendations. *Coaches Report, 1* (4), 10-14.

Bompa, T. (1985). *Theory and methodology of training.* Dubuque, IA: Kendall/Hunt.

Dick, F.W. (1989). *Sport training.* London: A&C Black.

Harre, D. (1982). *Principles of sport training.* Berlin: Sportverlag.

Matveyev, L. P. (1983). *Aspects fondamentaux de l'entrainement.* Paris: Vigot.

Nadori, L. (1986). *Az edzes elmelete es modszertana.* Budapest: Sport.

Platonov, V.N. (1988). *L'entrainement sportif: Theorie et methode.* Paris: Ed.EPS.

Sanderson, L. (1989). Growth and development considerations for the design of training plans for young athletes. *CAC, SPORTS, 10* (2).

Smith, M. (1990). Enhancing child development through play and sport. *CAC, Sports, 10* (7).

Thumm, H-P. (1987). The importance of the basic training for the development of performance. *New Studies in Athletics, 1,* 47-64.

Van Praagh, E. (Ed.). (1998). *Paediatric anaerobic performance.* Champaign, IL: Human Kinetics.

Viru, A, Loko, J., Volver, A., Laaneots, L., Karlesom, K., & Viru, M. (1998). Age periods of accelerated improvements of muscle strength, power, speed and endurance in age interval 6–18 years. *Biology of Sport, 15* (4), 211-227.

Wieneck, J. (1990). *Manuel d'entrainement.* Paris: Vigot.

17

Train to Compete

Angela's new training plan made her feel special. She was 17, and for the first time, her coach was working on a plan designed just for her. "Don't let it go to your head," her coach Stephan always joked with his athletes. "You're special, but not that special."

Angela's goal was to medal at the Olympics. Stephan was working on a realistic plan that saw her making the national team this year and potentially medaling at the following two games, but not just any coach could write it. He needed to know everything about Angela as a swimmer.

Stephan studied the notes from Angela's past coaches. He already knew she showed promise as a long-distance swimmer, and the two of them decided to build a competition schedule around long-distance events. But there were a number of other things to factor in. He had to consider how Angela had trained and what events she had competed in over her past four years with the club. He needed to know her mental and social habits and her physical status, and factor in data on her physical maturation, aerobic testing, and body composition. There was a good deal of pressure on Stephan; misreading any one of these factors could keep Angela from achieving her Olympic dream.

And there were concerns to address in Angela's plan. For instance, he wasn't sure she could complete the necessary strength and aerobic training in time for the state championships in January. She had also hurt her ankle doing dryland training last spring, and Stephan knew it would be difficult to get her training to the necessary volumes and intensities before some of this year's events. Notwithstanding, Angela's future looked promising. She had strong technique, was in good shape, and had a terrific work ethic.

After four hours on his computer, wrestling with questions of Angela's gym work, stroke technique, mental training, and nutritional planning, Stephan thought he had finished her plan. He would look over it in a few days with fresh eyes to make sure he hadn't missed anything (and there was a lot that could be missed). In the meantime, he moved onto his upcoming season's training plans for Zeke and Tabatha, both of whose regimens would look completely different from Angela's.

In the Train to Compete stage of the overall long-term athlete development (LTAD) framework, involvement in sport evolves markedly. This stage is about optimizing physical preparation. Over the course of this relatively broad and somewhat open-ended stage, the emphasis moves to a repetitive sequence of (1) prepare to compete, (2) execute the rehearsed and required performance, (3) recover, (4) review the performance, and (5) modify the training and competition plan. This time is for further developing sport, individual, event, or position-specific skills with help from a sport science and sports medicine support team. A basic tenet is that this developmental stage is as much about training, learning, improving, and executing a practiced behavior in competition as it is about the competition result.

The Train to Compete stage is both broad and open-ended because of a number of factors, including, but not limited to, sport specificity, gender, gaining experience at higher levels of competition, reliable and required performance levels in competition (performance on demand regardless of conditions or circumstances), and, of course, maturation. This final aspect is of great importance because a process that brings late maturers into the elite streams of sport is crucial to maximize the athlete pool. Late maturing athletes may require a slightly different programming time line than those on the mainstream path of the framework. By the same token, assuming there have been no deficiencies in fundamental programming and competencies (technical, physical, psychological), it can be argued that a true early maturer may also be moving along a specifically modified training and competition trajectory.

Train to Compete Basics

Athletes at the Train to Compete stage have a serious commitment to the pursuit of a goal. The allocation of resources from all involved in the process increases markedly and becomes more focused. Program and career planning have to move to a much higher level of sophistication that includes crucial nonsport aspects such as schooling and true downtime, as opposed to systematic recovery and regeneration programming (although these are not always mutually exclusive). This stage begins to lay out a clearer multiyear vision with objectives across a number of categories outside of performance outcomes (e.g., technical execution and decision making under pressure, and improvements in underlying physical attributes and ancillary capacities). This vision, a multiyear plan, is reviewed, modified, and improved with greater clarity as time progresses.

As with all stages of LTAD, the shifts into and out of the Train to Compete stage do not occur at clearly defined points in time. Rather, they come about as a result of a collection of key indicators such as underlying abilities and execution capability, biological development, and progress toward sport mastery, as well as the specific influences of the sport. The time frame of this stage varies from one athlete to another. In keeping with long-term thinking, the Train to Compete stage can be considered two seamlessly linked phases—an initial specialization period and a final specialization period. A key rationale for this two-phase concept is that usually the rate of performance improvement in the initial phase is still heavily influenced by physical growth and maturation, and not

aligned with the typical increases in training load seen over this period. Furthermore, it has to be stressed that the training-specific guidelines presented in the following bulleted list are targets to progress toward over the course of the entire stage and are not imposed at some initial chronological age.

Critical aspects and characteristics of this stage are identified here:

- Typical chronological ages: 16 to 23+ years for males and 15 to 21+ years for females (Ages are sport specific based on international normative data.)
- Improvement and maintenance of physical capacities
- Further development of technical, tactical, and performance, or playing, skills
- Increasing level of specialization (sport, position, discipline, or event)—stage classically moves from initial specialization to final specialization
- Modeling and relentless rehearsal of all aspects of training and performance, particularly the execution of required skills under a variety of conditions
- Integrated recovery and regeneration practices and periods as part of the training and competition process
- Attention paid to maximizing ancillary capacities and the education of the athlete (i.e., becoming a student of the sport)
- Ever-increasing level of program individualization
- Execution at the (predetermined) expected level (the focus of all behaviors and the program in general)
- Using single, double, or multiple periodized formats as dictated by the sport or the specific calendar year
- Sport-specific training (technical, tactical, and physical conditioning related) generally involving 9 to 15 programmed sessions per week
- Shift toward a more competition-based focus: broadly, 40 percent of available time to the development of technical and tactical skills and improving underlying

fitness, and 60 percent allocated to competition and competition-specific training

- Performance targets established according to a long-term plan based on a firm understanding of both the developmental performance level of the sport and the athlete's career path (i.e., projection and prediction)
- Target competitions: high-level provincial or state, national, development international, and relevant senior international (as per individualized athlete plan)
- Increased number of competitive starts across a range of competition levels throughout the stage

As with other stages of the LTAD framework, the overall annual volume of systematic training in the Train to Compete stage has a wide range (perhaps as large as 500 hours—from 400 to 900 hours). Training is gradually and individually increased in the early years of the stage and includes periods of consolidation. A marked increase in training time may occur once the athlete has reached the natural conclusion of the initial early specialization phase. Several authors have remarked that tracking the chronological relationship between competition performance level (output) and training load (input; especially the degree or amount of highly specific, intense competition training), both in reference to specific benchmarks (i.e., percentage of world-level performance and percentage of world-level training load), informs when to progress an athlete to the final specialization phase (Harmon Brown, 2009). Essentially, an assessment of when the rate of performance improvement diminishes in relation to the increase in training load is required (and must be understood) within the context of this stage and the long-term view.

As this stage progresses, the importance of developing appropriate behaviors, program content, and monitoring programs is easy to see, especially because these aspects are setting both the foundation for the next stage, Train to Win, and the concept of the 24-hour athlete. As with Train to Win, the assembly of multiple periodization within the cycles of the annual plan that meet the needs of training, competi-

tion, and recovery, with the final objectives in mind (optimal performance when needed), requires very careful planning and monitoring. The sequence of "analysis and understanding of task, planning and prescription, execution or implementation, evaluation and assessment, and adjustment (if warranted)" (Norris, 2009, p. 67), coupled with effective ongoing monitoring, as a continual cyclical procedure, is critical. Any deficiency displayed in this sequence or its composite parts will likely result in failure to attain the identified performance, competency, or execution level. The involvement of a supporting team of appropriately qualified and experienced experts from an array of disciplines (e.g., sports medicine, sport science, performance analysis, technology) will likely increase in importance as athletes move through this stage.

Key Training and Performance Characteristics

At the Train to Compete stage, the commitment is serious as resources of all forms combine to move the athlete to a much higher level of sophistication. The areas addressed in the following sections still need to be developed.

Skill Development

There is now a balance in training and competition among the four skills: fundamental movement skills, sport technical skills, strategies, and tactics. Athletes are refining their execution of a skill by combining it with other aspects within that skill (e.g., adding deception to the skill of dribbling a ball) and other skills, while also refining their tactics under conditions of game pressure and pace. Athletes also adapt skills to their own unique physiologies. For example, some basketball players may have the size and power to play the physical game under the net. Meanwhile, other players may come to rely on finer ball-handling skills or deception as they dribble to gain advantage on bigger, stronger opponents. Both player types may possess the same speed, but coaches design different strategies for them as they create tactics for matching up and beating opponents. As with all stages of skill development, many hours of practice are required in a variety of training and competitive settings to refine skills. The significant difference is that athletes refine their skills under increasing pressure as the speed and level of competition increases and the consequence of winning or losing can mean either more or less prestige, money, or media attention.

Following are the key skill development points of this stage:

- Refining skill execution
- Training with game pressure and pace
- Adapting skills to the athlete's characteristics
- Building on tactical awareness
- Increasing the level of competition

Psychology

In the previous stages, athletes worked on the basic mental skills that allowed them to be successful on representative teams leading to national championships. Now, at the Train to Compete stage, those basic skills are refined in situations of increased pressure and distraction.

Everything addressed in the Train to Train stage is worked on in more detail in the Train to Compete stage and is more specific to the competition situation of the athlete. Critical to improving these skills is increasing self-awareness by recording in training diaries how the skills are used in practice and competition.

The goal of this stage is to develop consistency in performance using the skills that have been developed.

Athletes, with their coaches' feedback, should evolve detailed competition preparation routines. These routines should include refocusing processes to use when routines are broken in situations such as delays, equipment problems, early poor performance, or preceding crashes by a competitor on the course they are about to run (e.g., Alpine skiing, luge, bobsleigh).

Journaling should now include performance tracking so athletes can better understand what creates personal best performances on demand. In addition to recording scores and

impressions of their personal play, their notes should indicate how they could perform better and what they should address in upcoming training sessions.

At this stage even more factors are introduced in athletes' training and competition. Jet lag, different food, and travel and living conditions can all result in athletes' not performing at their best as a result of physical and mental strain. Consistency of performance is an important objective. This can be achieved through high-quality training, which includes simulating a variety of conditions as well as actually competing under those conditions to better understand what happens, to record it, and to work to improve.

Following are the key points of this stage:

- Refining all basic skills
- Tracking performance
- Developing consistency
- Using personal mental training techniques

Recovery and Regeneration

To monitor recovery, athletes should now have a daily monitoring routine. Although many athletes have finished their growth spurt, their muscle size and strength will continue to increase (Calder, 2007).

Main recovery routines should now be periodized into athletes' training programs. Because training and competition demands are now varied, recovery techniques must suit the environments. This will allow the athlete to adapt to events away from home. Part of this involves managing travel fatigue effectively by learning to adapt to different climates and time zones. Yoga and meditation can be helpful recovery strategies, and massages can be increased to twice a week. During this stage and the next, the recovery program should be varied to avoid repetition.

Following are the key points of this stage:

- Periodizing main recovery routines into the athlete's training program
- Managing fatigue effectively with the help of yoga, meditation, and biweekly massages

Character

As discussed, the objective of this stage is to optimize the human engine and learn how to compete. An important component of that knowledge is to learn how to behave as an athlete who is spending most of the sport experience facing a variety of competitive conditions (East, 2010). At the same time, teenagers are becoming young adults, and their values are becoming more defined, but are still malleable. This is the time when the identification with older adults becomes more stable emotionally and independence is growing (e.g., economically).

A contrast in ethics can occur, though, between an athlete's personal values and the values within the sport. Through observation as well as interaction with coaches, teammates, opponents, and others in the sport system, athletes can be bombarded by different values and points of view. They may question their own values while searching for what will work best for them in achieving their goals.

The Train to Compete stage is particularly important because it may be the last chance for coaches to ensure that athletes resist the temptation to adopt unethical behaviors. Competition, or the competitive spirit, is the main value that should be reinforced at this stage. In fact, the competitive spirit should already have a strong foundation because the previous stage was about reinforcing the qualities of discipline, commitment, and fairness, which are essential components of competition. The key here is to ensure that athletes do not take on the attitude of winning at all costs. Thus, the various responsibilities inherent to respecting a sport will increase (e.g., doping control), and athletes need to be prepared to fulfill their responsibilities both at a social and a sport level.

Following are the key points of this stage:

- Competing in a healthy competitive environment
- Avoiding unethical behaviors
- Questioning values in the face of contrasting values
- Learning more about increased responsibilities

Females

To avoid injury, female athletes at this stage should still focus on the proper technical execution of lower-body and shoulder movements. Any injuries should be addressed and attended to by qualified health care staff, who should also provide preventative and corrective exercises to rehabilitate the athlete following treatment (Harber, 2007).

By this stage positive eating habits and refueling practices before, during, and after training should be established; in the case that they are not, they should be introduced. Some females at this stage have experienced disordered eating or eating disorders; for them, relearning positive habits and monitoring their habits are vital. The connection among energy intake, menstrual function, and bone mineral health should be understood or taught if not learned earlier. As in the previous stage, missing an occasional menstrual cycle is normal; however, if several periods are missed, a physician should be consulted to rule out causes associated with this irregularity.

Following are the key points of this stage:

- Reinforcing proper technique and addressing injuries with health care staff
- Relearning positive eating habits and monitoring eating habits
- Addressing delayed menarche (i.e., after 15 years of age) or other types of reproductive irregularities (e.g., amenorrhea) with a physician

Competition

This is the stage at which athletes are introduced to national-level competitions and are striving for new levels of performance. Exposing them to a number of competitive experiences will help refine their competition preparation techniques and strategies. Athletes may also start to travel internationally during this stage. It is not uncommon for athletes to leave their regular coaches at home and train under appointed national development team coach(es). Competitions are frequent, intense, and demanding, and the athlete and coach focus on competition

Train to Compete To-Do List

- Teach athletes to compete under any kind of condition or circumstance.
- Provide year-round, high intensity sport-, event-, or position-specific training.
- Teach athletes, who are now proficient at performing basic and sport-specific skills, to perform those skills under a variety of competitive conditions during training.
- Emphasize optimum preparation by modeling competitions in training.
- Optimize all training, competition, and recovery programs.
- Individually tailor physical conditioning programs, recovery programs, psychological preparation, and technical development to a greater degree.
- Emphasize preparation that addresses each athlete's individual strengths and weaknesses.
- Help athletes specialize in events or positions.
- Use single, double, triple, or multiple periodization as the national or international competition calendar dictates.
- Introduce quadrennial planning.
- Establish, monitor, and optimize a taper procedure.
- Change the training-to-competition (and competition-specific training) ratio to 40:60. Devote 40 percent of the available time to the development of technical and tactical skills and improving physical conditioning, and 60 percent of the time to competition and competition-specific training.
- Monitor and optimize ancillary capacities.

strategy and tactics. In many sports, a shift in the training-to-competition ratio occurs. Athletes who spend too much time practicing and not enough time competing at this stage will be at a disadvantage at competitions.

Athletes must have the opportunity to take part in competitions that are meaningful but do not have an impact on team selection so they can keep learning. Periodized plans will dictate which competitions to participate in.

A good focus on the training-to-competition ratio is a must. For the best long-term results in team sports, generally only 40 percent of time in the sport should be spent in training or practice, with 60 percent of the time spent on competition during this stage. The 60 percent ratio includes competition and competition-specific training (e.g., scrimmaging against an opposition). These percentages vary according to the sport and the individual athlete's needs,

especially in individual sports. Coaches and athletes must know the recommended training-to-competition ratio recommended by their sports' national organizations.

Following are the key points of this stage:

- Shifting training-to-competition ratios
- Optimizing training and competition environments to develop top international performers

Role of Parents

Teens are very committed to sport, and the dynamics of the family are often centered around this commitment. At this stage, the majority of the athlete's time, aside from school, is spent training or competing. Parents cannot expect that the family will eat many meals together or have time for many family holidays. A competitive athlete's schedule can be all consuming, so parents must find time for other family members and other children, and create a family environment in which members collectively support each other. Siblings may help out at sporting events, but it is important that parents encourage them to find their own roles and interests as well.

As the athlete becomes older and more independent and capable, parents may play a more passive role in managing the athlete's schedule, but still offer guidance and support when needed. They can support the coach and be sure that the athlete is following the correct regimen. Parents can still expect to be very busy attending competitions and volunteering. Overall costs may increase significantly, including the costs of training and competition, but also private or specialized coaching, nutritionists, physiotherapists, and psychologists. If the athlete is thinking about retiring or transitioning from the sport, parents can help in the exploration of career and educational options. At this time, the athlete is likely considering postsecondary education. Parents can help athletes explore their options regarding universities or other postsecondary institutions, scholarships, or other scenarios.

Following are the key points of this stage:

- Having an increasingly more passive role
- Acknowledging that the dynamics of the family are centered around the athlete's striving for excellence
- Recognizing the all-consuming nature of advanced sport for themselves and their other children
- Dealing with significantly increased costs
- Helping athletes in the stressful transition from high school to other opportunities (college?)

Summary

The Train to Compete stage is all about optimizing technical, tactical, mental, and physical preparation. This developmental stage is just as

concerned with learning, improving, training, and executing practiced behavior as it is with any specific competition result. Because of all the physiological and sport-related factors that influence this period, the time line is both broad and open-ended.

Maturation plays a big role in determining training schedules and periodization at this stage. As such, it is imperative to have a process in place that not only recognizes late maturers, but also offers them a pathway into elite sport streams. This is the only way to maximize the athlete pool. Late maturers often require an altered programming time line to ensure proper development and preparation.

Multiyear programs come into play at this time. For such programming and periodization to happen properly, the areas of an athlete's life outside of athletic involvement need to be addressed, too. As this stage progresses, the importance of developing suitable behaviors, program content, and analysis becomes apparent, especially because these aspects lay the foundation for the ascent to the international podium and the final competitive stage in LTAD—Train to Win.

Questions for Reflection

- Why is it necessary to have a process for late maturers, or late developers, to enter the excellence stream of a sport?
- What is the basic tenet of this developmental stage?
- What are the two seamlessly linked phases of this stage?

References

Calder, A. (2007). *Recovery and regeneration for long-term athlete development.* Vancouver, BC: Canadian Sport Centres.

East, J. (2010). LTAD-based character development. Unpublished manuscript.

Harber, V. (2007). *The female athlete perspective: Coach/parent/administrator guide.* Victoria, BC: Canadian Sport Centres. Retrieved from http://canadiansportforlife.ca/sites/default/files/flipbooks/TheFemaleAthletePerspective/TheFemaleAthletePerspective.html

Harmon Brown, C. (Ed.). (2009). *IAAF medical manual.* Monaco: International Association of Athletics Federations.

Norris, S. (2009). CS4L's "train to win": An advanced stage within LTAD. *Coaches Plan, 16* (2), 66-67.

To Learn More

Balyi, I. (1998) Long-term planning of athlete development: The training to compete phase. *FHS: The UK's Quarterly Coaching Magazine, 2,* 8-11.

Balyi, I. (1992). Beyond Barcelona: A contemporary critic of the theory of periodization. In *Beyond Barcelona, 4th Elite Coaches Seminar* (pp. 13-17). Canberra: Australian Coaching Council.

Balyi, I., & Hamilton, A. (2002). Key to success—Long-term athlete development: The training to compete stage. *Sports Coach, Australian Sports Commission, 25* (1), 24-27.

Banister, E.W. (1991). Modeling elite athletic performance. In D. MacDougall, et al. (Eds.), *Physiological testing of the high-performance athlete.* Champaign, IL: Human Kinetics.

Banister, E.W., & Calvert, T.W. (1980). Planning for future performance: Implication for long-term planning. *Canadian Journal of Applied Sport Sciences, 5* (3), 170-176.

Bompa, T.O. (1985). *Theory and methodology of training.* Dubuque, IA: Kendall.

Bompa, T.O., & Haff, G.G. (2009). *Perodization: Theory and methodology of training* (5th ed.). Champaign, IL: Human Kinetics.

Dick, F. (2007). *Sports training principles* (5th ed.). London: A & C Black Publishers.

Drabik, J. (1996). *Children and sport training: How your future champions should exercise to be healthy, fit, and happy.* Island Pond, VT: Stadion Publishing Company, Inc.

Farrow, D., Baker, J., & MacMahon, C. (Eds.). (2008). *Developing sport expertise: Researchers and coaches put theory into practice.* New York: Routledge.

Kunipers, J., & Keizer, H. A. (1988). Overtraining in elite athletes. *Sport Medicine,6,* 79-92.

Kurz, T. (2001) *Science of sports training: How to plan and control for peak performance* (2nd ed.). Island Pond, VT: Stadion Publishing Company, Inc.

Matveyev, L.P. (1983). *Aspects fondamentaux de l'entrainement.* Paris: Vigot.

Morrisey, B. (2010, October 15). *What is disordered eating?* Retrieved from www.eatingdisorderexpert.co.uk/what-disordered-eating.html

Nadori, L. (1986). *Az edzes elmelete es modszertana.* Budapest: Sport.

Nolte, V. (2011). *Rowing faster* (2nd ed.). Champaign, IL: Human Kinetics.

Norris, S. (2009). CS4L's "training to compete": It's not solely about winning. *Coaches Plan 16* (3), 28-29.

Platonov, V.N. (1988). *L'entrainement sportif: Theorie et methode.* Paris: Revue EPS.

Stafford, I. (2005). *Coaching for long-term athlete development: To improve participation and performance in sport.* West Yorkshire, UK: SportscoachUK & Coachwise Business Solutions.

Verkhoshansky, Y., & Siff, M.C. (2009). *Supertraining* (6th ed., expanded version). Self published.

18

Train to Win

At 29, Jamie was living his dream of playing professional golf on the PGA tour. He was making a good income in prize money and sponsorship deals and working toward his goal of winning the Masters in Augusta. But over the years, he'd learned that life as a professional golfer was not as easy as it looked on TV.

Jamie would be participating in over 40 events this year. With his livelihood resting on his performances, he had to train frequently; he could not afford to run out of steam or lose his game in the middle of the tour. As such, he'd been living by regimens for years. His periodization schedule had him spending 25 hours a week training and another 15 playing practice rounds. Factoring in tournaments, he guessed he must have been hitting 3,000 balls a week.

The commitment required of him didn't stop there. He followed a specific nutritional plan and worked with a number of sport experts, such as fitness trainers, physiologists, kinesiologists, physiotherapists, and psychologists, to avoid mental obstacles in the midst of an intense schedule. Four times a year, he had to perform biomechanical tests, the results of which always led to tweaks in his training regimen.

New challenges were always coming his way, too. Two years ago he had started media training after giving a TV interview completely unprepared at a tournament. He didn't know how to answer many of the questions, and the bad PR he knew would follow lingered in his head during the next day's round. Neither his interview nor his performance would look very appealing to potential sponsors. And even though his income allowed him to live comfortably, he found that the more money he made, the more he needed help managing it, mostly with regard to taxes and expenses.

Jamie often thought about how different golf was now compared to when he was 10, playing nine-hole courses for fun with his dad. Now, every stroke mattered, and pressure was always there. But although this took the fun and romance out of golfing for most, it didn't for Jamie. He lived for golf. He'd dedicated himself to getting the best result every time.

Train to Win evolves from Train to Compete. This stage encompasses both initial and final specialization of sport-specific elements, requiring intense training throughout the stage and involving more complex annual and multiyear planning. Furthermore, Train to Win precedes the Active for Life stage—the stage that caters to both athletes capable of pursuing competition at the highest national and international levels, and anyone else who engages in physical activity for life. High-performance athletes at the Active for Life stage are transitioning from systematic training regimens to the maintenance of health and recreational pursuits, possibly involving some level of masters competition. The Train to Win stage, although not the final stage of the overall pathway, is the ultimate performance stage and the period that should be used to determine the effectiveness of the long-term athlete development (LTAD) process from a high-performance standpoint.

Because Train to Win represents the final stage of athletic preparation, this is when sport- and position-specific skills and performances are maximized. An athlete's physical, technical, tactical (including decision-making skills), mental, and personal and lifestyle capacities are fully established at this stage. A support team of sport scientists should be fully integrated into the athlete's coaching team and contributing to the periodized plan. World-class able-bodied and disability sport performances require world-class equipment that is fine-tuned to the demands of the event and the requirements of the athlete.

Train to Win Basics

As with all stages of LTAD, the shift to the Train to Win stage is not a clearly defined point in time. It is triggered by a collection of indicators such as underlying abilities and execution capability, biological development, and progress toward sport mastery, as well as the specific influences of the sport. The time frame of the entire LTAD process varies from one athlete to another, although the greatest variation typically occurs at the early development stages and the Train to Win stage. In keeping with long-term thinking, the Train to Win stage can be broken down into two seamlessly linked phases: (1) a mastery period of world-class performances, podium performances, or finals qualifications and (2) the stabilization period in which the athlete maintains this performance level (or a level close to it).

The overall yearly volume for systematic training during this stage typically spans 800 to 1,400 hours. A peak occurs in the early to middle years of the stage, and a gradual decline to approximately 1,000 hours occurs as the stage moves to conclusion. The typical chronological age for entry into this stage, at least in sports in which athletes attain international performance levels later, is 19 and 18 for males and females, respectively. However, the sport-specific age range varies. For example, ages are 14 to 20 years for gymnastics, figure skating, tennis, and swimming (particularly for females); and 21 to 30 years for long-distance running, field events (athletics), cross-country skiing, golf, and wrestling. The initial suggestion of 19 and 18 years for males and females, respectively, fits with the majority of sports, which fall between 18 and 26 years of age for entry to this stage.

Critical aspects and characteristics of this stage are identified as follows:

- Typical chronological ages: 19 years (plus or minus) for males and 18 years (plus or minus) for females (Ages are sport specific based on international normative data.)
- Improvement and maintenance of physical capacities
- Further development of technical, tactical, and playing skills

- Modeling and relentless rehearsal of all aspects of training and performance
- Integrated recovery and regeneration practices and periods as part of the training and competition process
- Attention paid to maximizing ancillary capacities and educating the athlete (i.e., becoming a student of the sport)
- Ever-increasing levels of program individualization
- High performance as the focus of all behaviors and the program in general
- Targeting major events: Olympics, world championships, World Cup tours, and other multisport competitions (Specific professional or semiprofessional sports such as NHL, golf, and curling may adhere to different competition formats.)
- Planning encompassing single, double, triple, or multiple periodized formats as dictated by the sport or the specific calendar year
- Sport-specific, technical, tactical, and fitness-related training, typically requiring 9 to 15 programmed sessions per week
- Increased sport-specific training, typically in the region of 70 percent or more of total training volume
- Optimal number of competitive starts

Attention to detail concerning the organization of training and competition is critical in Train to Win. The assembly of multiple yearly cycles that meet training, competition, and recovery needs and keep the final objectives in mind requires very careful planning and monitoring. The sequence of "analysis and understanding of task, planning and prescription, execution (or implementation), evaluation and assessment, and adjustment (if warranted)" (Norris, 2009, p. 67), coupled with effective ongoing monitoring, as a continual cyclical procedure, is critical. Any deficiency displayed in this sequence or its composite parts will likely result in failure to attain the identified performance level. The involvement of a supporting team of appropriately qualified and experienced experts from an array of disciplines (e.g., sports medicine, sport science, performance analysis, and technology) may be a prerequisite to help the coach design, execute, and review the periodized plan at the highest performance levels.

Ultimately, the success of athletes at this stage will be largely influenced by the composition of their training programs. Creating an optimal program for a specific athlete requires a firm understanding of her strengths and weaknesses, together with clear knowledge of her responses to the range of training and environmental stimuli. This level of sophistication can be developed during this stage, but historical records from the Train to Compete stage, a critical period in training, show that tracking key performance areas from a training perspective can provide invaluable insight and information that will aid the Train to Win athlete. However, the real message here is that given the arrival of an athlete with the underlying abilities to move into the Train to Win stage, the chance of failure at critical times is very real, and athletes need to be willing to examine every facet of training and commit to kaizen, or continuous improvement.

Key Training and Performance Characteristics

This is the stage at which elite athletes with identified talents may pursue the most intense training suitable for international winning performances. Both athletes with disabilities and able-bodied athletes require world-class training methods, equipment, and facilities that meet the demands of their sports and themselves. The following areas must be addressed for this to happen.

Skill Development

At this stage, tactics take precedence while the other three skills—fundamental movement skills, sport technical skills, and strategies—are generally balanced during training and competition. Now athletes know their opponents' strengths and weaknesses as they vie for podium performances. Skills are constantly being perfected once they have completely adapted the skills to suit their particular physi-

ologies, because they have now reached their highest level of competition. The old saying *It's 90 percent mental* applies to athletes at this stage. Their fitness preparation is maximized and skills are refined, so reacting well tactically to a situation is the variable that can result in a competitive advantage. Experience under the greatest conditions of pressure and performance allows athletes to challenge themselves at their optimal limits as they continue to perfect every aspect of their skills so they can create peak performance on demand.

Following are the key skill development points of this stage:

- Developing further skills
- Maximizing fitness preparation
- Maximizing taper and peak (performance on demand)

Psychology

At this stage, all the skills have been refined to the point that the athlete has reached the international podium or top professional league. As a result of the level of performance, new pressures arise. At this stage winning is connected to living because athletes generate income from their performances. This increases mental stress as they work to maintain international excellence. Any weaknesses in athletes' mental preparation must be addressed so they can continue to build consistency into their podium or professional performances. This pressure tests every skill developed to date.

Following are the key psychological points of this stage:

- Being mentally prepared to perform in all conditions
- Embracing the stress of performing for a living

Recovery

Athletes at this stage travel often, sometimes without their home coaches. This distance is not a barrier to daily monitoring, because computer systems can graph athletes' responses and compare them against sport-specific data sets. The results can then be sent to coaches within moments. Athletes at this level require individualized testing and screening schedules to account for the complexities of the sport and recovery within the requirements of the competition calendar (Calder, 2007).

Athletes can now have a significant input into their recovery programs because they have acquired the necessary skills and experience throughout the previous stages. Strategies must be periodized and tailored to suit the competition schedule, with room for small adjustments depending on the environment. New recovery strategies should not be tested at major competitions.

Following are the key recovery points of this stage:

- Communicating with home coaches when travelling
- Periodizing recovery strategies and tailoring them to suit the competition schedule
- Avoiding testing new recovery strategies at major competitions

Character

This is the achievement stage of a young adult who possesses all the skills and capacities learned from previous stages. It is now the time to perform, to strive for excellence in terms of podium results. To keep building on the previous values (fun, discipline, respect, fairness, determination, responsibility, competition), athletes should now focus on a combination of excellence and health to maximize their potential (East, 2010).

The values and ethics of athletes at this stage are mostly solidified and change only as a result of experience. Athletes understand better the role of systems and rules in protecting their individual rights. However, they have a bigger role to play in helping the system achieve this by asking themselves whether their actions respect the rights of other athletes. Athletes now understand that they are responsible for their health, the quality of which affects their performance and goal achievement. They need to acquire healthy habits in areas such as eating, sleeping, and maintaining emotional balance.

Winning is obviously the result now, and the temptation to use shortcuts or adopt unethical behaviors is still present because the athlete can feel the power of glory. Elite athletes need reminders of the importance of respecting their own values and those of the people who have helped them reach this level of development. Unethical behaviors affect not only the athlete's reputation and life, but also their coaches, teammates, family, and friends. Cheating leads to isolation, both in the act itself and in the consequences. Nobody is proud to be a cheater, even those who make it to the podium by cheating. Coaches should reinforce to athletes the importance of excelling in a way that is fair in order to be proud and satisfied. This is the time when athletes become role models, even if they do not realize it. A solid reputation could help them stay attached to their sport and to give back to the community by helping young kids complete the same process they went through. The LTAD cycle then starts all over again.

Following are the key points of this stage:

- Striving to win, not at all costs, but in an ethical manner
- Being the best one can be; that's *real* excellence
- Being proud for having done one's best regardless of the result
- Staying healthy, respecting others, and starting to give back to younger participants

Females

By this stage, positive eating habits and refueling practices before, during, and after training should be well established; in the case that they are not, female athletes need to know the importance of fueling for training and competition. This is critical for competing at the highest levels internationally. All female athletes need encouragement and support to practice adequate energy replacement. For those having trouble meeting the energetic demand of their sport, health care professionals can help (Harber, 2007).

Some athletes during this stage become pregnant. Support and monitoring from a physician

---

Train to Win To-Do List

- Train athletes to peak for major competitions.
- Use minor competitions to model taper.
- Ensure that training is characterized by high intensity and high volume all year round.
- Allow frequent preventative breaks to avoid physical and mental burnouts.
- Use single, double, triple, or multiple periodization as national or international competition calendars dictate.
- Continue to refine modeling taper procedures.
- Continue to refine modeling quadrennial plans.
- Change the training-to-competition ratio to 25:75, and have the competition percentage include competition-specific training activities.
- Maximize ancillary capacities. Athletes who reach genetic ceiling limits can still improve their performances by using ancillary capacities to better advantage.

---

or other health care professionals is essential to ensure the safety of both athlete and baby. Following the pregnancy, an appropriate recovery period is required. Again, the support of a physician and other health care professionals is needed to guide athletes in their return to training and competition.

Following are the key points of this stage:

- Practicing positive eating habits
- When needed, having a pregnancy and prenatal support system in place

Competition

Major competition events define the training program in Train to Win. Other events serve as preparation and learning experiences for the major ones. Mastery of the sport is complete at this stage, and these athletes may be a source of national or sporting pride and role models for younger athletes. Winning at the highest level of competition is the goal at this stage.

The training-to-competition ratio continues to be important. For the best long-term results in team sports, generally only 25 percent of time in the sport should be spent in training or practice, and 75 percent of the time should be spent on competition. The 75 percent ratio includes competition and competition-specific training (e.g., scrimmaging against an opposition). These percentages vary according to the sport and the individual athlete's needs, especially in individual sports. Coaches and athletes must know the recommended training-to-competition ratio of their sports' national organizations. Athletes who spend too much time practicing at this stage and not enough time competing will be at a disadvantage when it comes to competing.

Following is the key point of this stage:

- Recognizing that one's chosen sport encompasses all aspects of one's life

Summary

The Train to Win stage represents the final level in an athlete's competitive pathway. As such, each component of the stage is geared toward preparing the athlete to step on, and stay on, the podium in international competition. This preparation often spans a number of years and requires a properly periodized plan and an expansive support network.

This stage can be seen as two seamlessly linked phases—(1) the *mastery* phase, at which an athlete attains world-class performances, podium performances, or finals qualification and (2) the *stabilization* phase, in which the athlete maintains this performance level. Although the typical chronological age for athletes who reach this stage is 19 for males and 18 for females, the age range varies across sports and individual athletes. The majority of late specialization athletes reach this stage between the ages of 18 and 26.

Attention to detail regarding training and competition organization is a major aspect of this stage. Assembling yearly cycles that meet the needs of training, competition, and recovery is necessary to help athletes reach peak performance levels. These programs cannot be created without a firm understanding of the athlete's strengths, weaknesses, and response capacities. Sport mastery and the training that enables an athlete to perform under any circumstances are pivotal, because the possibility of failure at critical times is magnified at this level. Improper recovery can be detrimental during Train to Win because athletes spend much time away from home and need their systems to be working faultlessly while competing.

Questions for Reflection

- What is the key objective of the Train to Win stage?
- How many years of structured training are required to reach the Train to Win stage?
- Why is double, triple, or multiple periodization during the Train to Win stage the recommended preparation framework?
- Why is a detailed analysis of the athlete's training requirements so important at this stage?
- Why is sport mastery so crucial at this stage?

- Why is monitoring recovery important during the Train to Win stage?

References

Calder, A. (2007). *Recovery and regeneration for long-term athlete development.* Retrieved from www.canadiansportforlife.ca

East, J. (2010). LTAD-based character development. Unpublished manuscript.

Harber, V. (2007). *The female athlete perspective: Coach/parent/administrator guide.* Victoria, BC: Canadian Sport Centres. Retrieved from www.physedandrec.ualberta.ca/Research/~/media/physedandrec/Documents/Research/Prof%20CVs/Harberfemaleathleteperspective.ashx

Norris, S. (2009). CS4L's "training to win": An advanced stage within LTAD. *Coaches Plan, 16* (2), 66-67.

To Learn More

Bompa, T. (1985). *Theory and methodology of training.* Dubuque, IA: Kendall/Hunt

Harre, D. (1982). *Principles of sports training: Introduction to the theory and methods of training.* Berlin: Sportverlag.

Harsanyi, L. (1992). *Az edzes egy even beluli szakaszai.* Budapest: OTSH.

Kenney, W.L., Wilmore, J., & Costill, D. (2012). *Physiology of sport and exercise* (5th ed.). Champaign, IL: Human Kinetics.

Nadori, L. (1989). *Theoretical and methodological basis of training planning with specific considerations within a microcycle.* Lincoln, NE: National Strength and Conditioning Association.

Norris, S.R., & Smith, D.J. (2002). Planning, periodization, and sequencing of training and competition: The rational for a competently planned, optimally executed training and competition program, supported by a multidisciplinary team. In M. Kellman (Ed.), *Enhancing recovery: Preventing underperformance in athletes* (pp.121-141). Champaign, IL: Human Kinetics.

Smith, D. (2000). A framework for understanding the training process leading to elite performance. *Sports Medicine, 33* (15), 1103-1126.

Wollstein, J. (1995). A new model of athletic development: Perceptual motor skill development programs for squash. *Australian Squash Coach, 3* (1), 5-8.

Active for Life

Dave watched Bernie effortlessly demonstrate the drill to the kids. Dave was head coach, but he had Bernie run through the drills because he was just so athletic. In all honesty, Dave envied Bernie. The kids looked up to Bernie because of the way he could perform so many sport skills. In fact, Dave couldn't think of a sport that Bernie wasn't good at. When Dave had taken Bernie to the golf club where he was a member, Bernie had played so well; his swing, so natural. Dave couldn't believe Bernie hardly ever played.

When Dave asked Bernie why he was so good, Bernie just shrugged his shoulders and explained that he had played a lot of sports as a kid. It seemed that any sport he tried came quite easily. Now, as an adult, Bernie was in demand—teams in a number of sports wanted him to join them. The guys wanted him to play pickup; the kids were always asking for tips; the moms wanted him to coach their kids. No doubt, the recognition made Bernie feel really good about himself.

For Bernie, it just felt good that he could help out. He really wanted the kids to have a positive experience in sport so that they could be physically active and feel good about themselves. Although sport didn't define Bernie, his participation sure made life more fulfilling.

This chapter covers the ultimate stage of long-term athlete development (LTAD)—Active for Life. Sport and physical activity should be designed according to situations and the people involved, who can range from those who are obese and sedentary to those who are extremely fit and competing at the highest levels.

Active for Life has three streams. The first two, competitive for life and fit for life, relate to the participant and are available to everyone. The third, sport and physical activity leaders, is leadership based. Regardless of the stream, being a nation with a population that is active for life plays a role in education and health; it affects the economy and is important to sustainable development by way of a healthy work force.

Active for Life is also guided by five primary actions: retaining participants in sport and physical activity for life; motivating less active or sedentary people to participate in physical activity; transitioning highly competitive athletes into more involvement-based roles; facilitating continued participation as children become youths; and recruiting, developing, and retaining sport and physical activity leaders.

Active for Life Basics

Not everyone wants, or is able, to compete at the highest level, but everyone benefits from healthy, lifelong involvement in sport and physical activity—whether as an athlete, coach, official, administrator, or volunteer. This chapter describes what needs to be done to encourage a smooth transition after developing physical literacy and from high performance sport to other forms of engagement, and how to make continued involvement attractive for those who love the sport and want to stay in it.

After physical literacy is developed through the first three stages of LTAD, athletes choose their level of interest and competition, whereas coaches select those they see as talented to advance to the Train to Train stage of sport-specific models. Those who are not in representative teams are described as active for life. In this stage participants have opportunities to learn new skills, be part of sport groups, or try new sports (see the discussion of transfer sports in chapter 4), which allows them to move back into the excellence pathway.

For those who want to try new aspects of sports, there are opportunities for coaching, officiating, volunteering, and working in the sport. Active for Life is for all people, regardless of their level of participation in sport and physical activity. New participants—even at advanced ages, as well as athletes with disabilities—can be active for life.

The Active for Life stage contains three streams, two that are participant based and one that is leadership based.

Participant Based

- **Competitive for life.** This stream includes participation in sports for the love of the game and includes recreational league play through championship competitions. It does not include athletes who are still in the excellence pathway striving for Olympic glory or professional contracts.

- **Fit for life.** This stream includes all physical activities such as hiking, gardening, yoga, aerobics, skiing, and walking, as well as nonorganized sports (with self-determined rules) such as pickup games in the schoolyard or park.

Leadership Based

- **Sport and physical activity leaders.** This stream is about contributors who enable sport and physical activity to take place.

All three streams should be considered when designing programs to meet the specific needs of participants. This is in contrast to traditional programs that superimpose adult and male programs on children and females. The Active for Life stage provides sport experiences appropriate for specific participants. As an example, most high school sport programs are guided by a philosophy of overall student-athlete development synonymous with competitive for life. However, in some programs, the athletes are coached as if they are in the Train to Win stage of the excellence pathway because of the emphasis on winning instead of skill develop-

ment. On the other hand, some programs claim to be in the excellence stream, yet the training and competition environment actually matches the competitive for life phase and is not a pathway to international excellence.

Importance of Active for Life

Government organizations, businesses, social organizations, and individuals all have a need to reverse the alarming trend of decreasing physical activity and increasing obesity. Engineers, urban planners, workplace designers, and technology programmers have been effective in minimizing the need to move—to be active. Advancements in design and technology have put exercise and play on the bench. Parental concern regarding the safety of streets and playgrounds has resulted in kids' staying indoors on couches in front of screens. They seem to have forgotten that a sedentary lifestyle is dangerous to health and wellness also, and that there are many benefits to being active for life.

Lifelong education, sport, and physical activity contribute to a child's ability to learn. Evidence shows that physically active, fit children perform better in the classroom, and that daily physical education does not hinder academic performance. In fact, an increase in physical activity levels maintains and occasionally enhances academic performance, despite a reduction in study time (Sallis et al., 1999; Shephard, 1996, 1997).

Youth who receive supplementary physical activity often exhibit benefits such as heightened brain function and nourishment, elevated energy and concentration levels, advances in body build leading to increased self-esteem, and better behavior, which may all aid cognitive learning (Cocke, 2002; Dwyer, Coonan, Leitch, Hetzel, & Baghurst, 1983; Morgan & Hansen, 2008; Scheuer & Mitchell, 2003; Shephard, 1997).

Physical activity enhances cognitive ability and information processing, and may help delay or prevent cognitive deterioration and dementia. Older adults who practice regular physical activity display sharper decision-making processes, memory, and problem-solving skills than their less physically active contemporaries (Hillman, Belopolsky, Snook, Kramer, & McAuley, 2004).

According to the World Health Organization (WHO), "physical inactivity is ranked as the fourth leading risk factor for all deaths globally, contributing to 1.9 million deaths each year" (WHO, 2010). The Global Advocacy Council for Physical Activity (GAPA 2010) goes a couple of steps further with its 2010 *Toronto Charter for Physical Activity: A Global Call to Action* by asserting that physical inactivity adversely affects not only health, but also the environment and the economy. In response, however, GAPA outlines ways the promotion and implementation of physical activity can remedy these issues.

Regarding health, physical activity is good for everyone. It can help combat the increasing level of childhood and adult obesity by promoting healthy growth and social development in children. Physical activity also improves mental health and reduces the risk of chronic disease in adults. People can become physically active at any time. Older adults can benefit from the reduced risk of falls and fractures, protection from age-related diseases, and the functional independence that comes from increased physical activity (GAPA, 2010). WHO has determined that the most efficient and sustainable way to reduce lifestyle-related diseases and all their associated costs—both financial and psychosocial—is through increased physical activity (WHO, 2001).

In terms of the economy, sport and physical activity contribute to the productivity and health of populations. A society that is active for life results in increased social cohesion, improved health, a reduction in chronic diseases, and an increase in the overall quality of life. And that is in addition to the workplace productivity that comes from employees' increased ability to work (WHO, 2003). Evidence shows that the benefits of sport go far beyond the positive health effects that have long been understood. "A growing body of research points to community sport's fundamental role as a primary generator of social capital and related benefits across a broad spectrum of societal goals including education, child and youth development, social inclusion, crime prevention, economic development and environmental sustainability" (Mulholland, 2008, pp. 1-2).

When it comes to sustainable development, active modes of travel such as walking and cycling can reduce the air pollution and greenhouse gas emissions that also negatively affect health. Urban redevelopment aimed at reducing dependence on motor vehicles can also lead to increased physical activity. This is particularly true in developing countries experiencing rapid urbanization and growth. Increased opportunities for active travel can also increase mobility options for citizens with disabilities (GAPA, 2010). Sport can do more than simply manage environmental impacts—it can also build stronger, more resilient, and more sustainable communities. The pursuit of sustainable sport leads, inevitably, to a more sustainable economy and more sustainable communities (Bloom, Grant, & Watt, 2005).

Competitive for Life Basics

Competitive athletes within the Active for Life stage fall into the competitive for life stream. These athletes are dedicated to success in their chosen sport(s), but differ from those in the excellence pathway because they are not competing for international podium performances. The competitive for life stream includes high school athletes and top university athletes who, for any reason, are not on the pathway to represent their countries on senior national teams. All competitive athletes who are not competing at the highest level fit into the competitive for life stage of Active for Life.

Also included in competitive for life are the world's top masters athletes. Although these outstanding athletes have many of the training requirements of Olympic athletes, they are not training to win medals at the Olympics and open world championships. In some cases, competitive for life participants may discover other sports or activities, and having entered late into them, move through the early stages into the excellence pathway, striving for international podium success.

The following points guide the athletic director, coach, club executive, and league convener when designing a program. Again, it is important to ask whether the competitive sport program is meeting the desires of the athletes or whether it is mimicking high-performance programs that do not fit the needs of the athletes. Use these points to evaluate the program design.

Competition

- **Meaningful competition.** The competition design is appropriate to the age, ability, and level of engagement of the individual.
- **Appropriate competition.** Aspirations and rules are modified to match the abilities of the participant and address the social aspect of the participant's involvement.

Training

- **Situational coaching.** Qualified coaches interact based on the age, ability, and level of engagement of participants.
- **Specific training.** Training should be specific to participant's goals. Age and past sporting experience should be considered when designing training programs.
- **Appropriate training.** Physical training follows appropriate recommendations to promote continued activity, depending on the option taken. Endurance, speed, strength, and flexibility training programs depend on the athlete's goals.
- **Skill training.** Technical training may present new skills, or it may simply focus on maintaining the skills already acquired. Basic tactics are sufficient to enjoy the activity, and the mental focus is on having fun, releasing stress, and maintaining a fitness discipline.
- **Well instructed.** Athletes may range from those who are new to sport to seasoned competitors; therefore, they should be instructed about the benefits of regular quality physical activity, and the importance of a proper warm-up, cool-down, and stretching routine in a safe environment.

- **Recovery and rehabilitation.** Proper recovery and rehabilitation should be considered, allowing the participant to maintain a healthy lifestyle. Coaches should encourage strength and flexibility training to prevent sore muscles and injuries.
- **Proper sustenance.** Proper hydration and proper nutrition and eating habits are essential for Active for Life athletes to maintain their physical health. As athletes age, metabolism slows, decreasing overall caloric output. Older athletes must take care to eat less so they don't gain unwanted weight.

Program Design

- **Inclusion.** Participants have an opportunity to play regardless of economic status, geography, culture, language, or time.
- **Different situations.** Sport leaders need to appreciate the variety of situations people face, recognizing that forcing conformity can result in exclusion.
- **A place for newcomers.** Ensure sport is a welcoming place for people without a sport background. Design remedial programs (extra training) for newcomers to catch up to their peers.
- **Flexibility.** As society becomes more accommodating to personal demands, sport remains rigid by usually dictating the time and place of play. Design programs that are flexible for the many people who have time restraints and find it difficult to participate in sport or to support the participation of others.

Holistic

- **Knowledge transfer.** Many lessons learned from overcoming the physical and emotional challenges experienced in sports can be applied in everyday life.

- **Enjoyment.** Last on the list, but most important of all, is enjoyment. Fun and social interaction ensure that athletes continue to participate regardless of their ability.

Fit for Life Basics

Once people have developed physical literacy through the first three stages of LTAD, many opportunities exist for furthering their involvement in sport and physical activity. Fit for life encompasses all forms of physical activity excluding organized, competitive sport. In this stream, people enjoy a lifestyle that supports being active to the extent they desire. Depending on their preferences, they follow one of these options:

- **Active living.** People maintain a healthy lifestyle through daily physical activity. Their daily behaviors center on activities such as walking or cycling to work, maintaining a garden, or having an occupation that involves physical work.

- **Active recreation.** People maintain a healthy lifestyle through planned activities that are extraneous to their daily behaviors. They may participate in physical activities such as jogging, working out at the gym, hiking, or playing pickup games in the park.

The following points guide the recreation programmer, instructor, fitness coordinator, or parks manager when designing a program. The list helps to align the desires of the participants with the program design.

Fitness

- **Heart healthy.** Participants should do a minimum of 60 minutes of moderate physical activity or 30 minutes of intense physical activity three times a week.
- **It's not only about calories.** For some people, simply burning calories is not enough to sustain continued engagement in physical activity.
- **Enjoyment.** People must enjoy the activity enough to continue. It must be in a fun and positive environment. Remember, people differ in what they enjoy or consider fun.

- **Specific activity.** Training should be specific to the goals of the participant. The participant's age, ability, and level of fitness should be considered when designing a training program. In some cases doctors' recommendations also need to be considered.

- **Instruction.** Many participants may be new to physical activity; therefore, they should be instructed about the benefits of regular quality physical activity and the importance of a proper warm-up, a proper cool-down, and stretching in a safe environment.

- **Recovery and rehabilitation.** Time set aside for recovery and rehabilitation will help participants maintain healthy lifestyles. Coaches should encourage athletes to do strength and flexibility training to prevent sore muscles and injuries.

- **Proper sustenance.** Proper hydration, nutrition, and eating habits are essential for Active for Life athletes to maintain their physical health. As athletes age, metabolism slows, decreasing overall caloric output. Older athletes must take care to eat less to avoid unwanted weight gain.

Program Design

- **Inclusion.** People's lack of participation may be the result of a variety of factors including economic status, geography, culture, language, time, and confidence.
- **Different situations.** Fitness leaders should appreciate the variety of situations people face, and recognize that forcing conformity can result in exclusion.
- **Welcoming.** Programs should provide a welcoming place for people who don't have a physical activity background.
- **Flexibility.** As society becomes more accommodating to personal demands,

sport remains rigid by usually dictating the time and place of play. People often have time constraints, making it difficult to participate in sport or to support the participation of others.

- **Appropriately challenging.** The level of skill required, whether it be for yoga or mountain climbing, should be appropriate for the participant to provide an opportunity for success.

Holistic

- **Knowledge transfer.** Many of the physical and emotional challenges experienced in sport can be applied in everyday life.
- **Social.** Fun and social interaction ensure that people continue to participate, regardless of their ability.

Sport and Physical Activity Leaders

At as early as 10 years old, people participating in sport will be recruited to contribute to sport and physical activity in a variety of ways. It may start with a young athlete being asked to lead the warm-up or to step up to referee younger kids. That early involvement as a sport or physical activity leader may then last for more than 70 years. Through the many stages of life, the connection with sport will change and can be tremendously fulfilling. Opportunities to be active for life can involve a variety of roles such as the following:

- Coaching and instructing
- Officiating
- Administrating (volunteer and professional)
- Working in sport science or sports medicine

LTAD logically leads to the following:

- Long-term coaching development
- Long-term officials' development
- Long-term volunteer development

Paid sport administrators, sport scientists, and sport physicians are trained through college or university programs, and therefore enter their pathways with the fundamentals of their professions already in place. Volunteers do not usually have this experience. The professional administrator's role is comparable to that of a superintendent of a school district, who is ultimately responsible for providing a quality education for every child. Similarly, professional administrators are accountable for ensuring that every child has a quality sport or physical activity experience. Thus, extensive training and education at the college or university level is required. This is true to an even greater degree for sport scientists and sport physicians because they require years of university education.

Long-Term Coaching (and Instructor) Development (LTCD)

The quality of a sport or physical activity depends on the quality of the person leading it. Developing successful, quality coaches and instructors is an ongoing challenge for countries, many of which have designed, implemented, revised, and abandoned various methods of training coaches, resulting in a wide range of training and instructional approaches to coaching certification. However, many people who coach children still have no training. LTAD and the development of defined sport-specific athlete curricula is changing sport coaching both philosophically and programmatically; thus, coach certification agencies are challenged to update their programs.

The optimal LTCD model starts when people are still active athletes, since the manner in which they are coached influences their competency to coach later in life. LTCD promotes coach education and training for young people, while they are active athletes, to improve their own athletic success and to make them better coaches if they choose the profession.

The following points are characteristics of a high-quality LTCD plan:

- **Quality coaching.** Coaches need to be able to coach their athletes at the LTAD stage they are in. (*Note:* Some great coaches of children are not very good at coaching teens, and coaches of Olympians are not necessarily the best at coaching children.)

- **Experiential learning.** Leadership can start in the Learn to Train stage by having athletes lead drills until the transition from athlete to coach is complete. Years of experience are then required to refine the art and science of coaching.

- **Continuous improvement (professional development).** Professional development is important and can be grouped into three strands:
  - **Federations.** Certified training programs offered by national or international sport federations
  - **Enterprises.** Education, training programs, and certifications offered by multisport organizations or private enterprises
  - **Institutions.** Degree and diploma programs through universities and colleges

- **Technology is the coach's friend.** In this rapidly changing world, various emerging tools are becoming crucial to coaching success.

- **Once a coach, always a coach.** As coaches learn the art and science of coaching, it is important that they pass along their experiences by teaching the following generations through mentoring programs.

Long-Term Officials' Development (LTOD)

Officials play vital roles in the delivery of sport programs at all stages of LTAD except Active Start, which does not involve competition. Their contributions have a significant impact on the quality of athletes' experience. Officiating is a challenging job, but one that, when handled correctly, is enormously enriching and satisfying.

The best sport officials are those who have an understanding of the spirit and the intent of the rules based on the stage of the athletes they are officiating, and how to enforce those rules with that age group. They must possess outstanding communication skills to interact with players and coaches in a developmentally appropriate manner. Similar to LTCD, the optimal LTOD model starts when people are still active athletes, suggesting that how they are officiated has some influence on the kind of officials they will be. LTOD advises that officials' training be available to young athletes to improve their own athletic success and make them better officials if they choose that path.

The following points are characteristics of a high-quality LTOD plan:

- **Recognition of unique pathways.** There are several types of officials—referees (team sports), judges (artistic sports), time keepers (timed sports), and scorers (target and racket sports).

- **Success takes time.** Becoming an excellent official takes time. The number of hours required to be very good is unique to the person, sport, and type of officiating.

- **Continuous improvement.** The desire to continually reflect on and study officiating keeps officials improving.

- **Excellence.** Officials need to strive to be the best they can be, regardless of the stage of the athletes they work with.

- **Flexibility.** Officials need to adapt to the needs of participants and changes in the game, such as new rules or the use of video technology.

- **Collaboration.** Collaboration may be difficult in some sports because of the confrontational culture between officials and coaches or parents. Officials, as well as coaches and parents, must always recognize that officials are valued partners in creating successful sport experiences.

Active for Life To-Do List

To keep participants in sport and physical activity programs throughout their lives, designers should do the following (GAPA, 2010):

- Recognize that sport and physical activity must be modified to suit the needs of the individual, or group of similar individuals.
- Develop skills and abilities, encouraging continued participation and increased self-esteem.
- Consider cost; keep it reasonable and appropriate to the targeted demographic.
- Be prepared with the right clothing and equipment. Correctly fitting shoes, bicycles, or other sport-specific equipment can mean the difference between an enjoyable experience and an experience that does not motivate continued participation.
- Create a safe environment in areas such as the field of play itself, the quality of officiating, and even parking.
- Encourage a social atmosphere in which people can engage with others for fun and enjoyment. In our society, in which technology-driven social networking has become predominant, sport and physical activity has a role to play in building communities.
- Provide meaningful, appropriate competition.
- Regardless of the level of play, ensure that sport is safe, is fun, and takes place in an inspiring environment.

Motivating Less Active or Sedentary People

In addition to the preceding, program designers looking to motivate less active or sedentary people to participate in sport and physical activity should do the following:

- Make sure sport and physical activity is fun! This cannot be emphasized enough. Implement any modifications required to make sure sport is fun for everyone involved.
- Many people have not developed fundamental movement and sport skills at the appropriate time, limiting their sport and physical activity options. Programming should provide opportunities to participate in activities in which success can be achieved, as well as opportunities in which to develop fundamental skills.
- Recognize the issues surrounding body image and create an environment that diminishes this concern (e.g., women-only classes or activities restricted to "big guys").
- Recognize and honor cultural differences.
- Appreciate the variety of fears people have of being active. Fears range from being attacked while walking on a trail to slipping on ice. Each person's fears need to be addressed to encourage participation.
- Leave guilt out of messaging. Motivating people to act based on guilt results in missing the essentials of the preceding points. Guilt is not fun.

> continued

> *continued*

Transitioning Athletes to Be Active for Life

To transition highly competitive athletes to the Active for Life stage, designers must offer programs to help them do the following:

- Move from one sport to another (e.g., via talent transfer programs). For example, a gymnast can become a freestyle aerial skier; a sprinter can take up bobsledding; or a basketball player can discover rowing.

- Move from one aspect of sport to another. For example, a middle-distance runner can become a guide runner for blind athletes, or a cyclist can ride tandem at the Paralympic Games.

- Move from competitive sport to active activities such as hiking and cycling.

- Move from highly competitive sport to lifelong competitive sport through age group competitions such as masters games.

- Upon retiring from sport, move to sport-related careers such as coaching, officiating, sport administration, small business enterprises, or media.

- Move from competitive sport to volunteering as coaches, officials, volunteers, or professional administrators and scientists.

Continuing Participation as Children Become Youths and Adults

Parents, coaches, and other sport leaders can help children continue to participate in sport and physical activity as they become youths.

- Coaches and parents should ensure that sport and physical activity are positive experiences during childhood. This is the key to keeping people active when they transition from Learn to Train to either Train to Train or Active for Life.

- Adults can help children experience a wide range of sports and physical activities during late childhood so they have many choices. Some may be competitive; others may develop fitness.

- Adults can help children choose activities by using tools such as SportFit (find more information at www.sportfitcanada.com). A few simple tests direct children to sports in which they may be particularly successful.

- Parents continue to support involvement in sport and physical activity as children enter their teen years. They should not reduce support simply because their children will clearly not become college-level or professional athletes!

- Regardless of the level of play, sport should offer a safe, fun, and inspiring environment.

Recruiting, Developing, and Retaining Sport and Physical Activity Leaders

- Coaches, officials, and volunteers:
  - Ensure leaders identify, challenge, and eliminate barriers.
  - Educate parents and fans about the value of contributing to sport and physical activity.

- Coaches and officials:
  - Offer a tutorship or mentorship program to complement educational courses.
  - Make sure coaches and officials acquire, refine, and maintain their knowledge and skills to optimize their performances at every game or event.
  - Improve the quality of coaching and officiating at every stage, which may mean keeping a coach or official at a particular stage because he is good at that stage, but not necessarily at the next.
  - Develop uniformity and consistency nationally so parents and athletes can become better informed consumers of sport and physical activity.

- Officials:
  - Develop uniformity in the interpretation of the rules, their implementation, the situational positioning of officials, and visual communication signals.

- Volunteers:
  - Ensure that volunteers who are in control of designing, planning, and scheduling competitions understand LTAD and abide by it.
  - Develop consistent, high-quality sport messaging nationally so parents and athletes can become better informed consumers of sport and physical activity.

Long-Term Volunteer Development (LTVD)

Simply put, volunteers make sport happen. Furthering the quality of volunteers' knowledge, skills, and attitudes results in a better experience for participants. Similar to coaching and officiating, volunteering can start at an early stage. Many elementary schools introduce volunteering by having children as young as 9 and 10 take responsibility and contribute to organizations. However, volunteer engagement is generally random over time; thus, the need for LTVD. Although volunteers in sport are indispensable, there is a dearth of systematic research in volunteer retention (Kim, Chelladurai, & Trail, 2007).

A variety of volunteer training programs exist, but organizations seldom require them. In addition to high-quality volunteers in local sport clubs, high-quality volunteer league administrators and event organizers are also needed. Just as it takes a significant amount of time for athletes to reach the highest levels of sport, so are many hours of involvement required for sport administrators to progress to international governing bodies. Along the way, those administrators often follow a pathway similar to that of athletes—first, by getting involved at the club level, then by moving on to bigger roles in larger jurisdictions, until finally contributing nationally, which can lead to international involvement.

The following points are characteristics of a high-quality LTVD plan:

- **Continuous improvement based on standards.** Club volunteers should seek standards they can measure themselves against to ensure quality. Accreditation encourages local organizations to adopt better, more organized systems and structures, thus helping them to run more effectively and efficiently.

- **Using LTAD as a foundation.** Designing community programs based on sport for life or LTAD helps clubs attract and retain quality volunteers, thereby building a strong organization.
- **Retaining members.** Creating an LTAD-based culture promotes quality sport results and boosts the morale of participants, thus ensuring that volunteers are excited, having fun, and being recognized for their contributions.
- **Basing decisions on values and principles.** All volunteers must consider the values and principles they use to make decisions. When parents are in governance positions, a clash of values can arise (e.g., what is best for my child is best for the club). Therefore, a strong set of values is needed to make good decisions.
- **Time investment.** In the case of volunteers, 10,000 hours is a gross underestimate of the time required to attain a position of governing a sport at the international level. Advancing to this level takes a long time and requires a huge commitment.

Using LTAD, with its purpose of improving the quality of sport, guides organizations when creating and delivering programs, not only for athletes, but also for coaches, officials, and volunteers. Although sport and physical activity leaders often are not practicing heart-healthy pursuits while engaged as coaches, officials, or volunteers, they *are* filling a valued role that improves the quality of many lives, as well as their own.

Summary

Even though we cannot all be professional or Olympic athletes, we can all benefit from a healthy, physically active lifestyle. The final stage of LTAD, Active for Life, consists of three streams. Fit for life and competitive for life represent the two streams participants can follow. Sport and physical activity leaders is the third, leadership-based option. Lifelong physical activity has positive effects on education, health, the economy, and sustainable development.

Active for Life is also guided by five main actions: retaining participants; motivating less active people to participate; transitioning highly competitive athletes; ensuring continued participation as children grow up; and recruiting, developing, and retaining physical activity leaders.

Athletes in the competitive for life stream differ from those in the excellence stream because they do not compete for international podium status. Any competitive athlete not involved at the highest level fits into this category.

Once people have passed through the first three stages of LTAD and developed physical literacy, they then have the wherewithal to enter the fit for life stream. After they have had the opportunity to participate in sport and physical activity for some time, Active for Life gives them the chance to try out new aspects. They can pursue coaching, officiating, volunteering, and working in the sport.

To enter Active for Life and remain there, people must take certain steps, which depend on their experience and lifestyle. Participants must either be retained, encouraged, or transitioned—whatever it takes to keep them involved.

Questions for Reflection

- Is the sport or physical activity fun, and does it satisfy personal objectives?
- Why is being active for life important?
- What are the three streams that make up Active for Life?
- What are the five main actions that guide Active for Life?
- How does competitive for life differ from Train to Compete and Train to Win?
- What is required to be fit for life? When in their lives can people become fit for life?

- What new aspects or roles within sport can people try during this stage?
- What are five ways of retaining participants in heart-healthy activities?
- What are four approaches to motivating less active or sedentary people?
- What three things can be done to transition highly competitive athletes to the Active for Life stage?
- How can we ensure continued participation as children become youths and adults?

References

Bloom, M., Grant, M., & Watt, D. (2005). *Strengthening Canada: The socio-economic benefits of sport participation in Canada.* Retrieved from www.sportmatters.ca/Groups/SMG%20Resources/Reports%20and%20Surveys/2005-Strengthening%20canada-%20The%20socio%20economic%20benefits%20of%20sport.pdf

Cocke, A. (2002). Brain may also pump up from workout. *Brainwork: The Neuroscience Newsletter, 12* (1), 6-7.

Dwyer, T., Coonan, W., Leitch, D., Hetzel, B., & Baghurst, R. (1983). An investigation of the effects of daily physical activity on the health of primary school students in South Australia [Abstract]. *International Journal of Epidemiologists, 12* (3), 308-313. doi: 10.1093/ije/12.3.308

Global Advocacy Council for Physical Activity, International Society for Physical Activity and Health. (2010). *The Toronto Charter for Physical Activity: A global call for action.* Retrieved from www.globalpa.org.uk/pdf/torontocharter-eng-20may2010.pdf

Hillman, C.H., Belopolsky, A.V., Snook, E.M., Kramer, A.F., & McAuley, E. (2004). Physical activity and executive control: Implications for increased cognitive health during older adulthood. *Research Quarterly for Exercise and Sport, 75* (2), 176-185.

Kim, M., Chelladurai, P., & Trail, G.T. (2007). A model of volunteer retention in youth sport. *Journal of Sport Management, 21* (2), 151-171.

Morgan, P.J., & Hansen, V. (2008). Physical education in primary schools: Classroom teachers' perceptions of benefits and outcomes. *Health Education Journal, 67* (3), 196-207.

Mulholland, E. (2008, September). *What sport can do: The true sport report.* Retrieved from www.cces.ca/files/pdfs/TS_report_EN_webdownload.pdf

Sallis, J., McKenzie, J., Kolody, B., Lewis, M., Marshall, S., & Rosengard, P. (1999). Effects of health-related physical education on academic achievement: Project SPARK. *Research Quarterly for Exercise and Sport, 70,* 127-134.

Scheuer, L.J., & Mitchell, D. (2003, May). *Does physical activity influence academic performance.* Retrieved from www.sportsmedia.org/sportapolisnewsletter19.htm

Shephard, R.J. (1996). Habitual physical activity and academic performance. *Nutrition Review, 54* (4), S32-S36.

Shephard, R.J. (1997). Curricular physical activity and academic performance. *Pediatric Exercise Science, 9,* 113-126.

World Health Organization. (2001). *Diet, physical activity and health.* Retrieved from http://apps.who.int/gb/archive/pdf_files/EB109/eeb10914.pdf

World Health Organization. (2003). *Health and development through physical activity and sport.* Retrieved from http://whqlibdoc.who.int/hq/2003/WHO_NMH_NPH_PAH_03.2.pdf

World Health Organization. (2010). *WHO and the International Olympic Committee sign agreement to improve healthy lifestyles: Physical activity can reduce the risk of noncommunicable diseases* [Press release]. Retrieved from www.who.int/mediacentre/news/releases/2010/ioc_20100721/en/index.html

To Learn More

Australia Sport Commission. (n.d.). *National talent search.* Retrieved from www.ausport.gov.au/news/fact_sheets/national_talent_search

Canadian Association for the Advancement of Women and Sport and Physical Activity. (2007, April). *Focus group report: Physical activity and women 55-70.* Retrieved from http://caaws-women55to70plus.ca/pdfs/FocusGroupReportWomen55-70.pdf

Corbin, C.B., & Lindsey, L. (2007). *Fitness for life* (5th ed.). Champaign, IL: Human Kinetics.

Journal of Physical Activity and Health, Human Kinetics.

Journal of Aging and Physical Activity, Human Kinetics.

Journal of Active Aging Today, Human Kinetics.

Sallis, J., & Owen, N. (1999). *Physical activity and behavioral medicine.* Thousand Oaks, CA: Sage.

UK Sport. (n.d.). *Pitch2Podium.* Retrieved from www.uksport.gov.uk/pages/pitch2podium

Way, R., & O'Leary, D. (2006). Long-term coach development concept. *Coaches PLAN du Coach, 12* (3), 24-32.

Epilogue

Top 10 LTAD Takeaways

The long-term athlete development (LTAD) model with its stages and factors offers an opportunity to look at sport and physical activity through a new lens. You must consider that no experiment in the real world would place young athletes in traditional or LTAD pathways and then develop those athletes within those pathways for the decade or two required for full development. LTAD is a model that is based in logic given what we know about youth and about sport and physical activity. This is important to keep in mind as you take on the challenge of making your sport program or organization as successful as it can be for your constituents and especially for your athletes. As this book ends and your actions to improve the quality of sport or physical activity in your community begin, we leave you with our top 10 LTAD takeaways.

1. **Kaizen:** Of all the factors outlined in LTAD, kaizen, or continuous improvement, is one of the most important. We are only beginning to understand what is required for improving the quality of sport and physical activity sufficiently to meet the demands of modern society. Advancing knowledge is a collective effort in which various people and organizations have different roles. As we work with sport organizations from the community level through the international level, we find innovators and critics, skeptics and champions. All are needed to ensure that we progress toward a vision of quality that constitutes developmentally appropriate sport for all, sport for life.

2. **Three key outcomes:** LTAD will contribute to a healthier, happier, and more successful society through the achievement of these key outcomes:
   - All children become physically literate by developing fundamental movement and sport skills and the confidence to use them.
   - More athletes reach higher levels of excellence through a systematic pathway of developmentally appropriate training, competition, and recovery programming.
   - Increased numbers of participants are active for life as the result of improved quality of sport and physical activity programs.

3. **Physical literacy:** Movement is a child's first language. Physical literacy is the foundation for the LTAD model. Physically literate individuals do the following:
   - Demonstrate a variety of basic human movements, fundamental movement skills, and foundational sport skills with confidence, competence, and creativity in different physical environments.
   - Develop the motivation and ability to understand, communicate, apply, and analyze different forms of movement.
   - Make choices that engage them in physical activity, recreation, or sport activities that enhance their

physical and psychological wellness and permit them to pursue sport excellence commensurate with their ability and motivation.

Physical literacy is the foundation for healthy development of the whole person. It helps to create a lifelong relationship with physical activity and sport performance to the best of one's ability. Physical literacy is the cornerstone for both participation in physical activity and excellence in sport. Ideally, physical literacy is developed before the adolescent growth spurt (Canadian Sport for Life expert definitions, 2012).

4. **Developmentally appropriate:** Programs that are based on developmental age rather than chronological age are the cornerstone of LTAD. Identifying early-, average-, and late-maturing athletes will dictate the content of all the activities, providing for the following:

- Developmentally appropriate fitness programs
- Developmentally appropriate technical and tactical programs
- Developmentally appropriate competitive programs
- Developmentally appropriate periodization programs for all stages of the pathway

LTAD challenges sport coaches and administrators to improve both the quality of the training and the competition environment for all participants. This can be threatening to sport leaders who believe their mandate is to identify and place talented youth into enriched situations, leaving the remaining participants to lower-quality training, competition, facilities, and coaching. Improving training and competition environments for all will result in more talent emerging at a greater variety of ages.

5. **Focus on the process:** Concentrating on the outcome in the next game or event is not what LTAD espouses. Whether developing high-performance athletes or participants who enjoy being fit for life, the key is to focus on the process of delivering high-quality sport expe-

riences on a daily basis. It's crucial that sport programs have properly periodized annual plans to ensure that sport not only is enjoyable but also develops participants' skills. Focusing on creating a great next practice will ignite children's passion for playing sport. Taking the focus off of winning in the short term allows kids to take risks to be creative—an important skill in high-performance athletes.

6. **Excellence takes time:** LTAD is an athlete-centered pathway that is about doing the right thing at the right time in the right way by the right people. Each participant has a unique pathway, but it is critical that children experience and be involved in a wide range of sports and activities from a young age and that they do not begin to specialize until the appropriate time as determined by each sport. Numerous factors affect the delivery of optimal training, competition, and recovery programs concerning individual needs. Evidence from the world of sport suggests that elite athletes require 8 to 12 years of practice to reach levels of excellence. The essential lesson is the same: There are no shortcuts to achieving excellence. Participant development is a long-term process, and elite participants will require approximately a decade or more of practice to achieve international standing.

7. **Person first, athlete second, player third:** LTAD focuses on developing a whole person as opposed to concentrating only on athletic development. The mental, cognitive, social, and emotional development of athletes is as important as physical, technical, and tactical development. Thus, building sport programs to develop the whole person is the first priority of LTAD-based activities. Second, LTAD highlights that developing athleticism comes before developing sport-specific skills. In the early LTAD stages the emphasis is on mastering skills before tactics.

8. **Collaboration drives success:** Many programs, organizations, and people are involved in getting children active and developing their abilities. As the movement to improve the quality of sport grows, we see Sport for Life and LTAD being embraced

not only by the sport community but also by other sectors such as health, recreation, and education. It takes a village to raise a healthy, athletic child. To be most efficient, sport, recreation, education, and health organizations need to work together at the local, regional, and national levels to ensure that youth and adults are given the opportunity to reach their potential. Organizations need to consider the multiple activities of each individual and must work with other organizations to ensure programs complement and build on each other. Through policy review and exploration of where one organization's mandate begins and another organization's ends, systems can be aligned so more coherent pathways are available for participants.

9. **Quality matters:** To ensure high-quality sport, implementation must be governed based on a solid set of values and led by qualified coaches, officials, and administrators. Sport leaders should use LTAD to ask pointed questions about the challenges facing sport. The principles of LTAD can be an asset when organizations look at the delivery of their sport or physical activity through this lens. Ultimately, our hope is that through implementation of LTAD, the quality of sport and physical activity will improve, which will result in both increased participation and improved performance. As we progress toward a vision of developmentally appropriate sport for all—sport for life—we can see that leaders in sport will need to shift their thinking from what a club can do to win a championship to what the sport can do for its participants and society in the long term.

10. **Catalyst for change:** Combining theory and practice into a single model is both the great strength of LTAD and the focus of criticism toward it. The model is an attempt to be roughly right about the whole process rather than attempt to be exactly right in every detail while risking missing the big picture. The LTAD model is often misunderstood because of misinterpretation of some of its more complex concepts. Focusing too heavily on the details can overshadow the simple message that we have just outlined: Taking action on these 10 key points will create better sport. LTAD should be used as a tool for reviewing current practices with the purpose of improving the quality of the experience of each participant.

Armed with these 10 takeaways and others you are sure to have learned from this text, you are ready to be a catalyst for change. *You* can make sport better. Go forward and be a champion for sport in your community and a catalyst for change to improve the quality of sport and physical activity worldwide.

Yearly Training Plan Chart

The blank chart on the following pages can be used to help plot a yearly training plan.

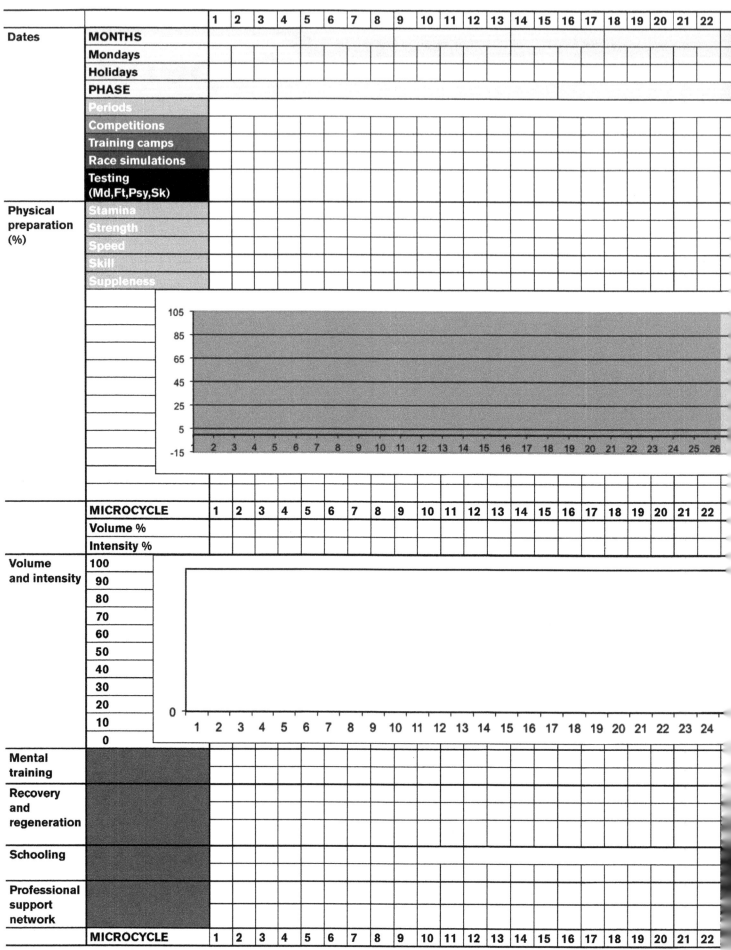

		1	2	3	4	5	6	7	8	9	10	11	12	13	14	15	16	17	18	19	20	21	22
Dates	MONTHS																						
	Mondays																						
	Holidays																						
	PHASE																						
	Periods																						
	Competitions																						
	Training camps																						
	Race simulations																						
	Testing (Md,Ft,Psy,Sk)																						
Physical preparation (%)	Stamina																						
	Strength																						
	Speed																						
	Skill																						
	Suppleness																						

	MICROCYCLE	1	2	3	4	5	6	7	8	9	10	11	12	13	14	15	16	17	18	19	20	21	22
	Volume %																						
	Intensity %																						
Volume and intensity																							

Mental training																							
Recovery and regeneration																							
Schooling																							
Professional support network																							
	MICROCYCLE	1	2	3	4	5	6	7	8	9	10	11	12	13	14	15	16	17	18	19	20	21	22

Md = medical; Ft = fitness; Psy = psychological; Sk = skills

| 23 | 24 | 25 | 26 | 27 | 28 | 29 | 30 | 31 | 32 | 33 | 34 | 35 | 36 | 37 | 38 | 39 | 40 | 41 | 42 | 43 | 44 | 45 | 46 | 47 | 48 | 49 | 50 | 51 | 52 |

Transition

Transition

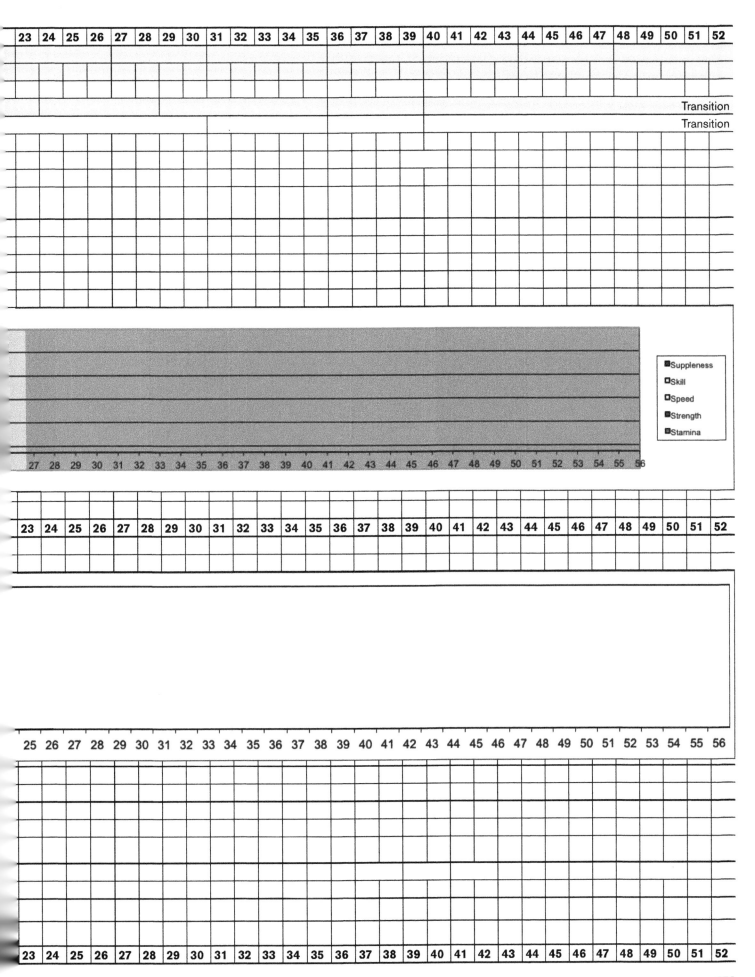

■Suppleness
□Skill
□Speed
■Strength
■Stamina

| 23 | 24 | 25 | 26 | 27 | 28 | 29 | 30 | 31 | 32 | 33 | 34 | 35 | 36 | 37 | 38 | 39 | 40 | 41 | 42 | 43 | 44 | 45 | 46 | 47 | 48 | 49 | 50 | 51 | 52 |

| 25 | 26 | 27 | 28 | 29 | 30 | 31 | 32 | 33 | 34 | 35 | 36 | 37 | 38 | 39 | 40 | 41 | 42 | 43 | 44 | 45 | 46 | 47 | 48 | 49 | 50 | 51 | 52 | 53 | 54 | 55 | 56 |

| 23 | 24 | 25 | 26 | 27 | 28 | 29 | 30 | 31 | 32 | 33 | 34 | 35 | 36 | 37 | 38 | 39 | 40 | 41 | 42 | 43 | 44 | 45 | 46 | 47 | 48 | 49 | 50 | 51 | 52 |

Step-by-Step Process for Creating an Annual Training, Competition, and Recovery Program for Developmental Athletes

Step 1: Evaluating (Feedback and Feedforward)

1. Profiling the athlete or team
   - 1.1. General training age
   - 1.2. Sport-specific training age
   - 1.3. Chronological or developmental age
     - 1.3.1. Monitor standing height, sitting height, arm span, and weight
       - 1.3.1.1. Identify the onset of PHV.
       - 1.3.1.2. Identify PHV.
       - 1.3.1.3. Identify post-PHV (deceleration of growth).
       - 1.3.1.4. Chart data.
     - 1.3.2. Identify prepubertal athletes (before the onset of PHV).
     - 1.3.3. Identify pubertal athletes (after the onset of PHV).
     - 1.3.4. Identify postpubertal athletes (post PHV).
     - 1.3.5. Register the onset of menarche for females.
     - 1.3.6. Identify early-, average-, and late-maturing athletes.
     - 1.3.7. Identify annual training and competition priorities.

2. Evaluate the last year's and earlier training, competition, and recovery programs.
   - 2.1. Training
     - 2.1.1. Physical components
     - 2.1.2. Technical components
     - 2.1.3. Tactical components
     - 2.1.4. Mental components
     - 2.1.5. Ancillary components (warm-up and cool-down, stretching, hydration and nutrition, regeneration, sociocultural)
   - 2.2. Performance
     - 2.2.1. Physical components
     - 2.2.2. Technical components
     - 2.2.3. Tactical components
     - 2.2.4. Mental components
     - 2.2.5. Ancillary components (warm-up and cool-down, stretching, hydration and nutrition, regeneration, taper and peak, sociocultural)

3. Strengths of the annual program
   - 3.1. Training
   - 3.2. Performance

4. Weaknesses of the annual program
   - 4.1. Training
   - 4.2. Performance

5. Opportunities

6. Threats

7. One major objective for the annual plan

    7.1. Align and sequence the timing of the secondary objectives.

8. Program planning for next year

    8.1. Calendar planning: select or identify all of the competitions of the next season (use appendix A).

    8.2. Optimize competition selection.

        8.2.1. Ensure that there are enough competitions before the major peak(s), to provide for optimum form.

        8.2.2. Ensure that there are not too many competitions and that athletes will not arrive to the major meet(s) in a fatigued state.

    8.3. Identify all training camps of the next season.

    8.4. Identify school holidays, examination periods, and all other activities that could have an impact on athlete or team preparations.

    8.5. Identify all sport science and sports medicine sessions for the preceding time periods.

        8.5.1. Sport science

        8.5.2. Sports medicine

        8.5.3. Others

Step 2: Drafting a Plan

1. Categorize selected competitions.

    1.1. Individual sports

        1.1.1. "Train-through" competitions

        1.1.2. "Lead-up" competitions

        1.1.3. Minor competitions

        1.1.4. Major competitions

        1.1.5. Major games (by calendar— e.g., world championships, Olympic Games)

2. Determine the competitive phases(s) of the annual plan.

    2.1. First and last competition of the annual cycle

    2.2. If implementing double, triple, or multiple periodization, act accordingly.

3. Determine the precompetitive phase(s) of the plan.

    3.1. If implementing double, triple, or multiple periodization, act accordingly.

4. Determine the specific preparatory phase(s) of the plan.

    4.1. If implementing double, triple, or multiple periodization, act accordingly.

5. Determine the general preparatory phase of the annual plan.

6. Calculate the optimum volume and intensity of the annual plan.

    6.1. Perform a retrospective analysis of the former years of training and performance.

        6.1.1. Competitive performances

        6.1.2. Training records

        6.1.3. Laboratory test results

        6.1.4. Field test results

        6.1.5. Injury and sickness reports

        6.1.6. Key factors affecting training and performance

    6.2. Test and monitor sessions prior to planning to identify priorities for planning.

        6.2.1. Laboratory tests

        6.2.2. Field tests

        6.2.3. Performance tests

        6.2.4. Psychological tests

        6.2.5. Medical checkup results

        6.2.6. Nutritional habits evaluation results

6.3. Identify, collect, and analyze sport- and event- or position-specific normative data.

    6.3.1. International normative data

    6.3.2. National normative data

    6.3.3. Provincial or state normative data

    6.3.4. Energy system contributions to training and performance

6.4. Based on 6.1, 6.2, and 6.3, identify individual or team needs, demands, goals, and objectives.

6.5. Design a plan to bridge the actual capacity of the athlete(s) or team(s) with the demands of national and provincial or state training and competition.

    6.5.1. If the gap is manageable, use a one-year plan.

    6.5.2. If the gap cannot be addressed in one annual cycle, establish a long-term plan to bridge the gap.

6.6. Based on 6.1 to 6.5, reevaluate the preliminary distribution of the general, specific, precompetitive, and competitive phase(s) of the annual plan.

7. Plot a preliminary chart of the volume and intensity of training on the yearly training plan (use appendix A).

Step 3: Planning Mesocycles and Microcycles

1. Design and work out the details of the mesocycle and microcycle distributions of the annual plan.

    1.1. Start a design with the last microcycle of the precompetitive phase and work backward to the last microcycle of the specific preparatory phase (SSP).

    1.2. Continue backward again from the last week of the specific preparatory phase to the first microcycle of the SSP phase.

    1.3. Continue backward from the last microcycle of the general preparatory phase until the first microcycle of the annual plan.

    1.4. Provide details about the microcycles between the first and last microcycles of the competition phase applying the principles of taper and peak, while maintaining physical and technical and tactical components.

    1.5. If implementing double, triple, or multiple periodization, start the design with the last or most important cycle of the annual plan and work back to the first cycle.

2. Reevaluate mesocycle and microcycle distribution from the point of view of the following:

    2.1. Training camps

    2.2. Regeneration cycles, or prophylactic breaks

    2.3. Official holidays of the seasons and the availability of training facilities

    2.4. School, college, or university exam periods

    2.5. "Train-through" competitions, minor and major competitions, optimum taper and peak

    2.6. Environmental factors (e.g., jet lag, heat, cold, humidity, altitude, pollution)

3. Finalize mesocycle and microcycle distribution keeping in mind that the training objectives of mesocycles are determined by the objectives of the long-term plan, followed by those of the annual plan, and then by the objectives of the particular period and phase of the annual plan!

    3.1. Identify mesocycle objectives.

        3.1.1. Introductory mesocycles

        3.1.2. Developmental or adaptation mesocycles

3.1.2.1. Metabolic, endurance, and strength endurance adaptation mesocycles

3.1.2.2. Speed (or neural), power, or skill adaptation mesocycles

3.1.2.3. Mixed metabolic–neural mesocycles

3.1.3. Stabilizing mesocycles

3.1.4. Taper mesocycles

3.1.5. Maintenance mesocycle

3.1.6. Recovery or restorative mesocycles

3.1.7. Transitional mesocycles

4. Based on the established mesocycle and microcycle values, record final volumes and intensities on the yearly training plan (appendix A). Ensure that the training and competition loads cover the technical, tactical, physical, mental, and recovery–regeneration components.

Step 4: Quantifying Training Loads, Volumes, and Intensities

1. Quantify the percentage contribution of the five Ss of training and performance for each phase of the annual plan.

   1.1. Stamina

   1.2. Strength

   1.3. Speed

   1.4. Skill

   1.5. Suppleness

2. Quantify the percentage contributions of the five Ss for each mesocycle of the general preparatory phase.

3. Quantify the percentage contributions of the five Ss of training and performance only for the microcycles of the first mesocycle of the annual plan. (Remember that you need to establish the structure of the annual training, but there are no guarantees that you will accomplish all of the adaptations you have planned. Therefore, only three to five weeks of training are quantified. After monitoring the effects of training, quantify the next segment taking into consideration the monitoring results!)

   3.1. Introductory microcycles

   3.2. Developmental microcycles

   3.3. Shock microcycles

   3.4. Stabilizing microcycles

   3.5. Competitive microcycles

      3.5.1. Taper microcycles

      3.5.2. Peak microcycles

      3.5.3. Competitive maintenance microcycles

   3.6. Modeling microcycles

   3.7. Restorative microcycles

   3.8. Transitional microcycles

4. Determine the number of weekly and daily training sessions of the microcycles of the first mesocycle, and sequence those sessions to provide optimum adaptation to training as well as to optimize recovery and regeneration.

   4.1. Higher-quality sessions must precede lower-quality sessions.

   4.2. Emphasized training components must precede maintained component(s).

5. Quantify the daily or weekly volume of training. When planning the sessions of a microcycle, always identify the goals of the session and the physical, technical, tactical, and mental component of the session, followed by the regeneration and nutritional components. The recovery component of the session is as important as the loading component! When planning the sessions, consider the following:

   5.1. Normative data

   5.2. Training logs and records

   5.3. Use the established guidelines to monitor adaptations to training.

   5.4. It is not recommended to quantify daily training programs longer then a mesocycle or three to five microcycles.

6. Identify the taper procedure to achieve peak performance.

   6.1. Perform a retrospective analysis of best performances.

   6.2. Determine the volume, intensity, and frequency of training during the taper.

   6.3. Determine the optimum number of "lead-up" competitions during the taper.

   6.4. Identify mental strategies and routines for final preparation and peak performance.

   6.5. Identify nutritional and hydration strategies for the taper.

   6.6. Identify recovery and regeneration strategies for the taper.

   6.7. Identify environmental strategies for the season (e.g., jet lag, late travel and arrival, heat, cold, insects, pollution, altitude).

Step 5: Monitoring and Evaluating

1. Monitor the adaptation processes regularly to ensure that the planned training effects are accomplished.

   1.1. Strategies for physiological monitoring

   1.2. Strategies for psychological monitoring or interventions

   1.3. Strategies for medical monitoring

   1.4. Strategies for other monitoring

2. Monitor and ensure that the ancillary capacities of athlete(s) are optimized.

Because there is no one formula to quantify short- or long-term training programs, the art and science of coaching lies in providing guidelines for the procedure. Ensure that sport science, sports medicine, and sport-specific technical and tactical activities are fully integrated and sequenced. Keep in mind that it is easy to compile a sophisticated plan; implementing a training, competition, and recovery plan is the real challenge!

Index

About the Authors

Istvan Balyi, MA, is a sport consultant and expert in Canadian Sport for Life and long-term athlete development. Balyi has served as a sport scientist in residence at the National Coaching Institute in Victoria, British Columbia, and remains involved in the program delivery of planning and periodization and LTAD.

As one of the architects of the long-term athlete development model, Balyi has served as an LTAD advisor for 50 sports in 7 countries and facilitated the use of LTAD for more than 20 countries. Balyi has worked with 17 Canadian national teams as a high-performance consultant and been responsible for athletic development planning and periodization for multiple Olympic medalists. In addition, Balyi has taught planning, periodization, and LTAD modules in Australia, Bahrain, Chile, England, Ireland, New Zealand, Northern Ireland, Portugal, Scotland, Singapore, South Africa, the United Sates, the Netherlands, and Wales.

Balyi resides in Victoria, British Columbia, where he enjoys reading, listening to music, and cooking.

Richard Way, MBA, is a project leader and expert in Canadian Sport for Life and long-term athlete development. He is also a principal of Citius Performance Corporation and serves on the faculty of the Institute for Global Studies at the University of Delaware.

Way developed the LTAD model along with Istvan Balyi and has served as a long-term athlete development advisor for 30 sports in 4 countries. He has also facilitated the use of LTAD in over 50 countries.

As a chartered professional coach, Way represented Canada as a luge racer and coach for over 10 years. Way holds a Medal of Honor for Exceptional Contributions to the Development of the International Luge Sport awarded by the Federation Internationale de Luge de Course (FIL). He received his advanced diploma in coaching in 2005 from the National Coaching Institute.

Way is president of the International Sport for Life Society. He was also the director of sport for Vancouver's successful 2010 Bid Corporation. Way enjoys spending time with his children in community sports, traveling, and playing soccer and hockey. He resides in Victoria, British Columbia.

Colin Higgs, PhD, is a sport consultant and expert in long-term athlete development. He has worked with many national governments and nongovernmental sport and disability sport organizations in North America, the Caribbean, southern Africa, and central Asia.

As a consultant, Higgs is currently involved in the redevelopment of the Caribbean Coaching Certification Program and the design, development, and implementation of a youth sport program in the Caribbean to reduce the incidence and impact of HIV/ AIDS. Higgs is working to transform the Canadian sport system with the goals of decreased negative medical consequences of physical inactivity and increased international sport performance for Canada's athletes.

Higgs is a frequent presenter at international conferences and has authored more than 60 publications on physical literary, long-term athlete development, and coaching with special emphasis on individuals with disabilities.

In 2013 Higgs was the inaugural recipient of the International Paralympic Committee's Sport Science Awards and also received the Queen's 60th Jubilee Medal for community service to Canada in support of reducing physical inactivity. He is a professor emeritus at Memorial University of Newfoundland in Canada. Higgs resides in Sydenham, Ontario, Canada.